THE FORBIDDEN GROVE

Book 2 in the  ELFQUEST Reader's Collection

WOLFRIDER BOOKS

Poughkeepsie
New York

THE FORBIDDEN GROVE

Reprinting **Elfquest: the original series**
comic book issue numbers 6 through 10
as published 1979-81

Story by Wendy & Richard Pini

Art by Wendy Pini

About the ELFQUEST Reader's Collection

The twenty year — and ongoing — saga that is Elfquest has been told in many different comic book titles. Some of this material has already been reprinted; these volumes go in and out of print over the years. The Elfquest Reader's Collection is our attempt to collect all the core stories in book form, so that readers new and old can follow the entire tale from its beginnings on up to the most recent work.

As planned the Elfquest Reader's Collection series — to see initial release throughout 1998 and 1999 — will include the following volumes:

#1 - Fire and Flight
#2 - The Forbidden Grove
#3 - Captives of Blue Mountain
#4 - Quest's End
> The story of Cutter, chief of the Wolfriders, and his tribe as they confront the perils of their primitive world, encounter new races of elves, and embark on a grand and dangerous quest to unveil the secret of their past.

#5 - Siege at Blue Mountain
#6 - The Secret of Two-Edge
> The adventures of the Wolfriders some years after the end of the first quest, as they face the machinations of a villainess from their past and her enigmatic half-elf, half-troll son.

#7 - The Cry from Beyond
#8 - Kings of the Broken Wheel
> The Wolfriders face their most daunting challenge when one of their number kidnaps Cutter's mate and children into future time, to prevent the very accident that first brought the elves to this world.

#8a - Dreamtime
> The visions of the Wolfriders as they slept for ten thousand years, waiting for the time when Cutter and his family can be united once more.

#9 - Rogue's Challenge
> Tales of the "bad guys" who have caused the Wolfriders so much trouble over the centuries.

#9a - Wolfrider!
> The tale of Cutter's sire Bearclaw, and how he brought two things to the Wolfriders — the enmity of humans and a monstrous tragedy, and a chief's son like no elf the tribe had ever known.

#10 - Shards
#11a - Legacy
#11b - Ascent
#12a - Huntress
#12b - Reunion
> Cutter and family are together again, but now a ruthless human warlord threatens the elves' very existence. The Wolfriders must become two tribes — one to fight a terrible war, the other to flee to ensure that the tribe continues. Volume #10 sets the stage; volumes #11a and #12a follow Cutter's daughter Ember as she leads the Wild Hunt elves into new lands; volumes #11b and #12b take Cutter and his warriors into the flames of battle.

#13a - the Rebels
#13b - Jink!
#14a - Skyward Shadow
#14b - Mindcoil
> In the far future of the World of Two Moons, human civilization has covered the planet — and the elves have disappeared. Where did they go? Volumes #13a and #14a follow the adventures of a group of young adventurers as they seek the answer. Volumes #13b and #14b tell the story of a mysterious woman who is more than she seems — for she may be the last remaining descendant of the missing elves.

THE FORBIDDEN GROVE

Book 2 in the _ELFQUEST_ Reader's Collection

Published by Warp Graphics, Inc.
under its Wolfrider Books imprint.

43 Haight Avenue
Poughkeepsie, New York 12603

ISBN 0-936861-56-8
Printed in USA

www.elfquest.com

COMMENTS ON THE QUEST

BY FRANK THORNE

Lucky you who are about to experience Elfquest for the first time. Luckier still are those of us who already know the wonder of the Pinis' creation. The Donning Company has chosen wisely in publishing Elfquest as the first in a series of graphic illustrated novels.

Elfquest is a rambunctious and poetic narrative that will be inevitably read as a sublime comic book. Critics are quick to call word and picture continuity in the comic book format low art. Elfquest fights this pigeonhole as doggedly as its elves persist against the evils of their world. As Cutter, the prime elf of the tale would say, "Let the wolves pick their bones!"

Elfquest is presented here as a graphic novel. It comes to book form after a remarkable record of success in its original publication as a small press magazine. The fans of Elfquest are legion. Some may grumble a bit at seeing their favorite stories presented as a novel. Hold a moment, Elfquest fans, it is more than it seems. It is indeed a graphic novel.

The graphic novel concept is not new. This curious hybrid of the publishing industry has been struggling to be born for decades. Many fine craftsmen have experimented with it. The mix has always been varied, exciting, outrageous, often boring and with few exceptions commercially unprofitable. From the surrealistic collage books of Max Ernst to Lynd Ward's graphic novels in woodcut, they remain on the fringe. How I love that fringe. You will always find me there, looking for truffles and tilling the soil. In the 20s and 30s Milt Gross, the American-born cartoonist, added his comic genius to the form. What wonderful stuff.

In Elfquest you will see a blending of the surreal, the illustrative and the comic styles of these forebears of the graphic novel. But typically, Wendy's work struggles mightily against demons. The demons of past visions.

There is a rage beneath the surface. A battling to define self and the cruelty of life. She cries, "I will have my own world!" This whirlpool of frustration has produced an animated film frozen in the amber of her prejudice and formed by her prodigious talents. I know her. I've known her for a thousand years. She is the most all-around talented woman ever to grace my existence. Elfquest in her hands becomes a buoyant indictment of life's passage. A personal eyeball-to-eyeball confrontation with destiny. It is more than autobiographical, it is a fist, a poem, a serenade by strangely voluptuous beings. They wonder at each other's gender. The sexual element abounds and is curved in strange ways. At times the Pinis' elves seem joyously androgynous. At other times darkly male or female. Wendy's eye will focus on a female elf and render it with such supreme skill that I begin to levitate, and worry. There's something there that's wandering naked in the predawn hours of my mind.

The special flavor of Elfquest could only have sprung from craftsmen who are rooted outside the mainstream of commercial comics. Their reverence for the form makes it valid and familiar and gives them a stage for their drama. The Pinis' words are clearly fantasy writing of a high order, but the completeness of creation and the grace of style in an Ursula LeGuin story is not here. The concept forbids it. Tolkien would be reduced to elongated boredom as a graphic novel. The voice must be at one with the picture. The energy and impact of moving from one frame to the next, page after page, demands a writing style that immolates itself in the fire of pictorial movement. It must be read as one, the picture and the word.

This is beginning to sound like a high-blown harangue. Much too scholarly. I fear I'll have you missing the pure fun in reading the adventures of Cutter, Skywise and company. The facial expressions and delicate characterizations are beyond intellectualizing. A troll is not a troll unless drawn by Wendy Pini. Her elves can amuse you, frighten you, break your heart and send you into the night to look for falling stars. For me, a practitioner of the drawing craft, watching Wendy's work develop in this first book is the rarest treat of all.

My esteem for the Pinis' work is within the cause of extreme partiality. It has not dimmed my judgement. I call Wendy and Richard friends and fellow craftsmen. My fondness for them allows no room for insincere flattery. Several years ago the three of us shared the wines of glory. Fate had chosen me as artist of Marvel Comics' Red Sonja series. Sonja was taking off, and upon the rise of that most splendid redhead's popularity was born a thing of dreams. I, a renegade haranguer was made a wizard. Wendy, a rising young fantasy artist became Red Sonja. Richard, alchemist, astronomer and writer became Cecil B. DeMille. Together, out of love for Red Sonja, we concocted the Wizard and Red Sonja Show. The multimedia presentation brought the great Hyrkanian swordswoman and her ancient world to life. It was Wendy, in her famous iron bikini, that made the show. Of all the many women who portrayed Sonja in her glory days none came close to matching Wendy's Sonja. It was a vivid, frightening and stunning impersonation. (Sounds like I'm talking about elves again. I am, but I'm getting ahead of my story.) The true wizardry in the show was Richard's handling of the special effects and everything else. It was a good piece of theater. We had the time of our lives.

In the climactic months traveling with the show, amid the whirlwind of TV appearances and national magazine coverage, Elfquest was born. As de facto midwife I can say it was ecstasy for the Pinis, ecstasy tinged with torture and frustration. Wendy was like a roller coaster. Such heights. Such depths. Publisher troubles, lurking fear of failure mixed with a festering toward a door that was finally opening for them.

One night in New York City we were all resting in my room at the Hilton Hotel. We had just finished our second Wizard and Red Sonja Show in the fabled Terrace Ballroom and were fresh from an interview on Eyewitness News. I was exhausted. As was our custom we left the costumes on for a bit of the afterglow. I'd wager that was the first time *that* rump-sprung wing chair had held a wizard in full garb. Richard was sitting on the dresser, brooding like a man jealous of King Priam and bent on creating his own Troy. Wendy was perched on the edge of the bed, still gorgeous in the Sonja outfit. She turned to me and asked, "What of Elfquest, Frank?"

Her voice was often husky after the show, but this time it had a different timbre. Instantly I knew it was Cutter who spoke those words. He was jealous too, and spoiling to have his world manifest.

BY C.C. BECK

When I was young—many, many years ago—we had the Brownies and the Teenie Weenies in the comics. The Brownies were ugly little things about six inches tall, and the Teenie Weenies were even smaller, about the size of mice or grasshoppers. In both strips there were Irishmen, Scotchmen, Bankers, Cooks, and such stock characters. The Brownies specialized in mischievous acts, while the Teenie Weenies made big productions of fixing up a tin can as a town hall and such nonsense. In both, the stress was always on how small everybody was. I suppose this was done in a mistaken belief that children are interested in small things, but to me, a very small person myself, it seemed pointless. I wanted to see big people, heroes, not cute little dolls playing around on the comic pages.

When modern comic books appeared in the late nineteen-thirties, science fiction and huge heroes became the rage. Elves and fairies and such were forgotten, although evil magicians and monsters were not. Now everything was drawn realistically, not in cartoon style. Nobody laughed while reading a comic book—drooling or breaking out in a cold sweat were more common reactions. Things became seriouser and seriouser, as Lewis Carroll might have said. They became so serious that comics became a new religion ... and nobody must laugh at a religion!

Then came Wendy and Richard Pini. Richard wrote with his tongue in cheek and Wendy made her drawings with a lighthearted touch that had not been used for many a dreary year in comics. Elfquest was funny, serious, real, impossible, and more fun to read than anything had been before. We old-timers often talk about the "good old days" and bemoan the present. Not this old-timer. There were plenty of bad things around in the old days, too. One of the worst was that there were none of Richard's and Wendy's marvelous elves, trolls, and other magical creatures around to brighten up our days.

Rejoice, people of today! We have Elfquest and I, for one, am glad that I lived long enough to enjoy it!

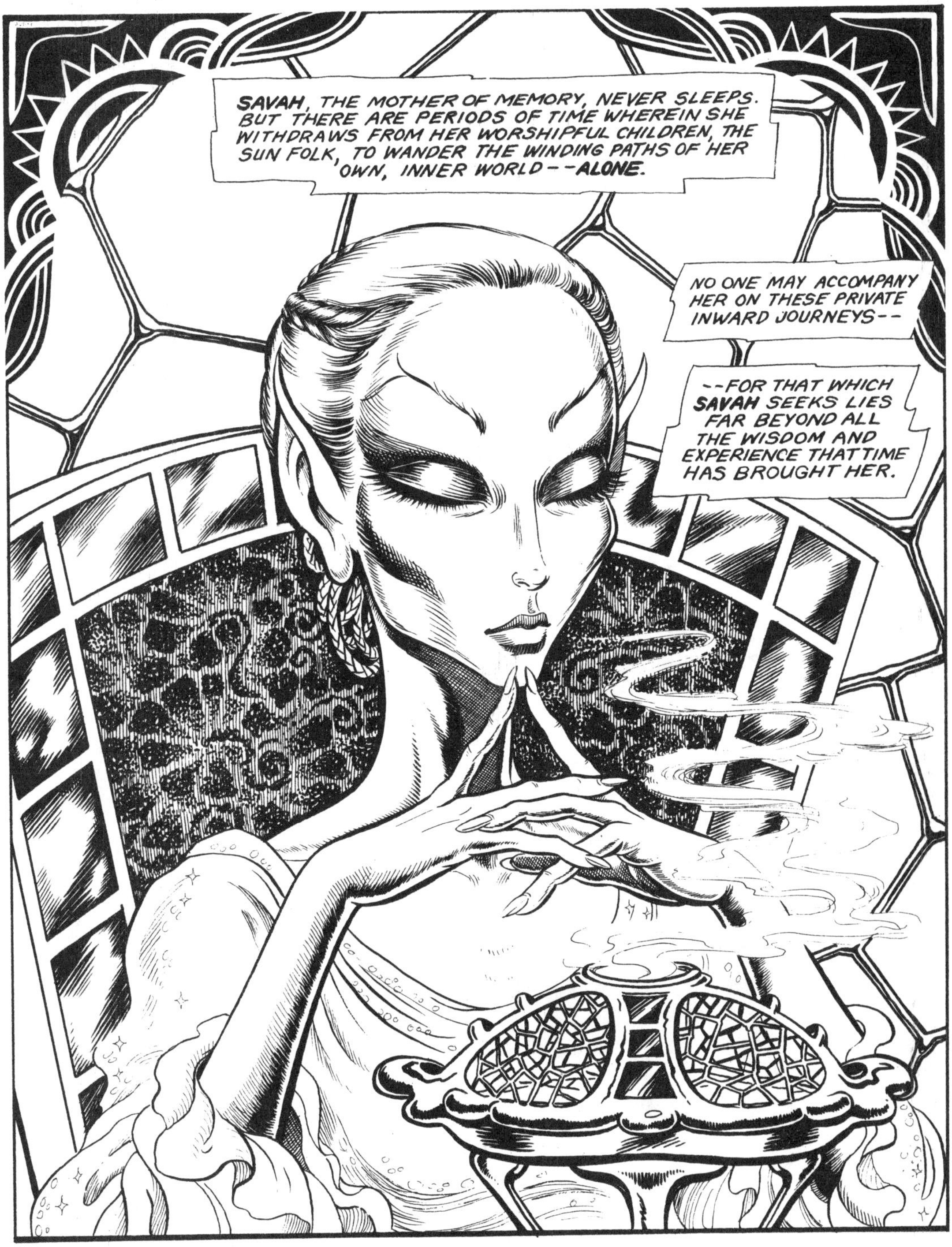
SAVAH, THE MOTHER OF MEMORY, NEVER SLEEPS. BUT THERE ARE PERIODS OF TIME WHEREIN SHE WITHDRAWS FROM HER WORSHIPFUL CHILDREN, THE SUN FOLK, TO WANDER THE WINDING PATHS OF HER OWN, INNER WORLD--ALONE.
NO ONE MAY ACCOMPANY HER ON THESE PRIVATE INWARD JOURNEYS--
--FOR THAT WHICH SAVAH SEEKS LIES FAR BEYOND ALL THE WISDOM AND EXPERIENCE THAT TIME HAS BROUGHT HER.

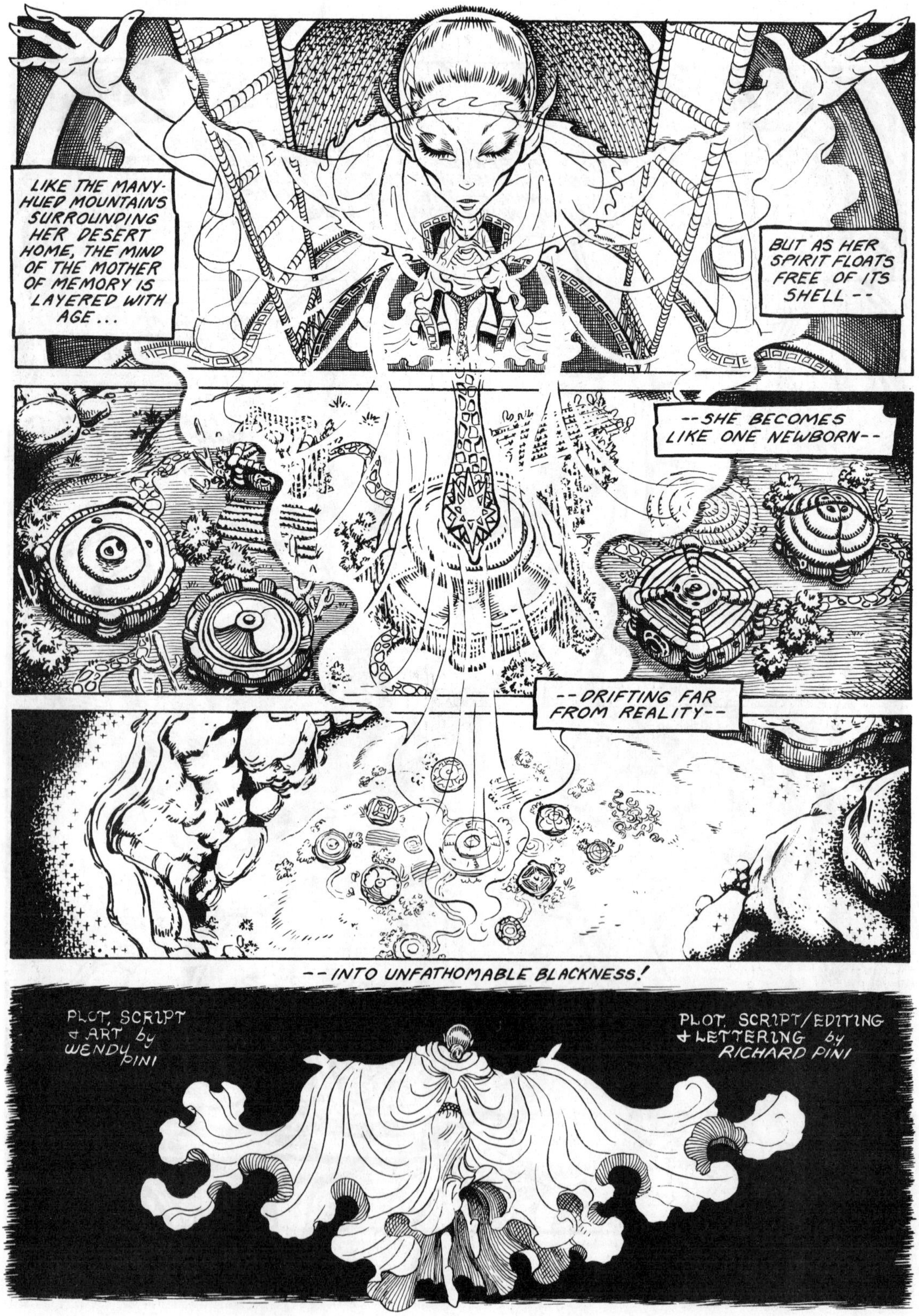
LIKE THE MANY-HUED MOUNTAINS SURROUNDING HER DESERT HOME, THE MIND OF THE MOTHER OF MEMORY IS LAYERED WITH AGE...
BUT AS HER SPIRIT FLOATS FREE OF ITS SHELL --
--SHE BECOMES LIKE ONE NEWBORN--
--DRIFTING FAR FROM REALITY--
--INTO UNFATHOMABLE BLACKNESS!
PLOT, SCRIPT & ART by WENDY PINI
PLOT, SCRIPT/EDITING & LETTERING by RICHARD PINI

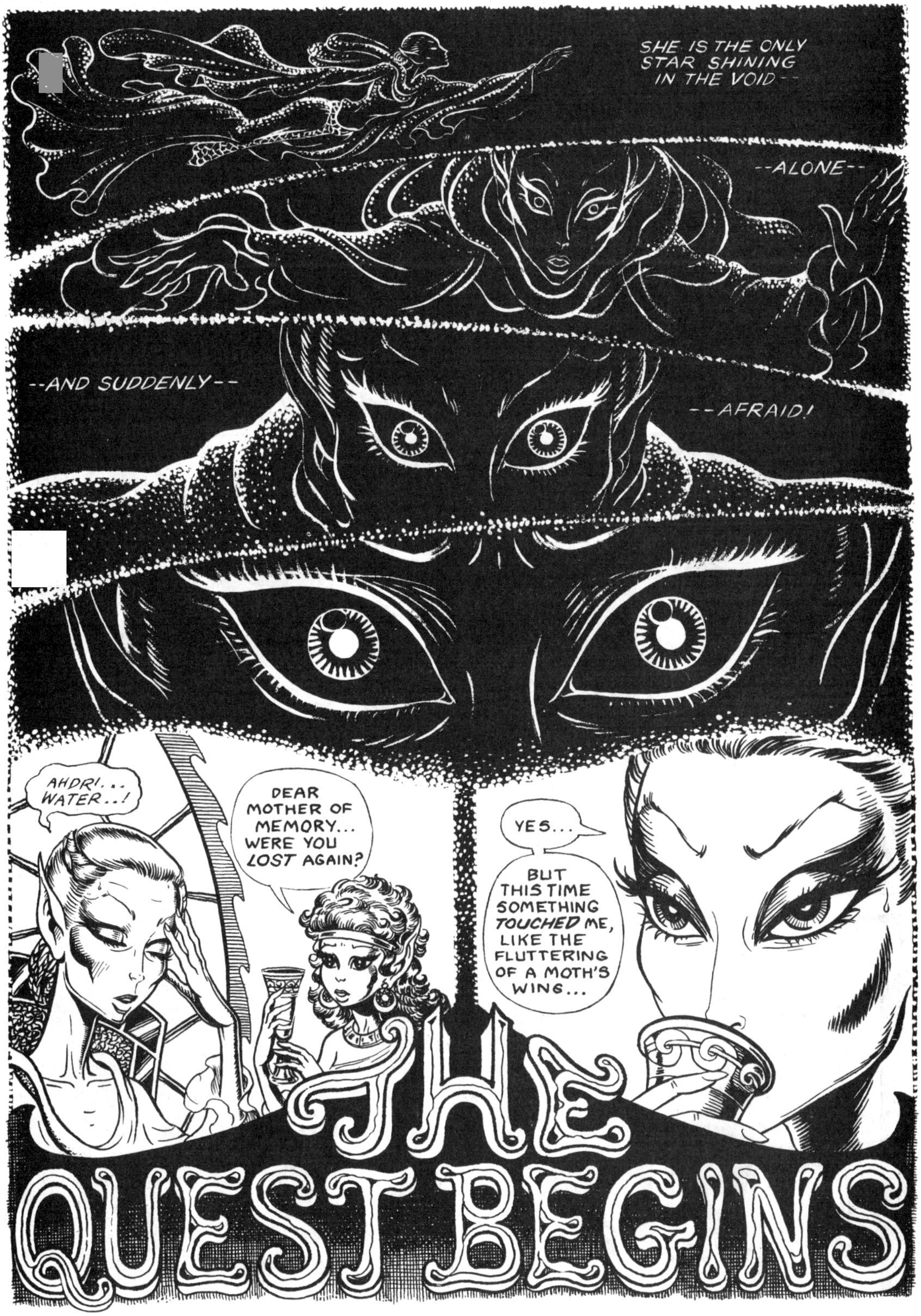

SHE IS THE ONLY STAR SHINING IN THE VOID--
--ALONE--
--AND SUDDENLY--
--AFRAID!
AHDRI... WATER..!
DEAR MOTHER OF MEMORY... WERE YOU LOST AGAIN?
YES...
BUT THIS TIME SOMETHING TOUCHED ME, LIKE THE FLUTTERING OF A MOTH'S WINGS...
THE QUEST BEGINS

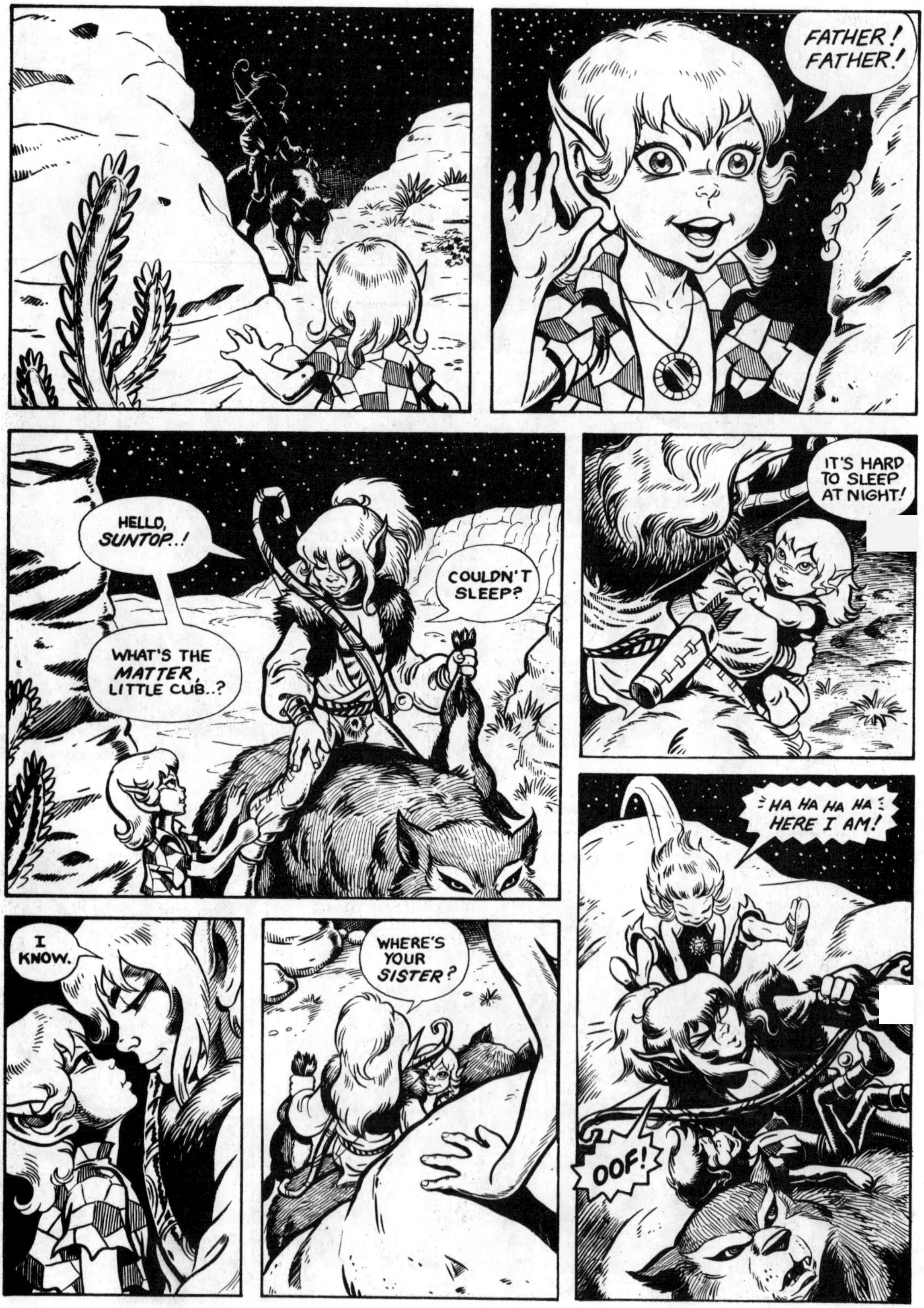
FATHER! FATHER!
HELLO, SUNTOP..!
WHAT'S THE MATTER, LITTLE CUB..?
COULDN'T SLEEP?
IT'S HARD TO SLEEP AT NIGHT!
I KNOW.
WHERE'S YOUR SISTER?
HA HA HA HA HERE I AM!
OOF!

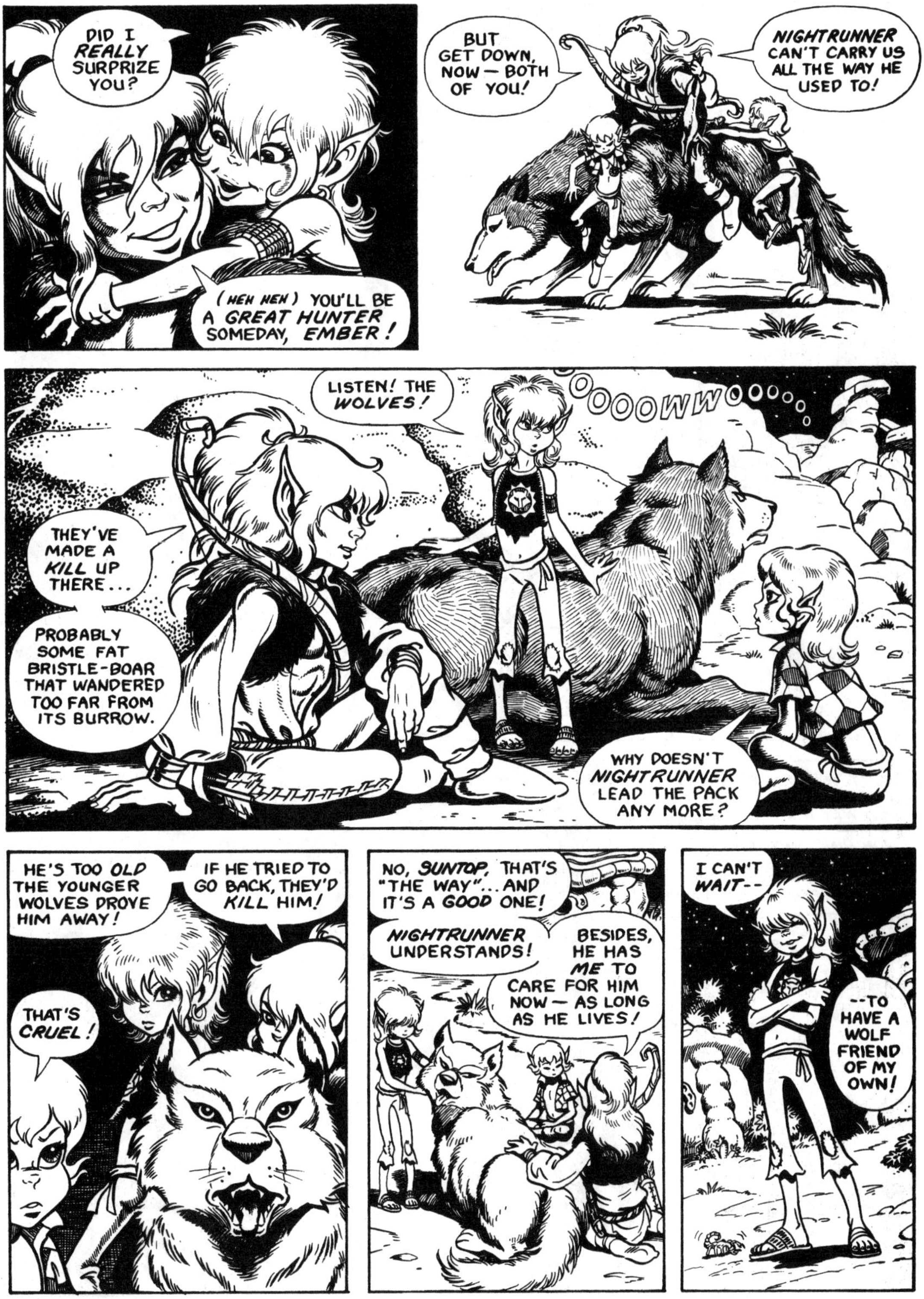
DID I REALLY SURPRIZE YOU?
(HEH HEH) YOU'LL BE A GREAT HUNTER SOMEDAY, EMBER!
BUT GET DOWN, NOW — BOTH OF YOU!
NIGHTRUNNER CAN'T CARRY US ALL THE WAY HE USED TO!
LISTEN! THE WOLVES!
OOOOWWOOOOOO
THEY'VE MADE A KILL UP THERE...
PROBABLY SOME FAT BRISTLE-BOAR THAT WANDERED TOO FAR FROM ITS BURROW.
WHY DOESN'T NIGHTRUNNER LEAD THE PACK ANY MORE?
HE'S TOO OLD THE YOUNGER WOLVES DROVE HIM AWAY!
IF HE TRIED TO GO BACK, THEY'D KILL HIM!
THAT'S CRUEL!
NO, SUNTOP, THAT'S "THE WAY"... AND IT'S A GOOD ONE!
NIGHTRUNNER UNDERSTANDS!
BESIDES, HE HAS ME TO CARE FOR HIM NOW — AS LONG AS HE LIVES!
I CAN'T WAIT--
--TO HAVE A WOLF FRIEND OF MY OWN!

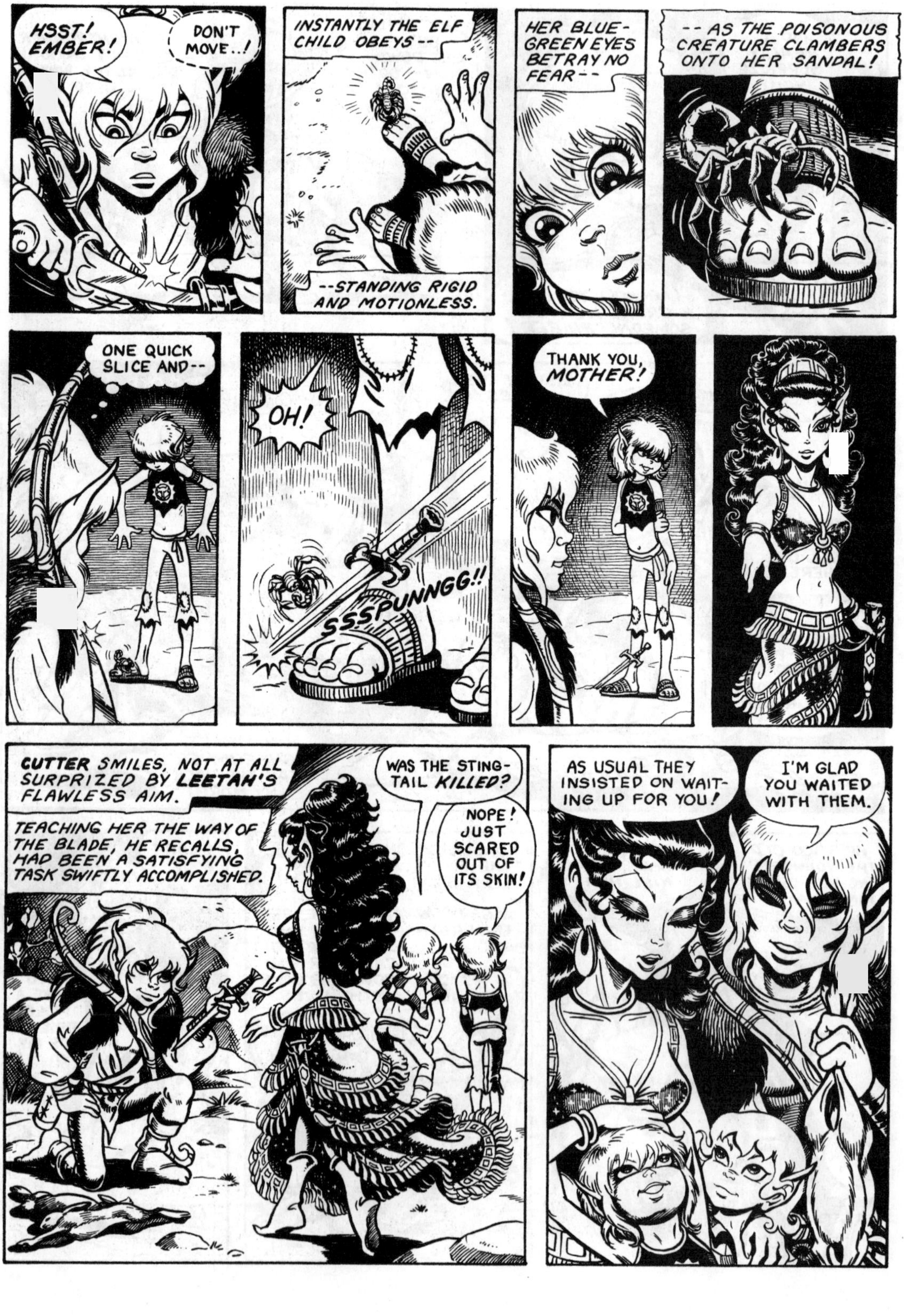
HSST! EMBER!
DON'T MOVE..!
INSTANTLY THE ELF CHILD OBEYS --
--STANDING RIGID AND MOTIONLESS.
HER BLUE-GREEN EYES BETRAY NO FEAR--
-- AS THE POISONOUS CREATURE CLAMBERS ONTO HER SANDAL!
ONE QUICK SLICE AND--
OH!
SSSPUNNGG!!
THANK YOU, MOTHER!
CUTTER SMILES, NOT AT ALL SURPRIZED BY LEETAH'S FLAWLESS AIM.
TEACHING HER THE WAY OF THE BLADE, HE RECALLS, HAD BEEN A SATISFYING TASK SWIFTLY ACCOMPLISHED.
WAS THE STING-TAIL KILLED?
NOPE! JUST SCARED OUT OF ITS SKIN!
AS USUAL THEY INSISTED ON WAITING UP FOR YOU!
I'M GLAD YOU WAITED WITH THEM.

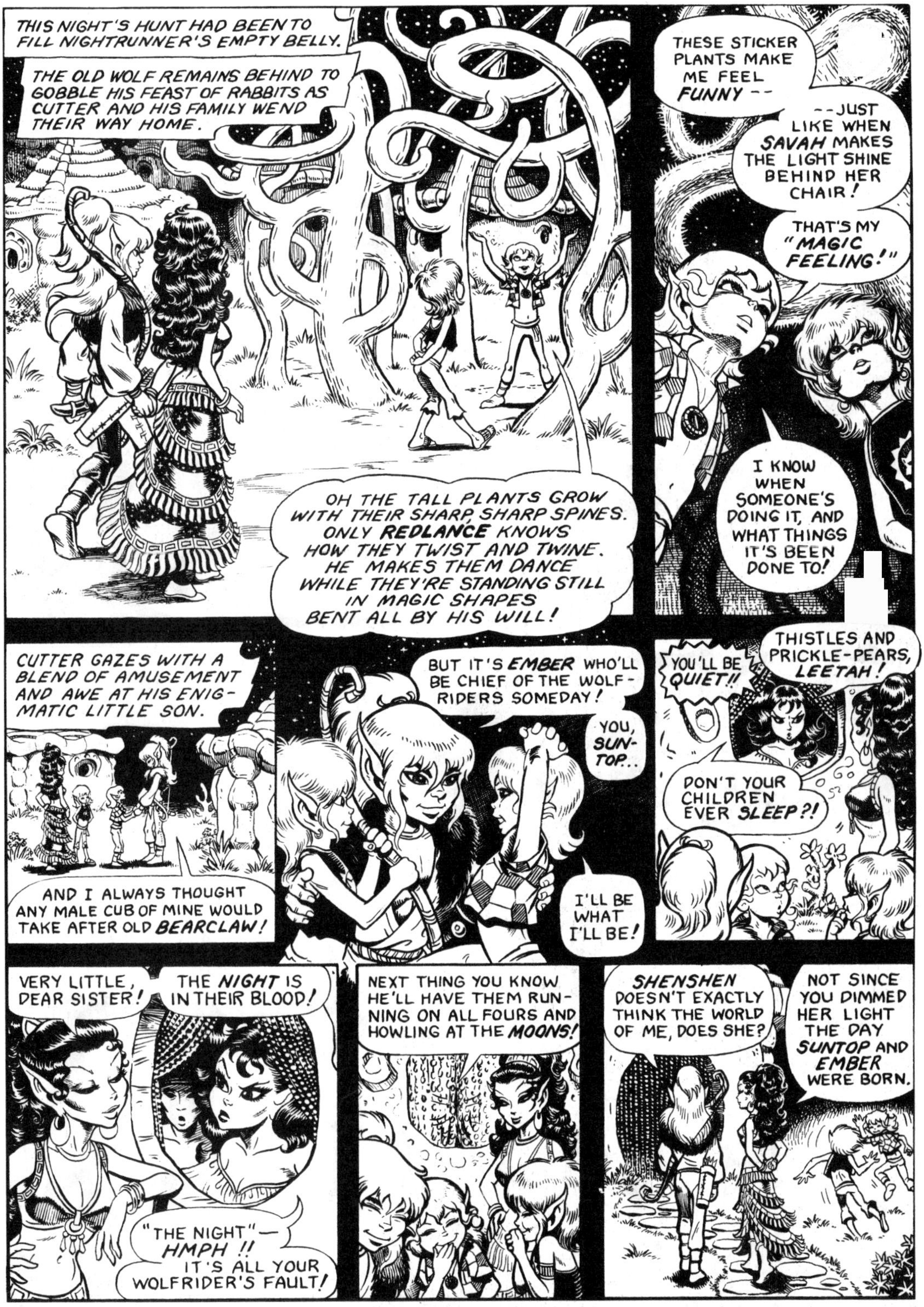
THIS NIGHT'S HUNT HAD BEEN TO FILL NIGHTRUNNER'S EMPTY BELLY.
THE OLD WOLF REMAINS BEHIND TO GOBBLE HIS FEAST OF RABBITS AS CUTTER AND HIS FAMILY WEND THEIR WAY HOME.
OH THE TALL PLANTS GROW WITH THEIR SHARP, SHARP SPINES. ONLY REDLANCE KNOWS HOW THEY TWIST AND TWINE. HE MAKES THEM DANCE WHILE THEY'RE STANDING STILL IN MAGIC SHAPES BENT ALL BY HIS WILL!
THESE STICKER PLANTS MAKE ME FEEL FUNNY --
-- JUST LIKE WHEN SAVAH MAKES THE LIGHT SHINE BEHIND HER CHAIR!
THAT'S MY "MAGIC FEELING!"
I KNOW WHEN SOMEONE'S DOING IT, AND WHAT THINGS IT'S BEEN DONE TO!
CUTTER GAZES WITH A BLEND OF AMUSEMENT AND AWE AT HIS ENIGMATIC LITTLE SON.
AND I ALWAYS THOUGHT ANY MALE CUB OF MINE WOULD TAKE AFTER OLD BEARCLAW!
BUT IT'S EMBER WHO'LL BE CHIEF OF THE WOLFRIDERS SOMEDAY!
YOU, SUNTOP...
I'LL BE WHAT I'LL BE!
THISTLES AND PRICKLE-PEARS, LEETAH!
YOU'LL BE QUIET!!
DON'T YOUR CHILDREN EVER SLEEP?!
VERY LITTLE, DEAR SISTER!
THE NIGHT IS IN THEIR BLOOD!
"THE NIGHT"— HMPH!! IT'S ALL YOUR WOLFRIDER'S FAULT!
NEXT THING YOU KNOW HE'LL HAVE THEM RUNNING ON ALL FOURS AND HOWLING AT THE MOONS!
SHENSHEN DOESN'T EXACTLY THINK THE WORLD OF ME, DOES SHE?
NOT SINCE YOU DIMMED HER LIGHT THE DAY SUNTOP AND EMBER WERE BORN.

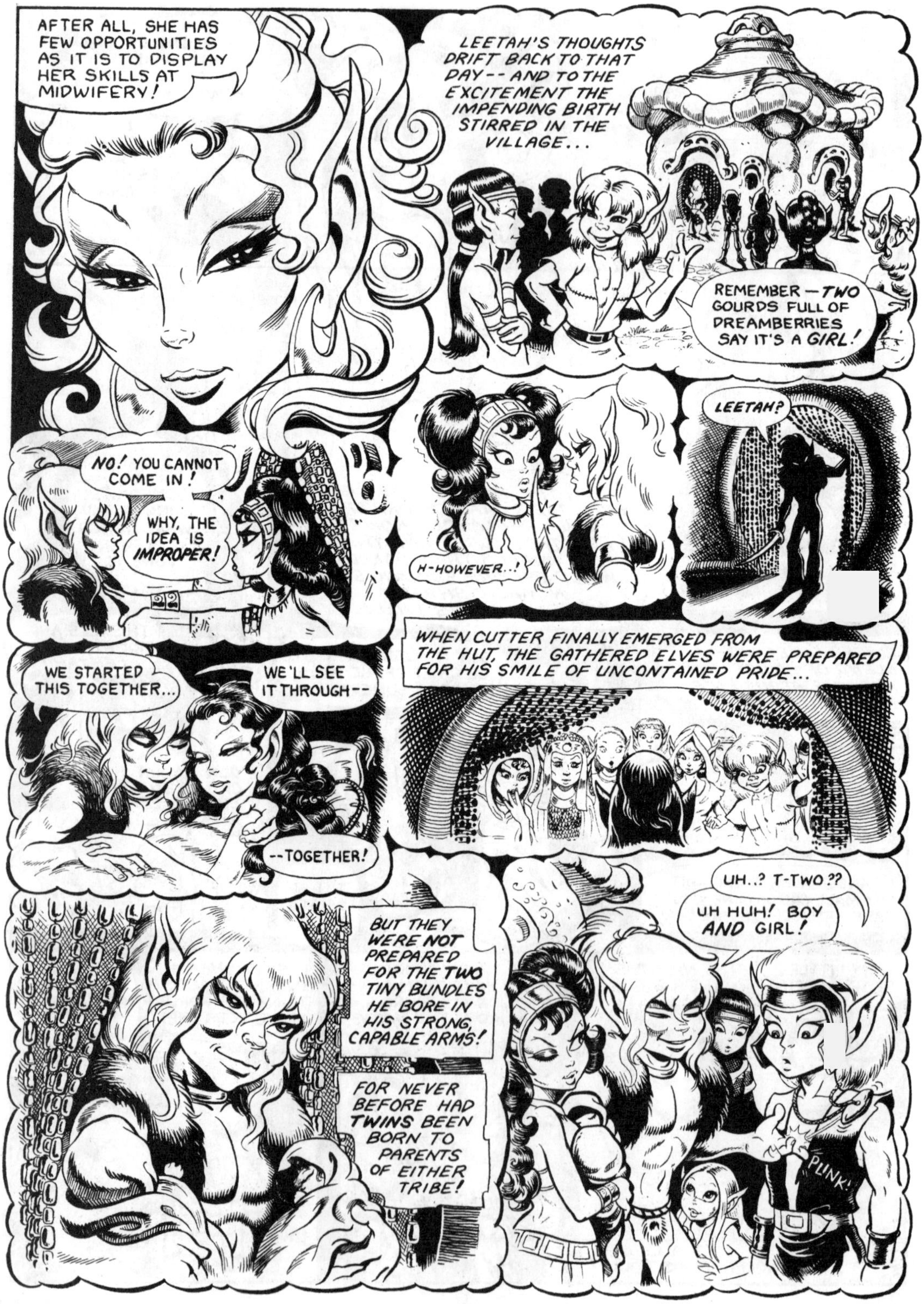
AFTER ALL, SHE HAS FEW OPPORTUNITIES AS IT IS TO DISPLAY HER SKILLS AT MIDWIFERY!
LEETAH'S THOUGHTS DRIFT BACK TO THAT DAY-- AND TO THE EXCITEMENT THE IMPENDING BIRTH STIRRED IN THE VILLAGE...
REMEMBER—TWO GOURDS FULL OF DREAMBERRIES SAY IT'S A GIRL!
NO! YOU CANNOT COME IN!
WHY, THE IDEA IS IMPROPER!
H-HOWEVER..!
LEETAH?
WE STARTED THIS TOGETHER...
WE'LL SEE IT THROUGH--
--TOGETHER!
WHEN CUTTER FINALLY EMERGED FROM THE HUT, THE GATHERED ELVES WERE PREPARED FOR HIS SMILE OF UNCONTAINED PRIDE...
BUT THEY WERE NOT PREPARED FOR THE TWO TINY BUNDLES HE BORE IN HIS STRONG, CAPABLE ARMS!
FOR NEVER BEFORE HAD TWINS BEEN BORN TO PARENTS OF EITHER TRIBE!
UH..? T-TWO??
UH HUH! BOY AND GIRL!
PLINK!

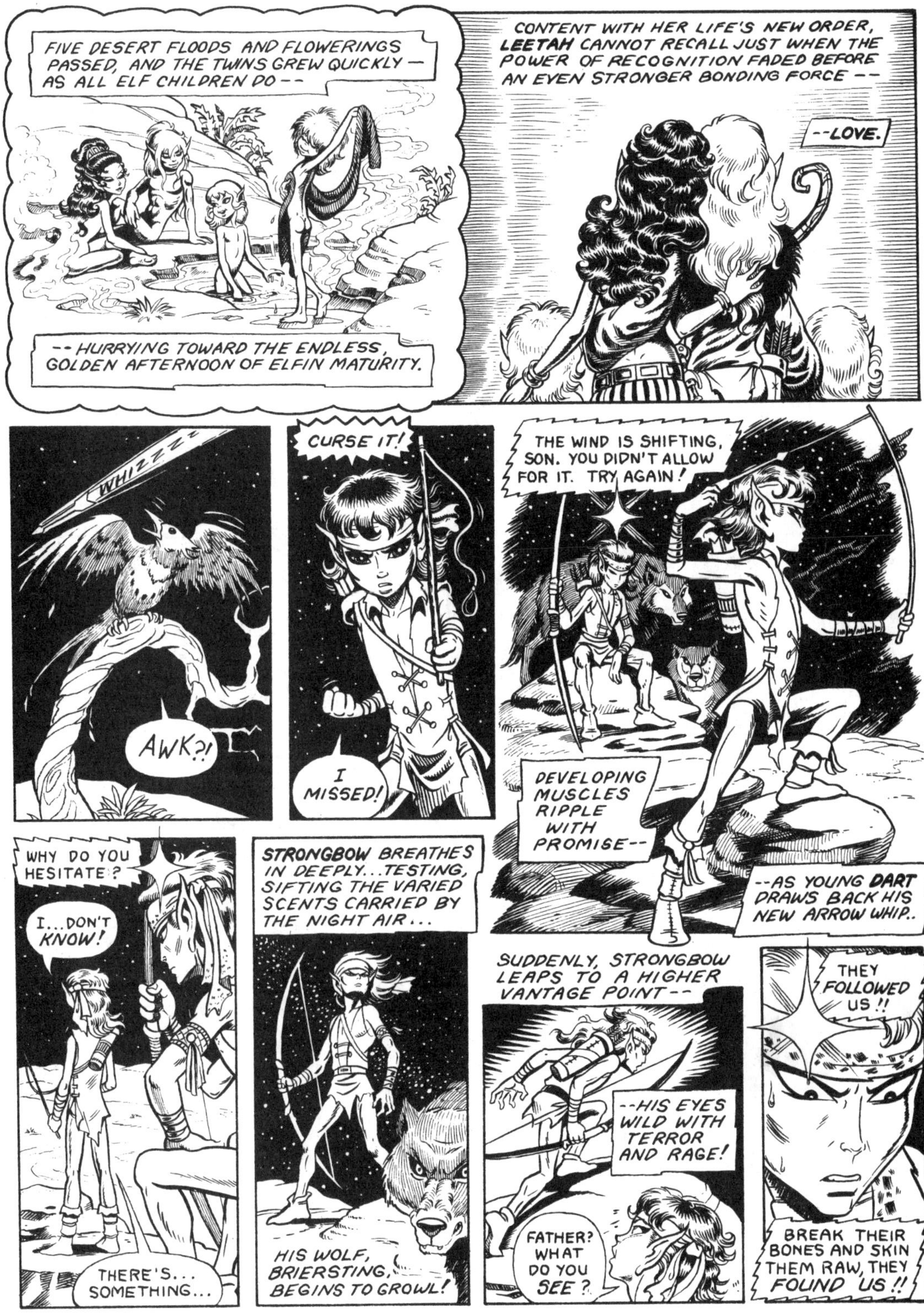
FIVE DESERT FLOODS AND FLOWERINGS PASSED, AND THE TWINS GREW QUICKLY — AS ALL ELF CHILDREN DO --
-- HURRYING TOWARD THE ENDLESS, GOLDEN AFTERNOON OF ELFIN MATURITY.
CONTENT WITH HER LIFE'S NEW ORDER, LEETAH CANNOT RECALL JUST WHEN THE POWER OF RECOGNITION FADED BEFORE AN EVEN STRONGER BONDING FORCE --
--LOVE.
WHIZZZZ
AWK?!
CURSE IT!
I MISSED!
THE WIND IS SHIFTING, SON. YOU DIDN'T ALLOW FOR IT. TRY AGAIN!
DEVELOPING MUSCLES RIPPLE WITH PROMISE--
--AS YOUNG DART DRAWS BACK HIS NEW ARROW WHIP..
WHY DO YOU HESITATE?
I...DON'T KNOW!
THERE'S... SOMETHING...
STRONGBOW BREATHES IN DEEPLY...TESTING, SIFTING THE VARIED SCENTS CARRIED BY THE NIGHT AIR...
HIS WOLF, BRIERSTING, BEGINS TO GROWL!
SUDDENLY, STRONGBOW LEAPS TO A HIGHER VANTAGE POINT --
--HIS EYES WILD WITH TERROR AND RAGE!
FATHER? WHAT DO YOU SEE?
THEY FOLLOWED US!!
BREAK THEIR BONES AND SKIN THEM RAW, THEY FOUND US!!

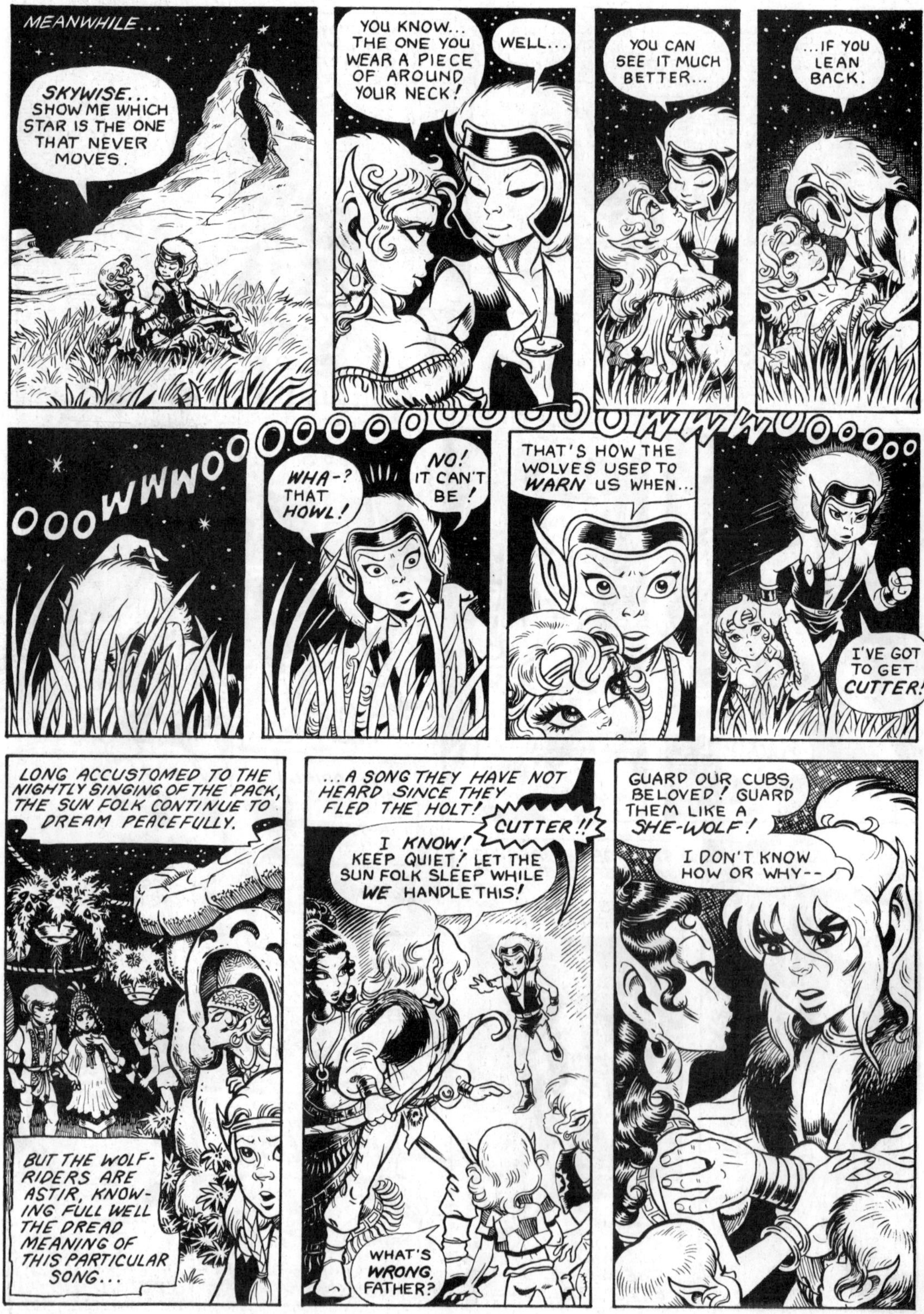

MEANWHILE...
SKYWISE... SHOW ME WHICH STAR IS THE ONE THAT NEVER MOVES.
YOU KNOW... THE ONE YOU WEAR A PIECE OF AROUND YOUR NECK!
WELL...
YOU CAN SEE IT MUCH BETTER...
...IF YOU LEAN BACK.
OOOWWWOOOOOOOOOOOOWWWOOOOOO
WHA-? THAT HOWL!
NO! IT CAN'T BE!
THAT'S HOW THE WOLVES USED TO WARN US WHEN...
I'VE GOT TO GET CUTTER!
LONG ACCUSTOMED TO THE NIGHTLY SINGING OF THE PACK, THE SUN FOLK CONTINUE TO DREAM PEACEFULLY.
BUT THE WOLF-RIDERS ARE ASTIR, KNOWING FULL WELL THE DREAD MEANING OF THIS PARTICULAR SONG...
...A SONG THEY HAVE NOT HEARD SINCE THEY FLED THE HOLT!
CUTTER!!
I KNOW! KEEP QUIET! LET THE SUN FOLK SLEEP WHILE WE HANDLE THIS!
WHAT'S WRONG, FATHER?
GUARD OUR CUBS, BELOVED! GUARD THEM LIKE A SHE-WOLF!
I DON'T KNOW HOW OR WHY--

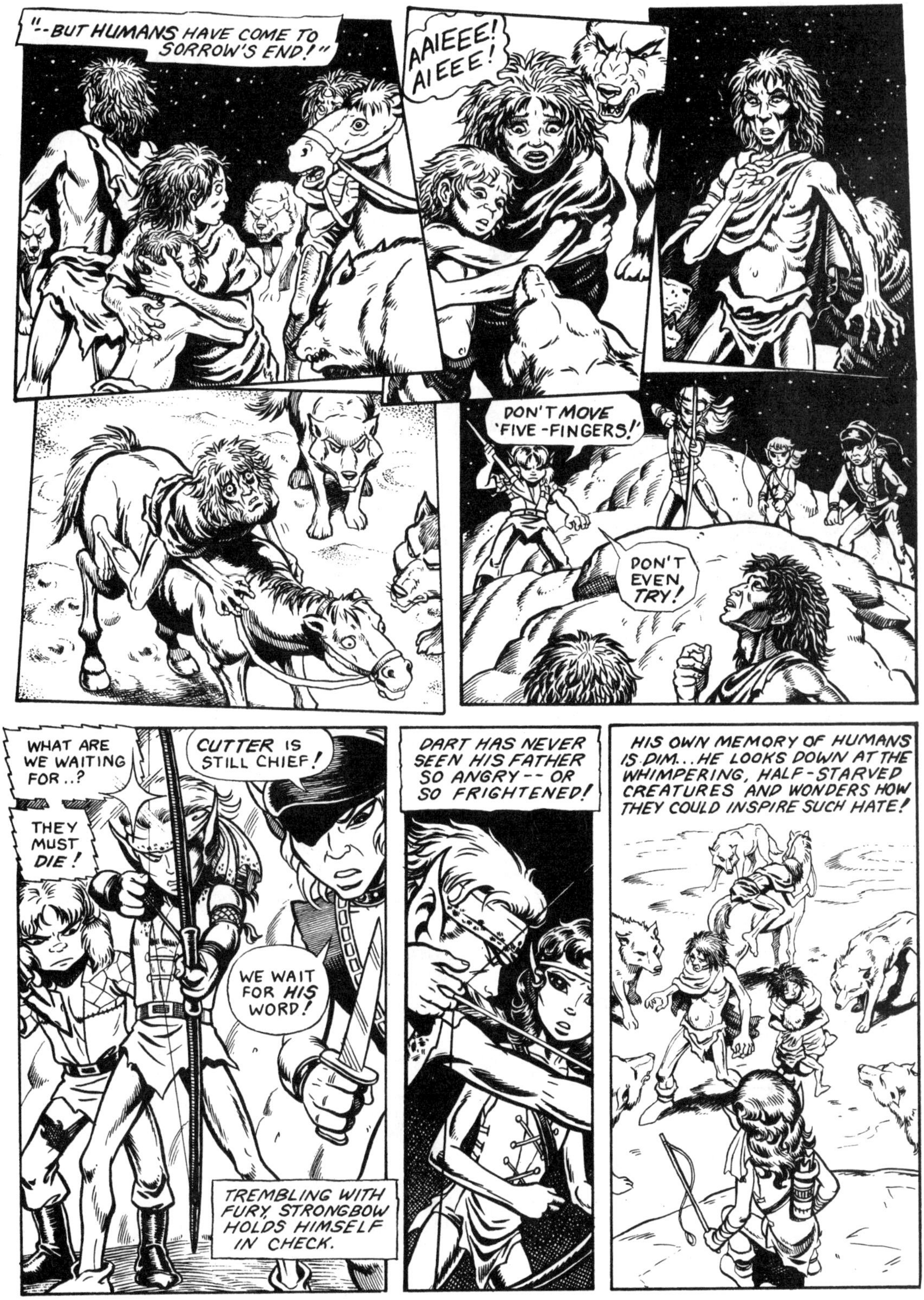
"--BUT HUMANS HAVE COME TO SORROW'S END!"
AAIEEE! AIEEE!
DON'T MOVE 'FIVE-FINGERS!'
DON'T EVEN TRY!
WHAT ARE WE WAITING FOR..?
THEY MUST DIE!
CUTTER IS STILL CHIEF!
WE WAIT FOR HIS WORD!
TREMBLING WITH FURY, STRONGBOW HOLDS HIMSELF IN CHECK.
DART HAS NEVER SEEN HIS FATHER SO ANGRY -- OR SO FRIGHTENED!
HIS OWN MEMORY OF HUMANS IS DIM... HE LOOKS DOWN AT THE WHIMPERING, HALF-STARVED CREATURES AND WONDERS HOW THEY COULD INSPIRE SUCH HATE!

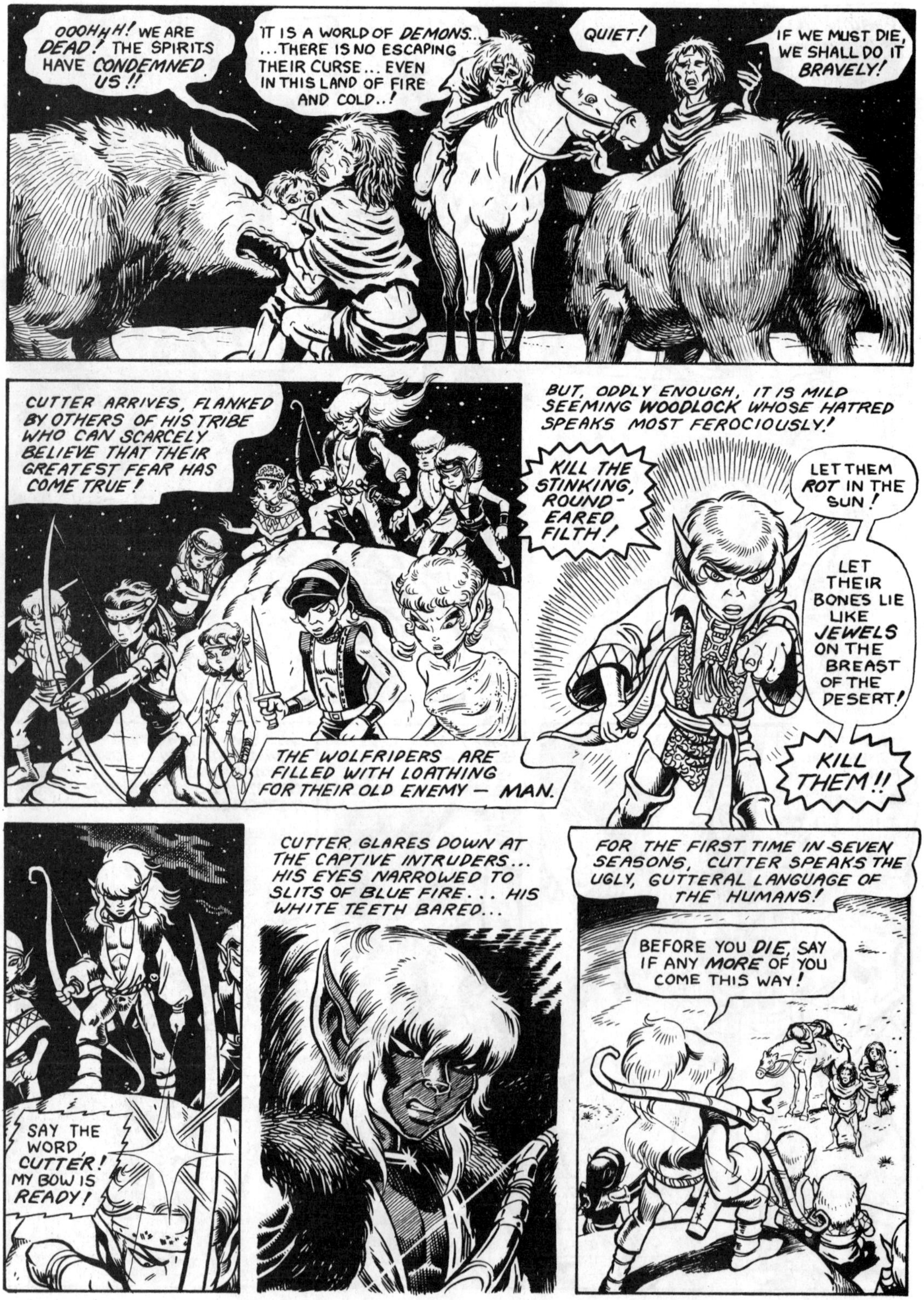

OOOHHH! WE ARE DEAD! THE SPIRITS HAVE CONDEMNED US!!
IT IS A WORLD OF DEMONS... ...THERE IS NO ESCAPING THEIR CURSE... EVEN IN THIS LAND OF FIRE AND COLD..!
QUIET!
IF WE MUST DIE, WE SHALL DO IT BRAVELY!
CUTTER ARRIVES, FLANKED BY OTHERS OF HIS TRIBE WHO CAN SCARCELY BELIEVE THAT THEIR GREATEST FEAR HAS COME TRUE!
THE WOLFRIDERS ARE FILLED WITH LOATHING FOR THEIR OLD ENEMY — MAN.
BUT, ODDLY ENOUGH, IT IS MILD SEEMING WOODLOCK WHOSE HATRED SPEAKS MOST FEROCIOUSLY!
KILL THE STINKING, ROUND-EARED FILTH!
LET THEM ROT IN THE SUN!
LET THEIR BONES LIE LIKE JEWELS ON THE BREAST OF THE DESERT!
KILL THEM!!
SAY THE WORD, CUTTER! MY BOW IS READY!
CUTTER GLARES DOWN AT THE CAPTIVE INTRUDERS... HIS EYES NARROWED TO SLITS OF BLUE FIRE... HIS WHITE TEETH BARED...
FOR THE FIRST TIME IN SEVEN SEASONS, CUTTER SPEAKS THE UGLY, GUTTERAL LANGUAGE OF THE HUMANS!
BEFORE YOU DIE, SAY IF ANY MORE OF YOU COME THIS WAY!

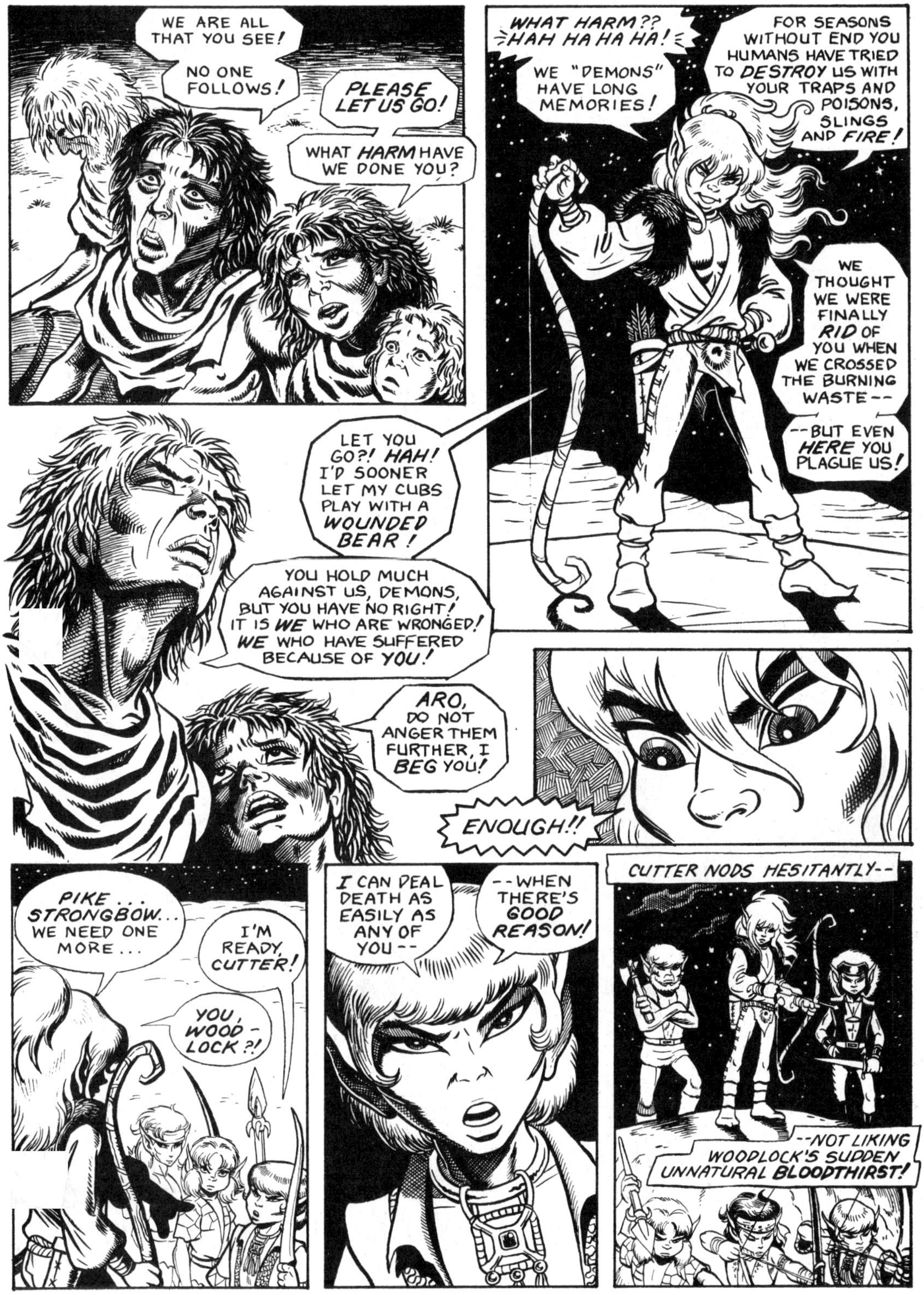
WE ARE ALL THAT YOU SEE!
NO ONE FOLLOWS!
PLEASE LET US GO!
WHAT HARM HAVE WE DONE YOU?
WHAT HARM?? HAH HA HA HA!
WE "DEMONS" HAVE LONG MEMORIES!
FOR SEASONS WITHOUT END YOU HUMANS HAVE TRIED TO DESTROY US WITH YOUR TRAPS AND POISONS, SLINGS AND FIRE!
WE THOUGHT WE WERE FINALLY RID OF YOU WHEN WE CROSSED THE BURNING WASTE--
--BUT EVEN HERE YOU PLAGUE US!
LET YOU GO?! HAH! I'D SOONER LET MY CUBS PLAY WITH A WOUNDED BEAR!
YOU HOLD MUCH AGAINST US, DEMONS, BUT YOU HAVE NO RIGHT! IT IS WE WHO ARE WRONGED! WE WHO HAVE SUFFERED BECAUSE OF YOU!
ARO, DO NOT ANGER THEM FURTHER, I BEG YOU!
ENOUGH!!
PIKE... STRONGBOW... WE NEED ONE MORE...
I'M READY, CUTTER!
YOU, WOODLOCK?!
I CAN DEAL DEATH AS EASILY AS ANY OF YOU--
--WHEN THERE'S GOOD REASON!
CUTTER NODS HESITANTLY--
--NOT LIKING WOODLOCK'S SUDDEN UNNATURAL BLOODTHIRST!

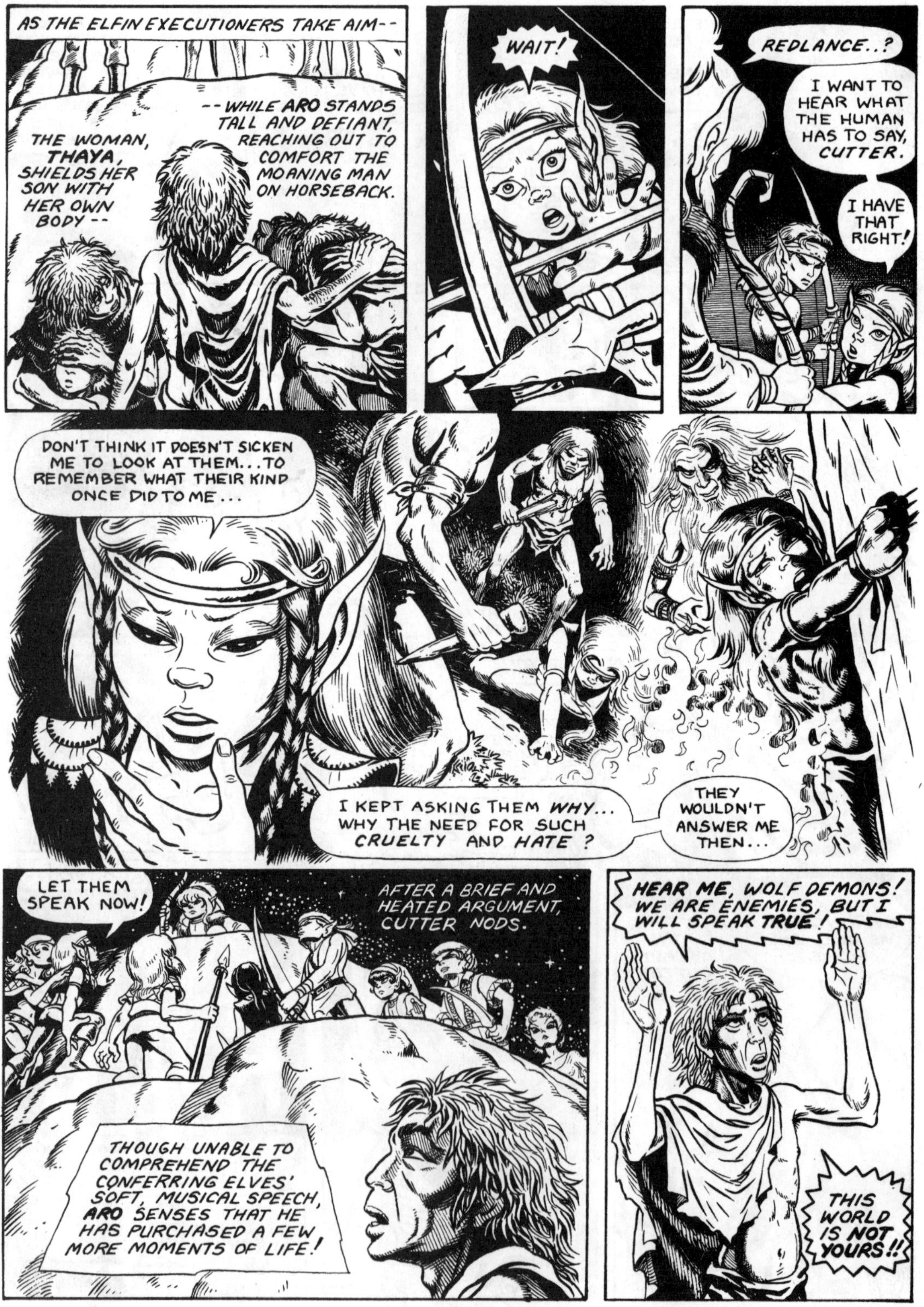
AS THE ELFIN EXECUTIONERS TAKE AIM--
THE WOMAN, THAYA, SHIELDS HER SON WITH HER OWN BODY --
-- WHILE ARO STANDS TALL AND DEFIANT, REACHING OUT TO COMFORT THE MOANING MAN ON HORSEBACK.
WAIT!
REDLANCE..?
I WANT TO HEAR WHAT THE HUMAN HAS TO SAY, CUTTER.
I HAVE THAT RIGHT!
DON'T THINK IT DOESN'T SICKEN ME TO LOOK AT THEM...TO REMEMBER WHAT THEIR KIND ONCE DID TO ME...
I KEPT ASKING THEM WHY... WHY THE NEED FOR SUCH CRUELTY AND HATE?
THEY WOULDN'T ANSWER ME THEN...
LET THEM SPEAK NOW!
AFTER A BRIEF AND HEATED ARGUMENT, CUTTER NODS.
THOUGH UNABLE TO COMPREHEND THE CONFERRING ELVES' SOFT, MUSICAL SPEECH, ARO SENSES THAT HE HAS PURCHASED A FEW MORE MOMENTS OF LIFE!
HEAR ME, WOLF DEMONS! WE ARE ENEMIES, BUT I WILL SPEAK TRUE!
THIS WORLD IS NOT YOURS!!

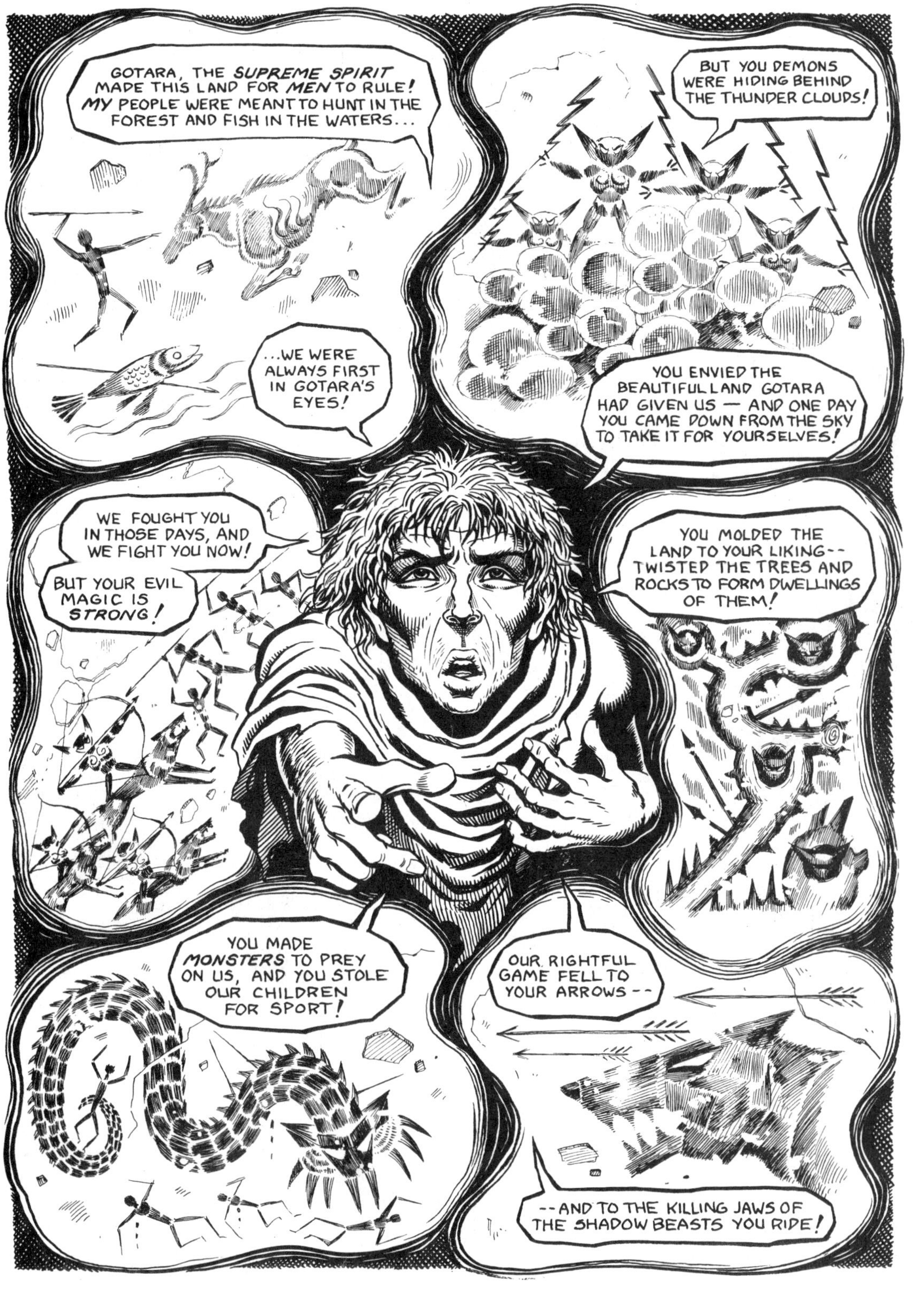
GOTARA, THE SUPREME SPIRIT MADE THIS LAND FOR MEN TO RULE! MY PEOPLE WERE MEANT TO HUNT IN THE FOREST AND FISH IN THE WATERS...
...WE WERE ALWAYS FIRST IN GOTARA'S EYES!
BUT YOU DEMONS WERE HIDING BEHIND THE THUNDER CLOUDS!
YOU ENVIED THE BEAUTIFUL LAND GOTARA HAD GIVEN US — AND ONE DAY YOU CAME DOWN FROM THE SKY TO TAKE IT FOR YOURSELVES!
WE FOUGHT YOU IN THOSE DAYS, AND WE FIGHT YOU NOW!
BUT YOUR EVIL MAGIC IS STRONG!
YOU MOLDED THE LAND TO YOUR LIKING-- TWISTED THE TREES AND ROCKS TO FORM DWELLINGS OF THEM!
YOU MADE MONSTERS TO PREY ON US, AND YOU STOLE OUR CHILDREN FOR SPORT!
OUR RIGHTFUL GAME FELL TO YOUR ARROWS--
--AND TO THE KILLING JAWS OF THE SHADOW BEASTS YOU RIDE!

CAN YOU WONDER, NOW, WHY WE *HATE* YOU?

YOU DO NOT *BELONG* HERE!

GO BACK! GO BACK INTO THE STORM!

GOTARA DESPISES YOU!!

SO... THAT'S IT!

I USED TO WONDER WHY THERE WAS ALWAYS AT LEAST *ONE* GROUP OF HUMANS CAMPED NEAR THE HOLT-- JUST LOOKING FOR TROUBLE.

THE FOREST WAS BIG! IT COULD HAVE FED AND SHELTERED US ALL! OUR PATHS NEVER HAD TO CROSS!

BUT *YOU* HAD YOUR SACRED DUTY TO *KILL* US, DIDN'T YOU!

AND WE LEARNED TO GIVE BACK AS GOOD AS WE GOT!

NO *WONDER* THIS FEUD HAS GONE ON FOR SO LONG!

CUTTER CROUCHES LOW-- TRANSFIXING ARO WITH HIS STRANGE, LUPINE STARE.

WELL? WASN'T IT ENOUGH THAT YOU DROVE US FROM OUR HOMES WITH *FIRE*?!

HAVE YOU COME ALL THIS WAY TO FINISH US OFF?

YOUR ALMIGHTY *GOTARA* HAS TRICKED YOU, HUMANS... YOU'RE IN *OUR* HANDS NOW!

IT IS OUR FINAL *PUNISHMENT* FOR DESTROYING THE FOREST!

YES... THAT MUST BE IT..!

FOR DAYS THE FLAMES BURNED HIGH!

WE FLOATED IN THE CENTER OF THE WIDE LAKE... PRAYING FOR *RAIN*...

...WHICH *GOTARA* FINALLY SENT US.

BLACK... BLACK... ASHES AND *DEATH!*

WE ARE WANDERERS IN THE BLACKNESS... SEARCHING FOR A BIT OF *GREEN*..!

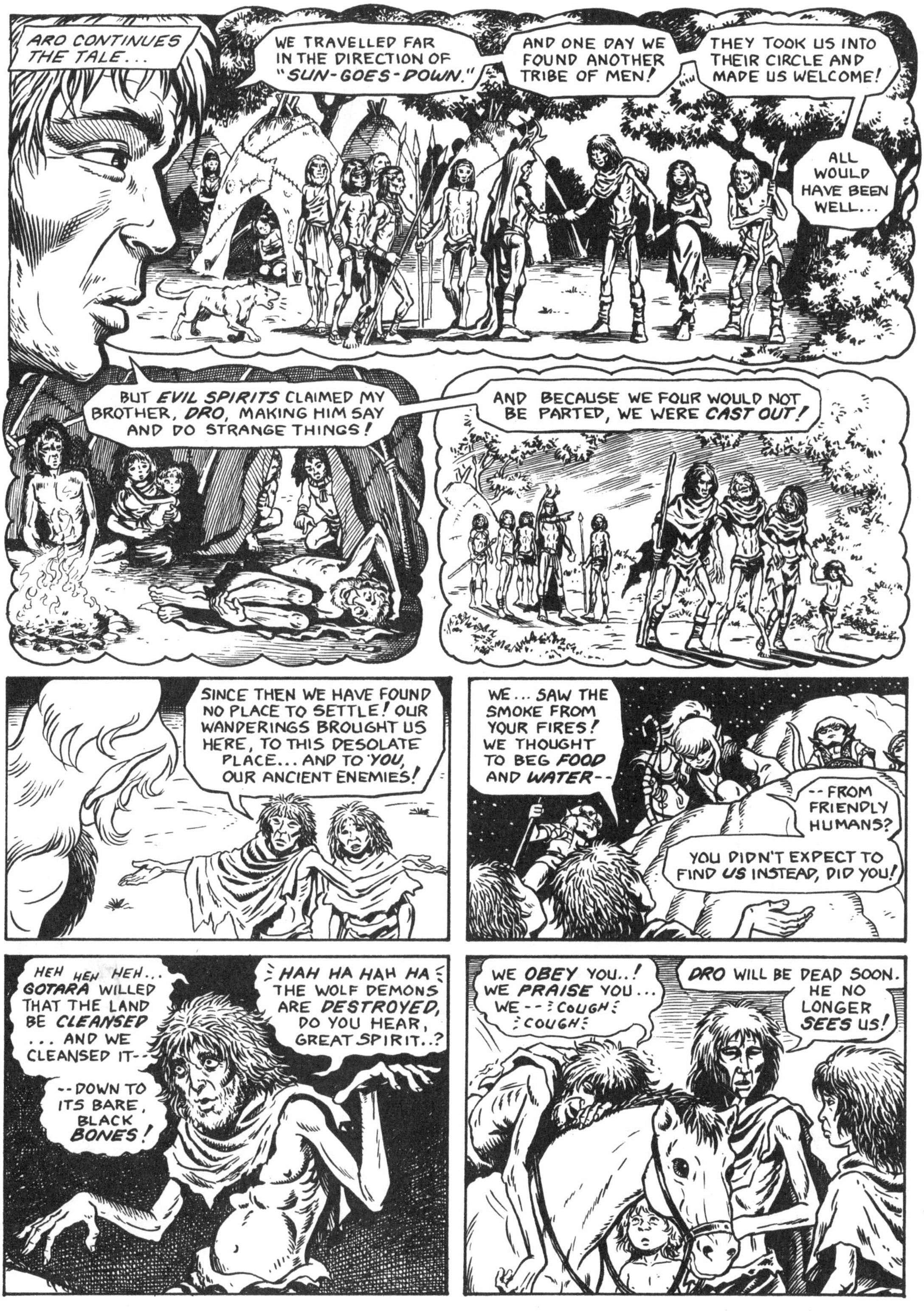
ARO CONTINUES THE TALE...
WE TRAVELLED FAR IN THE DIRECTION OF "SUN-GOES-DOWN."
AND ONE DAY WE FOUND ANOTHER TRIBE OF MEN!
THEY TOOK US INTO THEIR CIRCLE AND MADE US WELCOME!
ALL WOULD HAVE BEEN WELL...
BUT EVIL SPIRITS CLAIMED MY BROTHER, DRO, MAKING HIM SAY AND DO STRANGE THINGS!
AND BECAUSE WE FOUR WOULD NOT BE PARTED, WE WERE CAST OUT!
SINCE THEN WE HAVE FOUND NO PLACE TO SETTLE! OUR WANDERINGS BROUGHT US HERE, TO THIS DESOLATE PLACE... AND TO YOU, OUR ANCIENT ENEMIES!
WE... SAW THE SMOKE FROM YOUR FIRES! WE THOUGHT TO BEG FOOD AND WATER--
--FROM FRIENDLY HUMANS?
YOU DIDN'T EXPECT TO FIND US INSTEAD, DID YOU!
HEH HEH HEH... GOTARA WILLED THAT THE LAND BE CLEANSED ... AND WE CLEANSED IT--
--DOWN TO ITS BARE, BLACK BONES!
HAH HA HAH HA THE WOLF DEMONS ARE DESTROYED, DO YOU HEAR, GREAT SPIRIT..?
WE OBEY YOU..! WE PRAISE YOU... WE-- COUGH COUGH
DRO WILL BE DEAD SOON. HE NO LONGER SEES US!

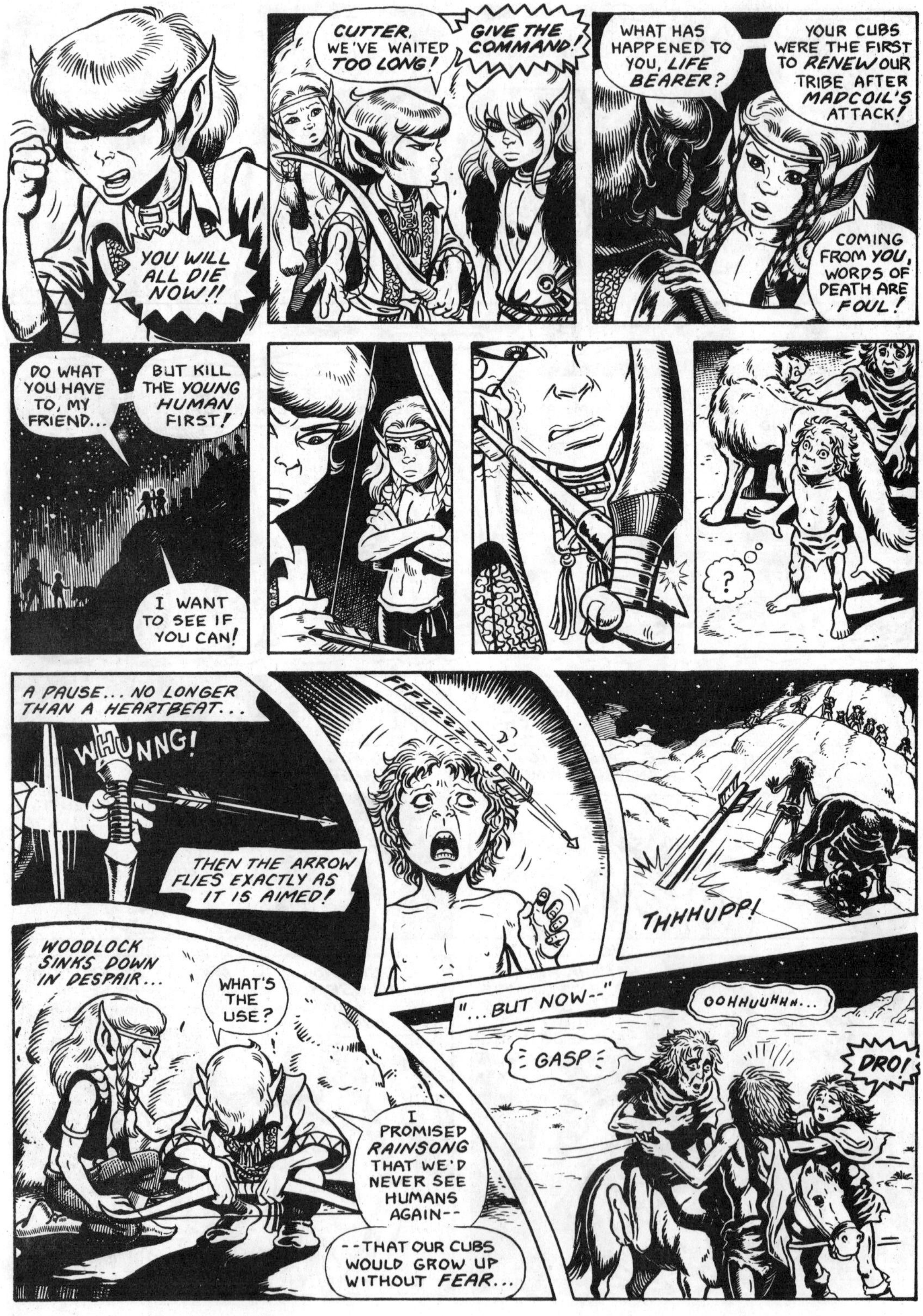
YOU WILL ALL DIE NOW!!
CUTTER, WE'VE WAITED TOO LONG!
GIVE THE COMMAND!
WHAT HAS HAPPENED TO YOU, LIFE BEARER?
YOUR CUBS WERE THE FIRST TO RENEW OUR TRIBE AFTER MADCOIL'S ATTACK!
COMING FROM YOU, WORDS OF DEATH ARE FOUL!
DO WHAT YOU HAVE TO, MY FRIEND...
BUT KILL THE YOUNG HUMAN FIRST!
I WANT TO SEE IF YOU CAN!
?
A PAUSE... NO LONGER THAN A HEARTBEAT...
WHUNNG!
THEN THE ARROW FLIES EXACTLY AS IT IS AIMED!
FFFZZZZT
THHHUPP!
WOODLOCK SINKS DOWN IN DESPAIR...
WHAT'S THE USE?
I PROMISED RAINSONG THAT WE'D NEVER SEE HUMANS AGAIN--
--THAT OUR CUBS WOULD GROW UP WITHOUT FEAR...
"...BUT NOW--"
OOHHUUHHH...
GASP
DRO!

HE IS DEAD, THAYA... AND SOON WE WILL JOIN HIM!

GO!!

LET THE DEAD ONE LIE THERE AS A WARNING! IF YOU OR OTHERS LIKE YOU EVER COME HERE AGAIN--

--WE'LL KILL YOU ON SIGHT!! UNDERSTAND?

GO QUICKLY, BEFORE I THINK TWICE!!

ARO DOES NOT QUESTION HIS GOOD FORTUNE--

--IF SUCH IT BE, FOR HE HAS NO PROVISIONS AND DARES ASK FOR NONE!

THE HUMANS AND THEIR STARVING PONY STAGGER AWAY INTO THE DARKNESS...THEY HAVE ONLY THEIR LIVES AND EACH OTHER... BUT IT IS MORE THAN THEY EXPECTED.

YOU...LET...THEM...GO!

CUTTER TURNS TO CONFRONT A SEETHING STRONGBOW! THEIR EYES MEET AND LOCK IN A STARE OF CHALLENGE!

WE HAD THEM HELPLESS AT OUR FEET, AND YOU LET THEM GO!

BEARCLAW WOULD HAVE CUT OUT THEIR LIVING HEARTS AND FED THEM TO THE WOLVES!!

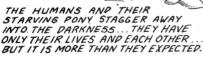

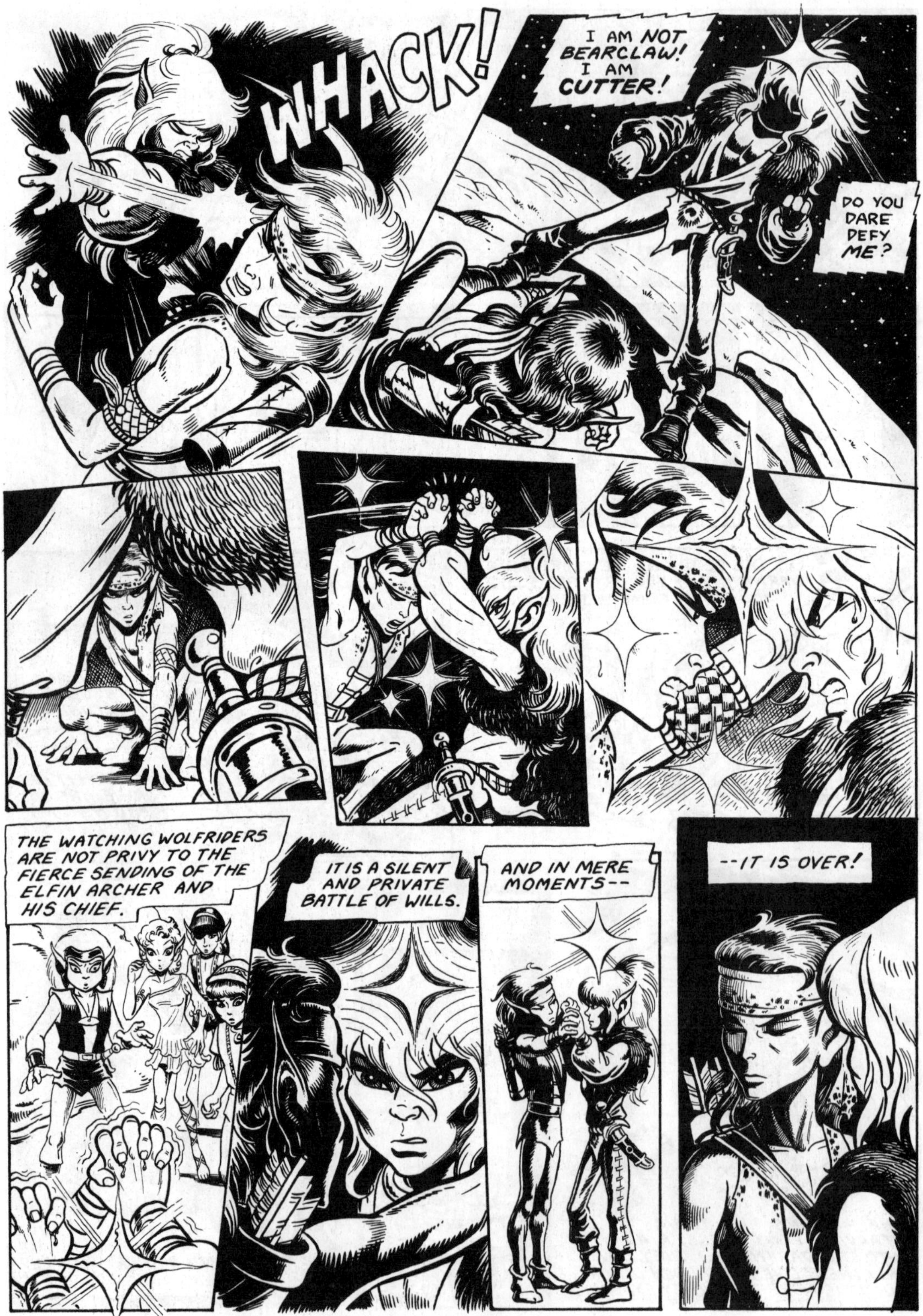
WHACK!
I AM NOT BEARCLAW! I AM CUTTER!
DO YOU DARE DEFY ME?
THE WATCHING WOLFRIDERS ARE NOT PRIVY TO THE FIERCE SENDING OF THE ELFIN ARCHER AND HIS CHIEF.
IT IS A SILENT AND PRIVATE BATTLE OF WILLS.
AND IN MERE MOMENTS--
--IT IS OVER!

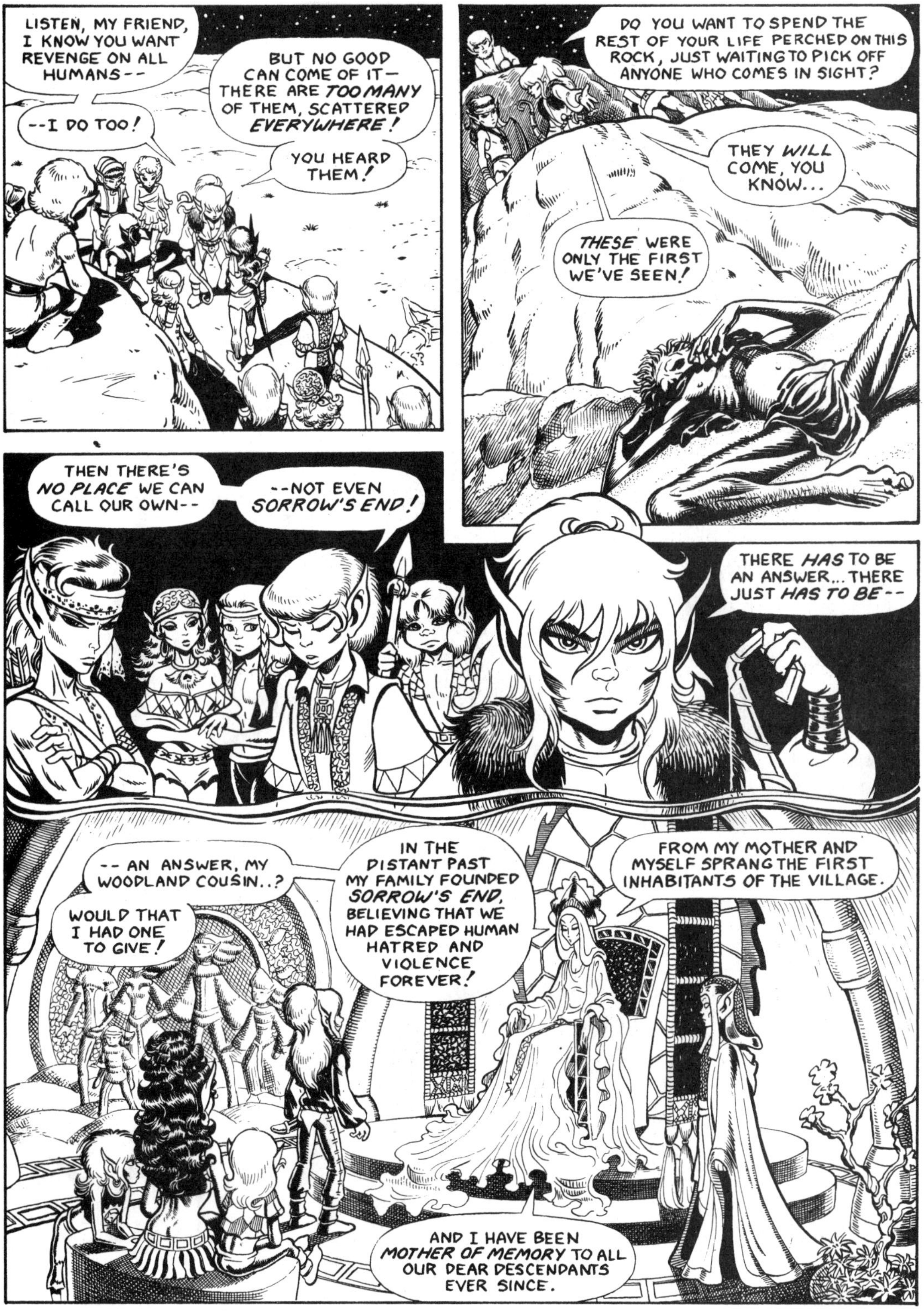
LISTEN, MY FRIEND, I KNOW YOU WANT REVENGE ON ALL HUMANS--
--I DO TOO!
BUT NO GOOD CAN COME OF IT— THERE ARE TOO MANY OF THEM, SCATTERED EVERYWHERE!
YOU HEARD THEM!
DO YOU WANT TO SPEND THE REST OF YOUR LIFE PERCHED ON THIS ROCK, JUST WAITING TO PICK OFF ANYONE WHO COMES IN SIGHT?
THEY WILL COME, YOU KNOW...
THESE WERE ONLY THE FIRST WE'VE SEEN!
THEN THERE'S NO PLACE WE CAN CALL OUR OWN--
--NOT EVEN SORROW'S END!
THERE HAS TO BE AN ANSWER... THERE JUST HAS TO BE--
-- AN ANSWER, MY WOODLAND COUSIN..?
WOULD THAT I HAD ONE TO GIVE!
IN THE DISTANT PAST MY FAMILY FOUNDED SORROW'S END, BELIEVING THAT WE HAD ESCAPED HUMAN HATRED AND VIOLENCE FOREVER!
FROM MY MOTHER AND MYSELF SPRANG THE FIRST INHABITANTS OF THE VILLAGE.
AND I HAVE BEEN MOTHER OF MEMORY TO ALL OUR DEAR DESCENDANTS EVER SINCE.

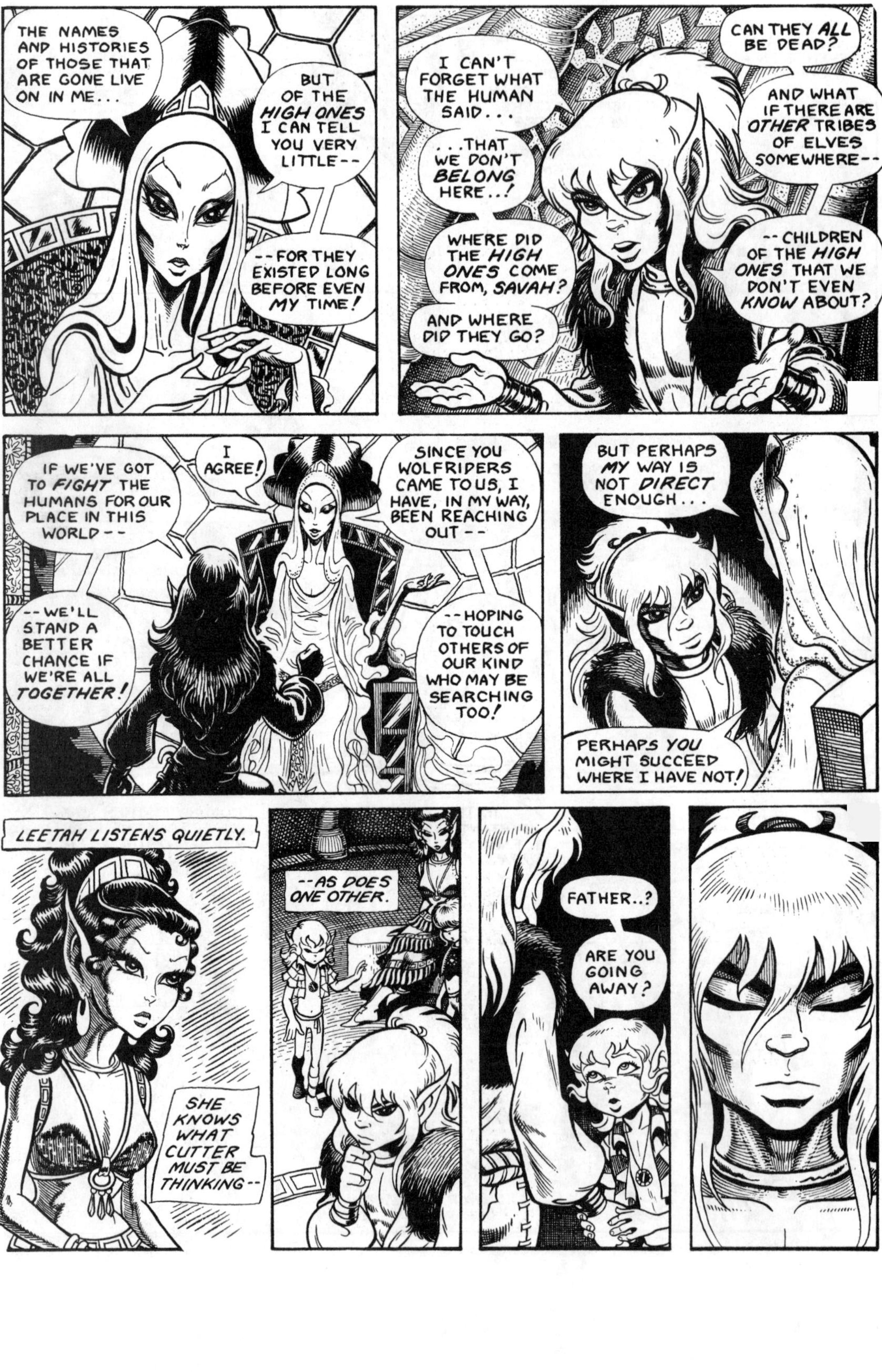

THE NAMES AND HISTORIES OF THOSE THAT ARE GONE LIVE ON IN ME...
BUT OF THE HIGH ONES I CAN TELL YOU VERY LITTLE--
--FOR THEY EXISTED LONG BEFORE EVEN MY TIME!
I CAN'T FORGET WHAT THE HUMAN SAID...
...THAT WE DON'T BELONG HERE...!
WHERE DID THE HIGH ONES COME FROM, SAVAH?
AND WHERE DID THEY GO?
CAN THEY ALL BE DEAD?
AND WHAT IF THERE ARE OTHER TRIBES OF ELVES SOMEWHERE--
--CHILDREN OF THE HIGH ONES THAT WE DON'T EVEN KNOW ABOUT?
IF WE'VE GOT TO FIGHT THE HUMANS FOR OUR PLACE IN THIS WORLD--
I AGREE!
--WE'LL STAND A BETTER CHANCE IF WE'RE ALL TOGETHER!
SINCE YOU WOLFRIDERS CAME TO US, I HAVE, IN MY WAY, BEEN REACHING OUT--
--HOPING TO TOUCH OTHERS OF OUR KIND WHO MAY BE SEARCHING TOO!
BUT PERHAPS MY WAY IS NOT DIRECT ENOUGH...
PERHAPS YOU MIGHT SUCCEED WHERE I HAVE NOT!
LEETAH LISTENS QUIETLY.
SHE KNOWS WHAT CUTTER MUST BE THINKING--
--AS DOES ONE OTHER.
FATHER..?
ARE YOU GOING AWAY?

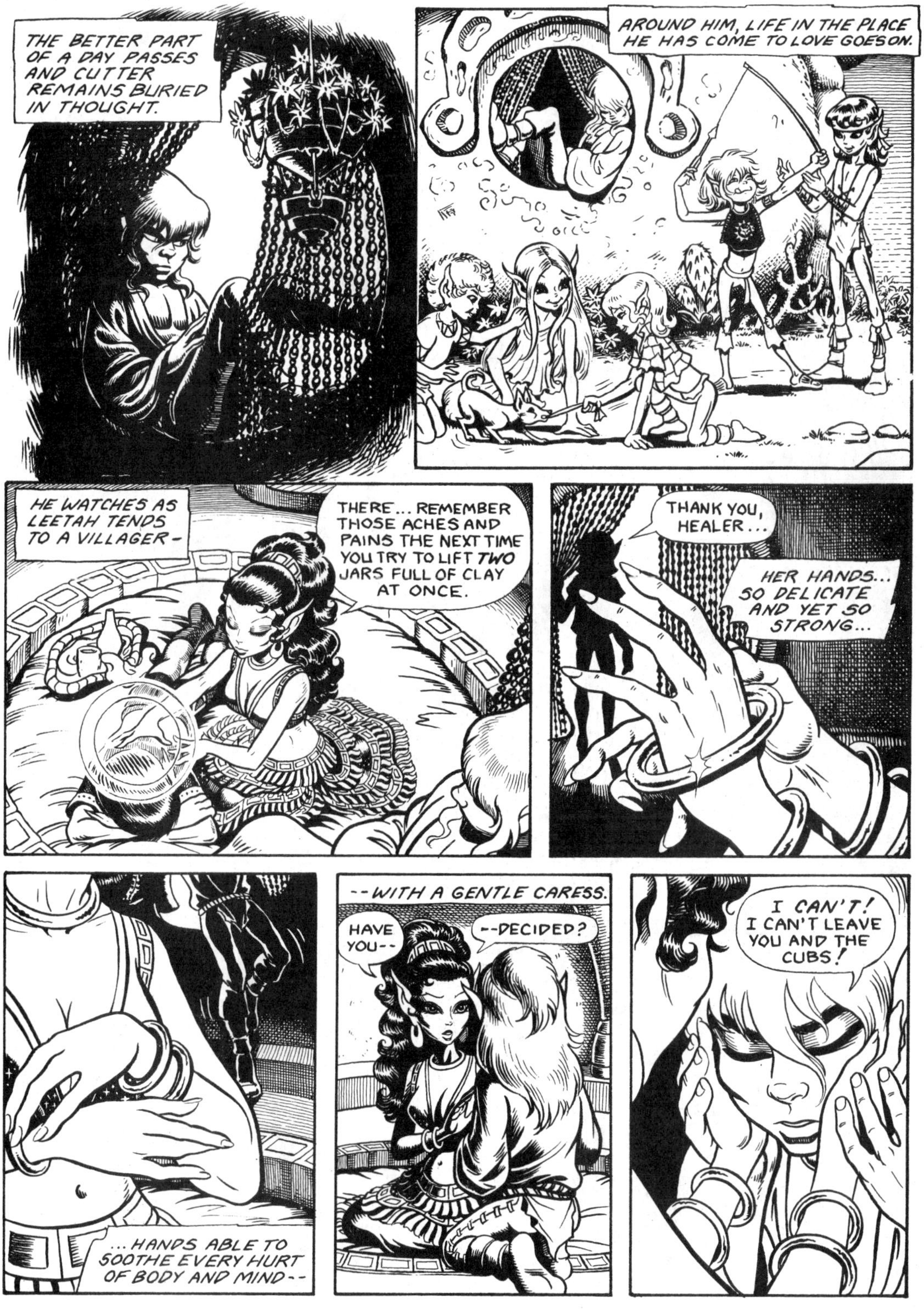
THE BETTER PART OF A DAY PASSES AND CUTTER REMAINS BURIED IN THOUGHT.
AROUND HIM, LIFE IN THE PLACE HE HAS COME TO LOVE GOES ON.
HE WATCHES AS LEETAH TENDS TO A VILLAGER-
THERE... REMEMBER THOSE ACHES AND PAINS THE NEXT TIME YOU TRY TO LIFT TWO JARS FULL OF CLAY AT ONCE.
THANK YOU, HEALER...
HER HANDS... SO DELICATE AND YET SO STRONG...
...HANDS ABLE TO SOOTHE EVERY HURT OF BODY AND MIND--
--WITH A GENTLE CARESS.
HAVE YOU--
--DECIDED?
I CAN'T! I CAN'T LEAVE YOU AND THE CUBS!

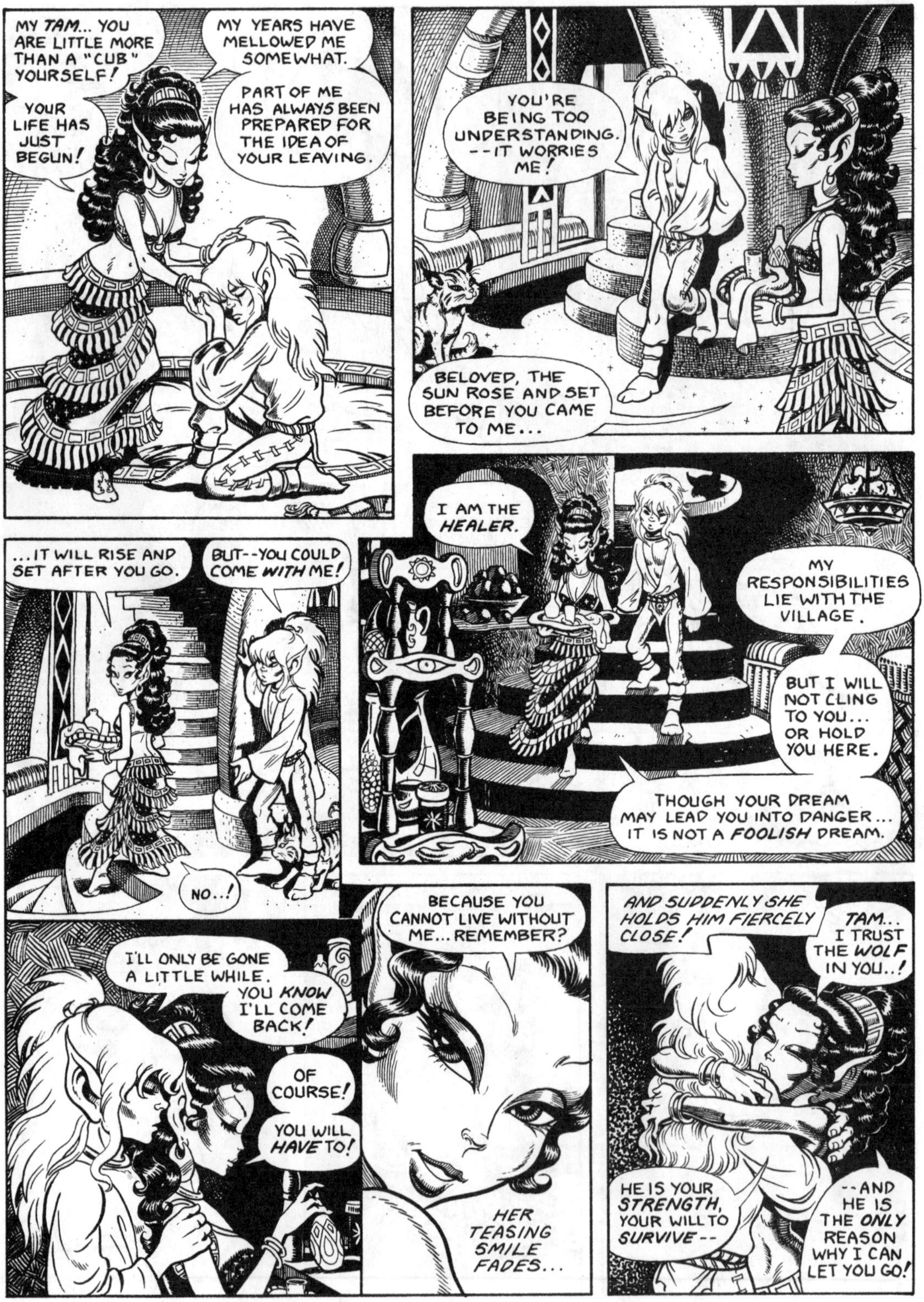
MY TAM... YOU ARE LITTLE MORE THAN A "CUB" YOURSELF!
YOUR LIFE HAS JUST BEGUN!
MY YEARS HAVE MELLOWED ME SOMEWHAT.
PART OF ME HAS ALWAYS BEEN PREPARED FOR THE IDEA OF YOUR LEAVING.
YOU'RE BEING TOO UNDERSTANDING. --IT WORRIES ME!
BELOVED, THE SUN ROSE AND SET BEFORE YOU CAME TO ME...
...IT WILL RISE AND SET AFTER YOU GO.
BUT--YOU COULD COME WITH ME!
NO..!
I AM THE HEALER.
MY RESPONSIBILITIES LIE WITH THE VILLAGE.
BUT I WILL NOT CLING TO YOU... OR HOLD YOU HERE.
THOUGH YOUR DREAM MAY LEAD YOU INTO DANGER... IT IS NOT A FOOLISH DREAM.
I'LL ONLY BE GONE A LITTLE WHILE.
YOU KNOW I'LL COME BACK!
OF COURSE!
YOU WILL HAVE TO!
BECAUSE YOU CANNOT LIVE WITHOUT ME... REMEMBER?
HER TEASING SMILE FADES...
AND SUDDENLY SHE HOLDS HIM FIERCELY CLOSE!
TAM... I TRUST THE WOLF IN YOU..!
HE IS YOUR STRENGTH, YOUR WILL TO SURVIVE--
--AND HE IS THE ONLY REASON WHY I CAN LET YOU GO!

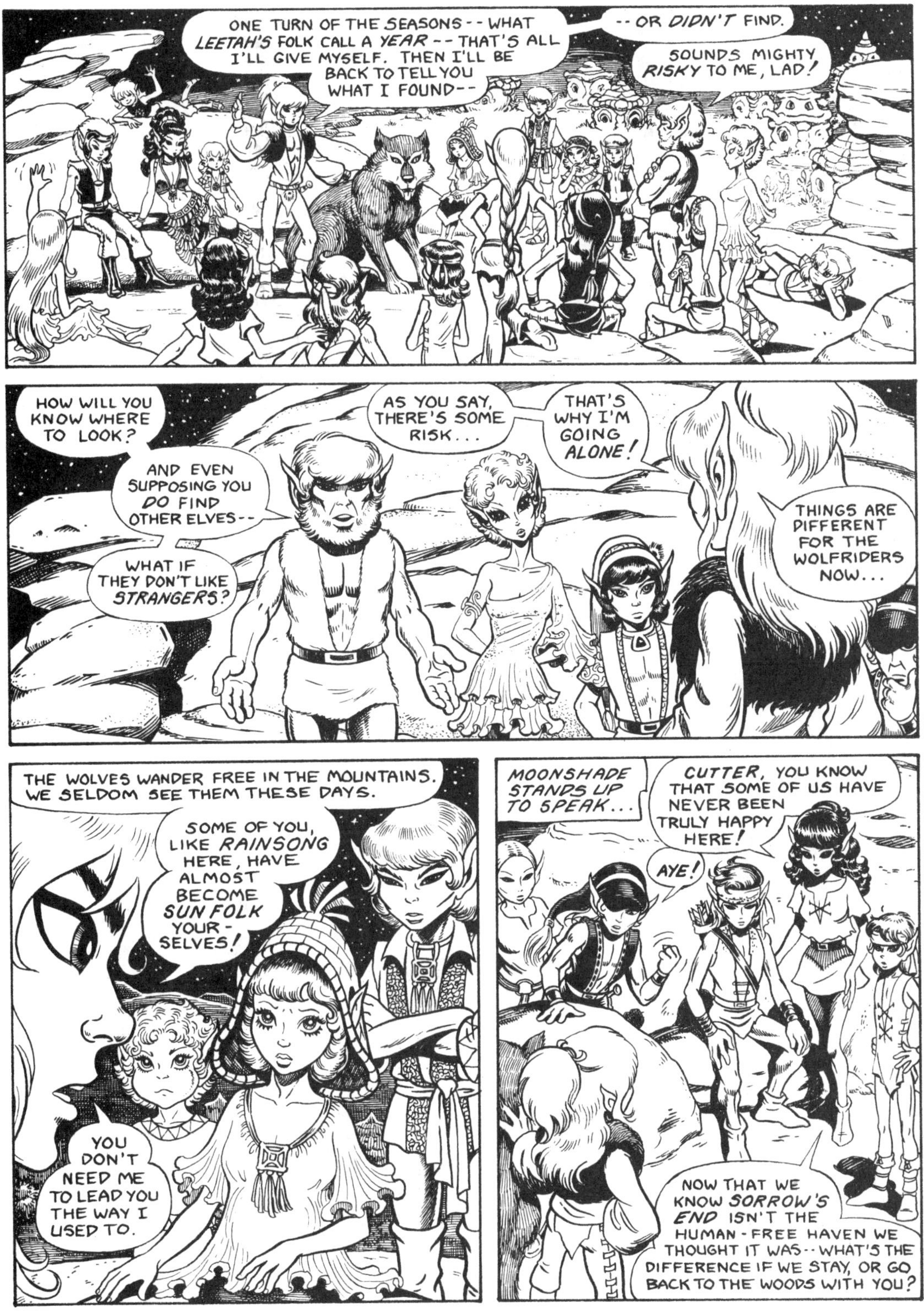
ONE TURN OF THE SEASONS -- WHAT LEETAH'S FOLK CALL A YEAR -- THAT'S ALL I'LL GIVE MYSELF. THEN I'LL BE BACK TO TELL YOU WHAT I FOUND--
-- OR DIDN'T FIND.
SOUNDS MIGHTY RISKY TO ME, LAD!
HOW WILL YOU KNOW WHERE TO LOOK?
AND EVEN SUPPOSING YOU DO FIND OTHER ELVES--
WHAT IF THEY DON'T LIKE STRANGERS?
AS YOU SAY, THERE'S SOME RISK...
THAT'S WHY I'M GOING ALONE!
THINGS ARE DIFFERENT FOR THE WOLFRIDERS NOW...
THE WOLVES WANDER FREE IN THE MOUNTAINS. WE SELDOM SEE THEM THESE DAYS.
SOME OF YOU, LIKE RAINSONG HERE, HAVE ALMOST BECOME SUN FOLK YOURSELVES!
YOU DON'T NEED ME TO LEAD YOU THE WAY I USED TO.
MOONSHADE STANDS UP TO SPEAK...
CUTTER, YOU KNOW THAT SOME OF US HAVE NEVER BEEN TRULY HAPPY HERE!
AYE!
NOW THAT WE KNOW SORROW'S END ISN'T THE HUMAN-FREE HAVEN WE THOUGHT IT WAS -- WHAT'S THE DIFFERENCE IF WE STAY, OR GO BACK TO THE WOODS WITH YOU?

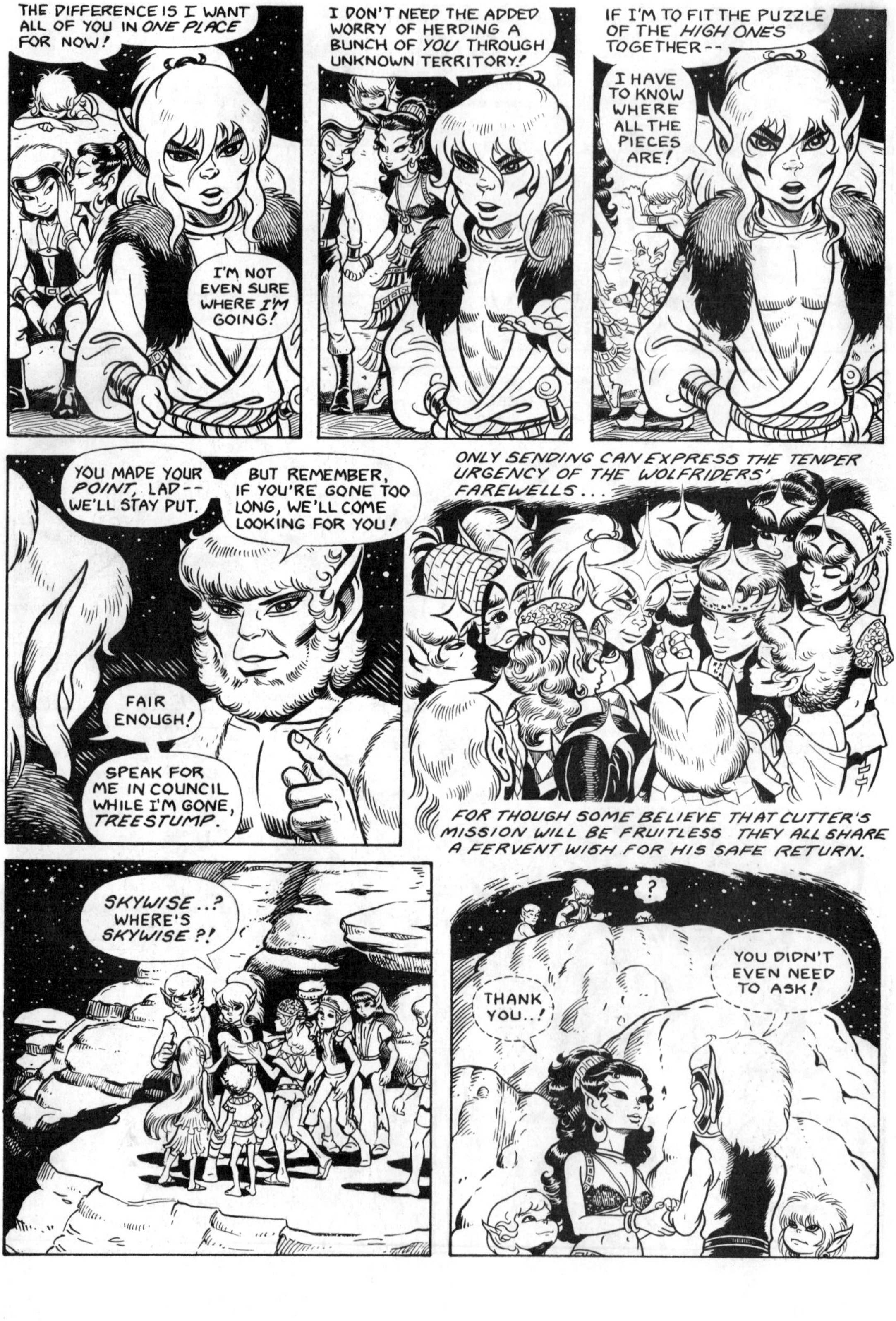
THE DIFFERENCE IS I WANT ALL OF YOU IN ONE PLACE FOR NOW!
I'M NOT EVEN SURE WHERE I'M GOING!
I DON'T NEED THE ADDED WORRY OF HERDING A BUNCH OF YOU THROUGH UNKNOWN TERRITORY!
IF I'M TO FIT THE PUZZLE OF THE HIGH ONES TOGETHER--
I HAVE TO KNOW WHERE ALL THE PIECES ARE!
YOU MADE YOUR POINT, LAD-- WE'LL STAY PUT.
BUT REMEMBER, IF YOU'RE GONE TOO LONG, WE'LL COME LOOKING FOR YOU!
FAIR ENOUGH!
SPEAK FOR ME IN COUNCIL WHILE I'M GONE, TREESTUMP.
ONLY SENDING CAN EXPRESS THE TENDER URGENCY OF THE WOLFRIDERS' FAREWELLS...
FOR THOUGH SOME BELIEVE THAT CUTTER'S MISSION WILL BE FRUITLESS THEY ALL SHARE A FERVENT WISH FOR HIS SAFE RETURN.
SKYWISE..? WHERE'S SKYWISE?!
?
THANK YOU..!
YOU DIDN'T EVEN NEED TO ASK!

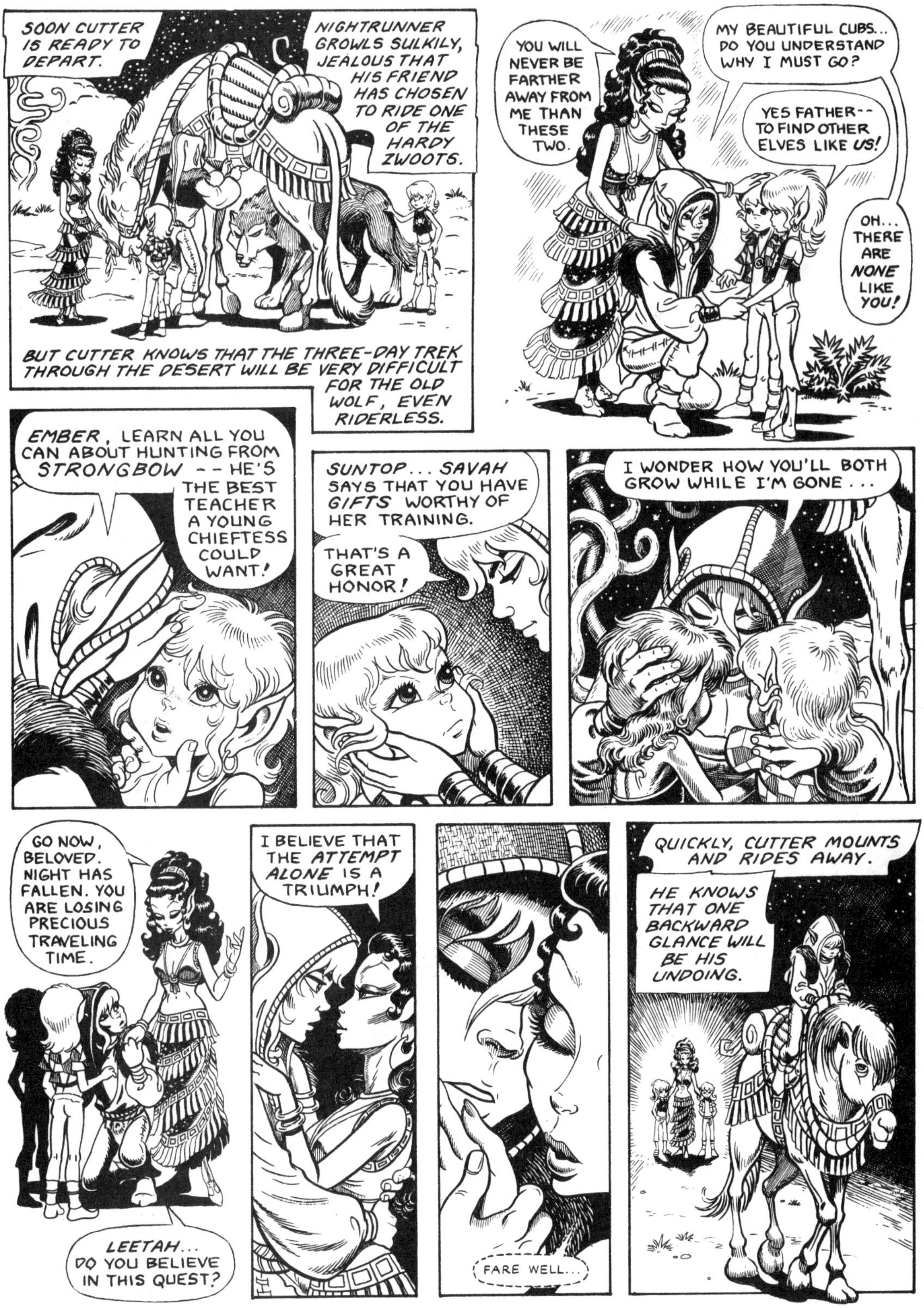
SOON CUTTER IS READY TO DEPART.
NIGHTRUNNER GROWLS SULKILY, JEALOUS THAT HIS FRIEND HAS CHOSEN TO RIDE ONE OF THE HARDY ZWOOTS.
BUT CUTTER KNOWS THAT THE THREE-DAY TREK THROUGH THE DESERT WILL BE VERY DIFFICULT FOR THE OLD WOLF, EVEN RIDERLESS.
MY BEAUTIFUL CUBS... DO YOU UNDERSTAND WHY I MUST GO?
YES FATHER-- TO FIND OTHER ELVES LIKE US!
OH... THERE ARE NONE LIKE YOU!
YOU WILL NEVER BE FARTHER AWAY FROM ME THAN THESE TWO.
EMBER, LEARN ALL YOU CAN ABOUT HUNTING FROM STRONGBOW -- HE'S THE BEST TEACHER A YOUNG CHIEFTESS COULD WANT!
SUNTOP... SAVAH SAYS THAT YOU HAVE GIFTS WORTHY OF HER TRAINING.
THAT'S A GREAT HONOR!
I WONDER HOW YOU'LL BOTH GROW WHILE I'M GONE...
GO NOW, BELOVED. NIGHT HAS FALLEN. YOU ARE LOSING PRECIOUS TRAVELING TIME.
LEETAH... DO YOU BELIEVE IN THIS QUEST?
I BELIEVE THAT THE ATTEMPT ALONE IS A TRIUMPH!
FARE WELL...
QUICKLY, CUTTER MOUNTS AND RIDES AWAY.
HE KNOWS THAT ONE BACKWARD GLANCE WILL BE HIS UNDOING.

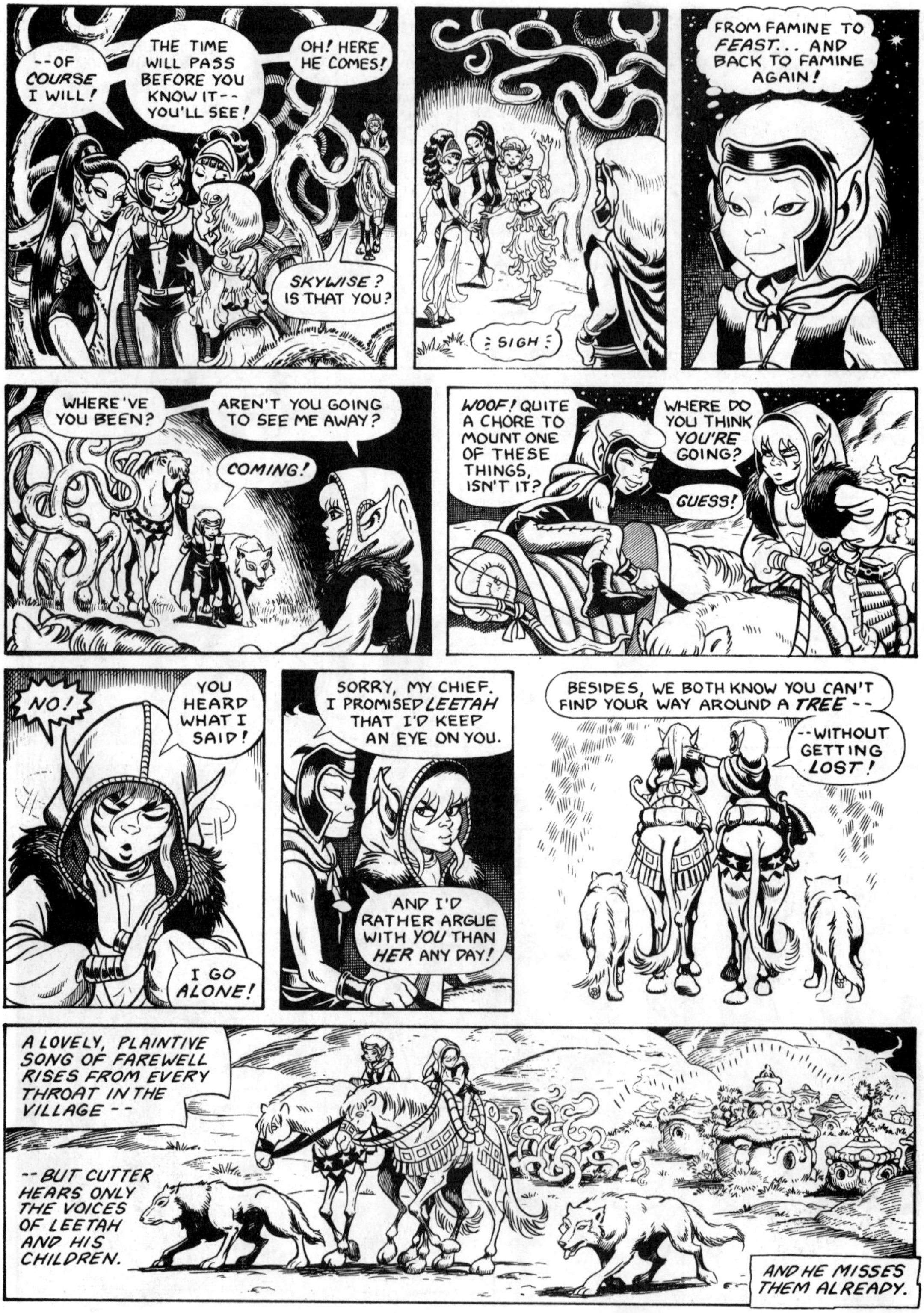
--OF COURSE I WILL!
THE TIME WILL PASS BEFORE YOU KNOW IT-- YOU'LL SEE!
OH! HERE HE COMES!
SKYWISE? IS THAT YOU?
SIGH
FROM FAMINE TO FEAST... AND BACK TO FAMINE AGAIN!
WHERE'VE YOU BEEN?
AREN'T YOU GOING TO SEE ME AWAY?
COMING!
WOOF! QUITE A CHORE TO MOUNT ONE OF THESE THINGS, ISN'T IT?
WHERE DO YOU THINK YOU'RE GOING?
GUESS!
NO!
YOU HEARD WHAT I SAID!
I GO ALONE!
SORRY, MY CHIEF. I PROMISED LEETAH THAT I'D KEEP AN EYE ON YOU.
AND I'D RATHER ARGUE WITH YOU THAN HER ANY DAY!
BESIDES, WE BOTH KNOW YOU CAN'T FIND YOUR WAY AROUND A TREE--
--WITHOUT GETTING LOST!
A LOVELY, PLAINTIVE SONG OF FAREWELL RISES FROM EVERY THROAT IN THE VILLAGE--
--BUT CUTTER HEARS ONLY THE VOICES OF LEETAH AND HIS CHILDREN.
AND HE MISSES THEM ALREADY.

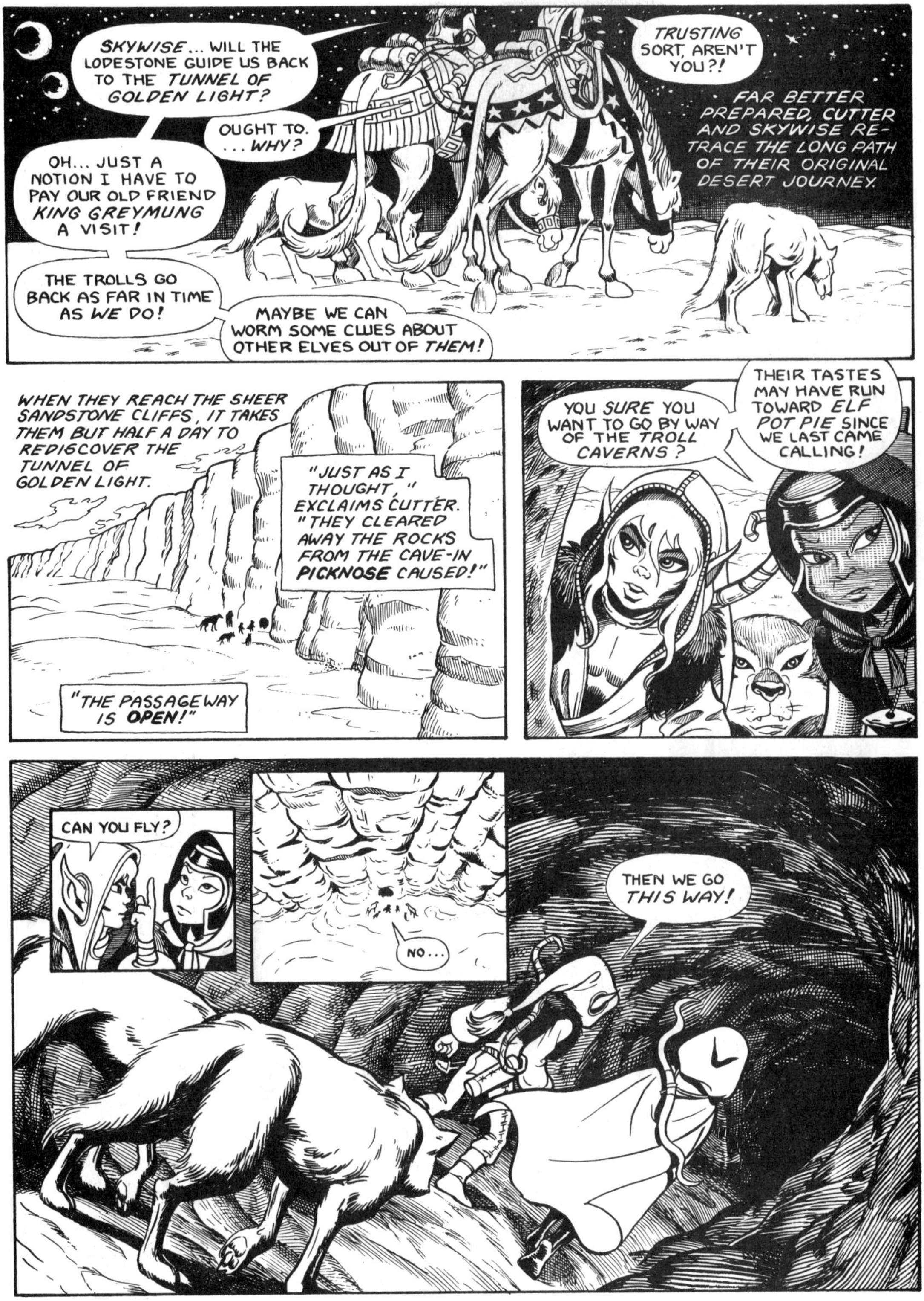
SKYWISE... WILL THE LODESTONE GUIDE US BACK TO THE TUNNEL OF GOLDEN LIGHT?
OUGHT TO. ...WHY?
OH... JUST A NOTION I HAVE TO PAY OUR OLD FRIEND KING GREYMUNG A VISIT!
THE TROLLS GO BACK AS FAR IN TIME AS WE DO!
MAYBE WE CAN WORM SOME CLUES ABOUT OTHER ELVES OUT OF THEM!
TRUSTING SORT, AREN'T YOU?!
FAR BETTER PREPARED, CUTTER AND SKYWISE RE-TRACE THE LONG PATH OF THEIR ORIGINAL DESERT JOURNEY.
WHEN THEY REACH THE SHEER SANDSTONE CLIFFS, IT TAKES THEM BUT HALF A DAY TO REDISCOVER THE TUNNEL OF GOLDEN LIGHT.
"JUST AS I THOUGHT," EXCLAIMS CUTTER. "THEY CLEARED AWAY THE ROCKS FROM THE CAVE-IN PICKNOSE CAUSED!"
"THE PASSAGEWAY IS OPEN!"
YOU SURE YOU WANT TO GO BY WAY OF THE TROLL CAVERNS?
THEIR TASTES MAY HAVE RUN TOWARD ELF POT PIE SINCE WE LAST CAME CALLING!
CAN YOU FLY?
NO...
THEN WE GO THIS WAY!

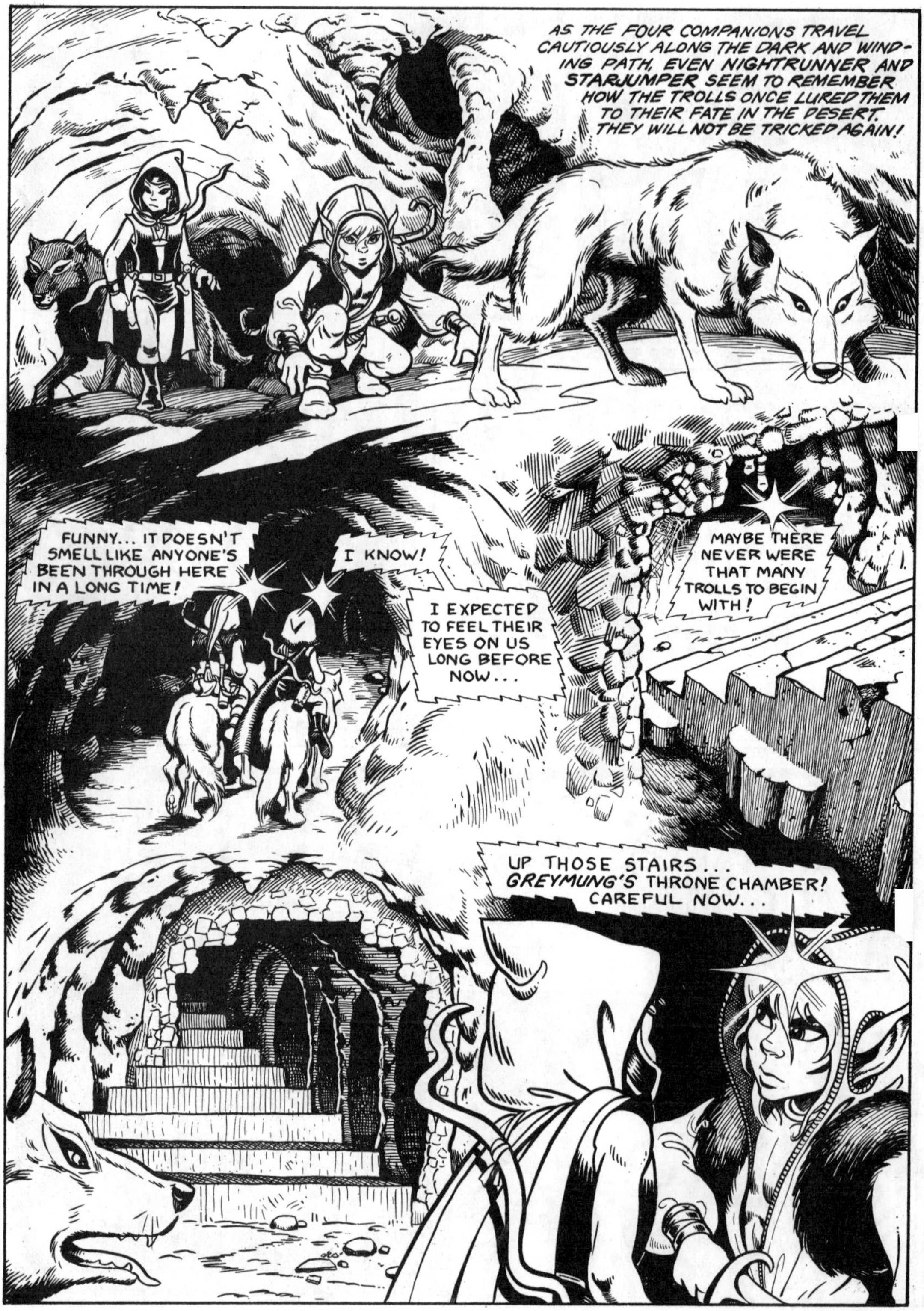
AS THE FOUR COMPANIONS TRAVEL CAUTIOUSLY ALONG THE DARK AND WINDING PATH, EVEN NIGHTRUNNER AND STARJUMPER SEEM TO REMEMBER HOW THE TROLLS ONCE LURED THEM TO THEIR FATE IN THE DESERT. THEY WILL NOT BE TRICKED AGAIN!
FUNNY... IT DOESN'T SMELL LIKE ANYONE'S BEEN THROUGH HERE IN A LONG TIME!
I KNOW!
I EXPECTED TO FEEL THEIR EYES ON US LONG BEFORE NOW...
MAYBE THERE NEVER WERE THAT MANY TROLLS TO BEGIN WITH!
UP THOSE STAIRS... GREYMUNG'S THRONE CHAMBER! CAREFUL NOW...

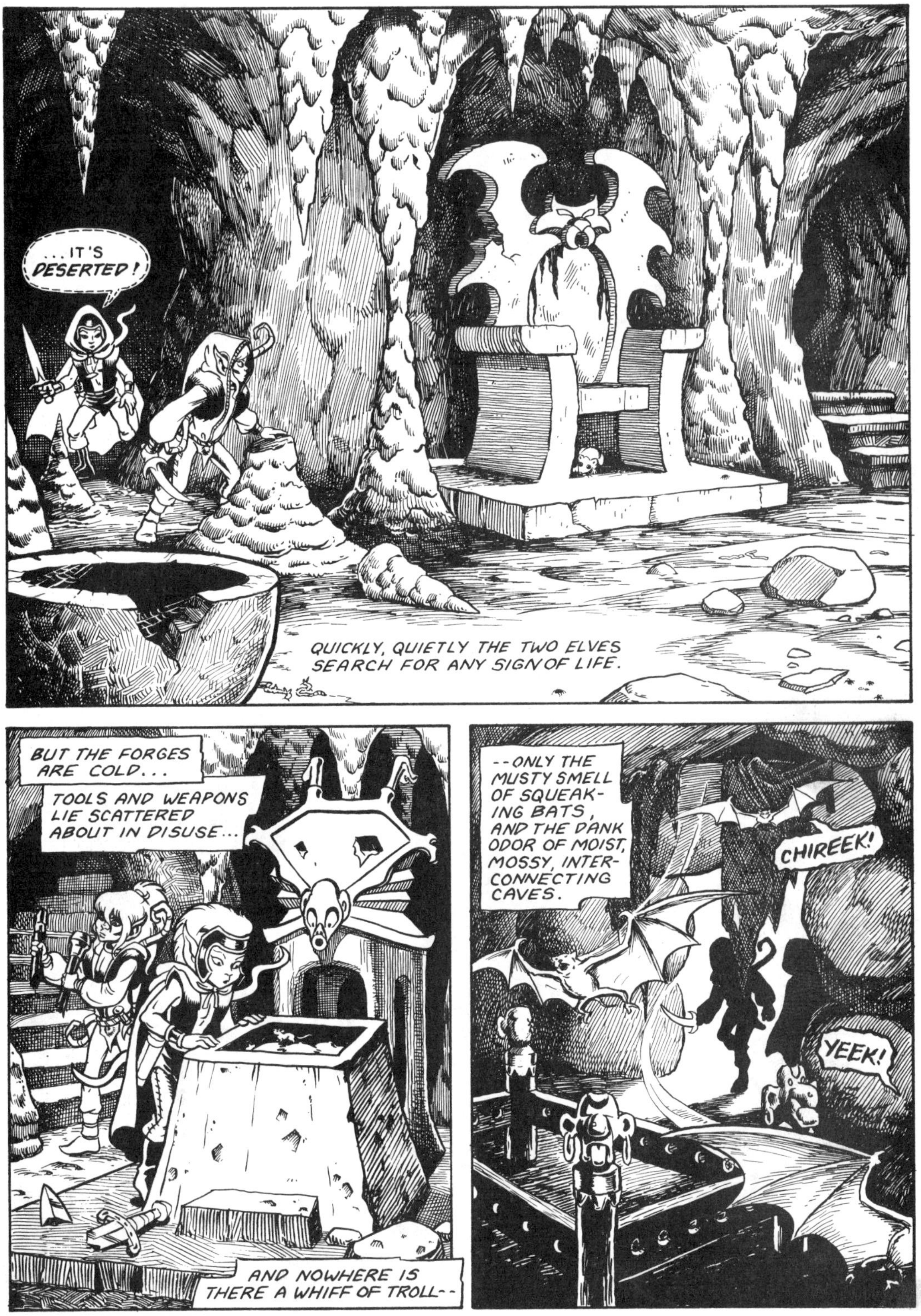
...IT'S DESERTED!
QUICKLY, QUIETLY THE TWO ELVES SEARCH FOR ANY SIGN OF LIFE.
BUT THE FORGES ARE COLD...
TOOLS AND WEAPONS LIE SCATTERED ABOUT IN DISUSE...
AND NOWHERE IS THERE A WHIFF OF TROLL--
--ONLY THE MUSTY SMELL OF SQUEAK-ING BATS, AND THE DANK ODOR OF MOIST, MOSSY, INTER-CONNECTING CAVES.
CHIREEK!
YEEK!

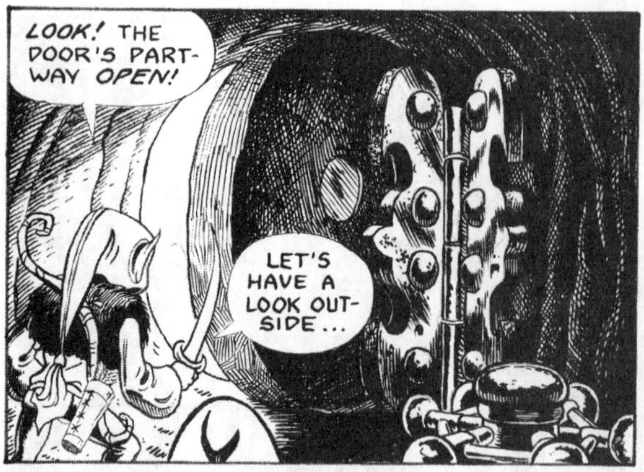
LOOK! THE DOOR'S PART-WAY OPEN!
LET'S HAVE A LOOK OUT-SIDE...

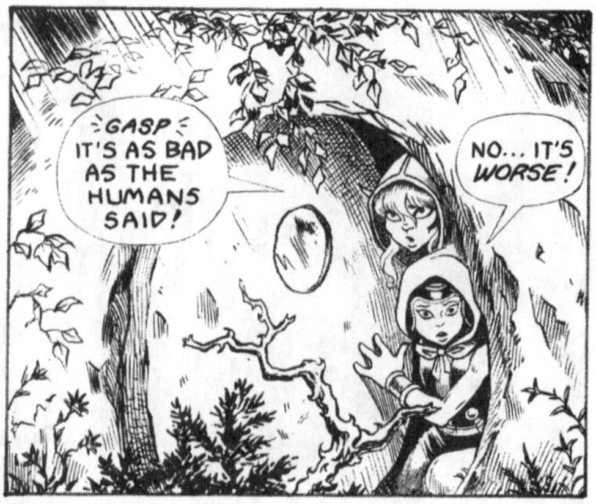
GASP IT'S AS BAD AS THE HUMANS SAID!
NO... IT'S WORSE!

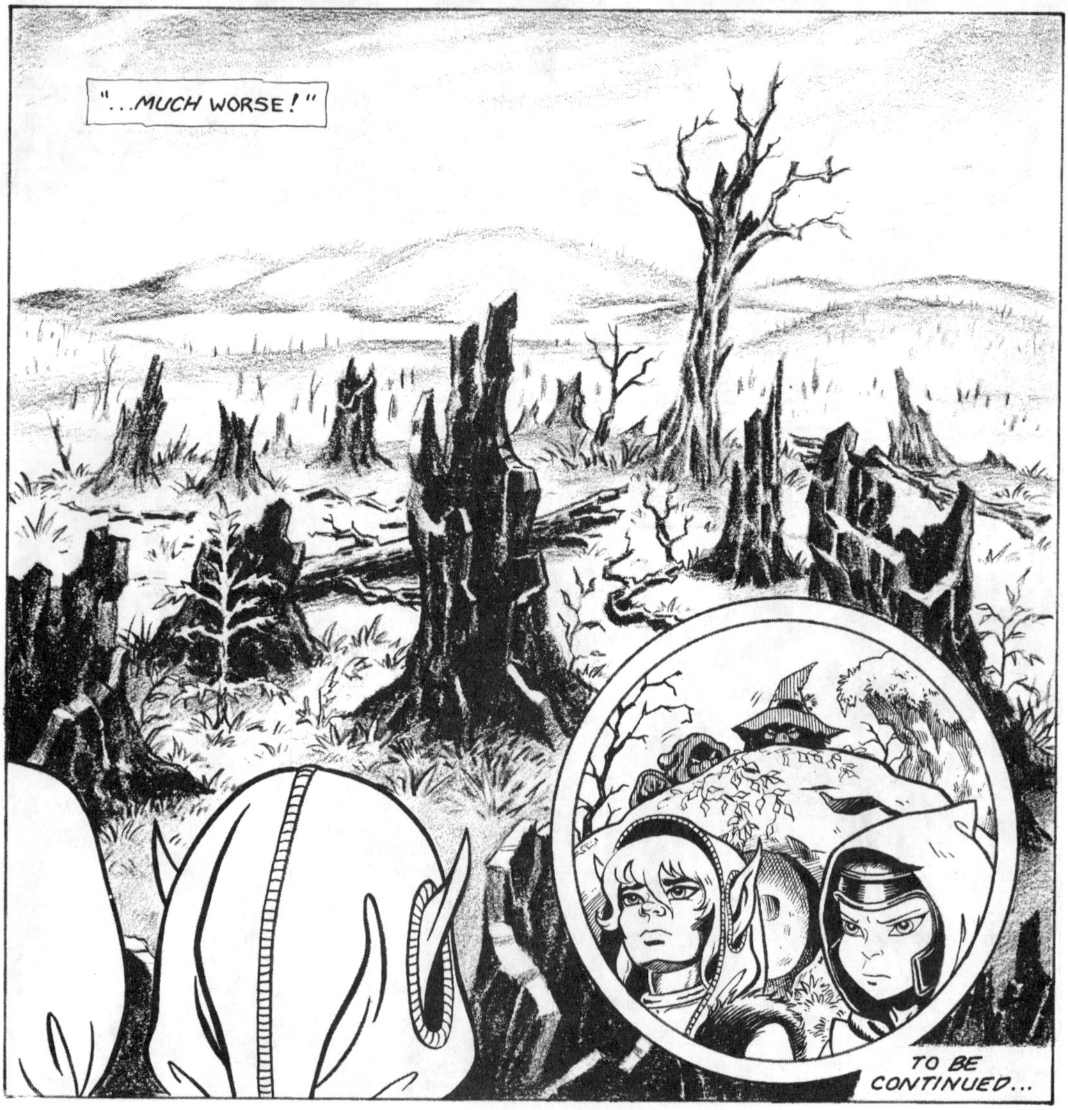
"...MUCH WORSE!"
TO BE CONTINUED...

AFTER SEVEN PEACEFUL YEARS OF LIFE IN THE OASIS-VILLAGE KNOWN AS **SORROW'S END**, CUTTER AND SKYWISE HAVE LEFT FAMILY AND FRIENDS TO SEARCH FOR OTHER KINDRED ELF TRIBES THAT MAY DWELL IN THE UNEXPLORED LANDS BEYOND THE DESERT. THEIR QUEST BEGINS, SADLY, AMID THE BLACKENED TREESTUMPS AND STRUGGLING VEGETATION THAT WAS ONCE THEIR FOREST HOME -- **THE HOLT**.

STORY & ART by WENDY PINI

STORY & LETTERING by RICHARD PINI

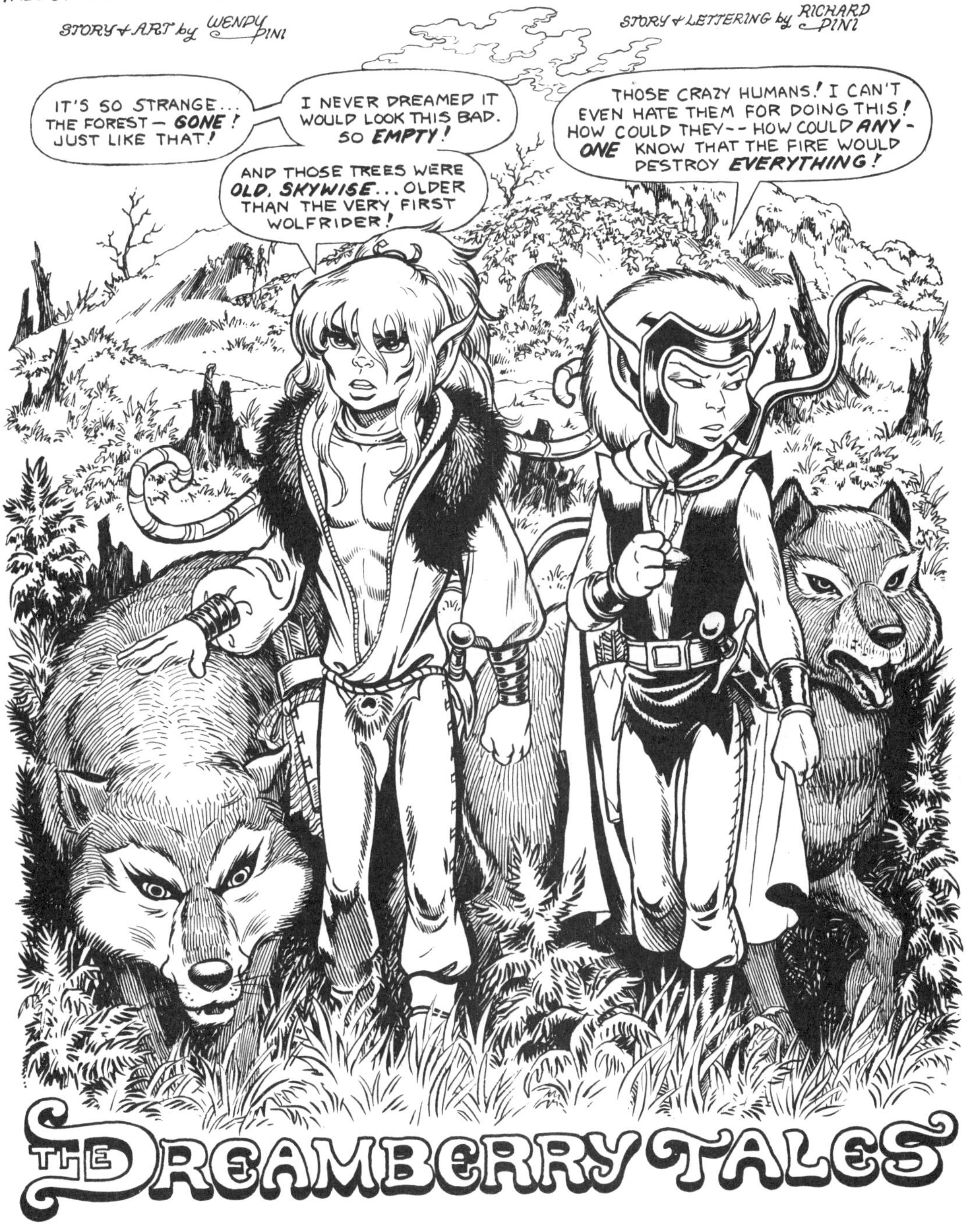
IT'S SO STRANGE... THE FOREST — **GONE**! JUST LIKE THAT!
I NEVER DREAMED IT WOULD LOOK THIS BAD. SO **EMPTY**!
AND THOSE TREES WERE **OLD, SKYWISE**... OLDER THAN THE VERY FIRST WOLFRIDER!
THOSE CRAZY HUMANS! I CAN'T EVEN HATE THEM FOR DOING THIS! HOW COULD THEY -- HOW COULD **ANY-ONE** KNOW THAT THE FIRE WOULD DESTROY **EVERYTHING**!

THE DREAMBERRY TALES

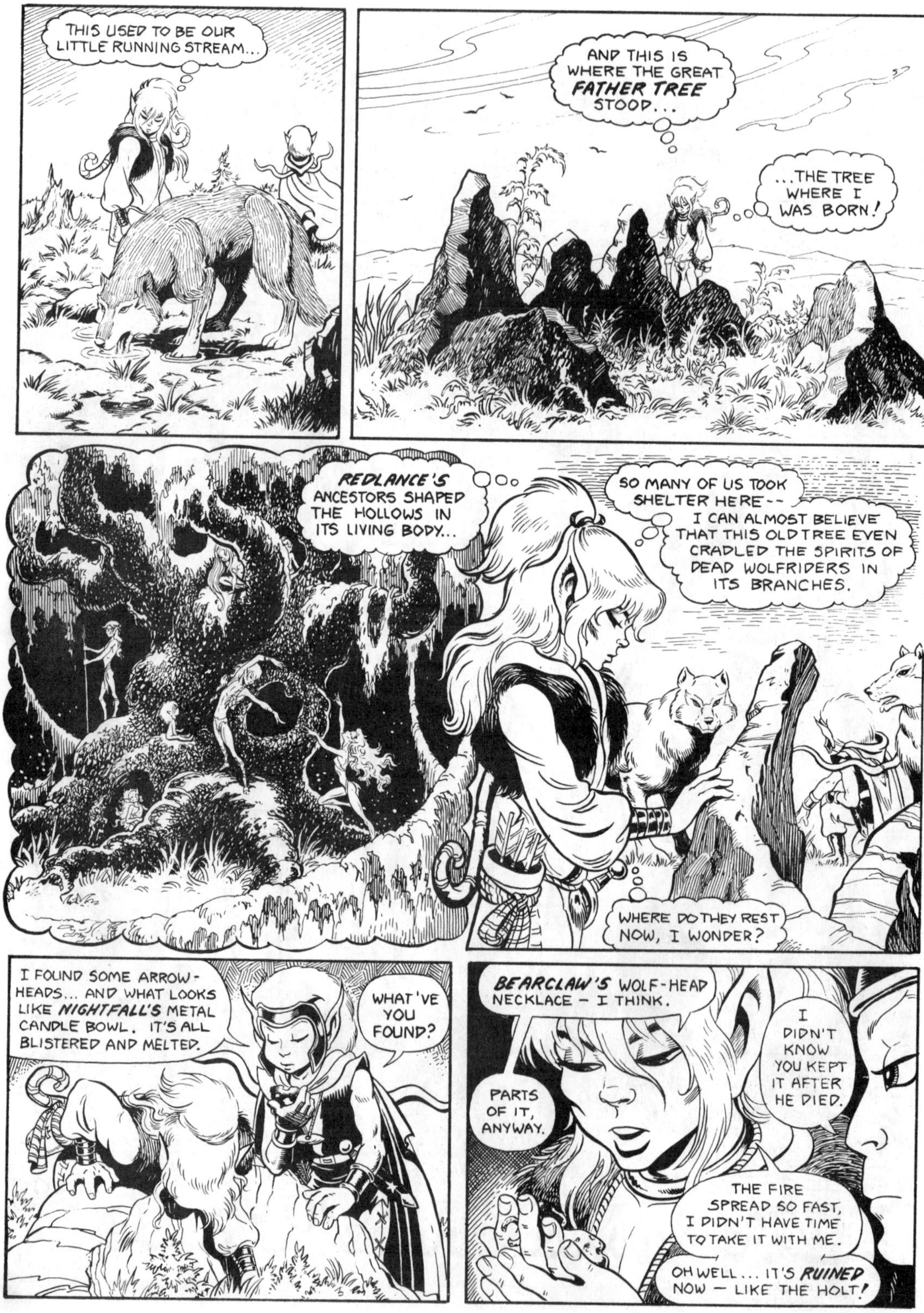
THIS USED TO BE OUR LITTLE RUNNING STREAM...
AND THIS IS WHERE THE GREAT FATHER TREE STOOD...
...THE TREE WHERE I WAS BORN!
REDLANCE'S ANCESTORS SHAPED THE HOLLOWS IN ITS LIVING BODY...
SO MANY OF US TOOK SHELTER HERE--
I CAN ALMOST BELIEVE THAT THIS OLD TREE EVEN CRADLED THE SPIRITS OF DEAD WOLFRIDERS IN ITS BRANCHES.
WHERE DO THEY REST NOW, I WONDER?
WHAT'VE YOU FOUND?
I FOUND SOME ARROW-HEADS... AND WHAT LOOKS LIKE NIGHTFALL'S METAL CANDLE BOWL. IT'S ALL BLISTERED AND MELTED.
BEARCLAW'S WOLF-HEAD NECKLACE - I THINK.
I DIDN'T KNOW YOU KEPT IT AFTER HE DIED.
PARTS OF IT, ANYWAY.
THE FIRE SPREAD SO FAST, I DIDN'T HAVE TIME TO TAKE IT WITH ME.
OH WELL... IT'S RUINED NOW — LIKE THE HOLT!

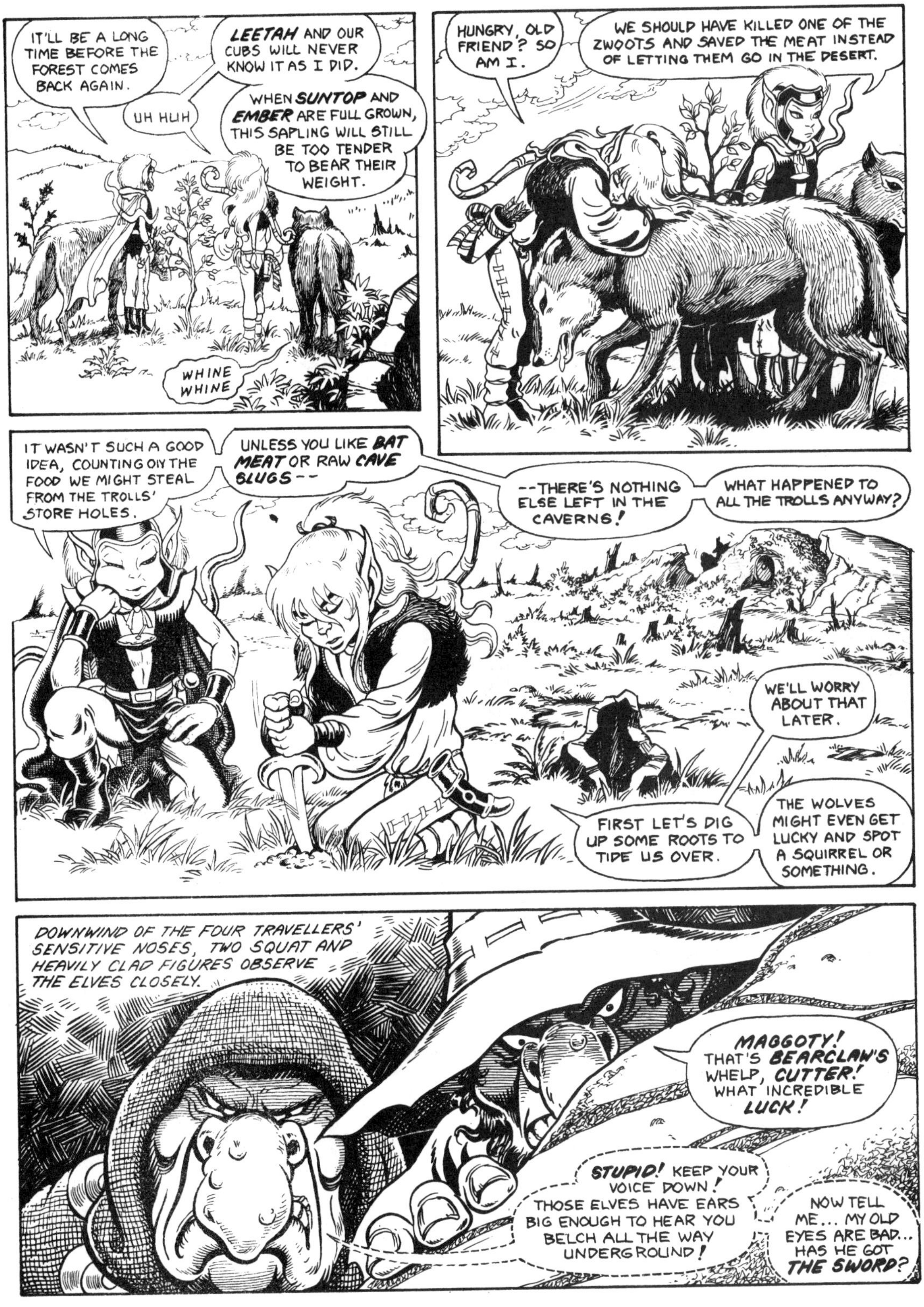
IT'LL BE A LONG TIME BEFORE THE FOREST COMES BACK AGAIN.
UH HUH
LEETAH AND OUR CUBS WILL NEVER KNOW IT AS I DID.
WHEN SUNTOP AND EMBER ARE FULL GROWN, THIS SAPLING WILL STILL BE TOO TENDER TO BEAR THEIR WEIGHT.
WHINE WHINE
HUNGRY, OLD FRIEND? SO AM I.
WE SHOULD HAVE KILLED ONE OF THE ZWOOTS AND SAVED THE MEAT INSTEAD OF LETTING THEM GO IN THE DESERT.
IT WASN'T SUCH A GOOD IDEA, COUNTING ON THE FOOD WE MIGHT STEAL FROM THE TROLLS' STORE HOLES.
UNLESS YOU LIKE BAT MEAT OR RAW CAVE SLUGS--
--THERE'S NOTHING ELSE LEFT IN THE CAVERNS!
WHAT HAPPENED TO ALL THE TROLLS ANYWAY?
WE'LL WORRY ABOUT THAT LATER.
FIRST LET'S DIG UP SOME ROOTS TO TIDE US OVER.
THE WOLVES MIGHT EVEN GET LUCKY AND SPOT A SQUIRREL OR SOMETHING.
DOWNWIND OF THE FOUR TRAVELLERS' SENSITIVE NOSES, TWO SQUAT AND HEAVILY CLAD FIGURES OBSERVE THE ELVES CLOSELY.
MAGGOTY! THAT'S BEARCLAW'S WHELP, CUTTER! WHAT INCREDIBLE LUCK!
STUPID! KEEP YOUR VOICE DOWN! THOSE ELVES HAVE EARS BIG ENOUGH TO HEAR YOU BELCH ALL THE WAY UNDERGROUND!
NOW TELL ME... MY OLD EYES ARE BAD... HAS HE GOT THE SWORD?

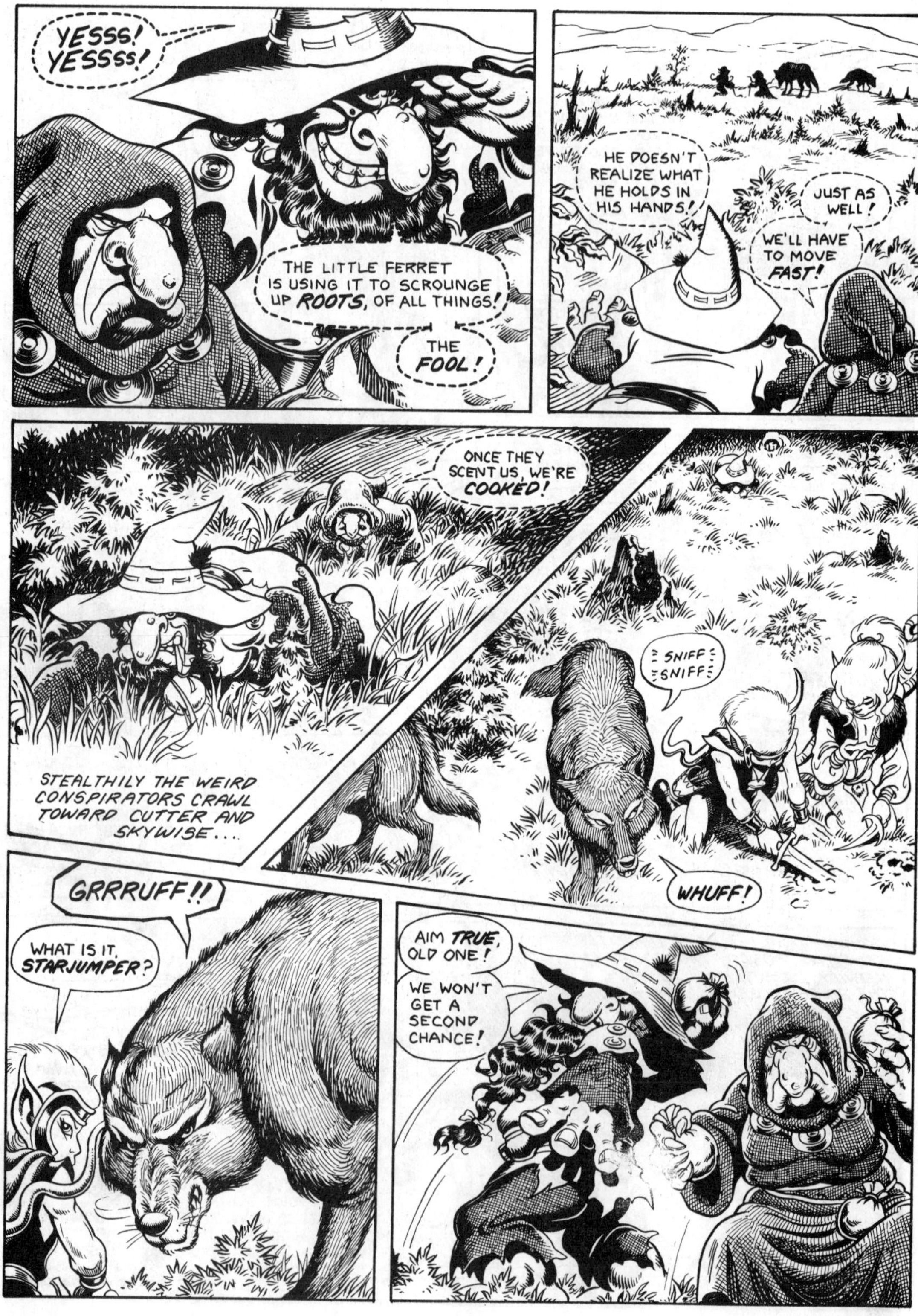
YESSS! YESSSS!
THE LITTLE FERRET IS USING IT TO SCROUNGE UP ROOTS, OF ALL THINGS!
THE FOOL!
HE DOESN'T REALIZE WHAT HE HOLDS IN HIS HANDS!
JUST AS WELL!
WE'LL HAVE TO MOVE FAST!
ONCE THEY SCENT US, WE'RE COOKED!
STEALTHILY THE WEIRD CONSPIRATORS CRAWL TOWARD CUTTER AND SKYWISE...
SNIFF SNIFF
WHUFF!
GRRRUFF!!
WHAT IS IT, STARJUMPER?
AIM TRUE, OLD ONE!
WE WON'T GET A SECOND CHANCE!

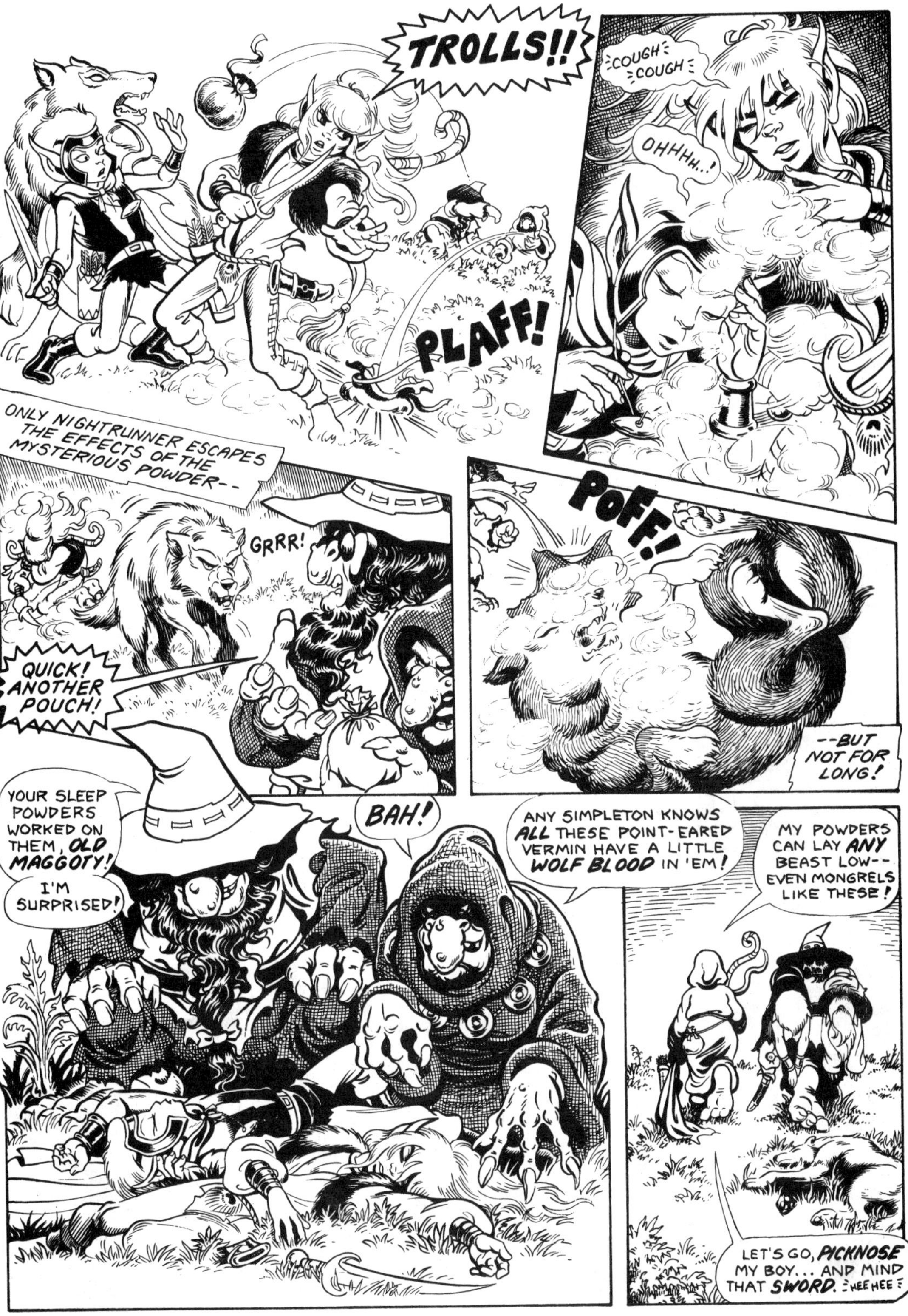
TROLLS!!
PLAFF!
COUGH COUGH
OHHHH..!
ONLY NIGHTRUNNER ESCAPES THE EFFECTS OF THE MYSTERIOUS POWDER--
GRRR!
QUICK! ANOTHER POUCH!
POFF!
--BUT NOT FOR LONG!
YOUR SLEEP POWDERS WORKED ON THEM, OLD MAGGOTY!
I'M SURPRISED!
BAH!
ANY SIMPLETON KNOWS ALL THESE POINT-EARED VERMIN HAVE A LITTLE WOLF BLOOD IN 'EM!
MY POWDERS CAN LAY ANY BEAST LOW-- EVEN MONGRELS LIKE THESE!
LET'S GO, PICKNOSE MY BOY... AND MIND THAT SWORD. HEE HEE

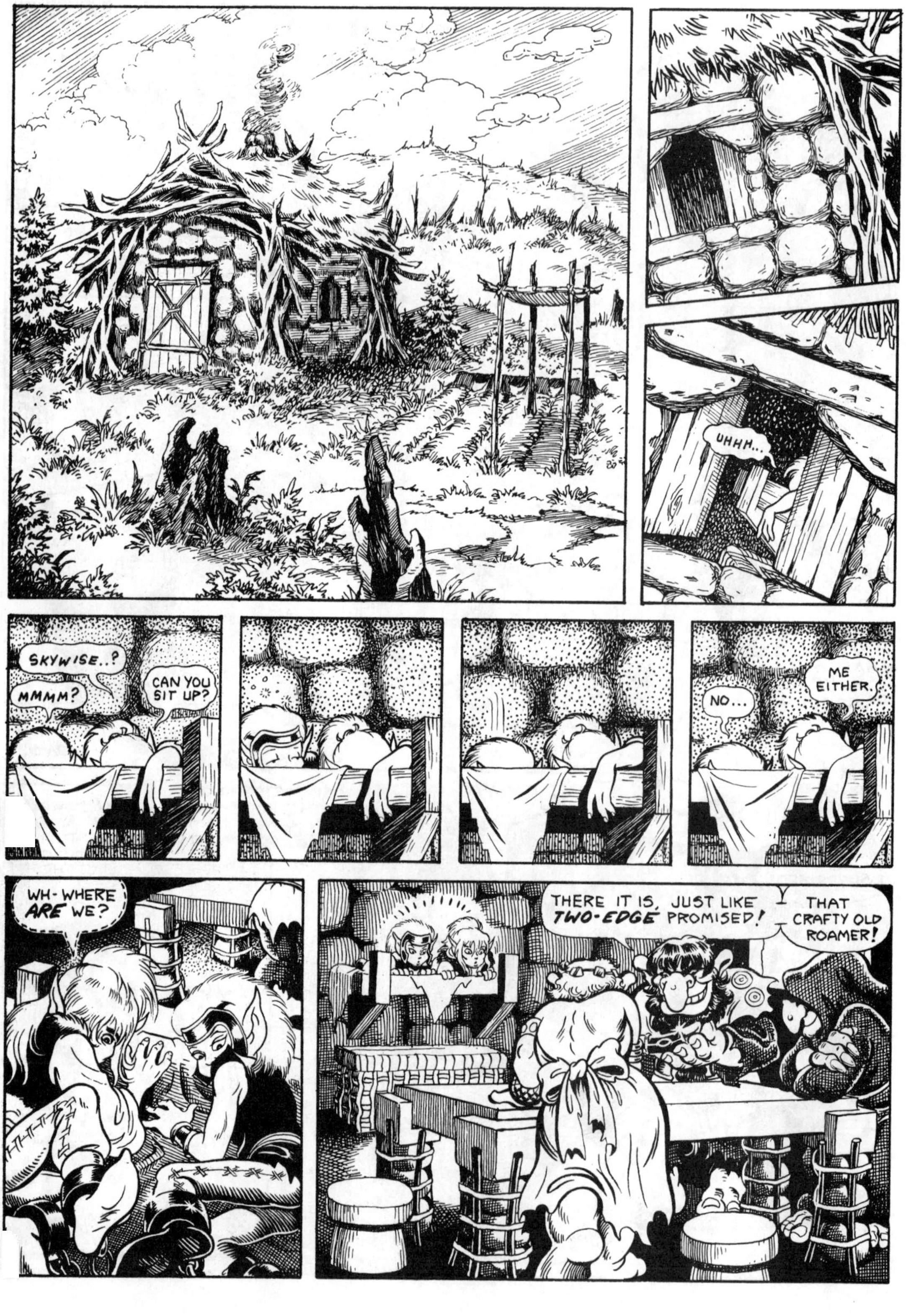
UHHM...
SKYWISE..?
MMMM?
CAN YOU SIT UP?
NO...
ME EITHER.
WH-WHERE ARE WE?
THERE IT IS, JUST LIKE TWO-EDGE PROMISED!
THAT CRAFTY OLD ROAMER!

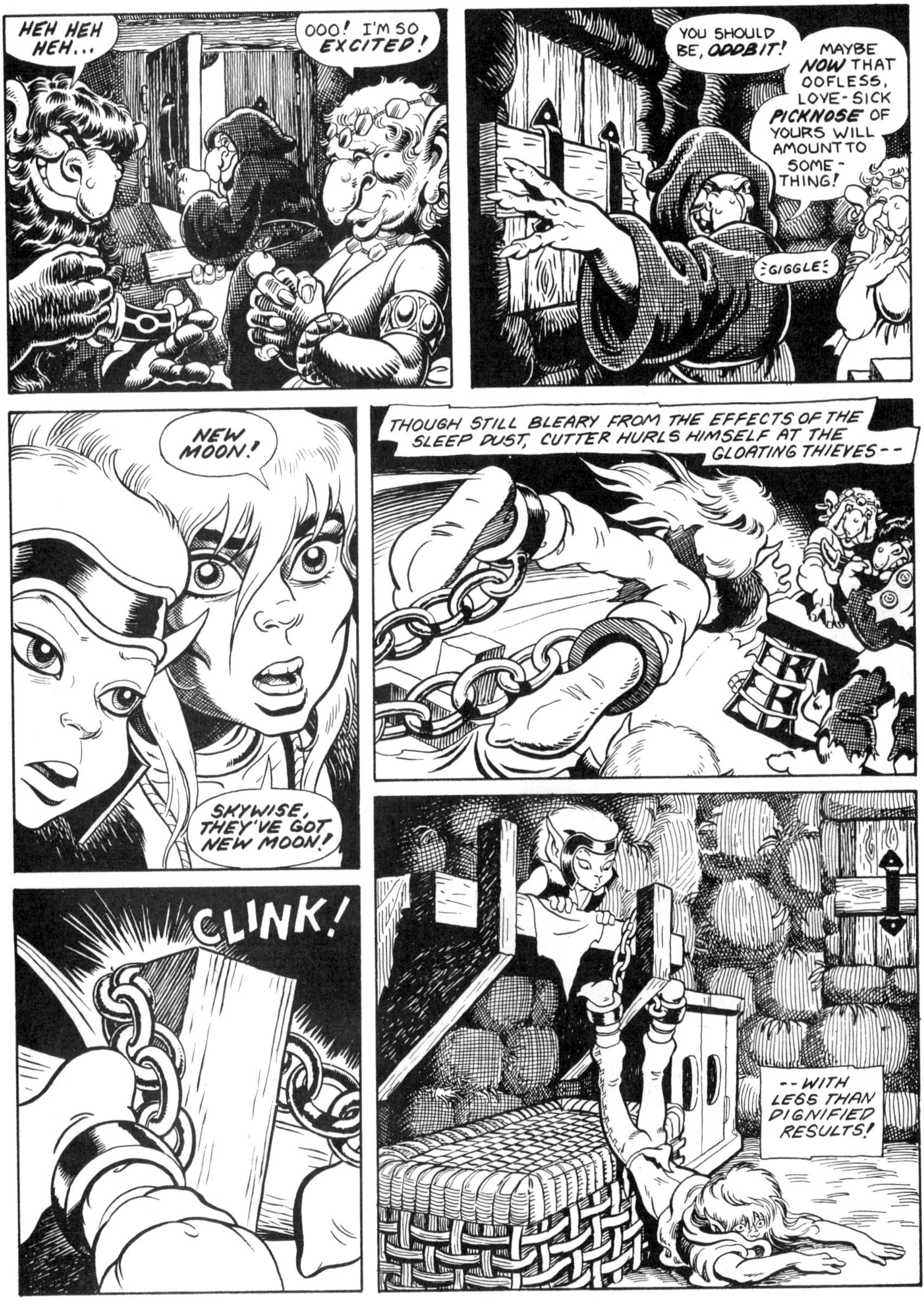
HEH HEH HEH...
OOO! I'M SO EXCITED!
YOU SHOULD BE, ODDBIT!
MAYBE NOW THAT OOFLESS, LOVE-SICK PICKNOSE OF YOURS WILL AMOUNT TO SOME-THING!
GIGGLE
NEW MOON!
SKYWISE, THEY'VE GOT NEW MOON!
THOUGH STILL BLEARY FROM THE EFFECTS OF THE SLEEP DUST, CUTTER HURLS HIMSELF AT THE GLOATING THIEVES--
CLINK!
--WITH LESS THAN DIGNIFIED RESULTS!

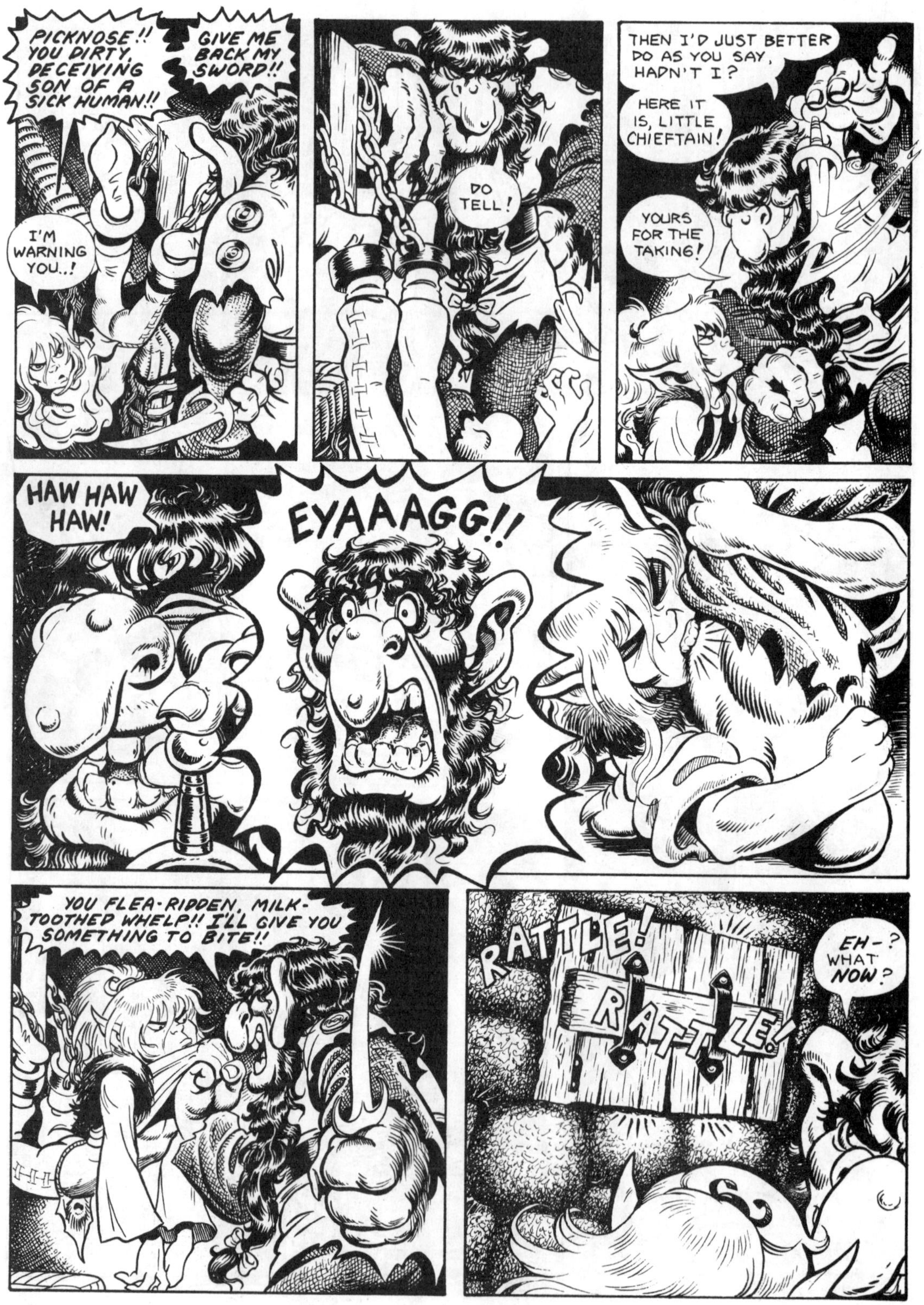
PICKNOSE!! YOU DIRTY, DECEIVING SON OF A SICK HUMAN!!
GIVE ME BACK MY SWORD!!
I'M WARNING YOU..!
DO TELL!
THEN I'D JUST BETTER DO AS YOU SAY, HADN'T I?
HERE IT IS, LITTLE CHIEFTAIN!
YOURS FOR THE TAKING!
HAW HAW HAW!
EYAAAGG!!
YOU FLEA-RIDDEN, MILK-TOOTHED WHELP!! I'LL GIVE YOU SOMETHING TO BITE!!
RATTLE! RATTLE!
EH-? WHAT NOW?

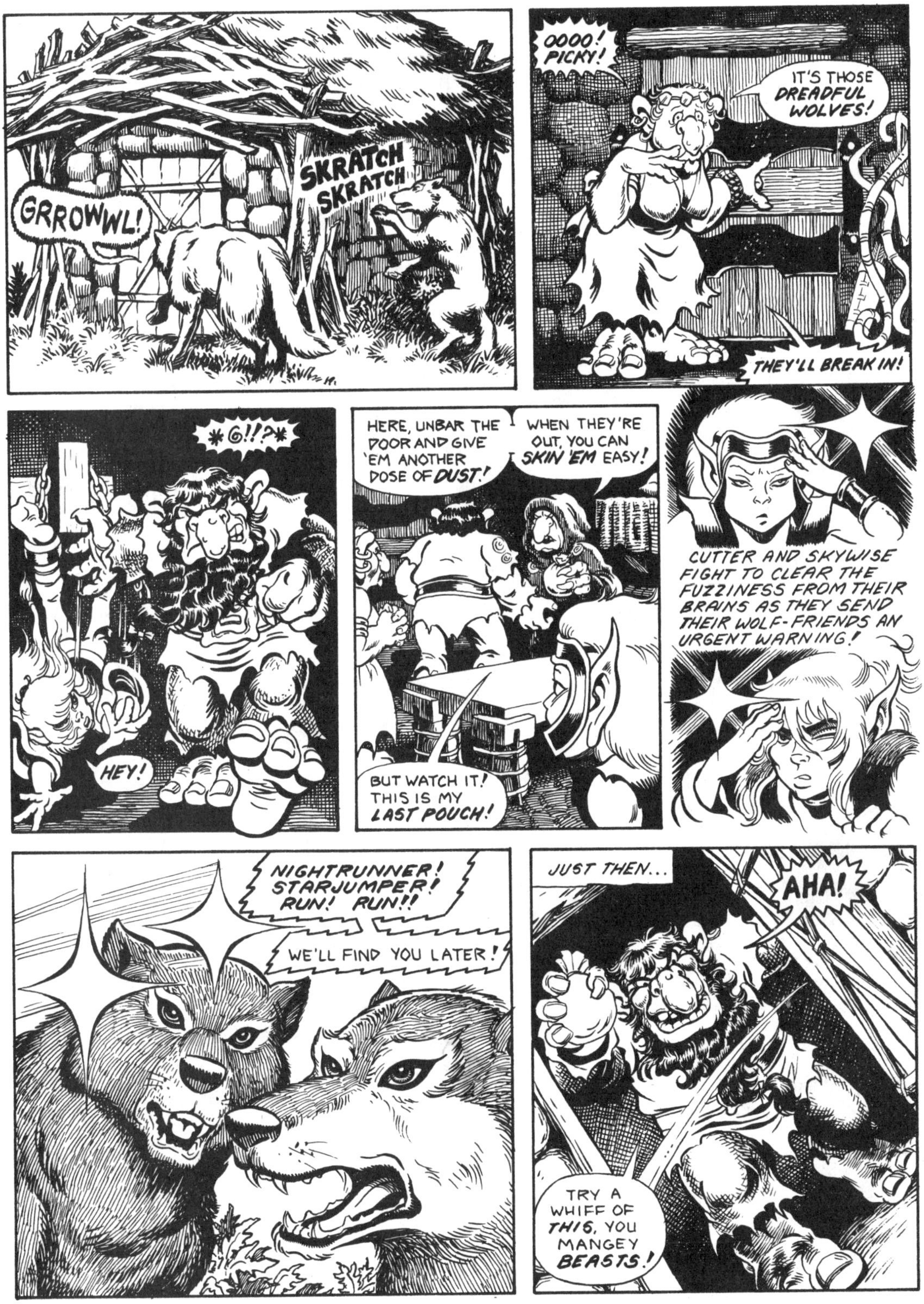
SKRATCH SKRATCH
GRROWWL!
OOOO! PICKY!
IT'S THOSE DREADFUL WOLVES!
THEY'LL BREAK IN!
G!!?
HEY!
HERE, UNBAR THE DOOR AND GIVE 'EM ANOTHER DOSE OF DUST!
WHEN THEY'RE OUT, YOU CAN SKIN 'EM EASY!
BUT WATCH IT! THIS IS MY LAST POUCH!
CUTTER AND SKYWISE FIGHT TO CLEAR THE FUZZINESS FROM THEIR BRAINS AS THEY SEND THEIR WOLF-FRIENDS AN URGENT WARNING!
NIGHTRUNNER! STARJUMPER! RUN! RUN!!
WE'LL FIND YOU LATER!
JUST THEN...
AHA!
TRY A WHIFF OF THIS, YOU MANGEY BEASTS!

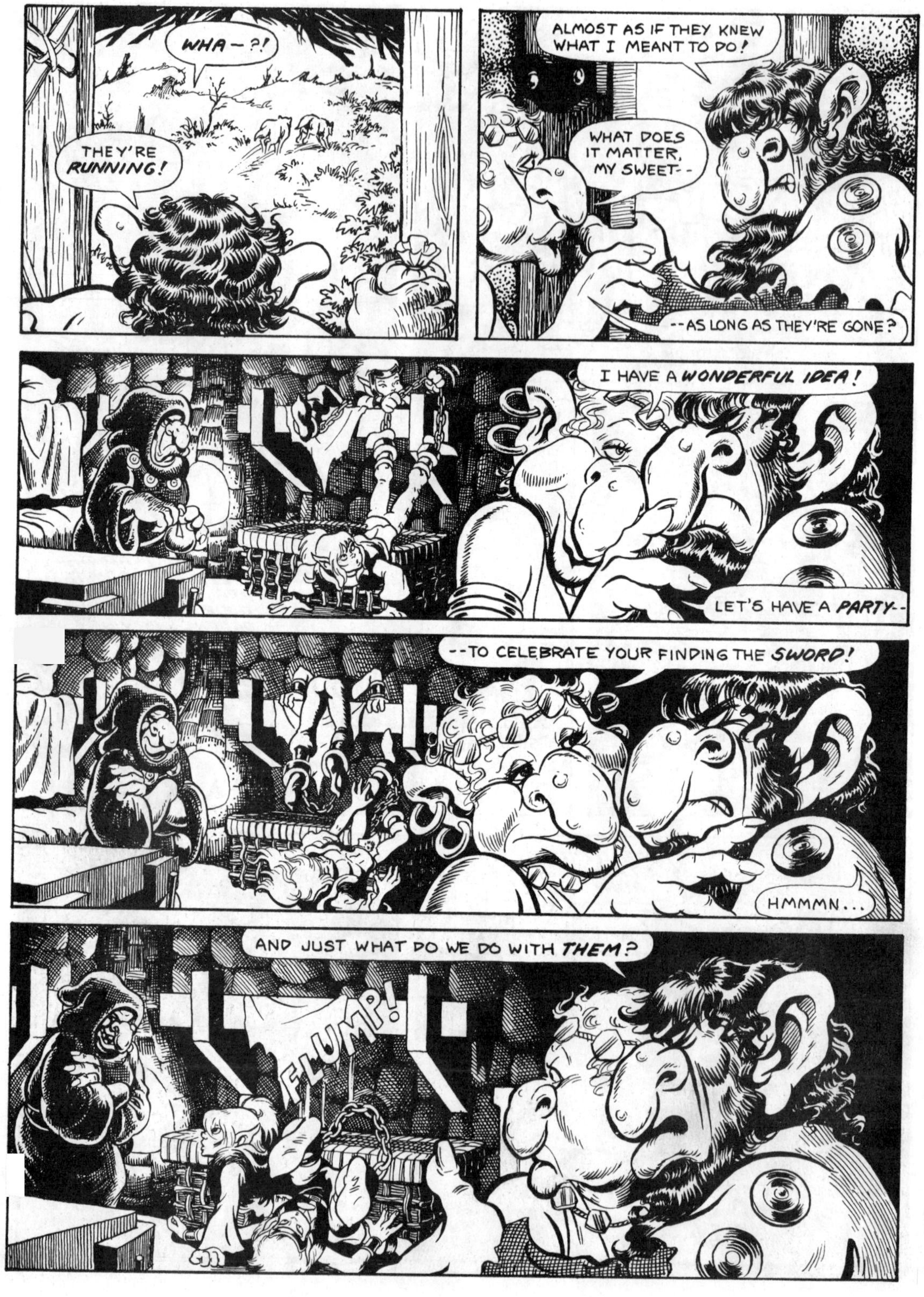
WHA-?!
THEY'RE RUNNING!
ALMOST AS IF THEY KNEW WHAT I MEANT TO DO!
WHAT DOES IT MATTER, MY SWEET--
--AS LONG AS THEY'RE GONE?
I HAVE A WONDERFUL IDEA!
LET'S HAVE A PARTY--
--TO CELEBRATE YOUR FINDING THE SWORD!
HMMMN...
AND JUST WHAT DO WE DO WITH THEM?
FLUMP!

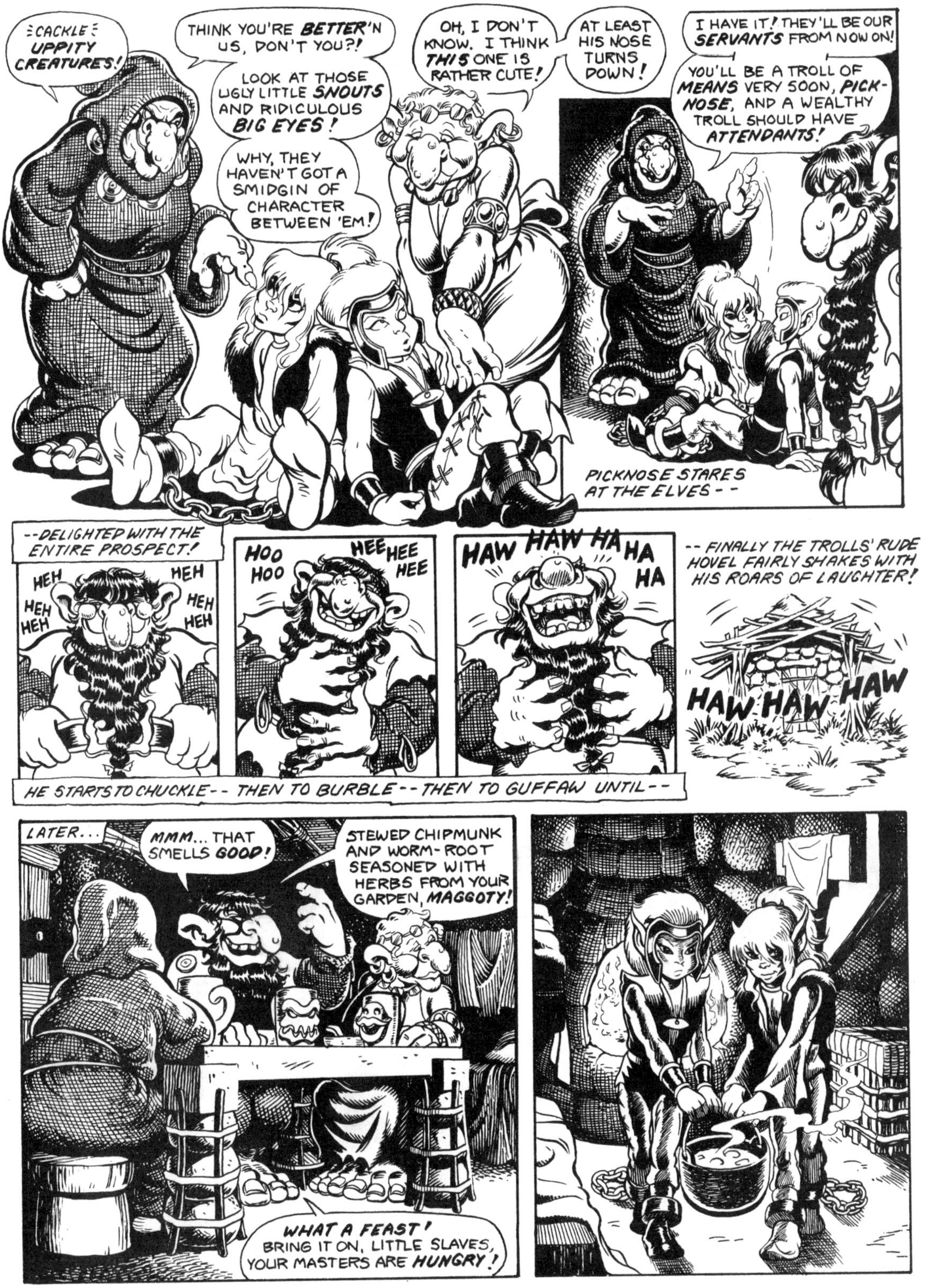

CACKLE UPPITY CREATURES!
THINK YOU'RE BETTER'N US, DON'T YOU?!
LOOK AT THOSE UGLY LITTLE SNOUTS AND RIDICULOUS BIG EYES!
WHY, THEY HAVEN'T GOT A SMIDGIN OF CHARACTER BETWEEN 'EM!
OH, I DON'T KNOW. I THINK THIS ONE IS RATHER CUTE!
AT LEAST HIS NOSE TURNS DOWN!
I HAVE IT! THEY'LL BE OUR SERVANTS FROM NOW ON!
YOU'LL BE A TROLL OF MEANS VERY SOON, PICK-NOSE, AND A WEALTHY TROLL SHOULD HAVE ATTENDANTS!
PICKNOSE STARES AT THE ELVES--
--DELIGHTED WITH THE ENTIRE PROSPECT!
HEH HEH HEH HEH HEH HEH HEH
HOO HOO HEE HEE HEE
HAW HAW HA HA HA
--FINALLY THE TROLLS' RUDE HOVEL FAIRLY SHAKES WITH HIS ROARS OF LAUGHTER!
HAW HAW HAW
HE STARTS TO CHUCKLE--THEN TO BURBLE--THEN TO GUFFAW UNTIL--
LATER...
MMM... THAT SMELLS GOOD!
STEWED CHIPMUNK AND WORM-ROOT SEASONED WITH HERBS FROM YOUR GARDEN, MAGGOTY!
WHAT A FEAST! BRING IT ON, LITTLE SLAVES, YOUR MASTERS ARE HUNGRY!

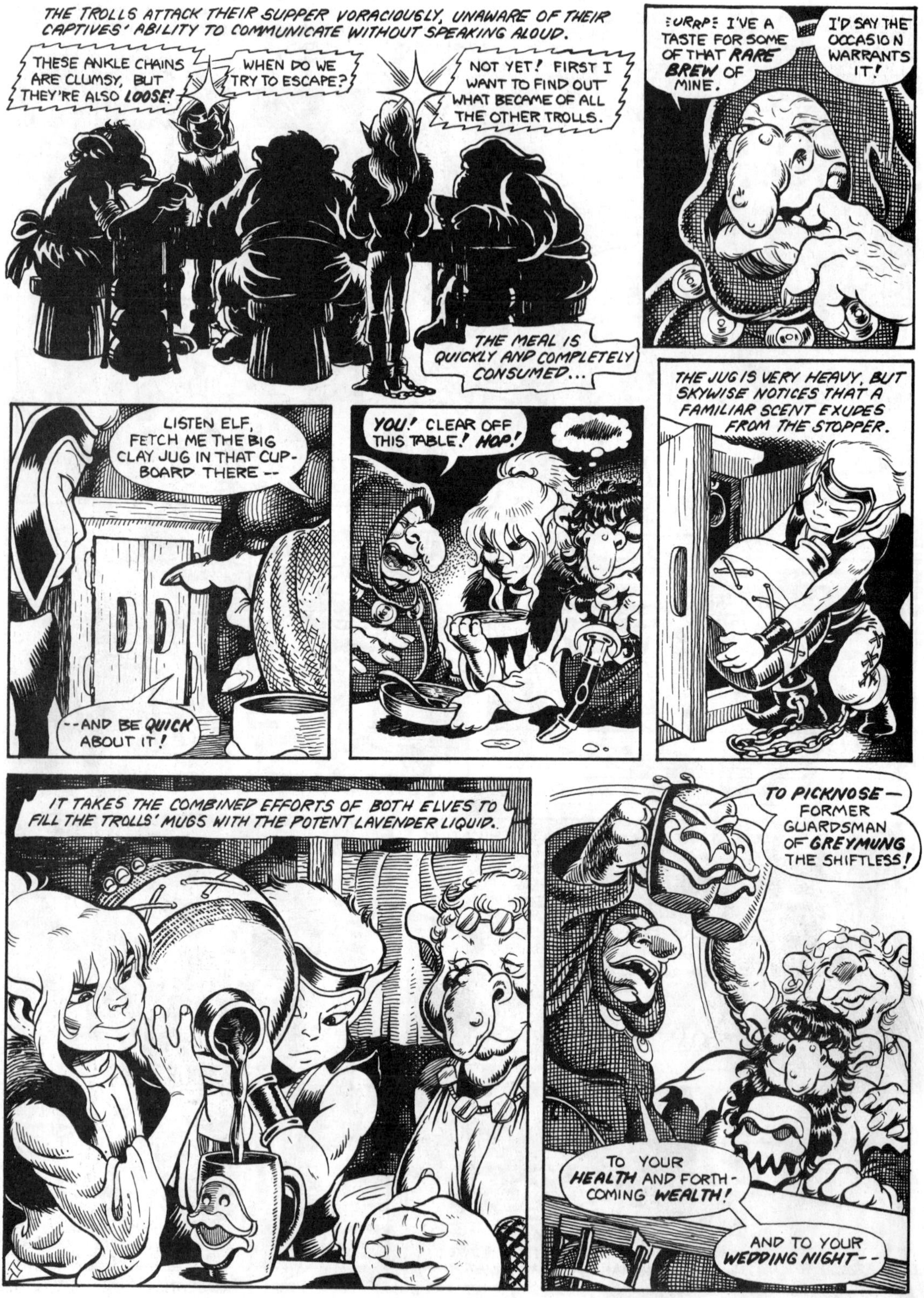
THE TROLLS ATTACK THEIR SUPPER VORACIOUSLY, UNAWARE OF THEIR CAPTIVES' ABILITY TO COMMUNICATE WITHOUT SPEAKING ALOUD.
THESE ANKLE CHAINS ARE CLUMSY, BUT THEY'RE ALSO LOOSE!
WHEN DO WE TRY TO ESCAPE?
NOT YET! FIRST I WANT TO FIND OUT WHAT BECAME OF ALL THE OTHER TROLLS.
URRP! I'VE A TASTE FOR SOME OF THAT RARE BREW OF MINE.
I'D SAY THE OCCASION WARRANTS IT!
THE MEAL IS QUICKLY AND COMPLETELY CONSUMED...
LISTEN ELF, FETCH ME THE BIG CLAY JUG IN THAT CUPBOARD THERE --
--AND BE QUICK ABOUT IT!
YOU! CLEAR OFF THIS TABLE! HOP!
THE JUG IS VERY HEAVY, BUT SKYWISE NOTICES THAT A FAMILIAR SCENT EXUDES FROM THE STOPPER.
IT TAKES THE COMBINED EFFORTS OF BOTH ELVES TO FILL THE TROLLS' MUGS WITH THE POTENT LAVENDER LIQUID.
TO PICKNOSE — FORMER GUARDSMAN OF GREYMUNG THE SHIFTLESS!
TO YOUR HEALTH AND FORTH-COMING WEALTH!
AND TO YOUR WEDDING NIGHT--

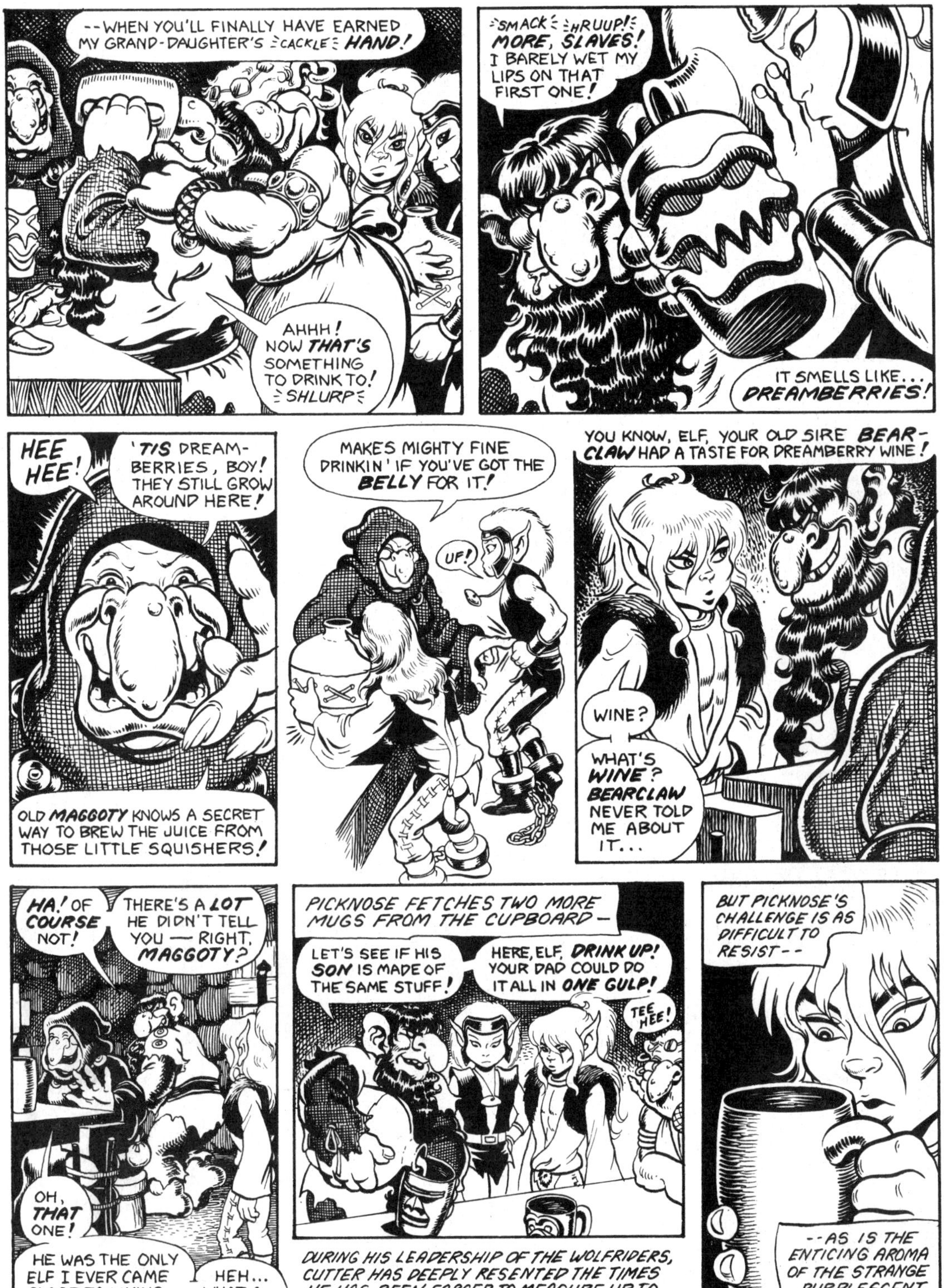
--WHEN YOU'LL FINALLY HAVE EARNED MY GRAND-DAUGHTER'S CACKLE HAND!
AHHH! NOW THAT'S SOMETHING TO DRINK TO! SHLURP
SMACK HRUUP! MORE, SLAVES! I BARELY WET MY LIPS ON THAT FIRST ONE!
IT SMELLS LIKE... DREAMBERRIES!
HEE HEE!
'TIS DREAMBERRIES, BOY! THEY STILL GROW AROUND HERE!
OLD MAGGOTY KNOWS A SECRET WAY TO BREW THE JUICE FROM THOSE LITTLE SQUISHERS!
MAKES MIGHTY FINE DRINKIN' IF YOU'VE GOT THE BELLY FOR IT!
UF!
YOU KNOW, ELF, YOUR OLD SIRE BEARCLAW HAD A TASTE FOR DREAMBERRY WINE!
WINE?
WHAT'S WINE? BEARCLAW NEVER TOLD ME ABOUT IT...
HA! OF COURSE NOT!
THERE'S A LOT HE DIDN'T TELL YOU — RIGHT, MAGGOTY?
OH, THAT ONE!
HE WAS THE ONLY ELF I EVER CAME CLOSE TO LIKING IN ALL MY DAYS!
HEH... WHAT A HOTSPUR!
PICKNOSE FETCHES TWO MORE MUGS FROM THE CUPBOARD—
LET'S SEE IF HIS SON IS MADE OF THE SAME STUFF!
HERE, ELF, DRINK UP! YOUR DAD COULD DO IT ALL IN ONE GULP!
TEE HEE!
DURING HIS LEADERSHIP OF THE WOLFRIDERS, CUTTER HAS DEEPLY RESENTED THE TIMES HE HAS BEEN FORCED TO MEASURE UP TO BEARCLAW'S COLORFUL REPUTATION...
BUT PICKNOSE'S CHALLENGE IS AS DIFFICULT TO RESIST--
--AS IS THE ENTICING AROMA OF THE STRANGE PURPLESCENT BREW.

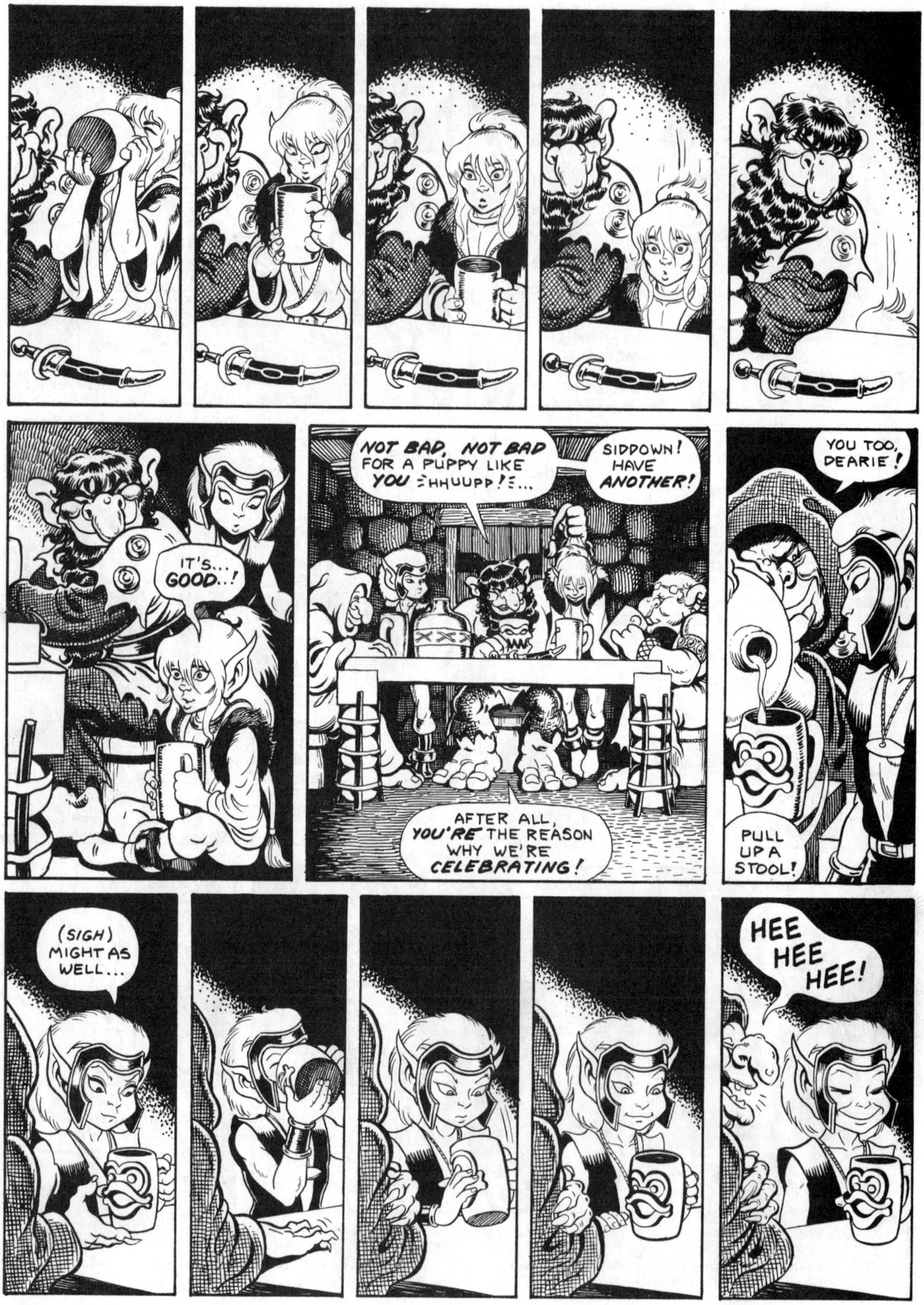
IT'S... GOOD..!
NOT BAD, NOT BAD FOR A PUPPY LIKE YOU HHUUPP!...
SIDDOWN! HAVE ANOTHER!
AFTER ALL, YOU'RE THE REASON WHY WE'RE CELEBRATING!
YOU TOO, DEARIE!
PULL UP A STOOL!
(SIGH) MIGHT AS WELL...
HEE HEE HEE!

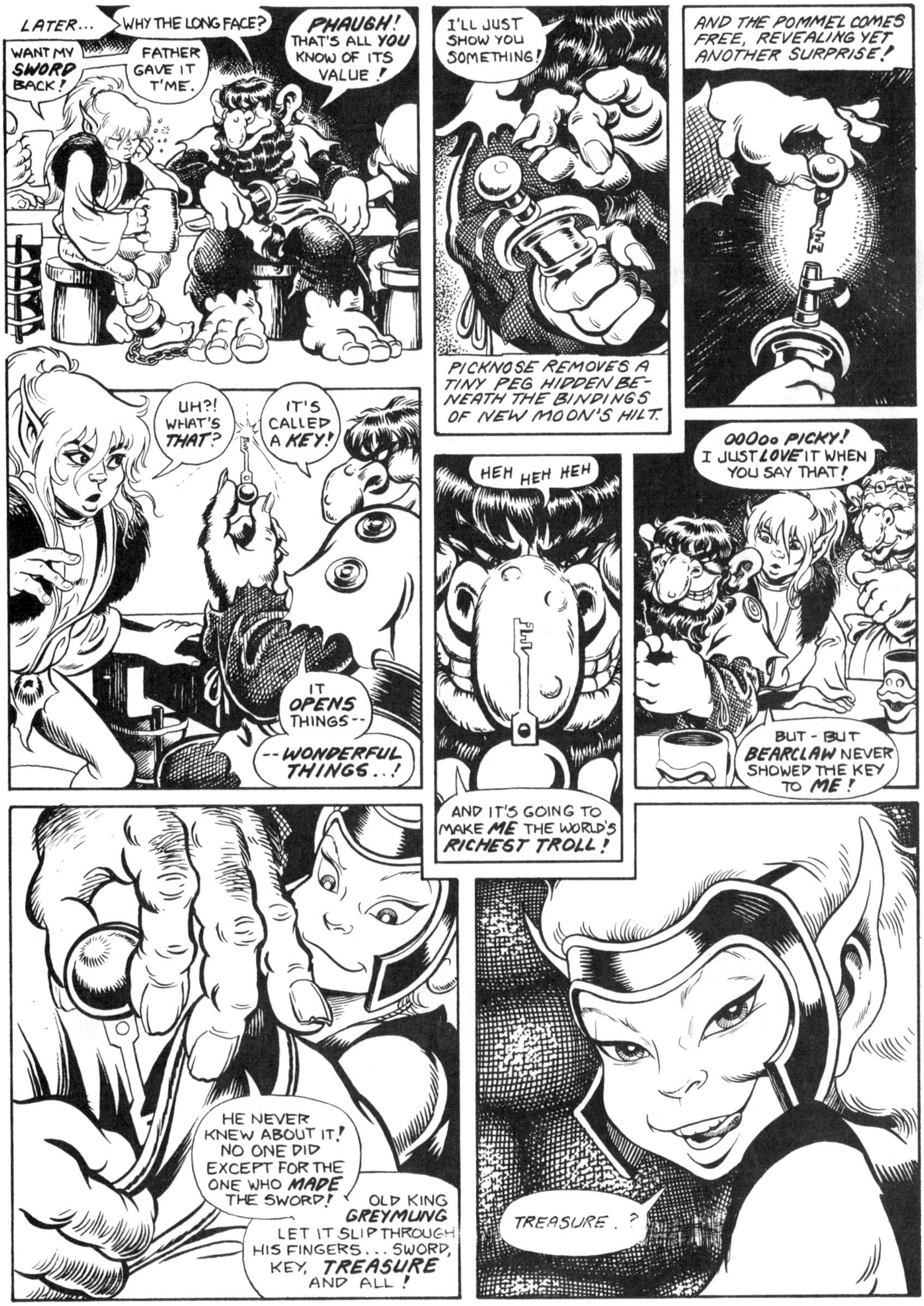
LATER...
WHY THE LONG FACE?
WANT MY SWORD BACK!
FATHER GAVE IT T'ME.
PHAUGH! THAT'S ALL YOU KNOW OF ITS VALUE!
I'LL JUST SHOW YOU SOMETHING!
PICKNOSE REMOVES A TINY PEG HIDDEN BENEATH THE BINDINGS OF NEW MOON'S HILT.
AND THE POMMEL COMES FREE, REVEALING YET ANOTHER SURPRISE!
UH?! WHAT'S THAT?
IT'S CALLED A KEY!
IT OPENS THINGS--
--WONDERFUL THINGS..!
HEH HEH HEH
AND IT'S GOING TO MAKE ME THE WORLD'S RICHEST TROLL!
OOOOo PICKY! I JUST LOVE IT WHEN YOU SAY THAT!
BUT - BUT BEARCLAW NEVER SHOWED THE KEY TO ME!
HE NEVER KNEW ABOUT IT! NO ONE DID EXCEPT FOR THE ONE WHO MADE THE SWORD!
OLD KING GREYMUNG LET IT SLIP THROUGH HIS FINGERS... SWORD, KEY, TREASURE AND ALL!
TREASURE. ?

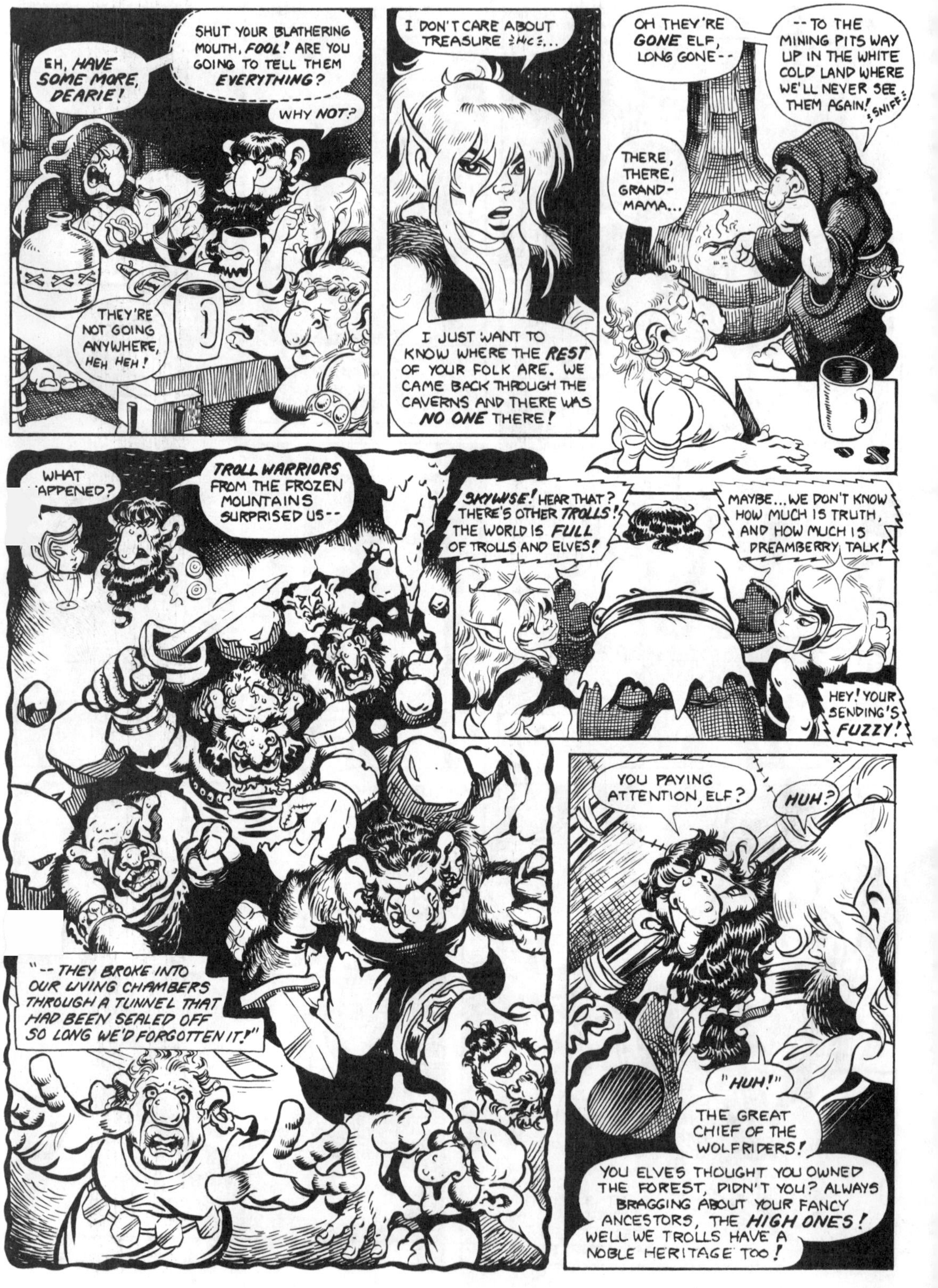
EH, HAVE SOME MORE, DEARIE!
SHUT YOUR BLATHERING MOUTH, FOOL! ARE YOU GOING TO TELL THEM EVERYTHING?
WHY NOT?
THEY'RE NOT GOING ANYWHERE, HEH HEH!
I DON'T CARE ABOUT TREASURE *HIC*...
I JUST WANT TO KNOW WHERE THE REST OF YOUR FOLK ARE. WE CAME BACK THROUGH THE CAVERNS AND THERE WAS NO ONE THERE!
OH THEY'RE GONE ELF, LONG GONE--
--TO THE MINING PITS WAY UP IN THE WHITE COLD LAND WHERE WE'LL NEVER SEE THEM AGAIN! *SNIFF*
THERE, THERE, GRAND-MAMA...
WHAT HAPPENED?
TROLL WARRIORS FROM THE FROZEN MOUNTAINS SURPRISED US--
"--THEY BROKE INTO OUR LIVING CHAMBERS THROUGH A TUNNEL THAT HAD BEEN SEALED OFF SO LONG WE'D FORGOTTEN IT!"
SKYWISE! HEAR THAT? THERE'S OTHER TROLLS! THE WORLD IS FULL OF TROLLS AND ELVES!
MAYBE... WE DON'T KNOW HOW MUCH IS TRUTH, AND HOW MUCH IS DREAMBERRY TALK!
HEY! YOUR SENDING'S FUZZY!
YOU PAYING ATTENTION, ELF?
HUH?
"HUH!"
THE GREAT CHIEF OF THE WOLFRIDERS!
YOU ELVES THOUGHT YOU OWNED THE FOREST, DIDN'T YOU? ALWAYS BRAGGING ABOUT YOUR FANCY ANCESTORS, THE HIGH ONES! WELL WE TROLLS HAVE A NOBLE HERITAGE TOO!

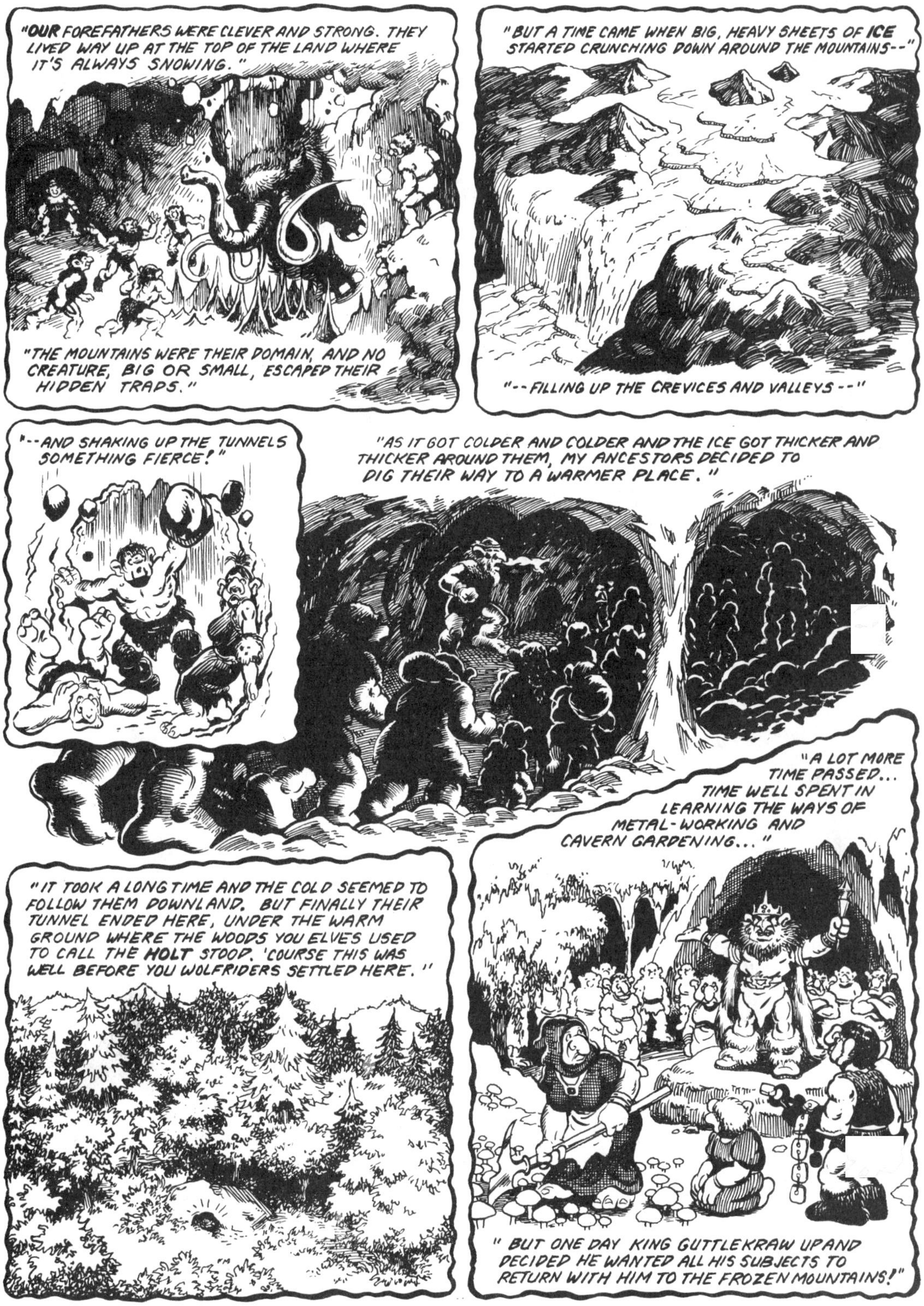
"OUR FOREFATHERS WERE CLEVER AND STRONG. THEY LIVED WAY UP AT THE TOP OF THE LAND WHERE IT'S ALWAYS SNOWING."
"THE MOUNTAINS WERE THEIR DOMAIN, AND NO CREATURE, BIG OR SMALL, ESCAPED THEIR HIDDEN TRAPS."
"BUT A TIME CAME WHEN BIG, HEAVY SHEETS OF ICE STARTED CRUNCHING DOWN AROUND THE MOUNTAINS--"
"--FILLING UP THE CREVICES AND VALLEYS--"
"--AND SHAKING UP THE TUNNELS SOMETHING FIERCE!"
"AS IT GOT COLDER AND COLDER AND THE ICE GOT THICKER AND THICKER AROUND THEM, MY ANCESTORS DECIDED TO DIG THEIR WAY TO A WARMER PLACE."
"IT TOOK A LONG TIME AND THE COLD SEEMED TO FOLLOW THEM DOWNLAND. BUT FINALLY THEIR TUNNEL ENDED HERE, UNDER THE WARM GROUND WHERE THE WOODS YOU ELVES USED TO CALL THE HOLT STOOD. 'COURSE THIS WAS WELL BEFORE YOU WOLFRIDERS SETTLED HERE."
"A LOT MORE TIME PASSED... TIME WELL SPENT IN LEARNING THE WAYS OF METAL-WORKING AND CAVERN GARDENING..."
"BUT ONE DAY KING GUTTLEKRAW UP AND DECIDED HE WANTED ALL HIS SUBJECTS TO RETURN WITH HIM TO THE FROZEN MOUNTAINS!"

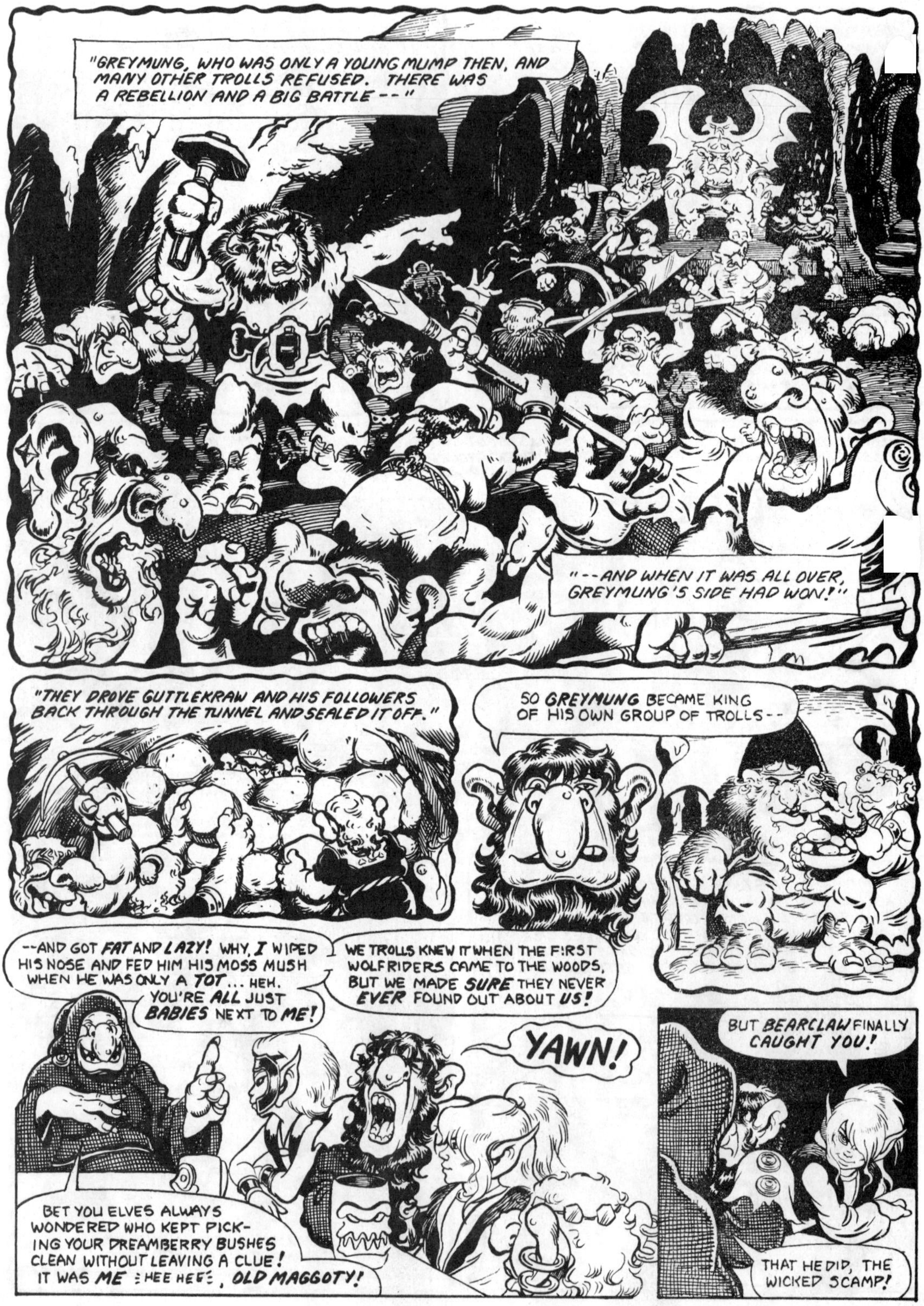
"GREYMUNG, WHO WAS ONLY A YOUNG MUMP THEN, AND MANY OTHER TROLLS REFUSED. THERE WAS A REBELLION AND A BIG BATTLE --"
"--AND WHEN IT WAS ALL OVER, GREYMUNG'S SIDE HAD WON!"
"THEY DROVE GUTTLEKRAW AND HIS FOLLOWERS BACK THROUGH THE TUNNEL AND SEALED IT OFF."
SO GREYMUNG BECAME KING OF HIS OWN GROUP OF TROLLS--
--AND GOT FAT AND LAZY! WHY, I WIPED HIS NOSE AND FED HIM HIS MOSS MUSH WHEN HE WAS ONLY A TOT... HEH. YOU'RE ALL JUST BABIES NEXT TO ME!
WE TROLLS KNEW IT WHEN THE FIRST WOLFRIDERS CAME TO THE WOODS, BUT WE MADE SURE THEY NEVER EVER FOUND OUT ABOUT US!
YAWN!
BET YOU ELVES ALWAYS WONDERED WHO KEPT PICKING YOUR DREAMBERRY BUSHES CLEAN WITHOUT LEAVING A CLUE! IT WAS ME -HEE HEE-, OLD MAGGOTY!
BUT BEARCLAW FINALLY CAUGHT YOU!
THAT HE DID, THE WICKED SCAMP!

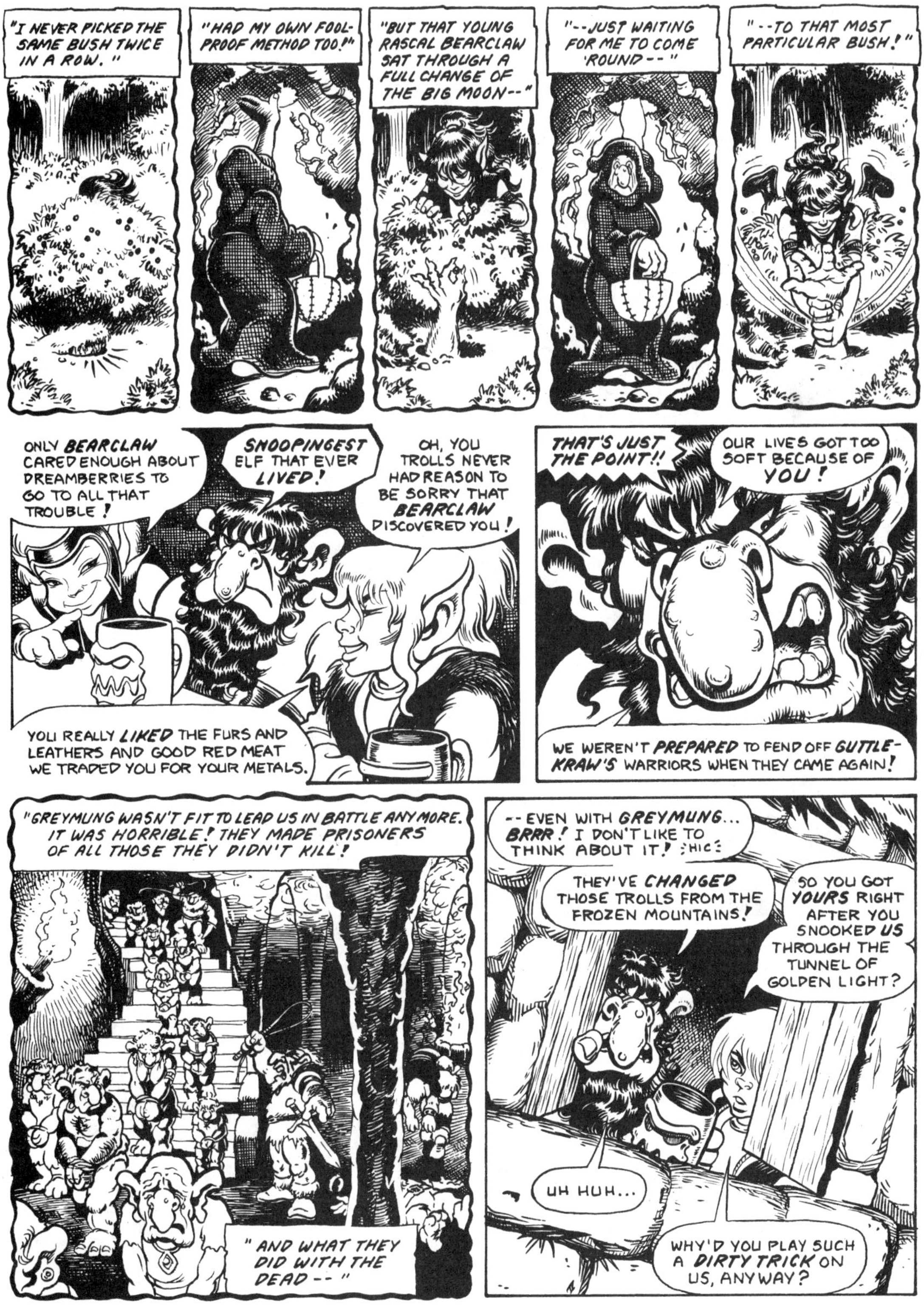
"I NEVER PICKED THE SAME BUSH TWICE IN A ROW."
"HAD MY OWN FOOL-PROOF METHOD TOO!"
"BUT THAT YOUNG RASCAL BEARCLAW SAT THROUGH A FULL CHANGE OF THE BIG MOON--"
"--JUST WAITING FOR ME TO COME 'ROUND--"
"--TO THAT MOST PARTICULAR BUSH!"
ONLY BEARCLAW CARED ENOUGH ABOUT DREAMBERRIES TO GO TO ALL THAT TROUBLE!
SNOOPINGEST ELF THAT EVER LIVED!
OH, YOU TROLLS NEVER HAD REASON TO BE SORRY THAT BEARCLAW DISCOVERED YOU!
YOU REALLY LIKED THE FURS AND LEATHERS AND GOOD RED MEAT WE TRADED YOU FOR YOUR METALS.
THAT'S JUST THE POINT!!
OUR LIVES GOT TOO SOFT BECAUSE OF YOU!
WE WEREN'T PREPARED TO FEND OFF GUTTLEKRAW'S WARRIORS WHEN THEY CAME AGAIN!
"GREYMUNG WASN'T FIT TO LEAD US IN BATTLE ANYMORE. IT WAS HORRIBLE! THEY MADE PRISONERS OF ALL THOSE THEY DIDN'T KILL!
"AND WHAT THEY DID WITH THE DEAD--"
--EVEN WITH GREYMUNG... BRRR! I DON'T LIKE TO THINK ABOUT IT! HIC
THEY'VE CHANGED THOSE TROLLS FROM THE FROZEN MOUNTAINS!
SO YOU GOT YOURS RIGHT AFTER YOU SNOOKED US THROUGH THE TUNNEL OF GOLDEN LIGHT?
UH HUH...
WHY'D YOU PLAY SUCH A DIRTY TRICK ON US, ANYWAY?

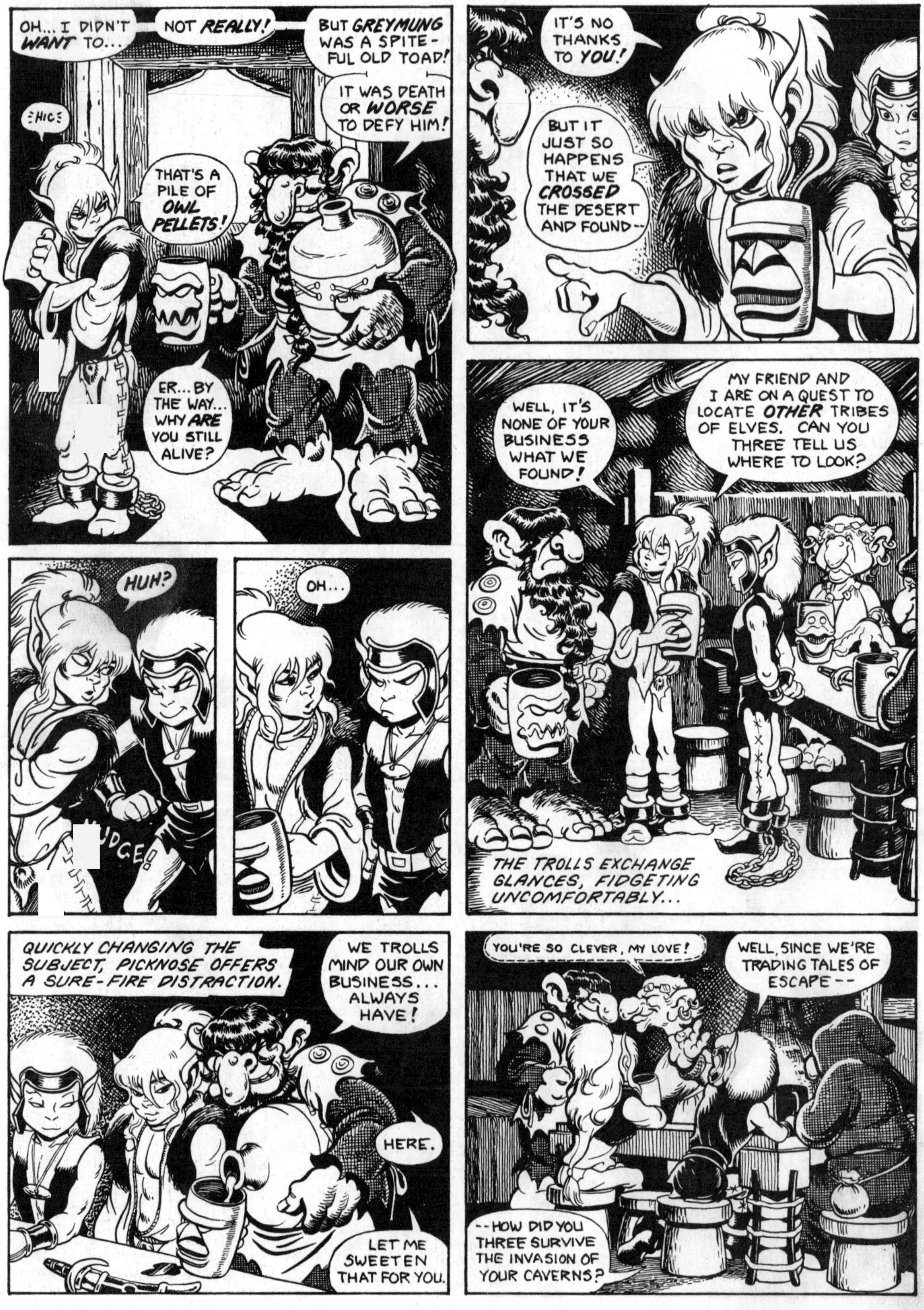
OH... I DIDN'T WANT TO...
NOT REALLY!
BUT GREYMUNG WAS A SPITE-FUL OLD TOAD!
IT WAS DEATH OR WORSE TO DEFY HIM!
HIC
THAT'S A PILE OF OWL PELLETS!
ER... BY THE WAY... WHY ARE YOU STILL ALIVE?
IT'S NO THANKS TO YOU!
BUT IT JUST SO HAPPENS THAT WE CROSSED THE DESERT AND FOUND--
HUH?
OH...
WELL, IT'S NONE OF YOUR BUSINESS WHAT WE FOUND!
MY FRIEND AND I ARE ON A QUEST TO LOCATE OTHER TRIBES OF ELVES. CAN YOU THREE TELL US WHERE TO LOOK?
THE TROLLS EXCHANGE GLANCES, FIDGETING UNCOMFORTABLY...
QUICKLY CHANGING THE SUBJECT, PICKNOSE OFFERS A SURE-FIRE DISTRACTION.
WE TROLLS MIND OUR OWN BUSINESS... ALWAYS HAVE!
HERE.
LET ME SWEETEN THAT FOR YOU.
YOU'RE SO CLEVER, MY LOVE!
WELL, SINCE WE'RE TRADING TALES OF ESCAPE --
--HOW DID YOU THREE SURVIVE THE INVASION OF YOUR CAVERNS?

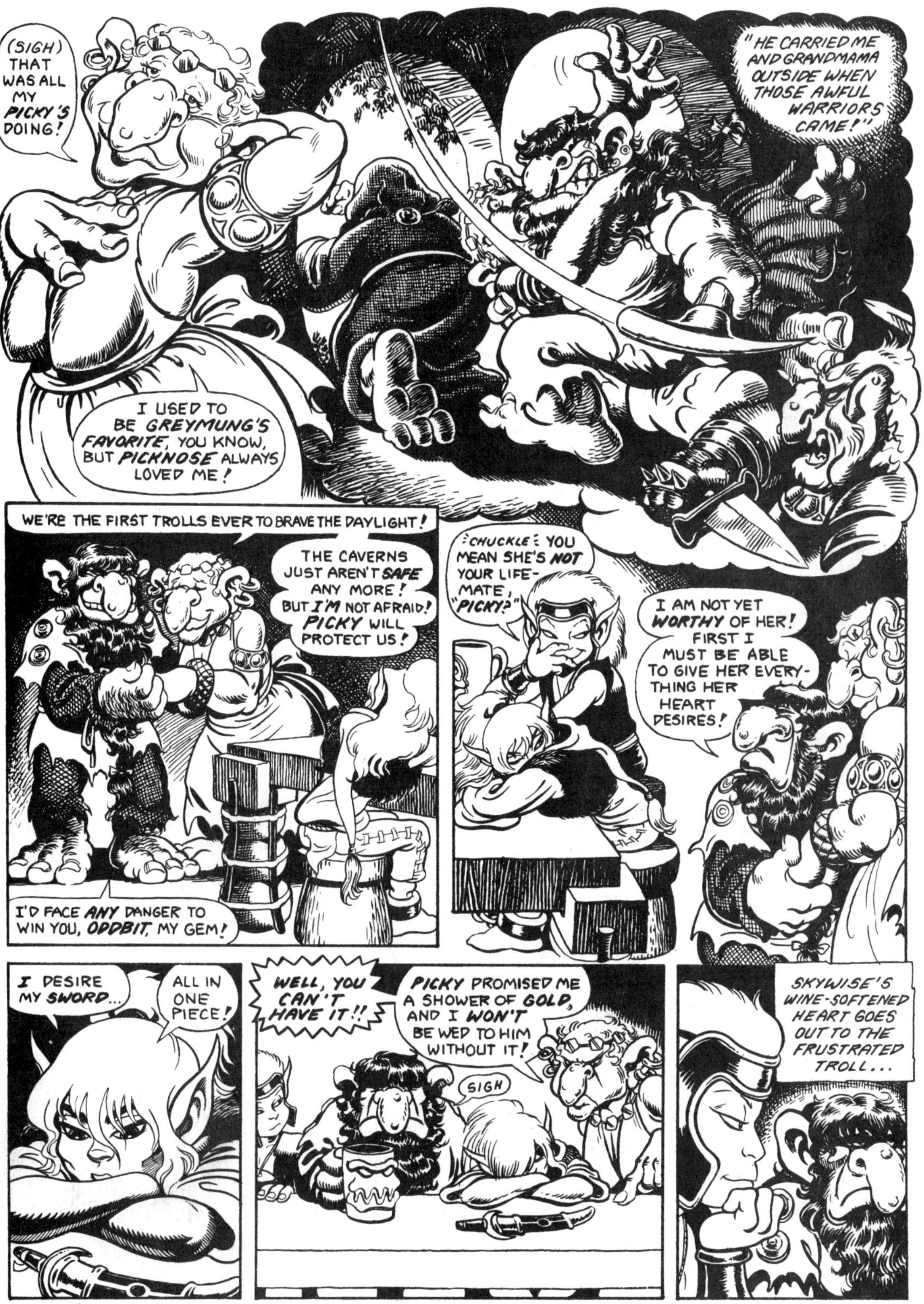
(SIGH) THAT WAS ALL MY PICKY'S DOING!
"HE CARRIED ME AND GRANDMAMA OUTSIDE WHEN THOSE AWFUL WARRIORS CAME!"
I USED TO BE GREYMUNG'S FAVORITE, YOU KNOW, BUT PICKNOSE ALWAYS LOVED ME!
WE'RE THE FIRST TROLLS EVER TO BRAVE THE DAYLIGHT!
THE CAVERNS JUST AREN'T SAFE ANY MORE! BUT I'M NOT AFRAID! PICKY WILL PROTECT US!
I'D FACE ANY DANGER TO WIN YOU, ODDBIT, MY GEM!
:CHUCKLE: YOU MEAN SHE'S NOT YOUR LIFE-MATE, "PICKY?"
I AM NOT YET WORTHY OF HER! FIRST I MUST BE ABLE TO GIVE HER EVERY-THING HER HEART DESIRES!
I DESIRE MY SWORD...
ALL IN ONE PIECE!
WELL, YOU CAN'T HAVE IT!!
PICKY PROMISED ME A SHOWER OF GOLD, AND I WON'T BE WED TO HIM WITHOUT IT!
SIGH
SKYWISE'S WINE-SOFTENED HEART GOES OUT TO THE FRUSTRATED TROLL...

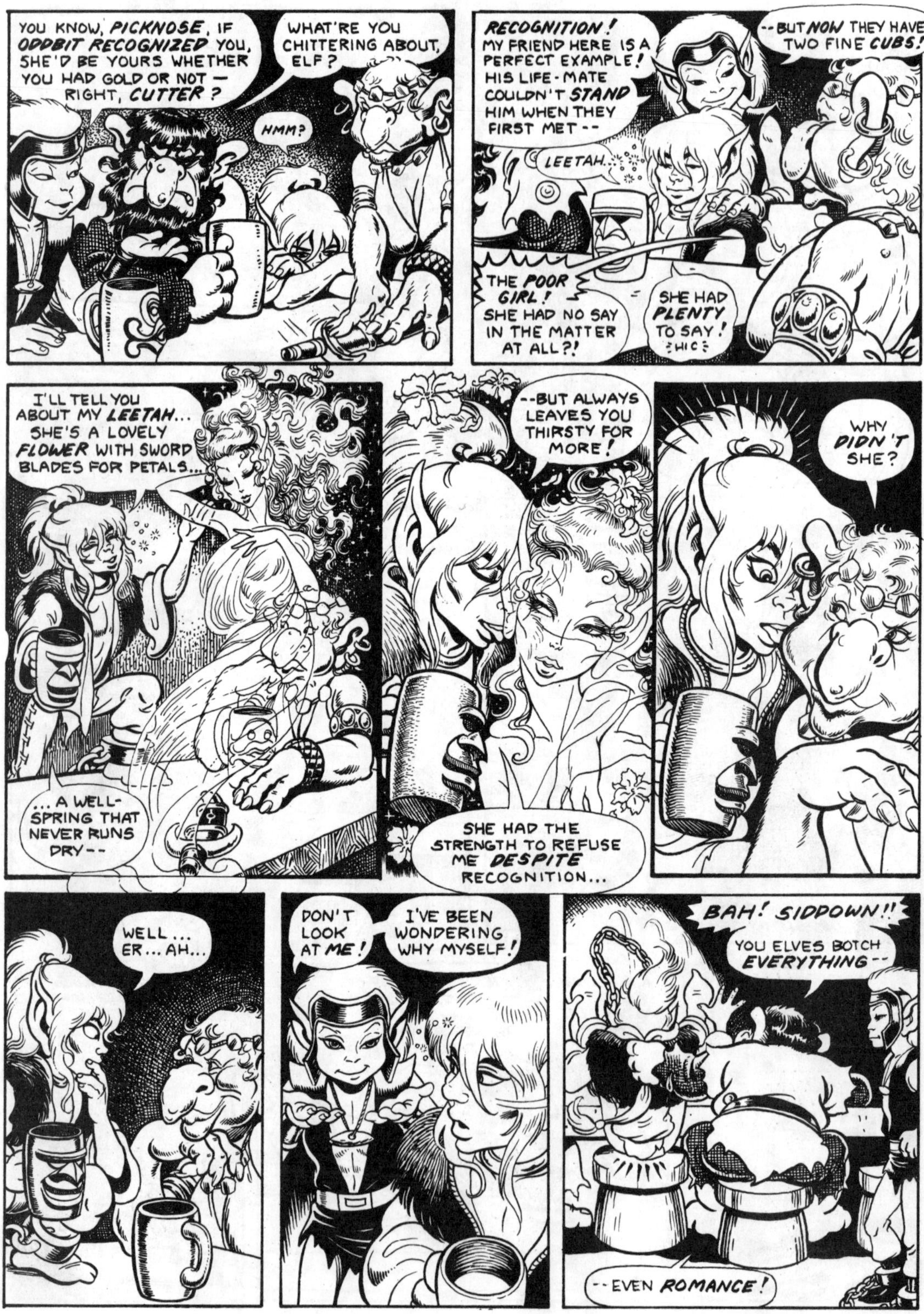
YOU KNOW, PICKNOSE, IF ODDBIT RECOGNIZED YOU, SHE'D BE YOURS WHETHER YOU HAD GOLD OR NOT — RIGHT, CUTTER?
WHAT'RE YOU CHITTERING ABOUT, ELF?
HMM?
RECOGNITION! MY FRIEND HERE IS A PERFECT EXAMPLE! HIS LIFE-MATE COULDN'T STAND HIM WHEN THEY FIRST MET --
--BUT NOW THEY HAVE TWO FINE CUBS!
LEETAH...
THE POOR GIRL! SHE HAD NO SAY IN THE MATTER AT ALL?!
SHE HAD PLENTY TO SAY! HIC
I'LL TELL YOU ABOUT MY LEETAH... SHE'S A LOVELY FLOWER WITH SWORD BLADES FOR PETALS...
...A WELL-SPRING THAT NEVER RUNS DRY--
--BUT ALWAYS LEAVES YOU THIRSTY FOR MORE!
SHE HAD THE STRENGTH TO REFUSE ME DESPITE RECOGNITION...
WHY DIDN'T SHE?
WELL... ER... AH...
DON'T LOOK AT ME!
I'VE BEEN WONDERING WHY MYSELF!
BAH! SIDDOWN!!
YOU ELVES BOTCH EVERYTHING--
--EVEN ROMANCE!

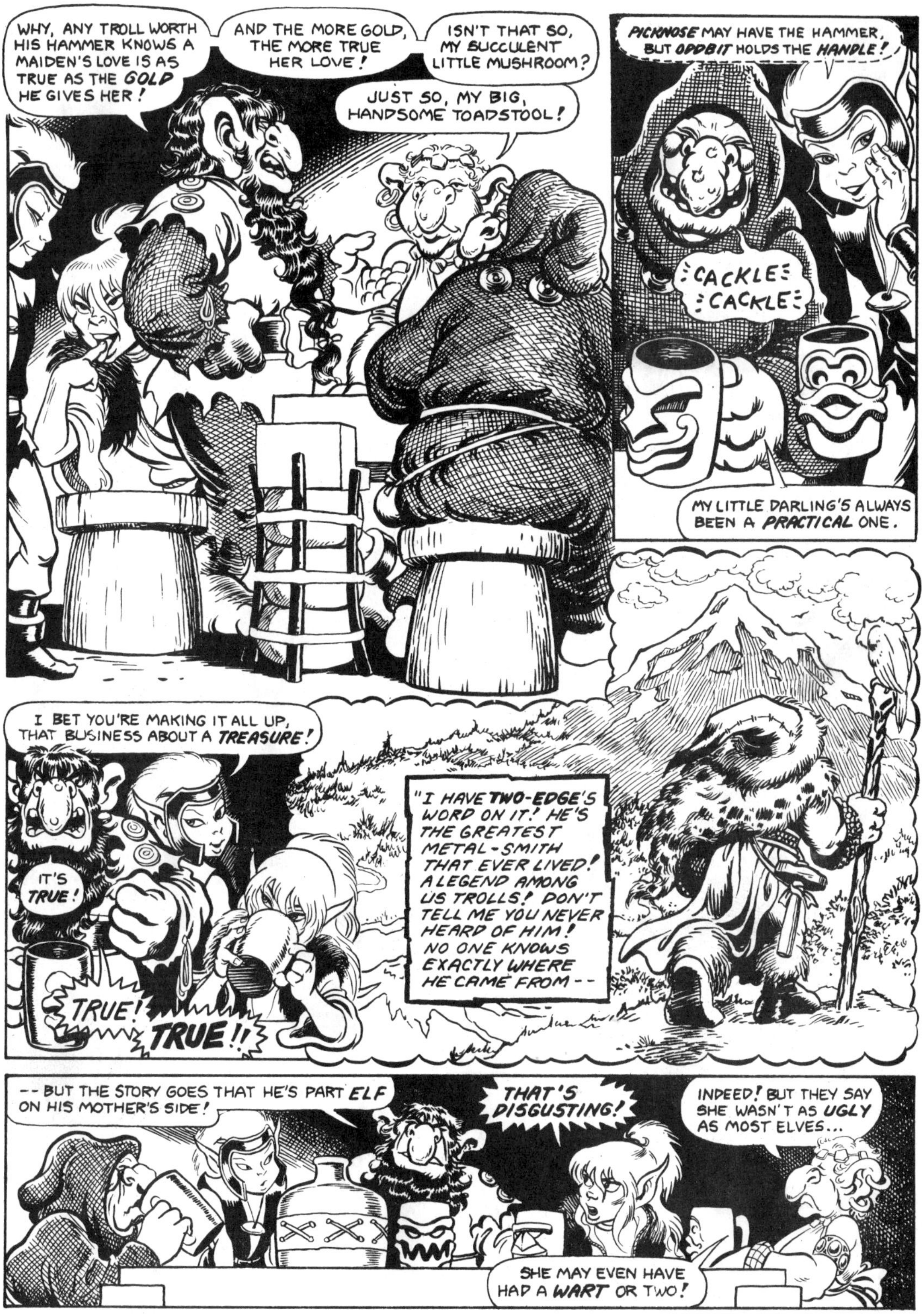

WHY, ANY TROLL WORTH HIS HAMMER KNOWS A MAIDEN'S LOVE IS AS TRUE AS THE GOLD HE GIVES HER!
AND THE MORE GOLD, THE MORE TRUE HER LOVE!
ISN'T THAT SO, MY SUCCULENT LITTLE MUSHROOM?
JUST SO, MY BIG, HANDSOME TOADSTOOL!
PICKNOSE MAY HAVE THE HAMMER, BUT ODDBIT HOLDS THE HANDLE!
CACKLE CACKLE
MY LITTLE DARLING'S ALWAYS BEEN A PRACTICAL ONE.
I BET YOU'RE MAKING IT ALL UP, THAT BUSINESS ABOUT A TREASURE!
IT'S TRUE!
TRUE! TRUE!!
"I HAVE TWO-EDGE'S WORD ON IT! HE'S THE GREATEST METAL-SMITH THAT EVER LIVED! A LEGEND AMONG US TROLLS! DON'T TELL ME YOU NEVER HEARD OF HIM! NO ONE KNOWS EXACTLY WHERE HE CAME FROM--
--BUT THE STORY GOES THAT HE'S PART ELF ON HIS MOTHER'S SIDE!
THAT'S DISGUSTING!
INDEED! BUT THEY SAY SHE WASN'T AS UGLY AS MOST ELVES...
SHE MAY EVEN HAVE HAD A WART OR TWO!

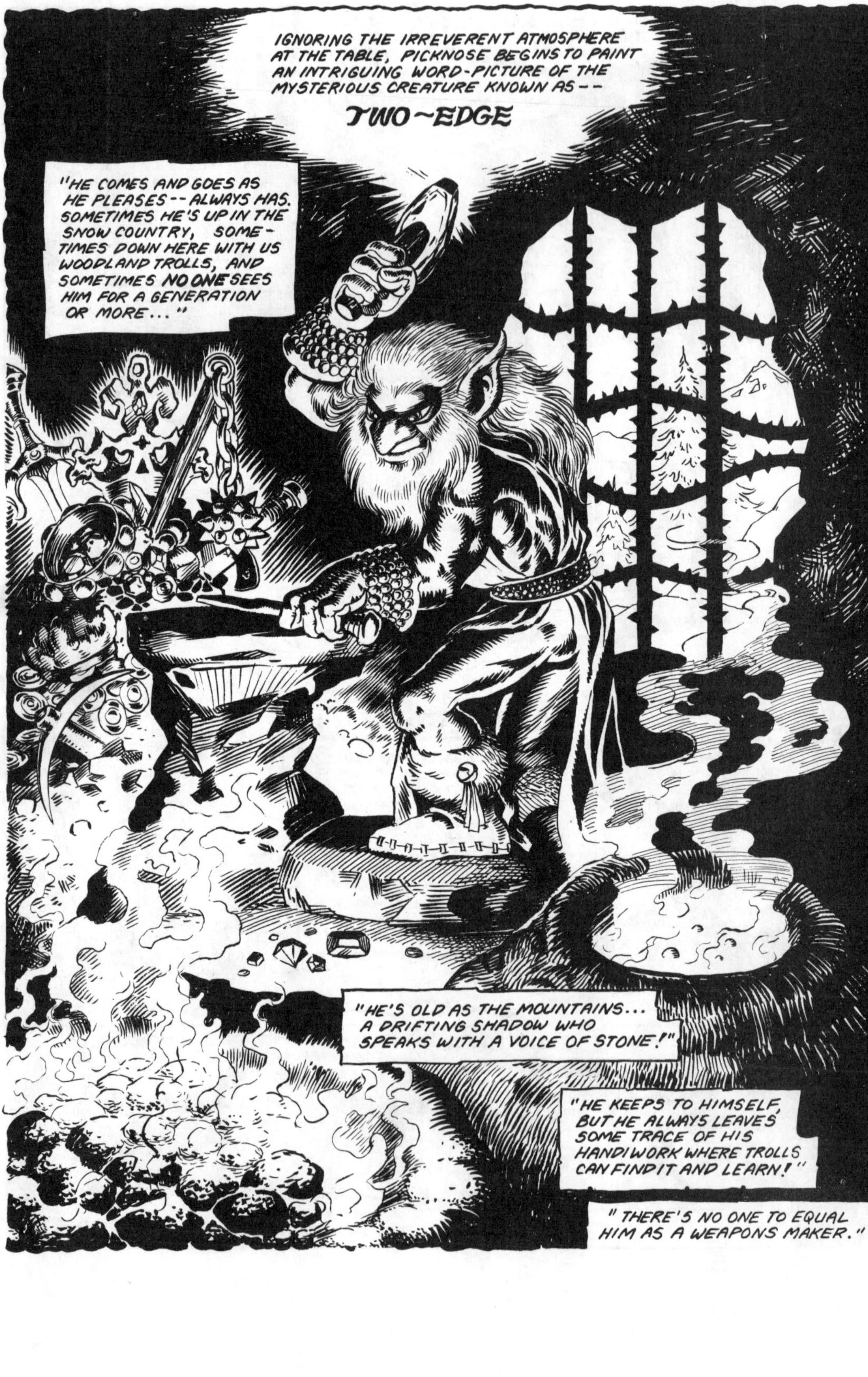
IGNORING THE IRREVERENT ATMOSPHERE AT THE TABLE, PICKNOSE BEGINS TO PAINT AN INTRIGUING WORD-PICTURE OF THE MYSTERIOUS CREATURE KNOWN AS--
TWO-EDGE
"HE COMES AND GOES AS HE PLEASES--ALWAYS HAS. SOMETIMES HE'S UP IN THE SNOW COUNTRY, SOMETIMES DOWN HERE WITH US WOODLAND TROLLS, AND SOMETIMES NO ONE SEES HIM FOR A GENERATION OR MORE..."
"HE'S OLD AS THE MOUNTAINS... A DRIFTING SHADOW WHO SPEAKS WITH A VOICE OF STONE!"
"HE KEEPS TO HIMSELF, BUT HE ALWAYS LEAVES SOME TRACE OF HIS HANDIWORK WHERE TROLLS CAN FIND IT AND LEARN!"
"THERE'S NO ONE TO EQUAL HIM AS A WEAPONS MAKER."

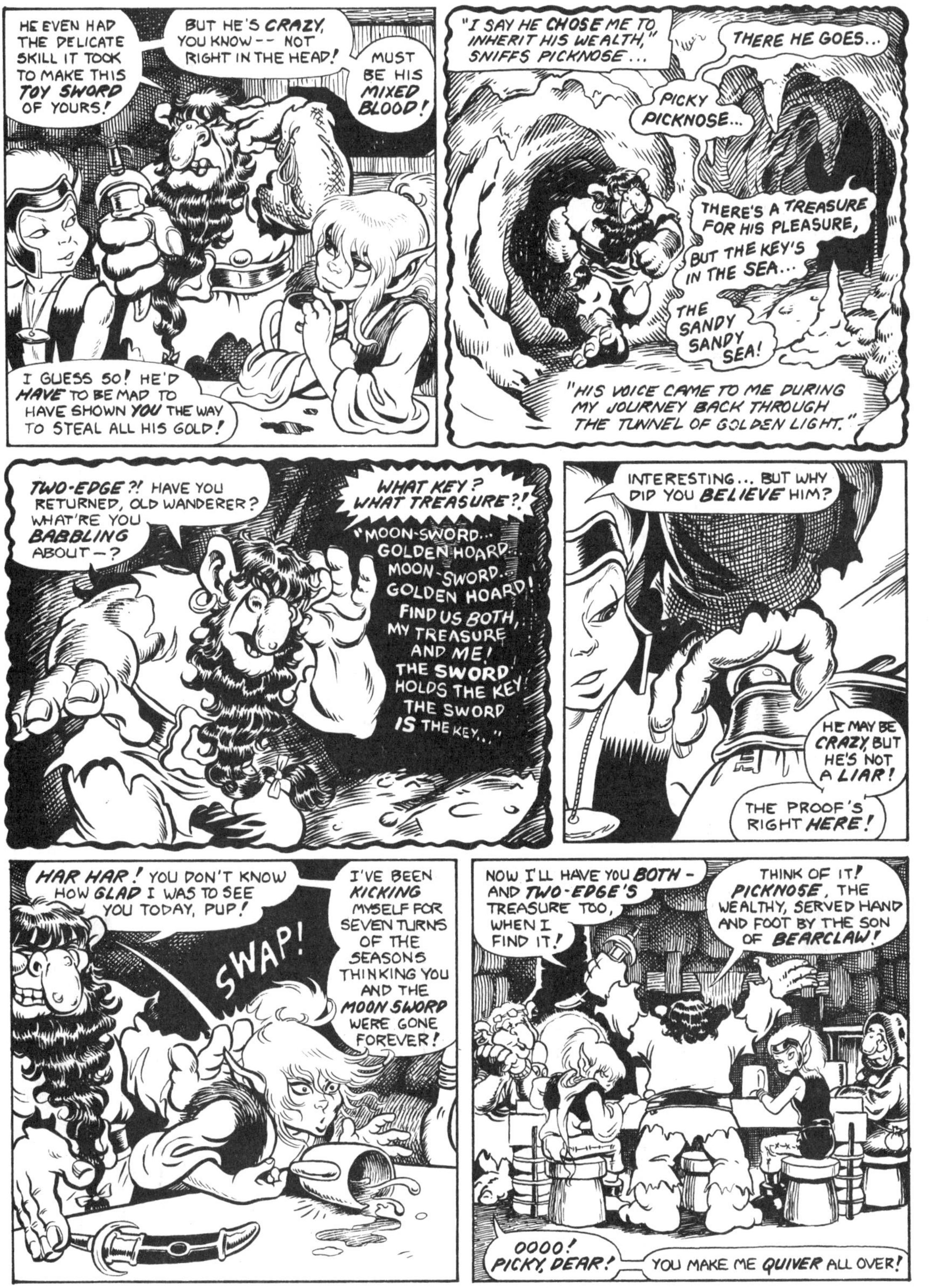
HE EVEN HAD THE DELICATE SKILL IT TOOK TO MAKE THIS TOY SWORD OF YOURS!
BUT HE'S CRAZY, YOU KNOW -- NOT RIGHT IN THE HEAD!
MUST BE HIS MIXED BLOOD!
I GUESS SO! HE'D HAVE TO BE MAD TO HAVE SHOWN YOU THE WAY TO STEAL ALL HIS GOLD!
"I SAY HE CHOSE ME TO INHERIT HIS WEALTH," SNIFFS PICKNOSE...
THERE HE GOES...
PICKY PICKNOSE...
THERE'S A TREASURE FOR HIS PLEASURE,
BUT THE KEY'S IN THE SEA...
THE SANDY SANDY SEA!
"HIS VOICE CAME TO ME DURING MY JOURNEY BACK THROUGH THE TUNNEL OF GOLDEN LIGHT."
TWO-EDGE?! HAVE YOU RETURNED, OLD WANDERER? WHAT'RE YOU BABBLING ABOUT--?
WHAT KEY? WHAT TREASURE?!
"MOON-SWORD... GOLDEN HOARD... MOON-SWORD... GOLDEN HOARD! FIND US BOTH, MY TREASURE AND ME! THE SWORD HOLDS THE KEY THE SWORD IS THE KEY..."
INTERESTING... BUT WHY DID YOU BELIEVE HIM?
HE MAY BE CRAZY, BUT HE'S NOT A LIAR!
THE PROOF'S RIGHT HERE!
HAR HAR! YOU DON'T KNOW HOW GLAD I WAS TO SEE YOU TODAY, PUP!
SWAP!
I'VE BEEN KICKING MYSELF FOR SEVEN TURNS OF THE SEASONS THINKING YOU AND THE MOON SWORD WERE GONE FOREVER!
NOW I'LL HAVE YOU BOTH -- AND TWO-EDGE'S TREASURE TOO, WHEN I FIND IT!
THINK OF IT! PICKNOSE, THE WEALTHY, SERVED HAND AND FOOT BY THE SON OF BEARCLAW!
OOOO! PICKY, DEAR!
YOU MAKE ME QUIVER ALL OVER!

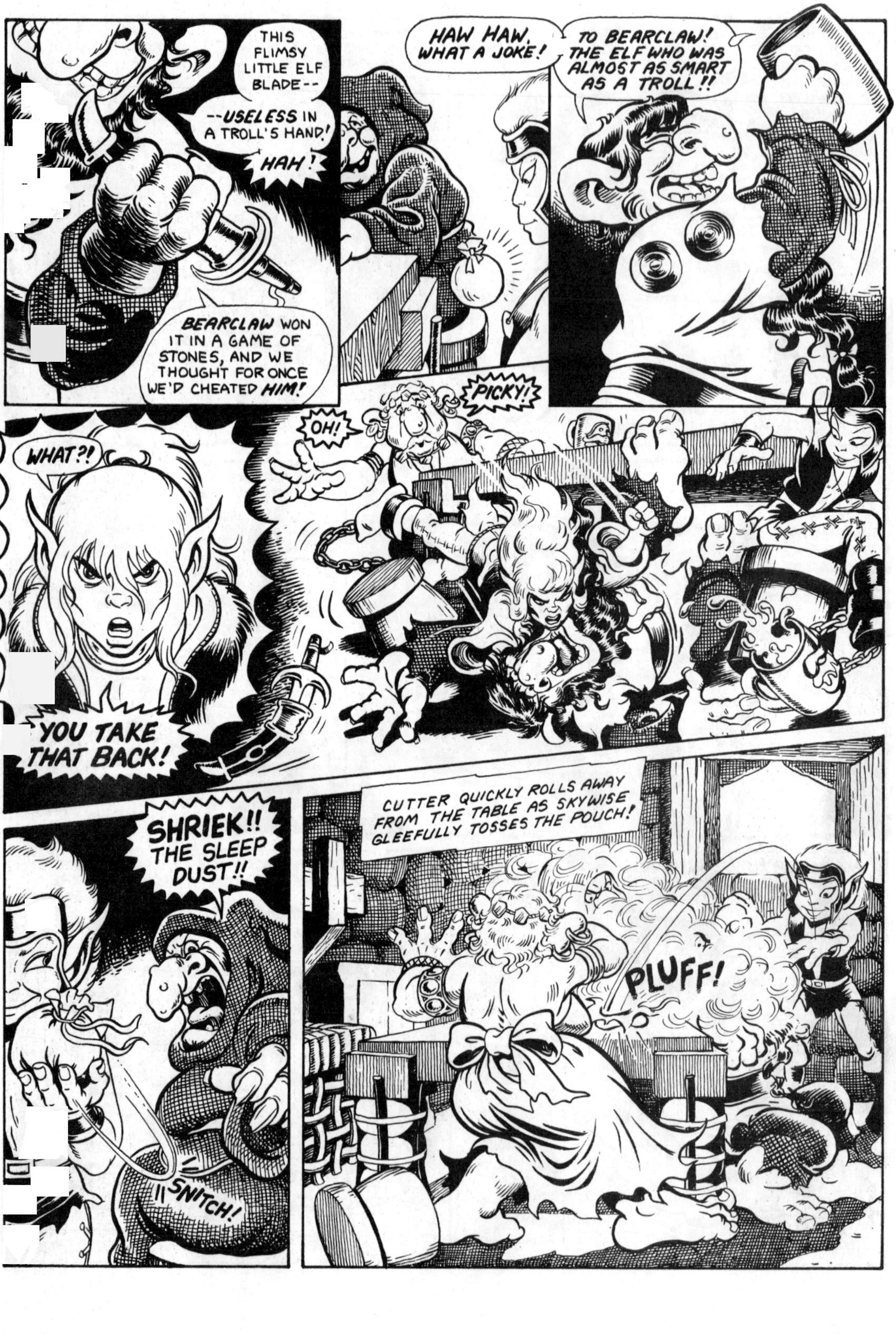
THIS FLIMSY LITTLE ELF BLADE--
--USELESS IN A TROLL'S HAND!
HAH!
BEARCLAW WON IT IN A GAME OF STONES, AND WE THOUGHT FOR ONCE WE'D CHEATED HIM!
HAW HAW. WHAT A JOKE!
TO BEARCLAW! THE ELF WHO WAS ALMOST AS SMART AS A TROLL!!
PICKY!
WHAT?!
YOU TAKE THAT BACK!
OH!
SHRIEK!! THE SLEEP DUST!!
SNITCH!
CUTTER QUICKLY ROLLS AWAY FROM THE TABLE AS SKYWISE GLEEFULLY TOSSES THE POUCH!
PLUFF!

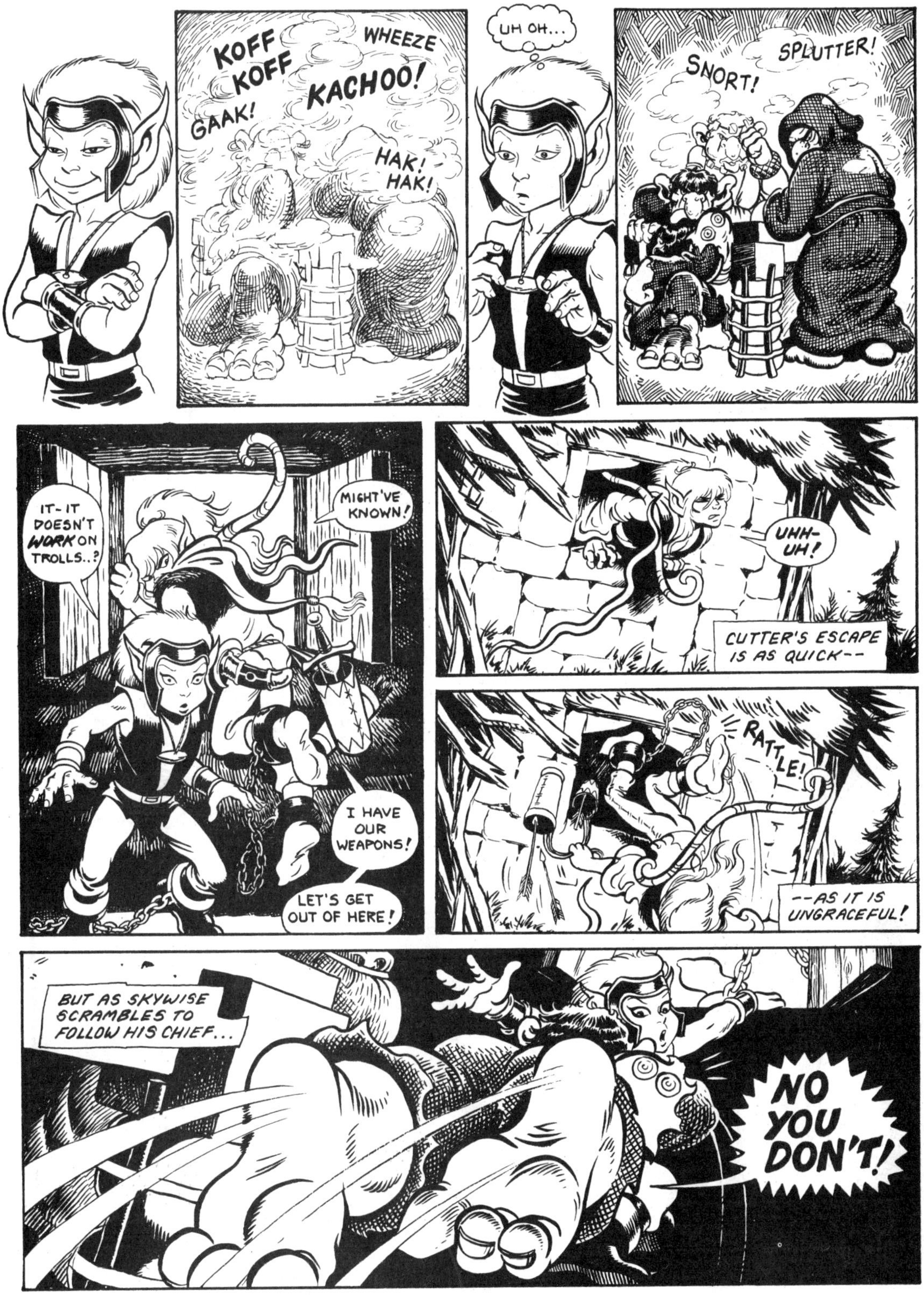
KOFF
KOFF
WHEEZE
KACHOO!
GAAK!
HAK! HAK!
UH OH...
SNORT!
SPLUTTER!
IT-IT DOESN'T WORK ON TROLLS..?
MIGHT'VE KNOWN!
I HAVE OUR WEAPONS!
LET'S GET OUT OF HERE!
UHH-UH!
CUTTER'S ESCAPE IS AS QUICK--
RATTLE!
--AS IT IS UNGRACEFUL!
BUT AS SKYWISE SCRAMBLES TO FOLLOW HIS CHIEF...
NO YOU DON'T!

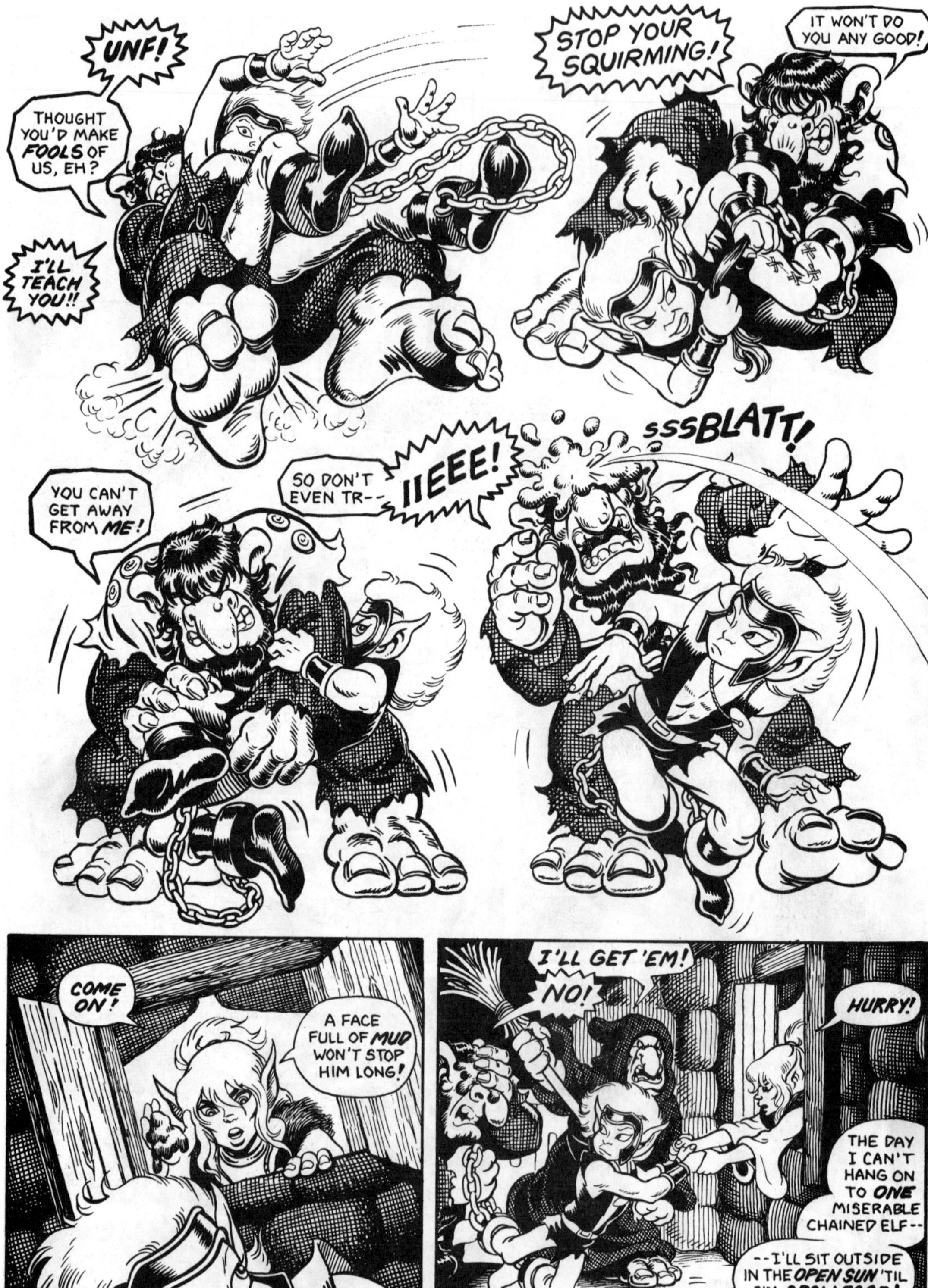
UNF!
THOUGHT YOU'D MAKE FOOLS OF US, EH?
I'LL TEACH YOU!!
STOP YOUR SQUIRMING!
IT WON'T DO YOU ANY GOOD!
YOU CAN'T GET AWAY FROM ME!
SO DON'T EVEN TR--
IIEEE!
SSSBLATT!
COME ON!
A FACE FULL OF MUD WON'T STOP HIM LONG!
I'LL GET 'EM!
NO!
HURRY!
THE DAY I CAN'T HANG ON TO ONE MISERABLE CHAINED ELF--
--I'LL SIT OUTSIDE IN THE OPEN SUN 'TIL I'M CROW FOOD!

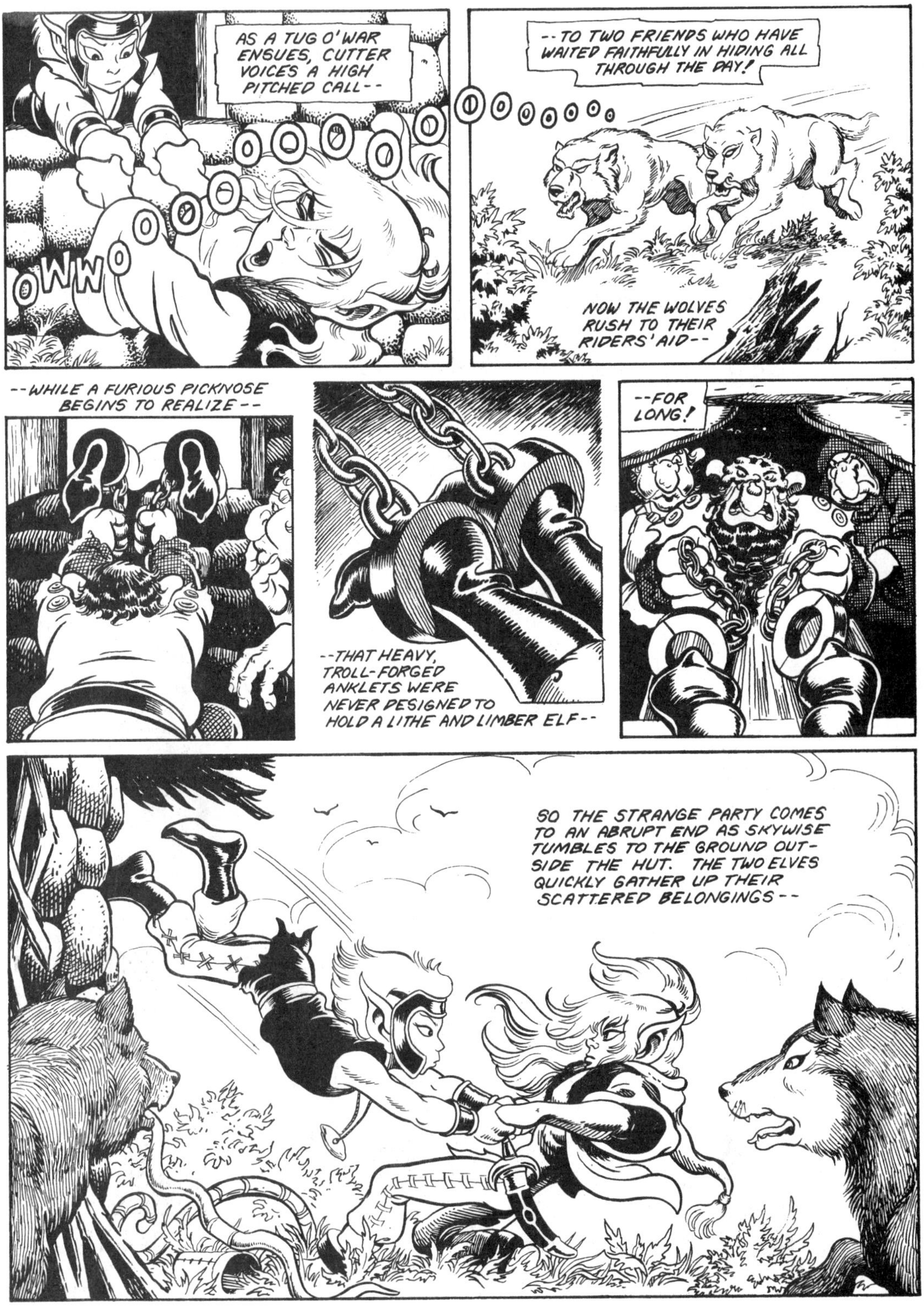
AS A TUG O' WAR ENSUES, CUTTER VOICES A HIGH PITCHED CALL--
OWWOOOOOOOOOOOOOOOOOOOOO
--TO TWO FRIENDS WHO HAVE WAITED FAITHFULLY IN HIDING ALL THROUGH THE DAY!
NOW THE WOLVES RUSH TO THEIR RIDERS' AID--
--WHILE A FURIOUS PICKNOSE BEGINS TO REALIZE--
--THAT HEAVY, TROLL-FORGED ANKLETS WERE NEVER DESIGNED TO HOLD A LITHE AND LIMBER ELF--
--FOR LONG!
SO THE STRANGE PARTY COMES TO AN ABRUPT END AS SKYWISE TUMBLES TO THE GROUND OUT-SIDE THE HUT. THE TWO ELVES QUICKLY GATHER UP THEIR SCATTERED BELONGINGS--

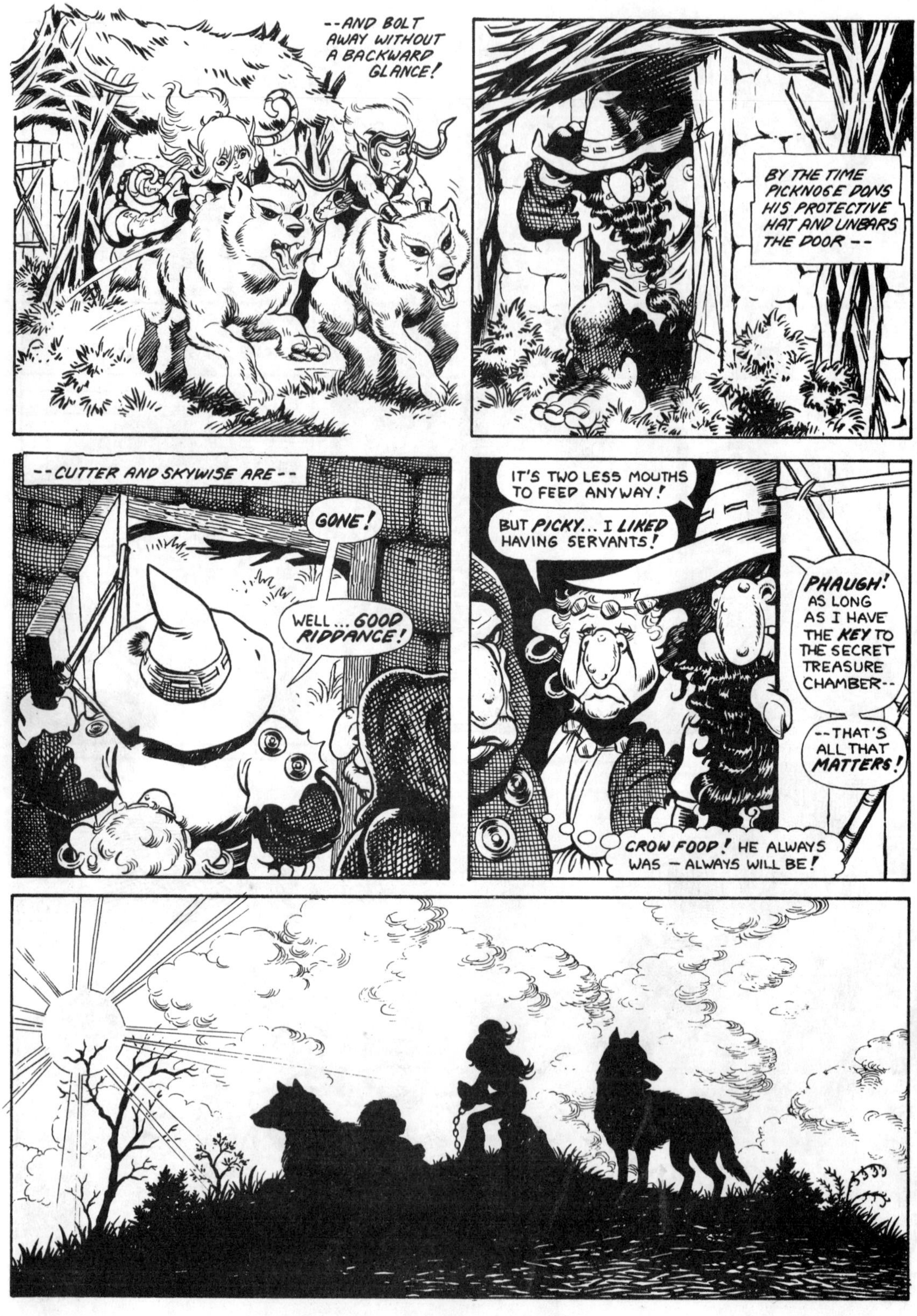
--AND BOLT AWAY WITHOUT A BACKWARD GLANCE!
BY THE TIME PICKNOSE DONS HIS PROTECTIVE HAT AND UNBARS THE DOOR --
--CUTTER AND SKYWISE ARE--
GONE!
WELL... GOOD RIDDANCE!
IT'S TWO LESS MOUTHS TO FEED ANYWAY!
BUT PICKY... I LIKED HAVING SERVANTS!
PHAUGH! AS LONG AS I HAVE THE KEY TO THE SECRET TREASURE CHAMBER--
--THAT'S ALL THAT MATTERS!
CROW FOOD! HE ALWAYS WAS — ALWAYS WILL BE!

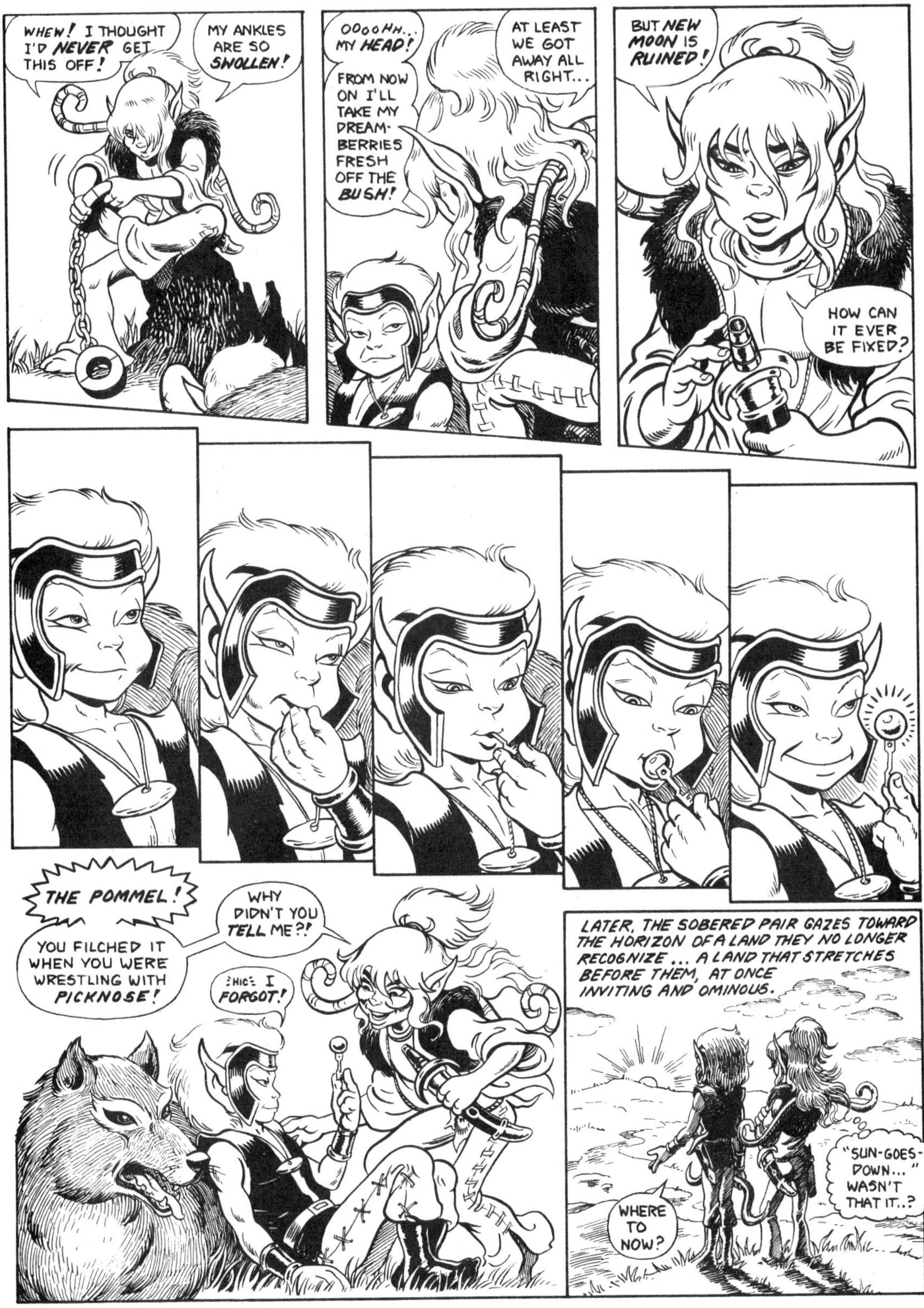
WHEW! I THOUGHT I'D NEVER GET THIS OFF!
MY ANKLES ARE SO SWOLLEN!
OOOOHH... MY HEAD!
FROM NOW ON I'LL TAKE MY DREAM-BERRIES FRESH OFF THE BUSH!
AT LEAST WE GOT AWAY ALL RIGHT...
BUT NEW MOON IS RUINED!
HOW CAN IT EVER BE FIXED?
THE POMMEL!
YOU FILCHED IT WHEN YOU WERE WRESTLING WITH PICKNOSE!
WHY DIDN'T YOU TELL ME?!
HIC I FORGOT!
LATER, THE SOBERED PAIR GAZES TOWARD THE HORIZON OF A LAND THEY NO LONGER RECOGNIZE ... A LAND THAT STRETCHES BEFORE THEM, AT ONCE INVITING AND OMINOUS.
WHERE TO NOW?
"SUN-GOES-DOWN..." WASN'T THAT IT..?

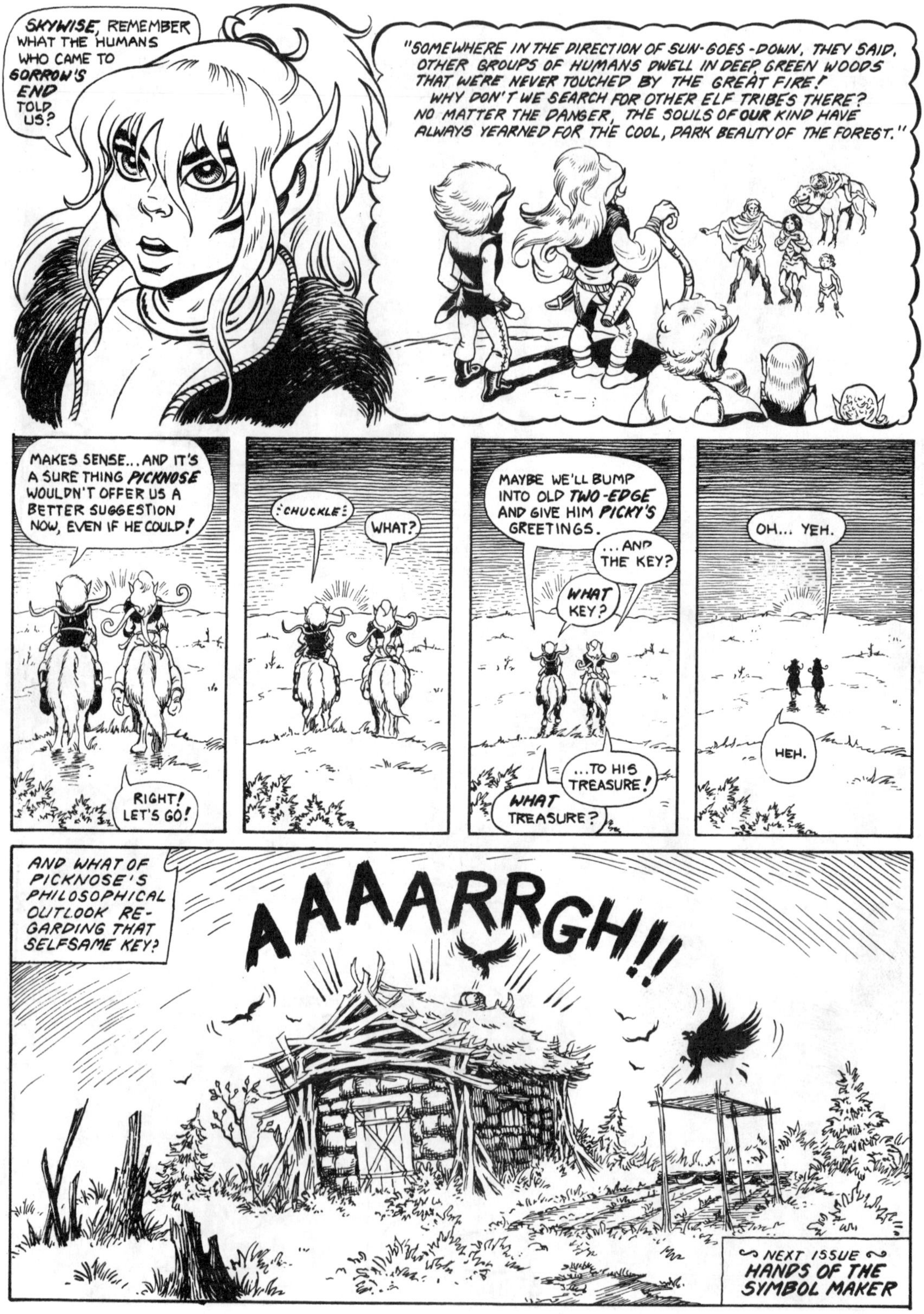
SKYWISE, REMEMBER WHAT THE HUMANS WHO CAME TO SORROW'S END TOLD US?
"SOMEWHERE IN THE DIRECTION OF SUN-GOES-DOWN, THEY SAID, OTHER GROUPS OF HUMANS DWELL IN DEEP, GREEN WOODS THAT WERE NEVER TOUCHED BY THE GREAT FIRE!
WHY DON'T WE SEARCH FOR OTHER ELF TRIBES THERE? NO MATTER THE DANGER, THE SOULS OF OUR KIND HAVE ALWAYS YEARNED FOR THE COOL, DARK BEAUTY OF THE FOREST."
MAKES SENSE... AND IT'S A SURE THING PICKNOSE WOULDN'T OFFER US A BETTER SUGGESTION NOW, EVEN IF HE COULD!
RIGHT! LET'S GO!
CHUCKLE
WHAT?
MAYBE WE'LL BUMP INTO OLD TWO-EDGE AND GIVE HIM PICKY'S GREETINGS.
...AND THE KEY?
WHAT KEY?
...TO HIS TREASURE!
WHAT TREASURE?
OH... YEH.
HEH.
AND WHAT OF PICKNOSE'S PHILOSOPHICAL OUTLOOK REGARDING THAT SELFSAME KEY?
AAAARRGH!!
NEXT ISSUE
HANDS OF THE SYMBOL MAKER

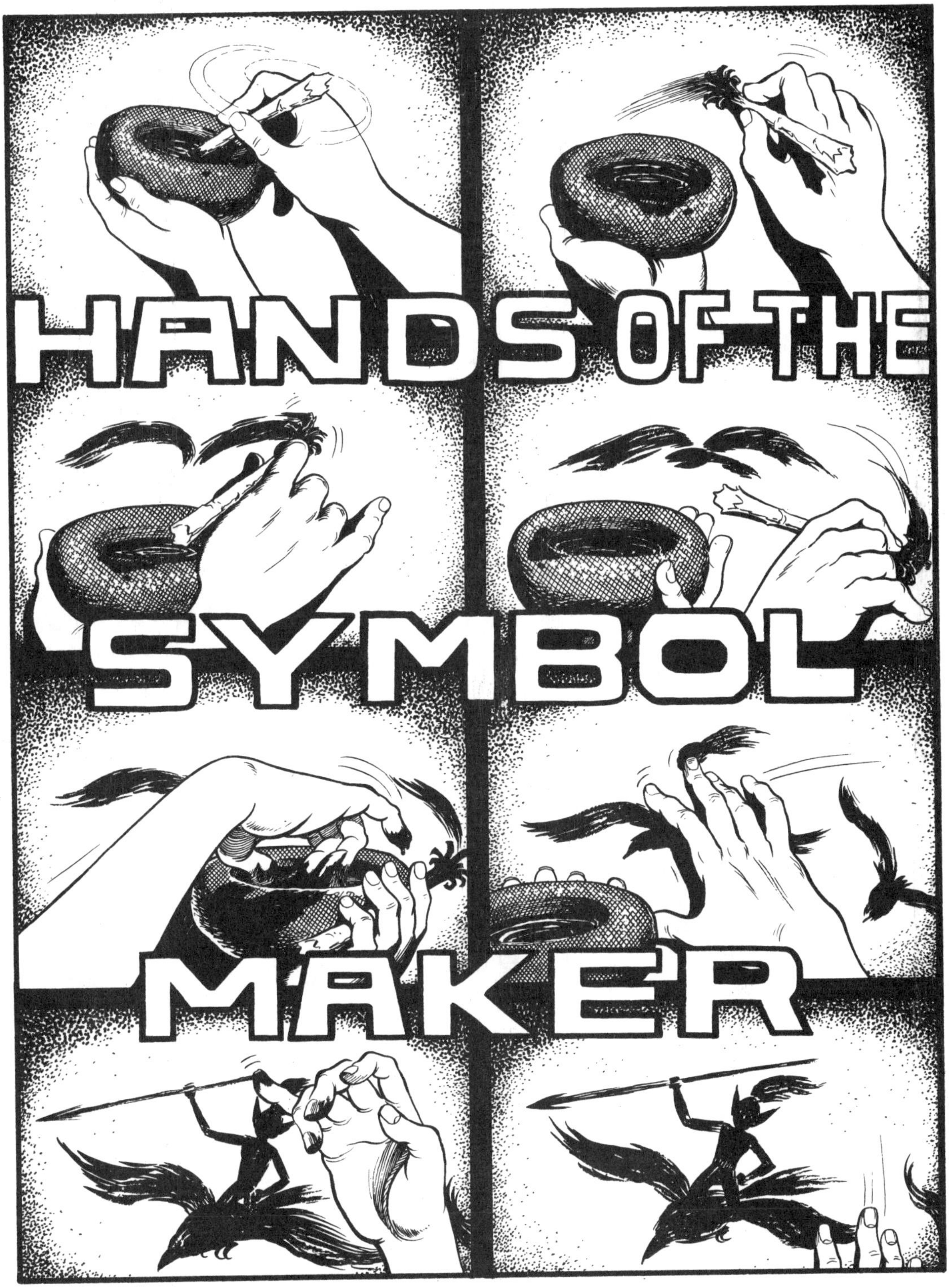
HANDS OF THE
SYMBOL
MAKER

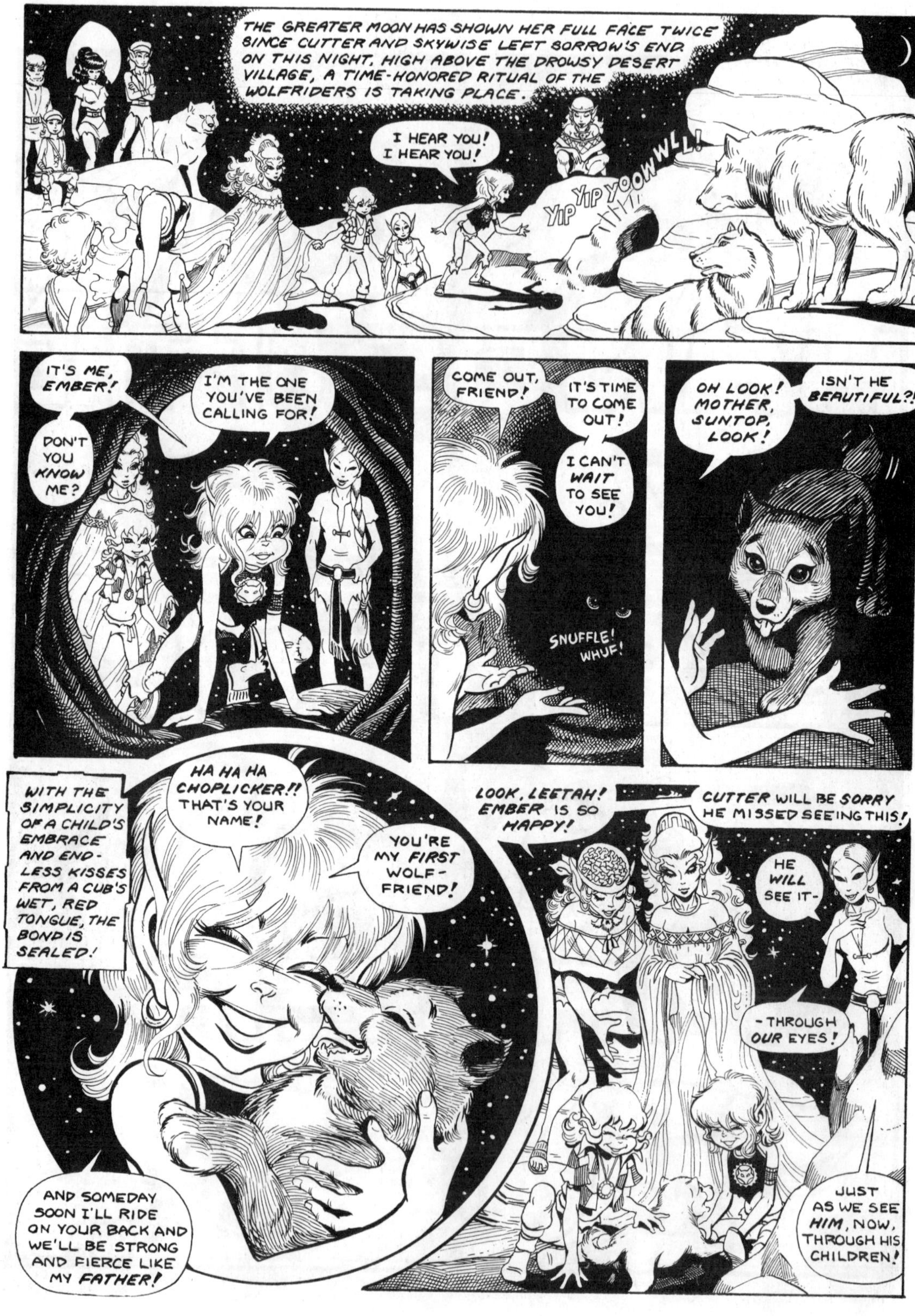
THE GREATER MOON HAS SHOWN HER FULL FACE TWICE SINCE CUTTER AND SKYWISE LEFT SORROW'S END. ON THIS NIGHT, HIGH ABOVE THE DROWSY DESERT VILLAGE, A TIME-HONORED RITUAL OF THE WOLFRIDERS IS TAKING PLACE.
I HEAR YOU! I HEAR YOU!
YIP YIP YOOOWLL!
IT'S ME, EMBER!
I'M THE ONE YOU'VE BEEN CALLING FOR!
DON'T YOU KNOW ME?
COME OUT, FRIEND!
IT'S TIME TO COME OUT!
I CAN'T WAIT TO SEE YOU!
SNUFFLE! WHUF!
OH LOOK! MOTHER, SUNTOP, LOOK!
ISN'T HE BEAUTIFUL?!
WITH THE SIMPLICITY OF A CHILD'S EMBRACE AND ENDLESS KISSES FROM A CUB'S WET, RED TONGUE, THE BOND IS SEALED!
HA HA HA CHOPLICKER!! THAT'S YOUR NAME!
YOU'RE MY FIRST WOLF-FRIEND!
AND SOMEDAY SOON I'LL RIDE ON YOUR BACK AND WE'LL BE STRONG AND FIERCE LIKE MY FATHER!
LOOK, LEETAH! EMBER IS SO HAPPY!
CUTTER WILL BE SORRY HE MISSED SEEING THIS!
HE WILL SEE IT-
-THROUGH OUR EYES!
JUST AS WE SEE HIM, NOW, THROUGH HIS CHILDREN!

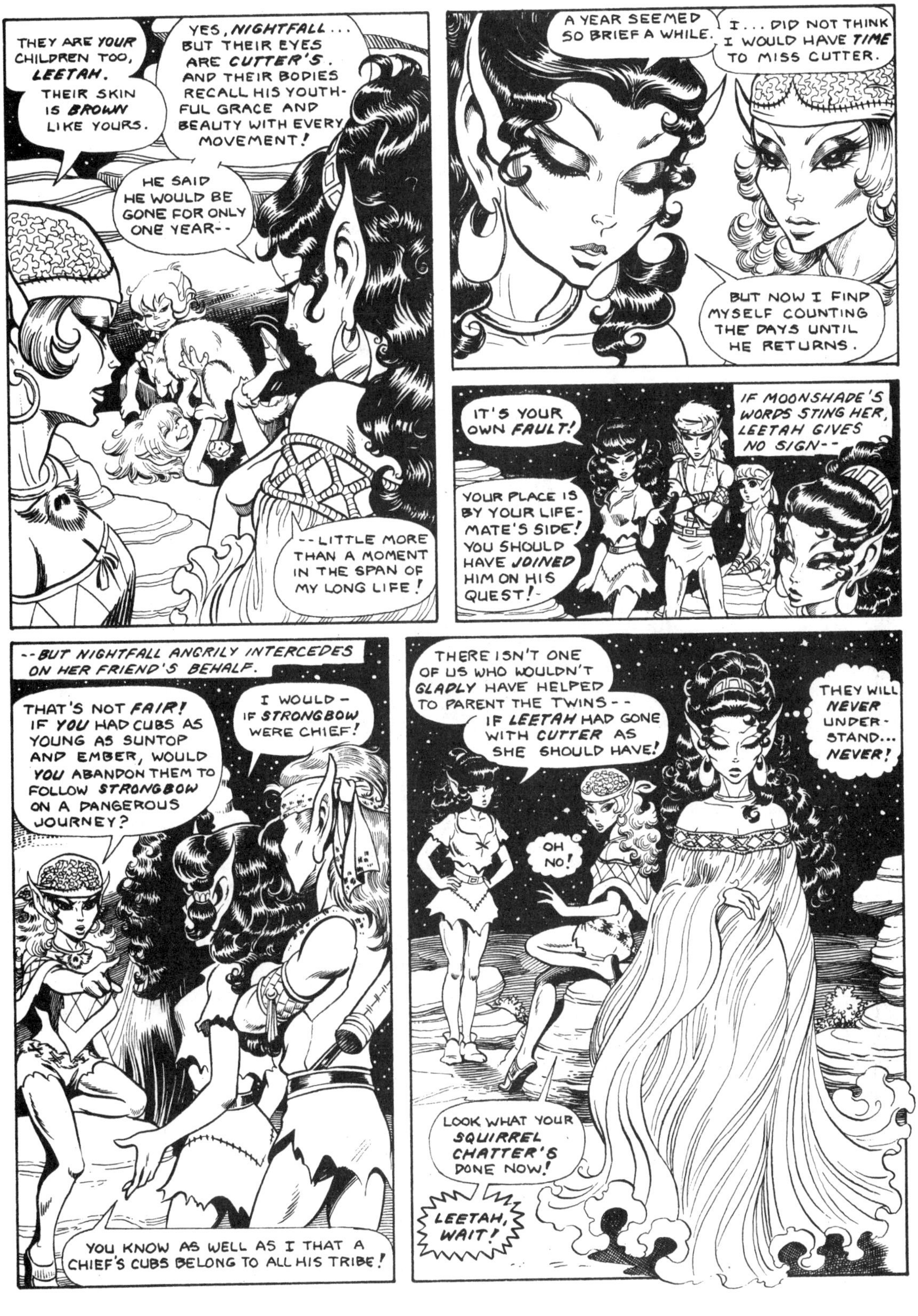
THEY ARE YOUR CHILDREN TOO, LEETAH. THEIR SKIN IS BROWN LIKE YOURS.
YES, NIGHTFALL... BUT THEIR EYES ARE CUTTER'S. AND THEIR BODIES RECALL HIS YOUTHFUL GRACE AND BEAUTY WITH EVERY MOVEMENT!
HE SAID HE WOULD BE GONE FOR ONLY ONE YEAR--
--LITTLE MORE THAN A MOMENT IN THE SPAN OF MY LONG LIFE!
A YEAR SEEMED SO BRIEF A WHILE.
I... DID NOT THINK I WOULD HAVE TIME TO MISS CUTTER.
BUT NOW I FIND MYSELF COUNTING THE DAYS UNTIL HE RETURNS.
IT'S YOUR OWN FAULT!
IF MOONSHADE'S WORDS STING HER, LEETAH GIVES NO SIGN--
YOUR PLACE IS BY YOUR LIFE-MATE'S SIDE! YOU SHOULD HAVE JOINED HIM ON HIS QUEST!
--BUT NIGHTFALL ANGRILY INTERCEDES ON HER FRIEND'S BEHALF.
THAT'S NOT FAIR! IF YOU HAD CUBS AS YOUNG AS SUNTOP AND EMBER, WOULD YOU ABANDON THEM TO FOLLOW STRONGBOW ON A DANGEROUS JOURNEY?
I WOULD - IF STRONGBOW WERE CHIEF!
YOU KNOW AS WELL AS I THAT A CHIEF'S CUBS BELONG TO ALL HIS TRIBE!
THERE ISN'T ONE OF US WHO WOULDN'T GLADLY HAVE HELPED TO PARENT THE TWINS--
IF LEETAH HAD GONE WITH CUTTER AS SHE SHOULD HAVE!
THEY WILL NEVER UNDERSTAND... NEVER!
OH NO!
LOOK WHAT YOUR SQUIRREL CHATTER'S DONE NOW!
LEETAH, WAIT!

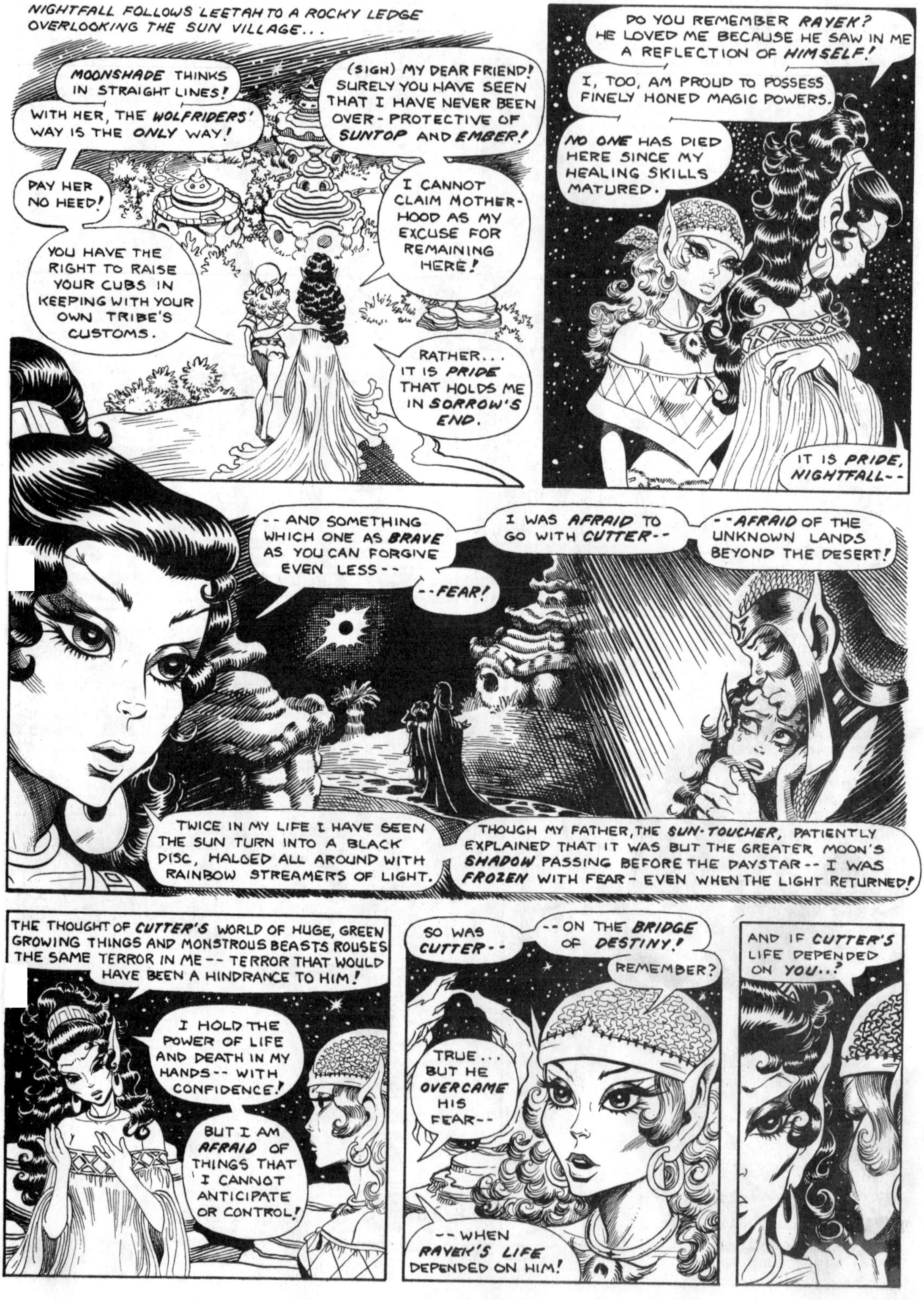
NIGHTFALL FOLLOWS LEETAH TO A ROCKY LEDGE OVERLOOKING THE SUN VILLAGE...
MOONSHADE THINKS IN STRAIGHT LINES!
WITH HER, THE WOLFRIDERS' WAY IS THE ONLY WAY!
PAY HER NO HEED!
YOU HAVE THE RIGHT TO RAISE YOUR CUBS IN KEEPING WITH YOUR OWN TRIBE'S CUSTOMS.
(SIGH) MY DEAR FRIEND! SURELY YOU HAVE SEEN THAT I HAVE NEVER BEEN OVER-PROTECTIVE OF SUNTOP AND EMBER!
I CANNOT CLAIM MOTHERHOOD AS MY EXCUSE FOR REMAINING HERE!
RATHER... IT IS PRIDE THAT HOLDS ME IN SORROW'S END.
DO YOU REMEMBER RAYEK? HE LOVED ME BECAUSE HE SAW IN ME A REFLECTION OF HIMSELF!
I, TOO, AM PROUD TO POSSESS FINELY HONED MAGIC POWERS.
NO ONE HAS DIED HERE SINCE MY HEALING SKILLS MATURED.
IT IS PRIDE, NIGHTFALL--
--AND SOMETHING WHICH ONE AS BRAVE AS YOU CAN FORGIVE EVEN LESS--
--FEAR!
I WAS AFRAID TO GO WITH CUTTER--
--AFRAID OF THE UNKNOWN LANDS BEYOND THE DESERT!
TWICE IN MY LIFE I HAVE SEEN THE SUN TURN INTO A BLACK DISC, HALOED ALL AROUND WITH RAINBOW STREAMERS OF LIGHT.
THOUGH MY FATHER, THE SUN-TOUCHER, PATIENTLY EXPLAINED THAT IT WAS BUT THE GREATER MOON'S SHADOW PASSING BEFORE THE DAYSTAR-- I WAS FROZEN WITH FEAR- EVEN WHEN THE LIGHT RETURNED!
THE THOUGHT OF CUTTER'S WORLD OF HUGE, GREEN GROWING THINGS AND MONSTROUS BEASTS ROUSES THE SAME TERROR IN ME-- TERROR THAT WOULD HAVE BEEN A HINDRANCE TO HIM!
I HOLD THE POWER OF LIFE AND DEATH IN MY HANDS-- WITH CONFIDENCE!
BUT I AM AFRAID OF THINGS THAT I CANNOT ANTICIPATE OR CONTROL!
SO WAS CUTTER--
--ON THE BRIDGE OF DESTINY!
REMEMBER?
TRUE... BUT HE OVERCAME HIS FEAR--
--WHEN RAYEK'S LIFE DEPENDED ON HIM!
AND IF CUTTER'S LIFE DEPENDED ON YOU..?

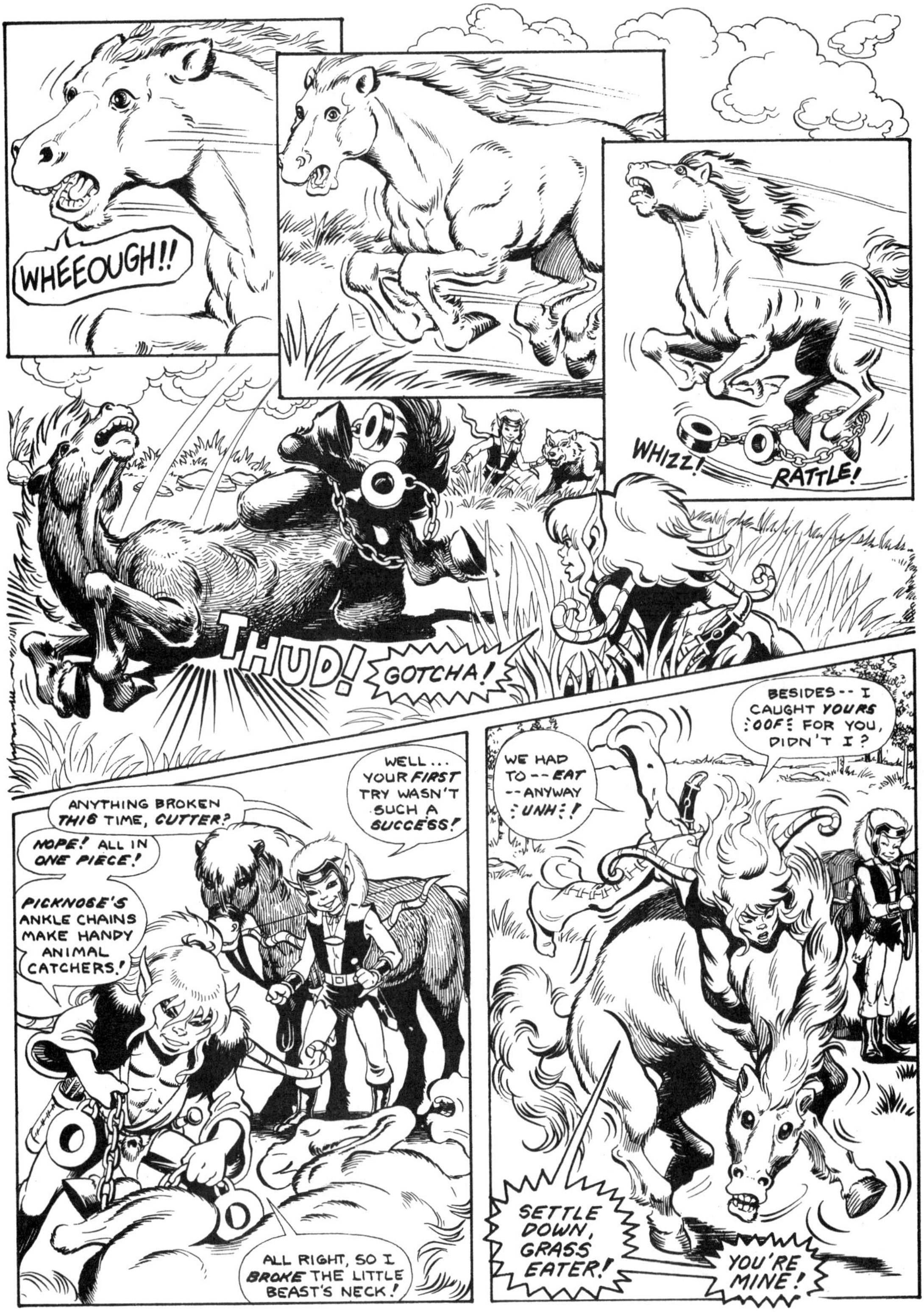

WHEEOUGH!!
WHIZZ!
RATTLE!
THUD!
GOTCHA!
ANYTHING BROKEN THIS TIME, CUTTER?
NOPE! ALL IN ONE PIECE!
PICKNOSE'S ANKLE CHAINS MAKE HANDY ANIMAL CATCHERS!
WELL... YOUR FIRST TRY WASN'T SUCH A SUCCESS!
ALL RIGHT, SO I BROKE THE LITTLE BEAST'S NECK!
WE HAD TO--EAT--ANYWAY UNH!
BESIDES--I CAUGHT YOURS OOF FOR YOU, DIDN'T I?
SETTLE DOWN, GRASS EATER!
YOU'RE MINE!

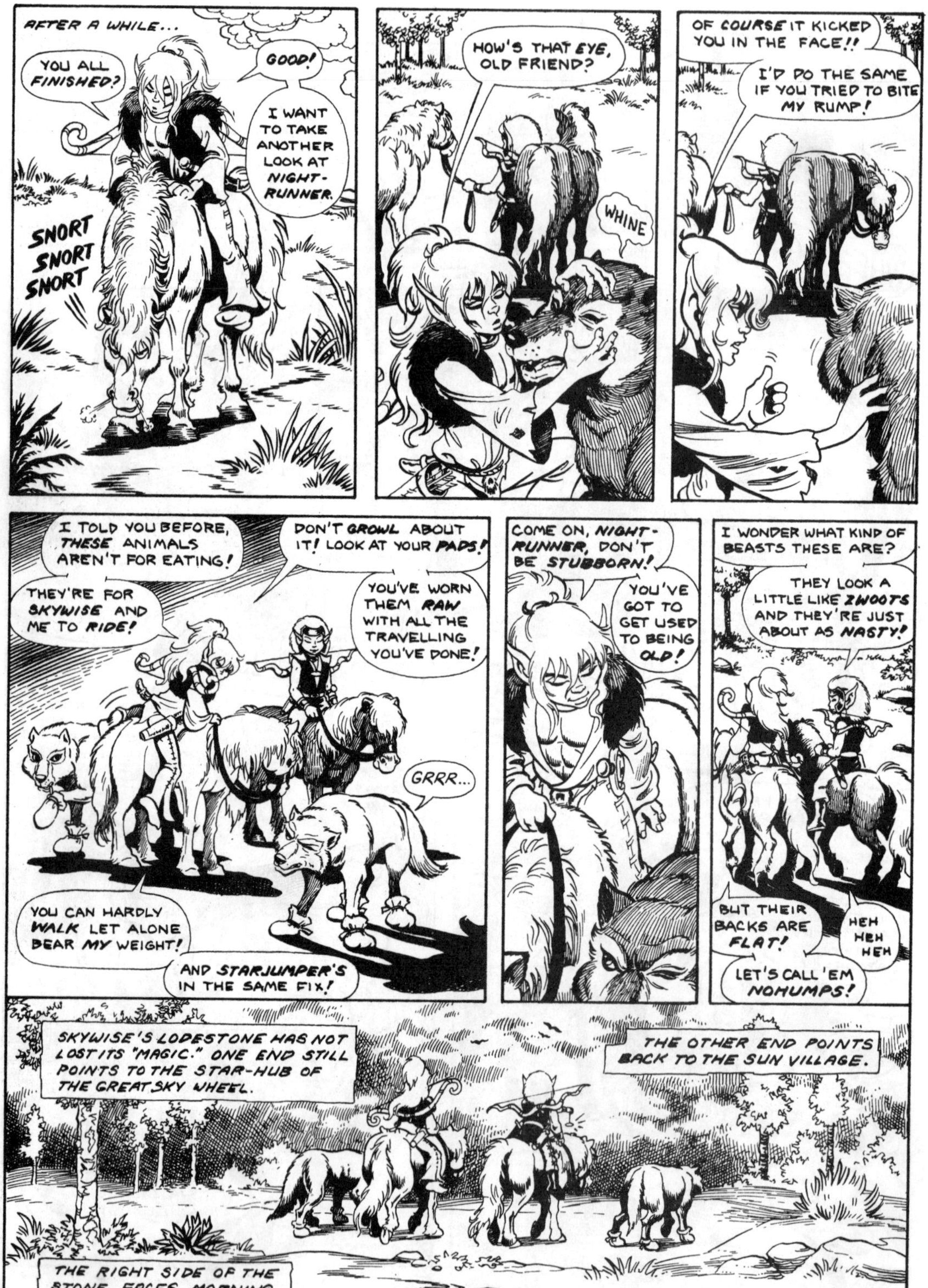
AFTER A WHILE...
YOU ALL FINISHED?
GOOD!
I WANT TO TAKE ANOTHER LOOK AT NIGHT-RUNNER.
SNORT SNORT SNORT
HOW'S THAT EYE, OLD FRIEND?
WHINE
OF COURSE IT KICKED YOU IN THE FACE!!
I'D DO THE SAME IF YOU TRIED TO BITE MY RUMP!
I TOLD YOU BEFORE, THESE ANIMALS AREN'T FOR EATING!
THEY'RE FOR SKYWISE AND ME TO RIDE!
DON'T GROWL ABOUT IT! LOOK AT YOUR PADS!
YOU'VE WORN THEM RAW WITH ALL THE TRAVELLING YOU'VE DONE!
GRRR...
YOU CAN HARDLY WALK LET ALONE BEAR MY WEIGHT!
AND STARJUMPER'S IN THE SAME FIX!
COME ON, NIGHT-RUNNER, DON'T BE STUBBORN!
YOU'VE GOT TO GET USED TO BEING OLD!
I WONDER WHAT KIND OF BEASTS THESE ARE?
THEY LOOK A LITTLE LIKE ZWOOTS AND THEY'RE JUST ABOUT AS NASTY!
BUT THEIR BACKS ARE FLAT!
HEH HEH HEH
LET'S CALL 'EM NOHUMPS!
SKYWISE'S LODESTONE HAS NOT LOST ITS "MAGIC." ONE END STILL POINTS TO THE STAR-HUB OF THE GREAT SKY WHEEL.
THE OTHER END POINTS BACK TO THE SUN VILLAGE.
THE RIGHT SIDE OF THE STONE FACES MORNING.
AND THE LEFT SIDE FACES--

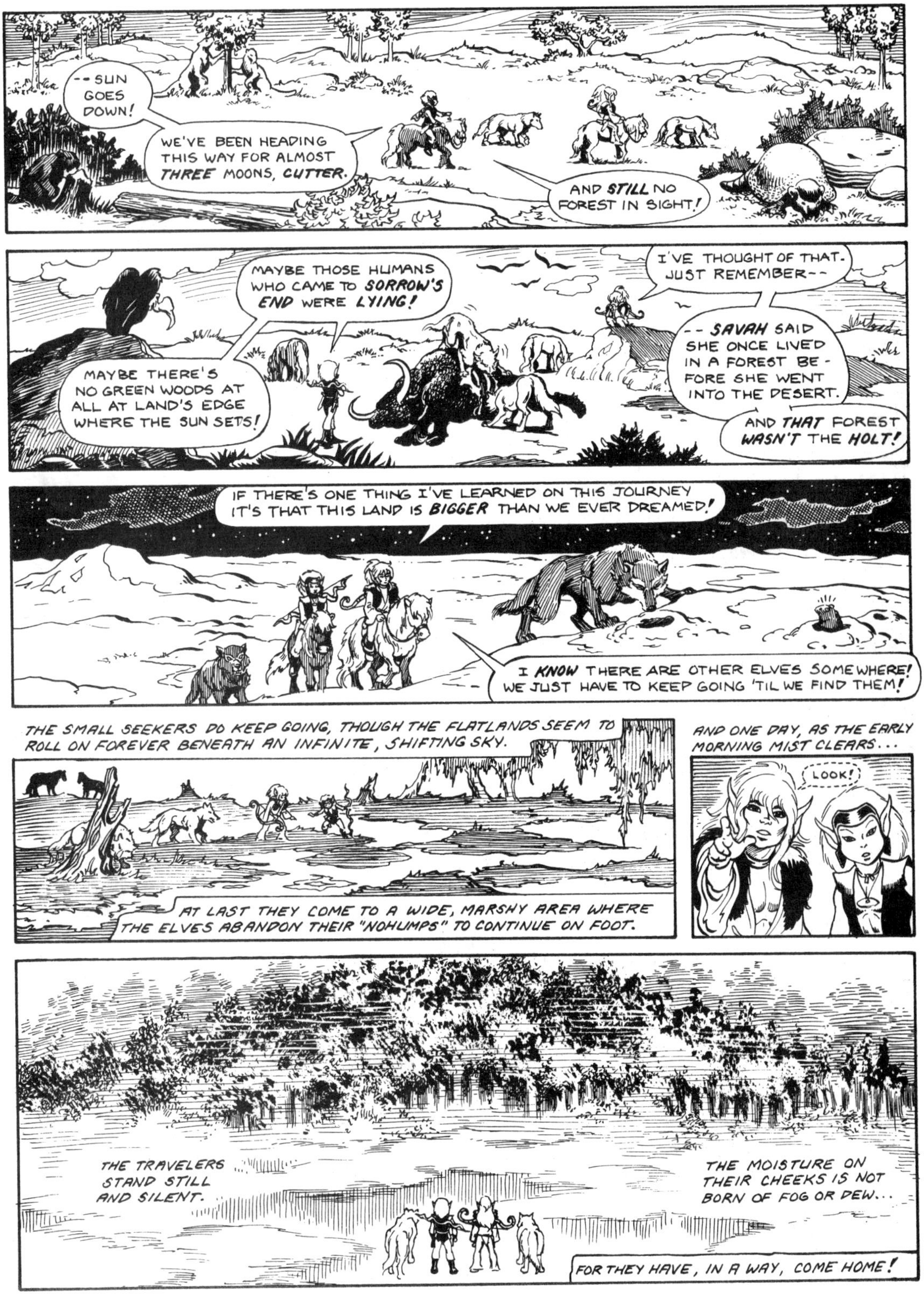
--SUN GOES DOWN!
WE'VE BEEN HEADING THIS WAY FOR ALMOST THREE MOONS, CUTTER.
AND STILL NO FOREST IN SIGHT!
MAYBE THOSE HUMANS WHO CAME TO SORROW'S END WERE LYING!
MAYBE THERE'S NO GREEN WOODS AT ALL AT LAND'S EDGE WHERE THE SUN SETS!
I'VE THOUGHT OF THAT. JUST REMEMBER--
--SAVAH SAID SHE ONCE LIVED IN A FOREST BE-FORE SHE WENT INTO THE DESERT.
AND THAT FOREST WASN'T THE HOLT!
IF THERE'S ONE THING I'VE LEARNED ON THIS JOURNEY IT'S THAT THIS LAND IS BIGGER THAN WE EVER DREAMED!
I KNOW THERE ARE OTHER ELVES SOMEWHERE! WE JUST HAVE TO KEEP GOING 'TIL WE FIND THEM!
THE SMALL SEEKERS DO KEEP GOING, THOUGH THE FLATLANDS SEEM TO ROLL ON FOREVER BENEATH AN INFINITE, SHIFTING SKY.
AT LAST THEY COME TO A WIDE, MARSHY AREA WHERE THE ELVES ABANDON THEIR "NOHUMPS" TO CONTINUE ON FOOT.
AND ONE DAY, AS THE EARLY MORNING MIST CLEARS...
LOOK!
THE TRAVELERS STAND STILL AND SILENT.
THE MOISTURE ON THEIR CHEEKS IS NOT BORN OF FOG OR DEW...
FOR THEY HAVE, IN A WAY, COME HOME!

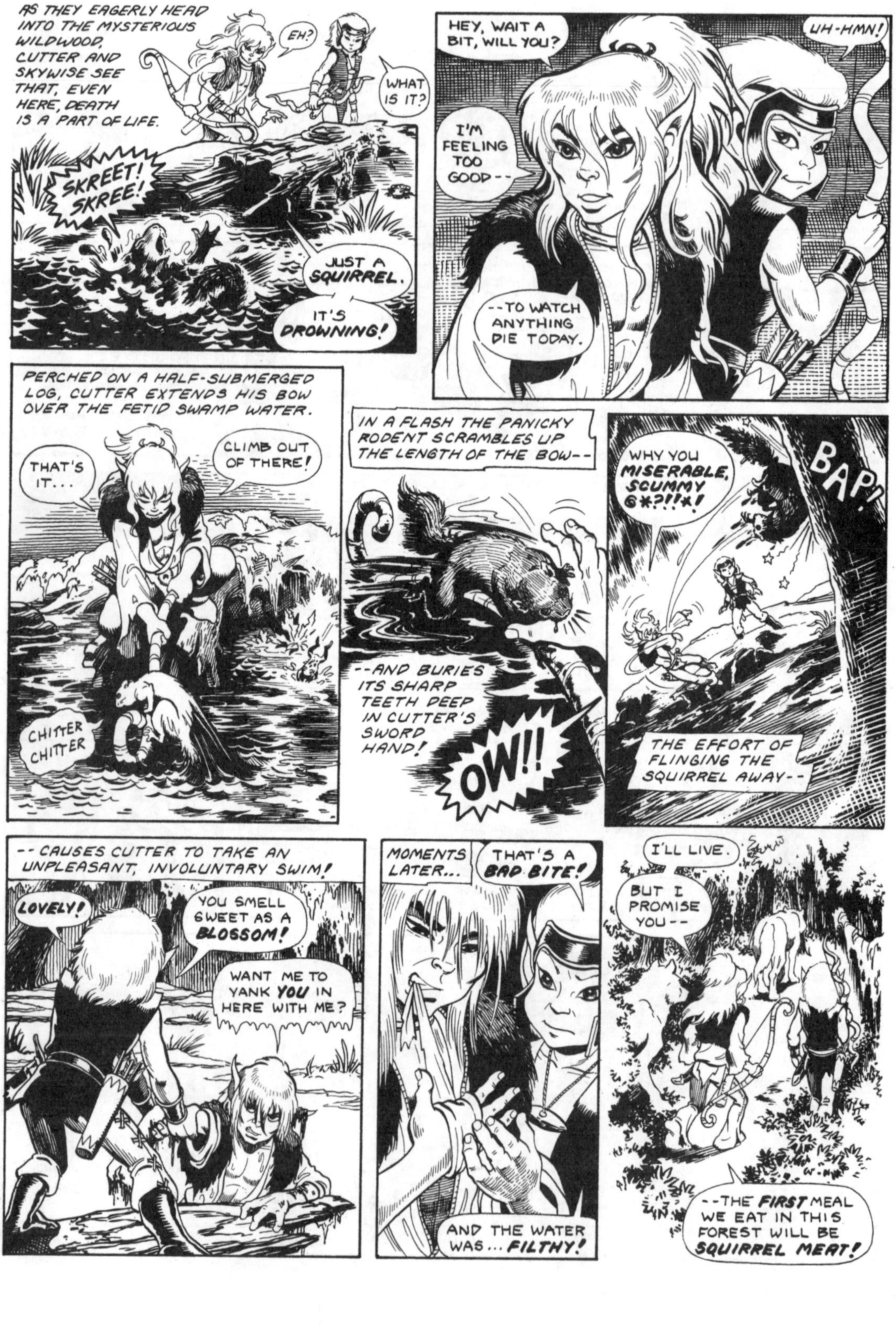
AS THEY EAGERLY HEAD INTO THE MYSTERIOUS WILDWOOD, CUTTER AND SKYWISE SEE THAT, EVEN HERE, DEATH IS A PART OF LIFE.
EH?
WHAT IS IT?
SKREET! SKREE!
JUST A SQUIRREL.
IT'S DROWNING!
HEY, WAIT A BIT, WILL YOU?
UH-HMN!
I'M FEELING TOO GOOD--
--TO WATCH ANYTHING DIE TODAY.
PERCHED ON A HALF-SUBMERGED LOG, CUTTER EXTENDS HIS BOW OVER THE FETID SWAMP WATER.
THAT'S IT...
CLIMB OUT OF THERE!
CHITTER CHITTER
IN A FLASH THE PANICKY RODENT SCRAMBLES UP THE LENGTH OF THE BOW--
--AND BURIES ITS SHARP TEETH DEEP IN CUTTER'S SWORD HAND!
OW!!
WHY YOU MISERABLE, SCUMMY 6*?!!*!
BAP!
THE EFFORT OF FLINGING THE SQUIRREL AWAY--
--CAUSES CUTTER TO TAKE AN UNPLEASANT, INVOLUNTARY SWIM!
LOVELY!
YOU SMELL SWEET AS A BLOSSOM!
WANT ME TO YANK YOU IN HERE WITH ME?
MOMENTS LATER...
THAT'S A BAD BITE!
AND THE WATER WAS... FILTHY!
I'LL LIVE.
BUT I PROMISE YOU--
--THE FIRST MEAL WE EAT IN THIS FOREST WILL BE SQUIRREL MEAT!

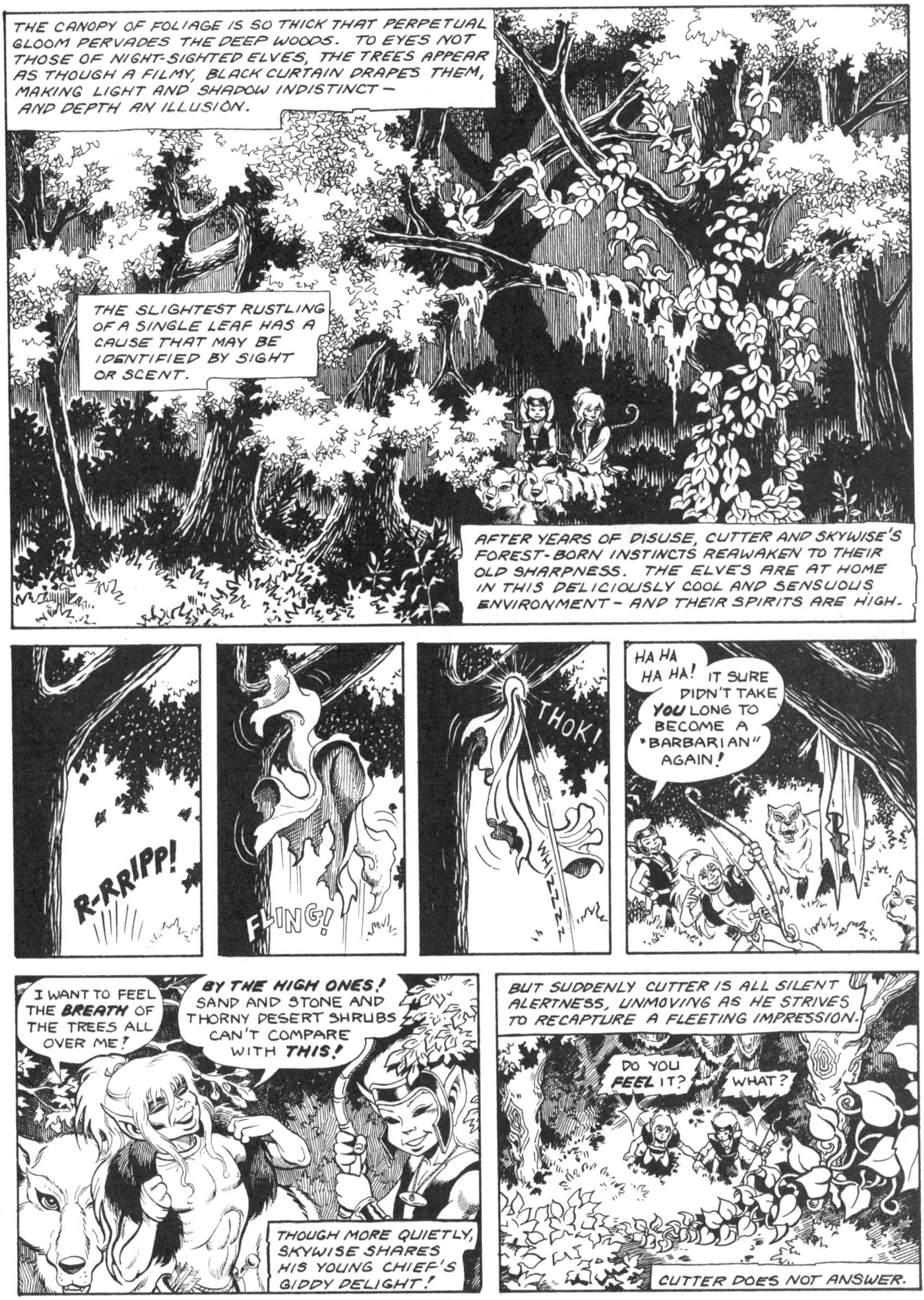
THE CANOPY OF FOLIAGE IS SO THICK THAT PERPETUAL GLOOM PERVADES THE DEEP WOODS. TO EYES NOT THOSE OF NIGHT-SIGHTED ELVES, THE TREES APPEAR AS THOUGH A FILMY, BLACK CURTAIN DRAPES THEM, MAKING LIGHT AND SHADOW INDISTINCT — AND DEPTH AN ILLUSION.
THE SLIGHTEST RUSTLING OF A SINGLE LEAF HAS A CAUSE THAT MAY BE IDENTIFIED BY SIGHT OR SCENT.
AFTER YEARS OF DISUSE, CUTTER AND SKYWISE'S FOREST-BORN INSTINCTS REAWAKEN TO THEIR OLD SHARPNESS. THE ELVES ARE AT HOME IN THIS DELICIOUSLY COOL AND SENSUOUS ENVIRONMENT - AND THEIR SPIRITS ARE HIGH.
R-RRIPP!
FLING!
THOK!
WHIZZZZZ
HA HA HA HA!
IT SURE DIDN'T TAKE YOU LONG TO BECOME A "BARBARIAN" AGAIN!
I WANT TO FEEL THE BREATH OF THE TREES ALL OVER ME!
BY THE HIGH ONES! SAND AND STONE AND THORNY DESERT SHRUBS CAN'T COMPARE WITH THIS!
THOUGH MORE QUIETLY, SKYWISE SHARES HIS YOUNG CHIEF'S GIDDY DELIGHT!
BUT SUDDENLY CUTTER IS ALL SILENT ALERTNESS, UNMOVING AS HE STRIVES TO RECAPTURE A FLEETING IMPRESSION.
DO YOU FEEL IT?
WHAT?
CUTTER DOES NOT ANSWER.

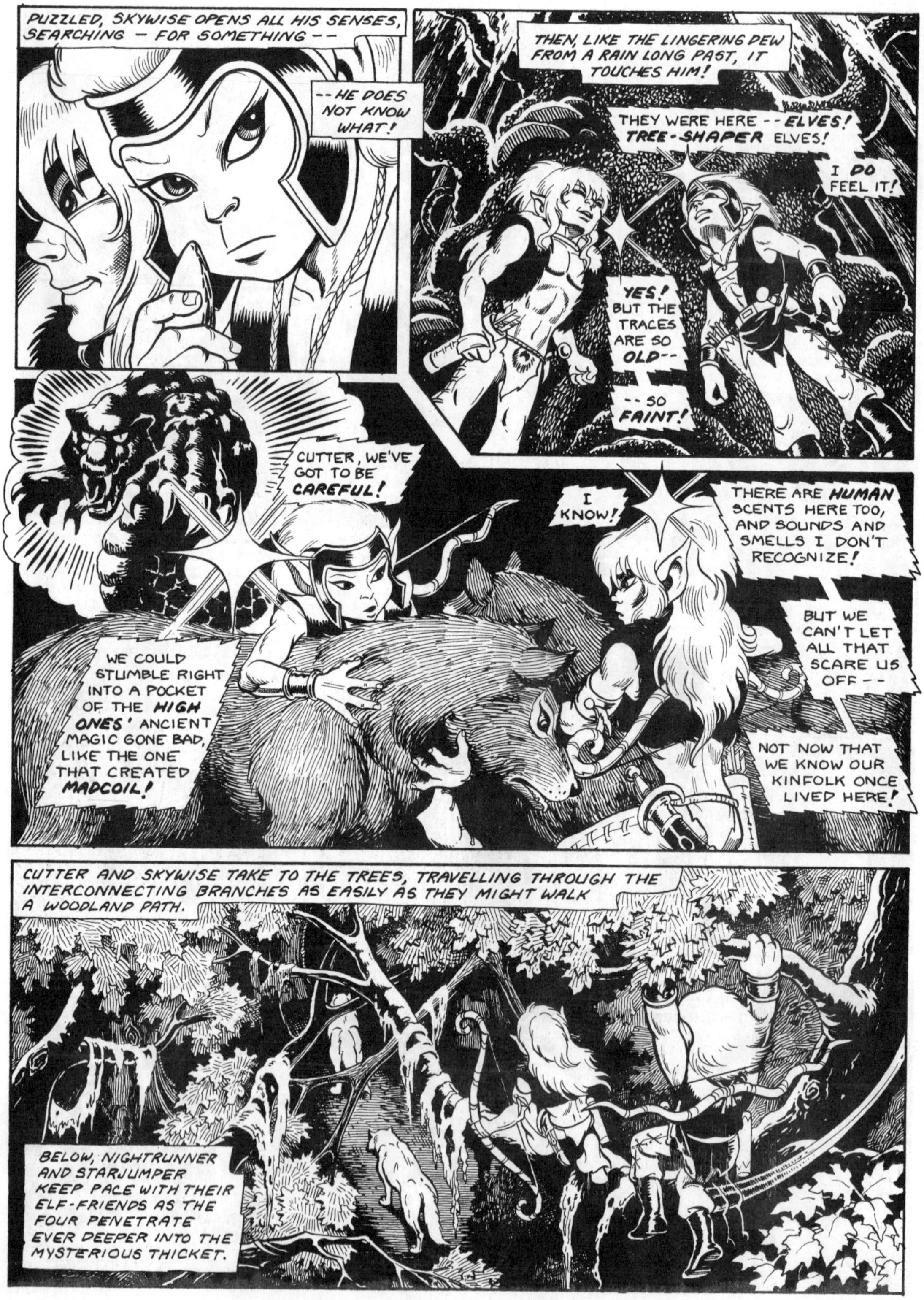
PUZZLED, SKYWISE OPENS ALL HIS SENSES, SEARCHING — FOR SOMETHING --
--HE DOES NOT KNOW WHAT!
THEN, LIKE THE LINGERING DEW FROM A RAIN LONG PAST, IT TOUCHES HIM!
THEY WERE HERE -- ELVES! TREE-SHAPER ELVES!
I DO FEEL IT!
YES! BUT THE TRACES ARE SO OLD--
--SO FAINT!
CUTTER, WE'VE GOT TO BE CAREFUL!
WE COULD STUMBLE RIGHT INTO A POCKET OF THE HIGH ONES' ANCIENT MAGIC GONE BAD, LIKE THE ONE THAT CREATED MADCOIL!
I KNOW!
THERE ARE HUMAN SCENTS HERE TOO, AND SOUNDS AND SMELLS I DON'T RECOGNIZE!
BUT WE CAN'T LET ALL THAT SCARE US OFF --
NOT NOW THAT WE KNOW OUR KINFOLK ONCE LIVED HERE!
CUTTER AND SKYWISE TAKE TO THE TREES, TRAVELLING THROUGH THE INTERCONNECTING BRANCHES AS EASILY AS THEY MIGHT WALK A WOODLAND PATH.
BELOW, NIGHTRUNNER AND STARJUMPER KEEP PACE WITH THEIR ELF-FRIENDS AS THE FOUR PENETRATE EVER DEEPER INTO THE MYSTERIOUS THICKET.

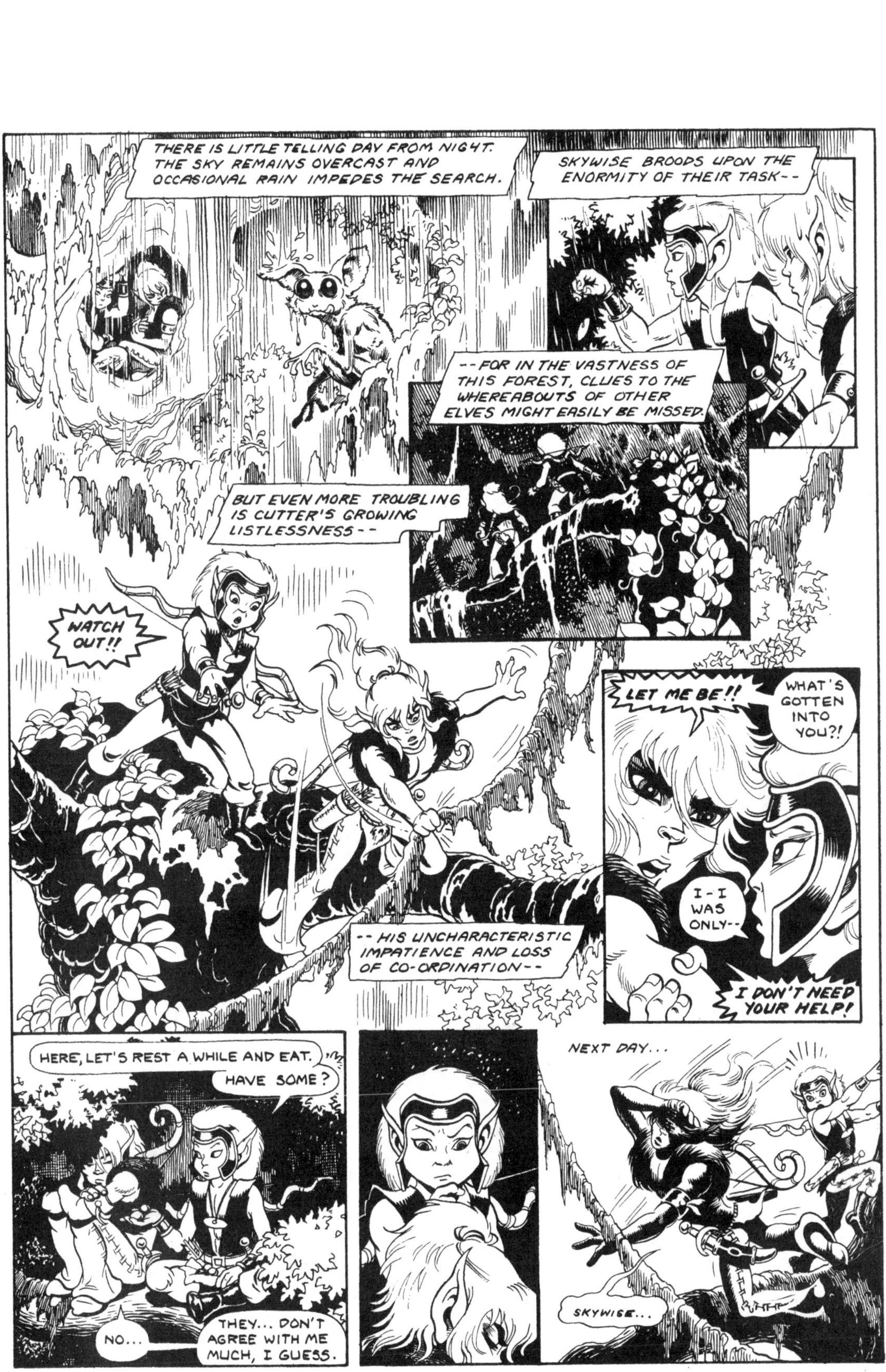
THERE IS LITTLE TELLING DAY FROM NIGHT. THE SKY REMAINS OVERCAST AND OCCASIONAL RAIN IMPEDES THE SEARCH.
SKYWISE BROODS UPON THE ENORMITY OF THEIR TASK--
--FOR IN THE VASTNESS OF THIS FOREST, CLUES TO THE WHEREABOUTS OF OTHER ELVES MIGHT EASILY BE MISSED.
BUT EVEN MORE TROUBLING IS CUTTER'S GROWING LISTLESSNESS--
WATCH OUT!!
--HIS UNCHARACTERISTIC IMPATIENCE AND LOSS OF CO-ORDINATION--
LET ME BE!!
WHAT'S GOTTEN INTO YOU?!
I-I WAS ONLY--
I DON'T NEED YOUR HELP!
HERE, LET'S REST A WHILE AND EAT.
HAVE SOME?
NO...
THEY... DON'T AGREE WITH ME MUCH, I GUESS.
NEXT DAY...
SKYWISE...

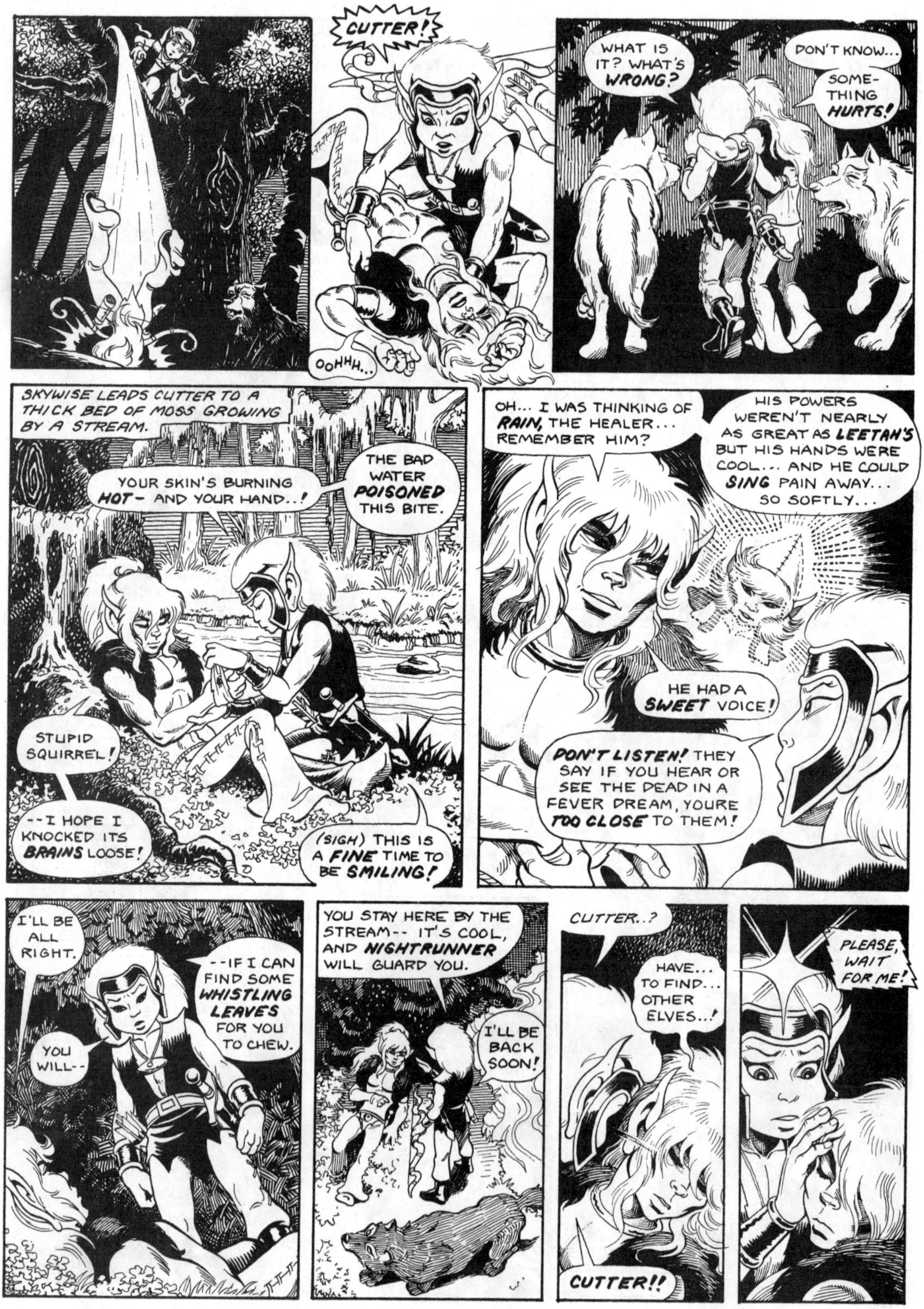
CUTTER!
OOHHH...
WHAT IS IT? WHAT'S WRONG?
DON'T KNOW... SOME-THING HURTS!
SKYWISE LEADS CUTTER TO A THICK BED OF MOSS GROWING BY A STREAM.
YOUR SKIN'S BURNING HOT- AND YOUR HAND..!
THE BAD WATER POISONED THIS BITE.
STUPID SQUIRREL!
--I HOPE I KNOCKED ITS BRAINS LOOSE!
(SIGH) THIS IS A FINE TIME TO BE SMILING!
OH... I WAS THINKING OF RAIN, THE HEALER... REMEMBER HIM?
HIS POWERS WEREN'T NEARLY AS GREAT AS LEETAH'S BUT HIS HANDS WERE COOL... AND HE COULD SING PAIN AWAY... SO SOFTLY...
HE HAD A SWEET VOICE!
DON'T LISTEN! THEY SAY IF YOU HEAR OR SEE THE DEAD IN A FEVER DREAM, YOURE TOO CLOSE TO THEM!
I'LL BE ALL RIGHT.
--IF I CAN FIND SOME WHISTLING LEAVES FOR YOU TO CHEW.
YOU WILL--
YOU STAY HERE BY THE STREAM-- IT'S COOL, AND NIGHTRUNNER WILL GUARD YOU.
I'LL BE BACK SOON!
CUTTER..?
HAVE... TO FIND... OTHER ELVES..!
CUTTER!!
PLEASE, WAIT FOR ME!

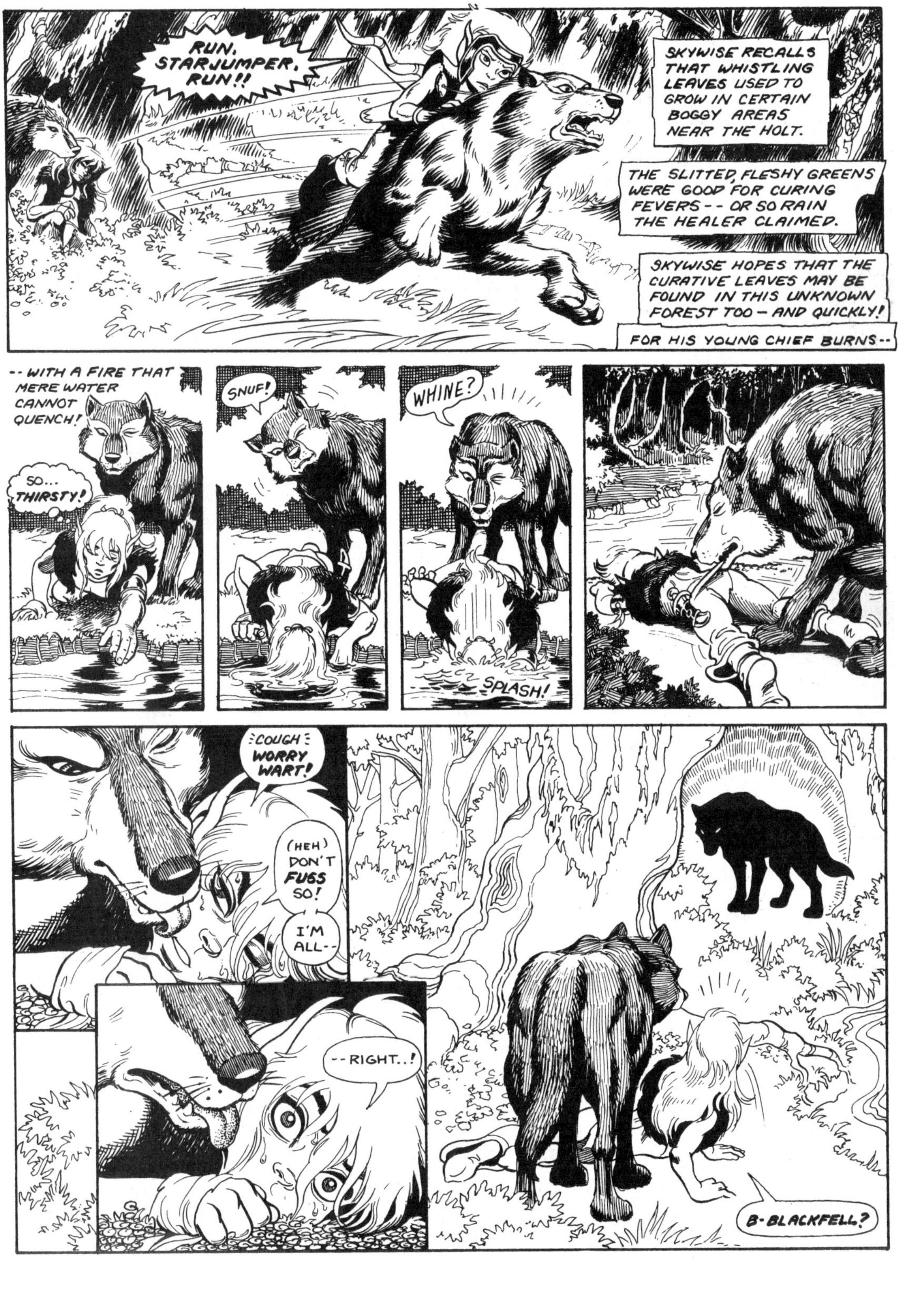

RUN, STARJUMPER, RUN!!
SKYWISE RECALLS THAT WHISTLING LEAVES USED TO GROW IN CERTAIN BOGGY AREAS NEAR THE HOLT.
THE SLITTED, FLESHY GREENS WERE GOOD FOR CURING FEVERS -- OR SO RAIN THE HEALER CLAIMED.
SKYWISE HOPES THAT THE CURATIVE LEAVES MAY BE FOUND IN THIS UNKNOWN FOREST TOO - AND QUICKLY!
FOR HIS YOUNG CHIEF BURNS--
--WITH A FIRE THAT MERE WATER CANNOT QUENCH!
SO... THIRSTY!
SNUF!
WHINE?
SPLASH!
COUGH WORRY WART!
(HEH) DON'T FUSS SO!
I'M ALL--
--RIGHT..!
B-BLACKFELL?

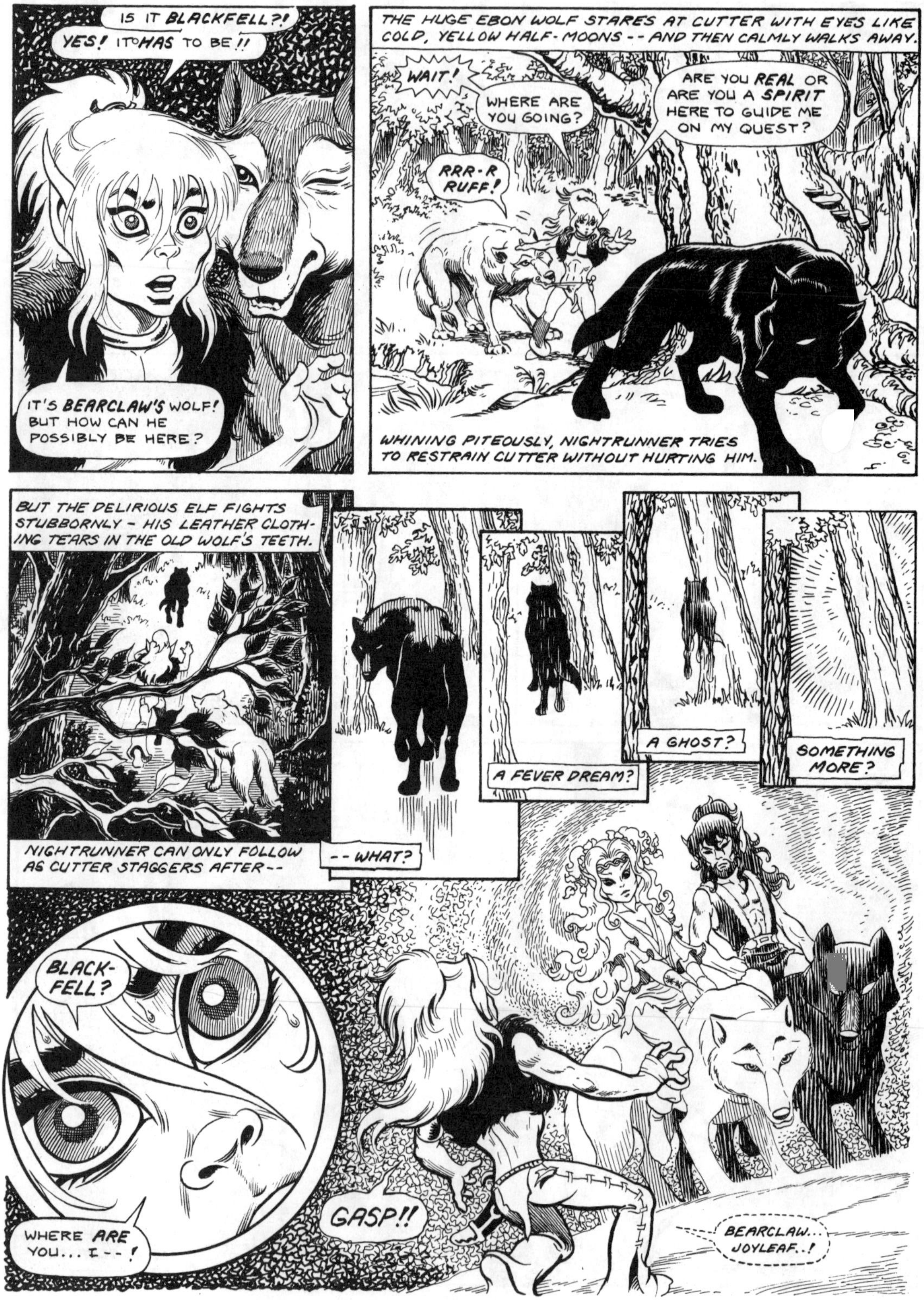
IS IT BLACKFELL?!
YES! IT HAS TO BE!!
IT'S BEARCLAW'S WOLF! BUT HOW CAN HE POSSIBLY BE HERE?
THE HUGE EBON WOLF STARES AT CUTTER WITH EYES LIKE COLD, YELLOW HALF-MOONS -- AND THEN CALMLY WALKS AWAY.
WAIT!
WHERE ARE YOU GOING?
ARE YOU REAL OR ARE YOU A SPIRIT HERE TO GUIDE ME ON MY QUEST?
RRR-R RUFF!
WHINING PITEOUSLY, NIGHTRUNNER TRIES TO RESTRAIN CUTTER WITHOUT HURTING HIM.
BUT THE DELIRIOUS ELF FIGHTS STUBBORNLY - HIS LEATHER CLOTHING TEARS IN THE OLD WOLF'S TEETH.
NIGHTRUNNER CAN ONLY FOLLOW AS CUTTER STAGGERS AFTER--
-- WHAT?
A FEVER DREAM?
A GHOST?
SOMETHING MORE?
BLACK-FELL?
WHERE ARE YOU... I--!
GASP!!
BEARCLAW... JOYLEAF..!

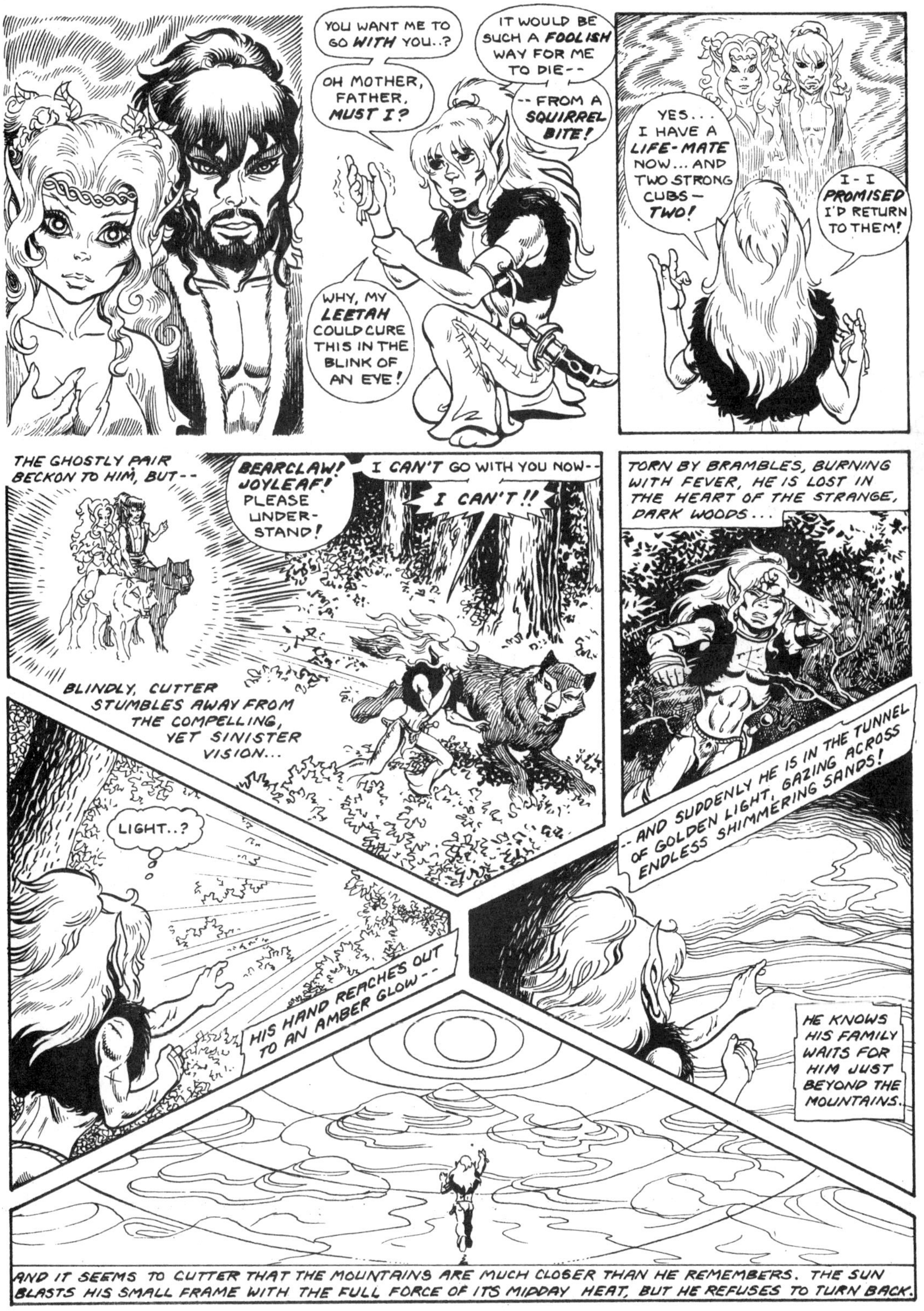
YOU WANT ME TO GO WITH YOU..?
OH MOTHER, FATHER, MUST I?
IT WOULD BE SUCH A FOOLISH WAY FOR ME TO DIE--
--FROM A SQUIRREL BITE!
WHY, MY LEETAH COULD CURE THIS IN THE BLINK OF AN EYE!
YES... I HAVE A LIFE-MATE NOW... AND TWO STRONG CUBS— TWO!
I-I PROMISED I'D RETURN TO THEM!
THE GHOSTLY PAIR BECKON TO HIM, BUT--
BEARCLAW! JOYLEAF! PLEASE UNDER-STAND!
I CAN'T GO WITH YOU NOW--
I CAN'T!!
TORN BY BRAMBLES, BURNING WITH FEVER, HE IS LOST IN THE HEART OF THE STRANGE, DARK WOODS...
BLINDLY, CUTTER STUMBLES AWAY FROM THE COMPELLING, YET SINISTER VISION...
LIGHT..?
HIS HAND REACHES OUT TO AN AMBER GLOW--
--AND SUDDENLY HE IS IN THE TUNNEL OF GOLDEN LIGHT, GAZING ACROSS ENDLESS SHIMMERING SANDS!
HE KNOWS HIS FAMILY WAITS FOR HIM JUST BEYOND THE MOUNTAINS.
AND IT SEEMS TO CUTTER THAT THE MOUNTAINS ARE MUCH CLOSER THAN HE REMEMBERS. THE SUN BLASTS HIS SMALL FRAME WITH THE FULL FORCE OF ITS MIDDAY HEAT, BUT HE REFUSES TO TURN BACK.

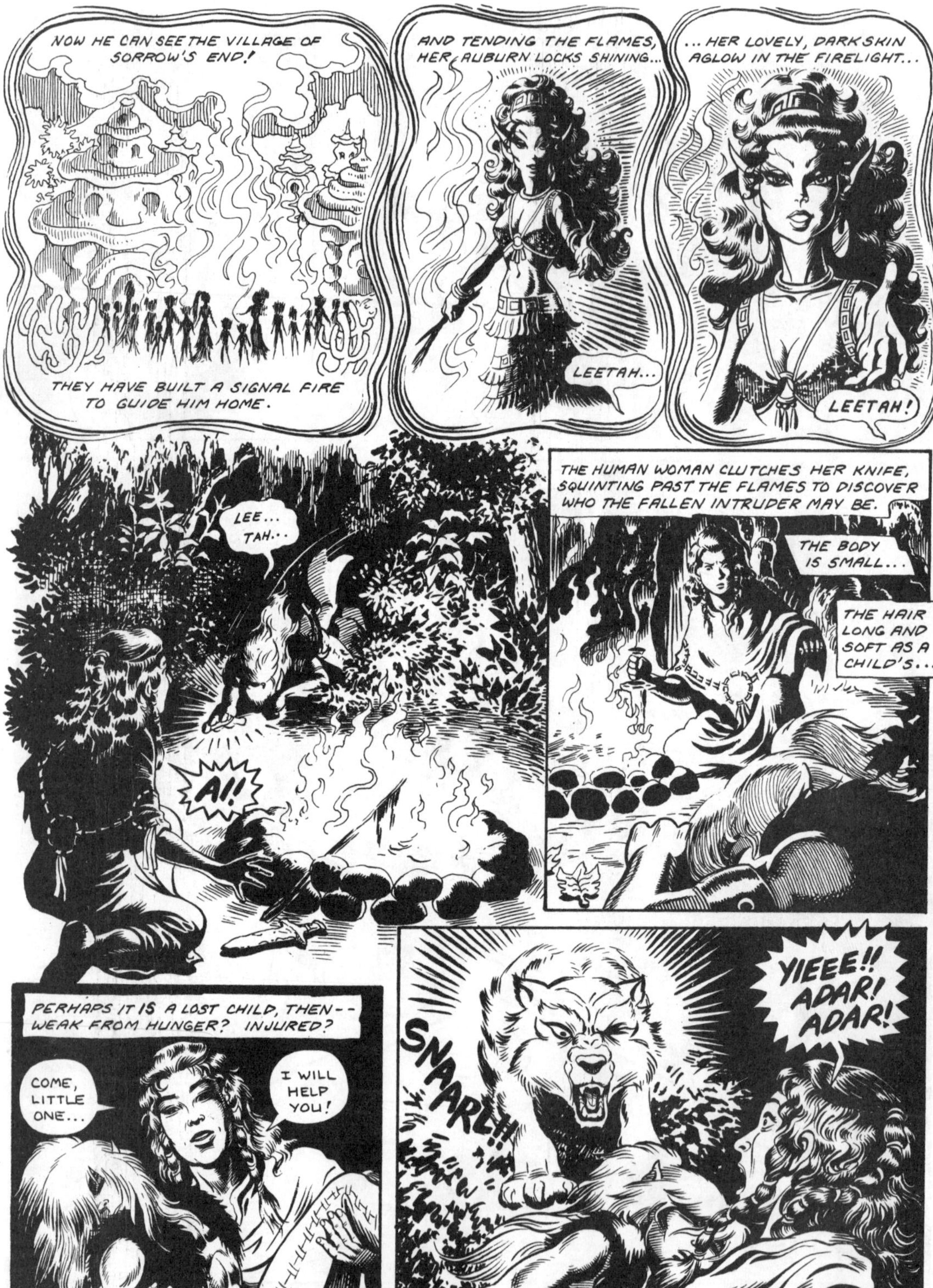
NOW HE CAN SEE THE VILLAGE OF SORROW'S END!
THEY HAVE BUILT A SIGNAL FIRE TO GUIDE HIM HOME.
AND TENDING THE FLAMES, HER AUBURN LOCKS SHINING...
LEETAH...
...HER LOVELY, DARKSKIN AGLOW IN THE FIRELIGHT...
LEETAH!
LEE... TAH...
AI!
THE HUMAN WOMAN CLUTCHES HER KNIFE, SQUINTING PAST THE FLAMES TO DISCOVER WHO THE FALLEN INTRUDER MAY BE.
THE BODY IS SMALL...
THE HAIR LONG AND SOFT AS A CHILD'S...
PERHAPS IT IS A LOST CHILD, THEN--WEAK FROM HUNGER? INJURED?
COME, LITTLE ONE...
I WILL HELP YOU!
SNAARLH!!
YIEEE!! ADAR! ADAR!

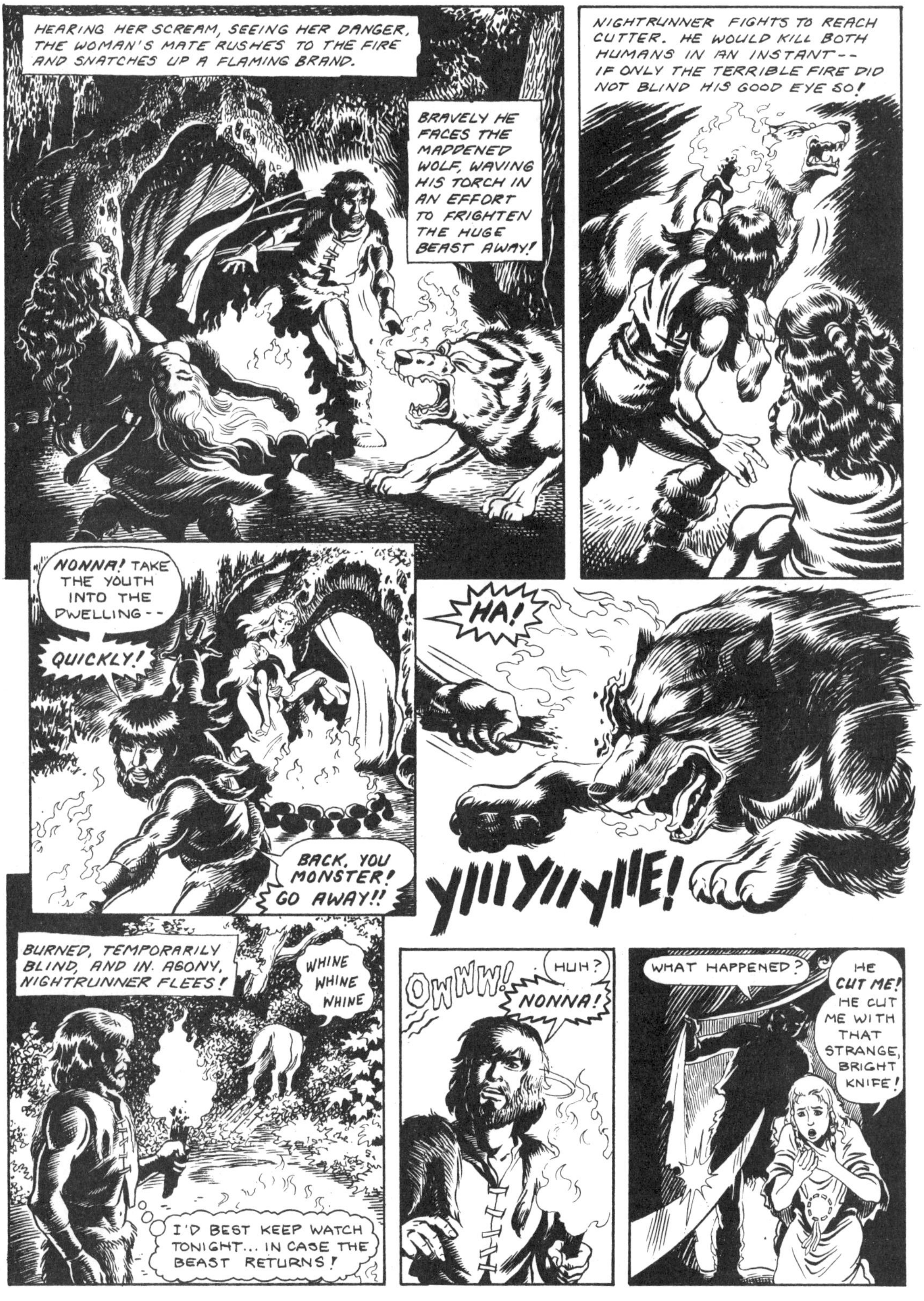
HEARING HER SCREAM, SEEING HER DANGER, THE WOMAN'S MATE RUSHES TO THE FIRE AND SNATCHES UP A FLAMING BRAND.
BRAVELY HE FACES THE MADDENED WOLF, WAVING HIS TORCH IN AN EFFORT TO FRIGHTEN THE HUGE BEAST AWAY!
NIGHTRUNNER FIGHTS TO REACH CUTTER. HE WOULD KILL BOTH HUMANS IN AN INSTANT-- IF ONLY THE TERRIBLE FIRE DID NOT BLIND HIS GOOD EYE SO!
NONNA! TAKE THE YOUTH INTO THE DWELLING--
QUICKLY!
BACK, YOU MONSTER! GO AWAY!!
HA!
YIIIYIIYIIE!
BURNED, TEMPORARILY BLIND, AND IN AGONY, NIGHTRUNNER FLEES!
WHINE WHINE WHINE
I'D BEST KEEP WATCH TONIGHT... IN CASE THE BEAST RETURNS!
OWWW!
HUH?
NONNA!
WHAT HAPPENED?
HE CUT ME! HE CUT ME WITH THAT STRANGE, BRIGHT KNIFE!

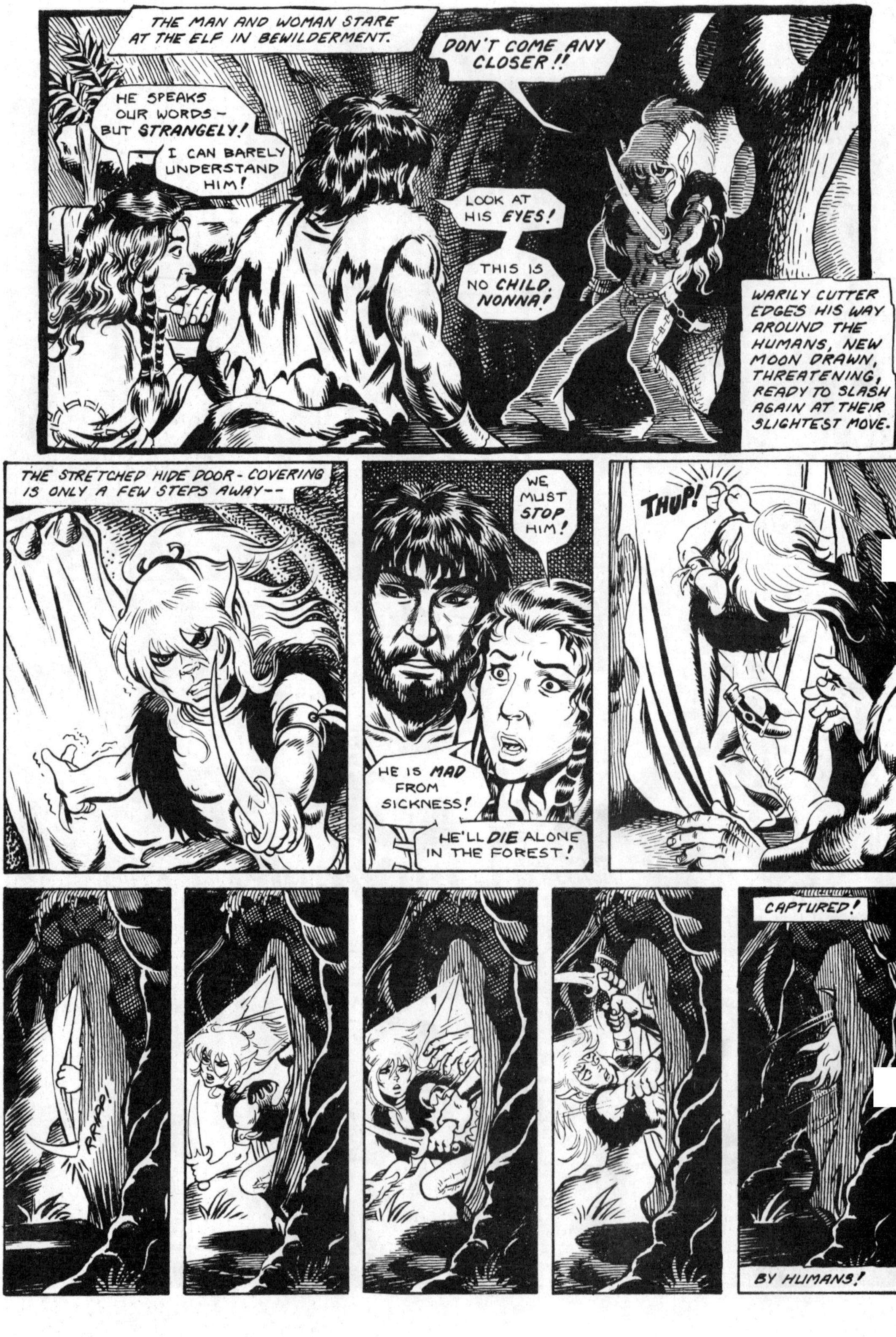

THE MAN AND WOMAN STARE AT THE ELF IN BEWILDERMENT.
DON'T COME ANY CLOSER!!
HE SPEAKS OUR WORDS - BUT STRANGELY!
I CAN BARELY UNDERSTAND HIM!
LOOK AT HIS EYES!
THIS IS NO CHILD, NONNA!
WARILY CUTTER EDGES HIS WAY AROUND THE HUMANS, NEW MOON DRAWN, THREATENING, READY TO SLASH AGAIN AT THEIR SLIGHTEST MOVE.
THE STRETCHED HIDE DOOR-COVERING IS ONLY A FEW STEPS AWAY--
WE MUST STOP HIM!
HE IS MAD FROM SICKNESS!
HE'LL DIE ALONE IN THE FOREST!
THUP!
RRIPP!
CAPTURED!
BY HUMANS!

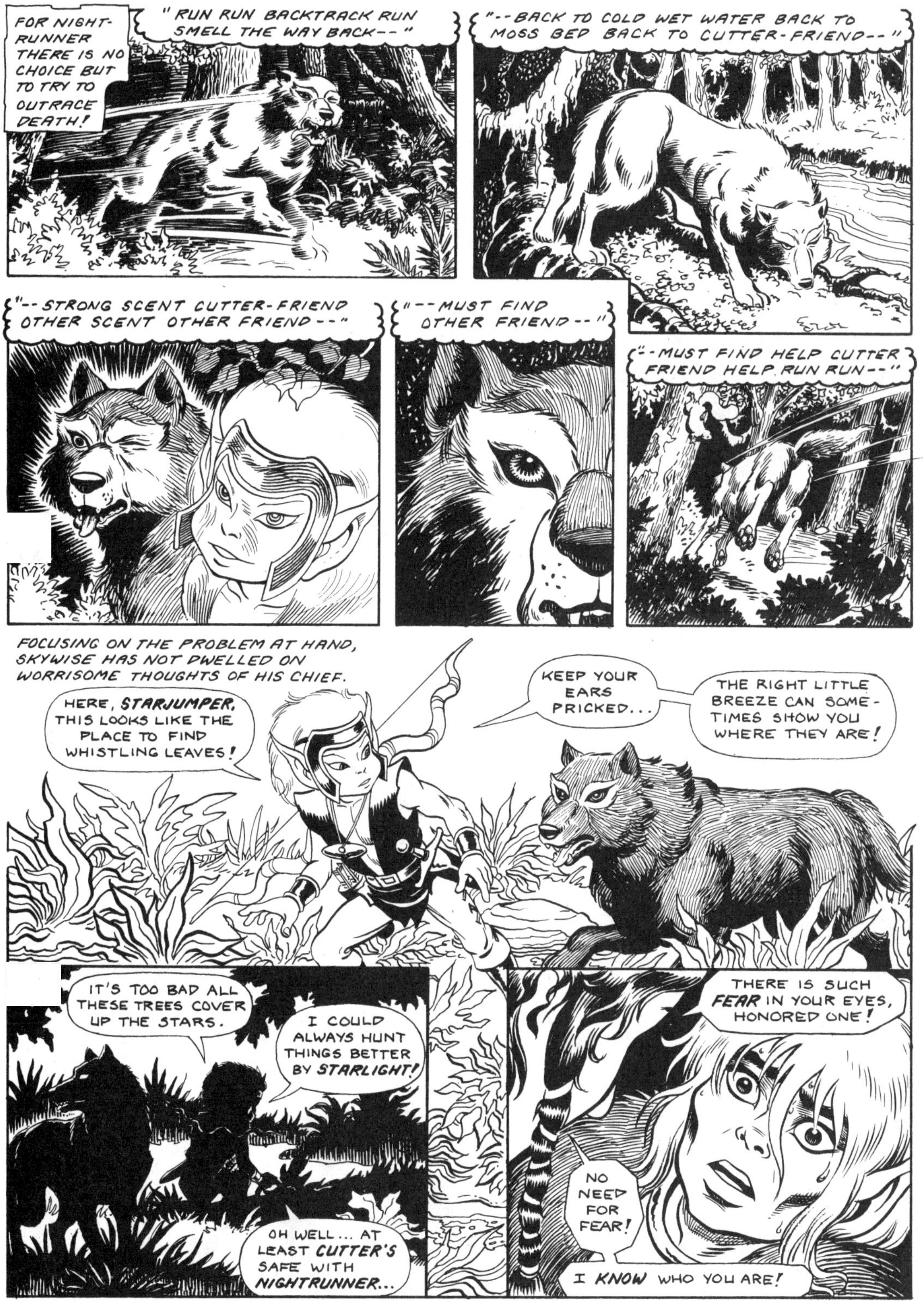
FOR NIGHT-RUNNER THERE IS NO CHOICE BUT TO TRY TO OUTRACE DEATH!
"RUN RUN BACKTRACK RUN SMELL THE WAY BACK--"
"--BACK TO COLD WET WATER BACK TO MOSS BED BACK TO CUTTER-FRIEND--"
"--STRONG SCENT CUTTER-FRIEND OTHER SCENT OTHER FRIEND--"
"--MUST FIND OTHER FRIEND--"
"--MUST FIND HELP CUTTER FRIEND HELP RUN RUN--"
FOCUSING ON THE PROBLEM AT HAND, SKYWISE HAS NOT DWELLED ON WORRISOME THOUGHTS OF HIS CHIEF.
HERE, STARJUMPER, THIS LOOKS LIKE THE PLACE TO FIND WHISTLING LEAVES!
KEEP YOUR EARS PRICKED...
THE RIGHT LITTLE BREEZE CAN SOMETIMES SHOW YOU WHERE THEY ARE!
IT'S TOO BAD ALL THESE TREES COVER UP THE STARS.
I COULD ALWAYS HUNT THINGS BETTER BY STARLIGHT!
OH WELL... AT LEAST CUTTER'S SAFE WITH NIGHTRUNNER...
THERE IS SUCH FEAR IN YOUR EYES, HONORED ONE!
NO NEED FOR FEAR!
I KNOW WHO YOU ARE!

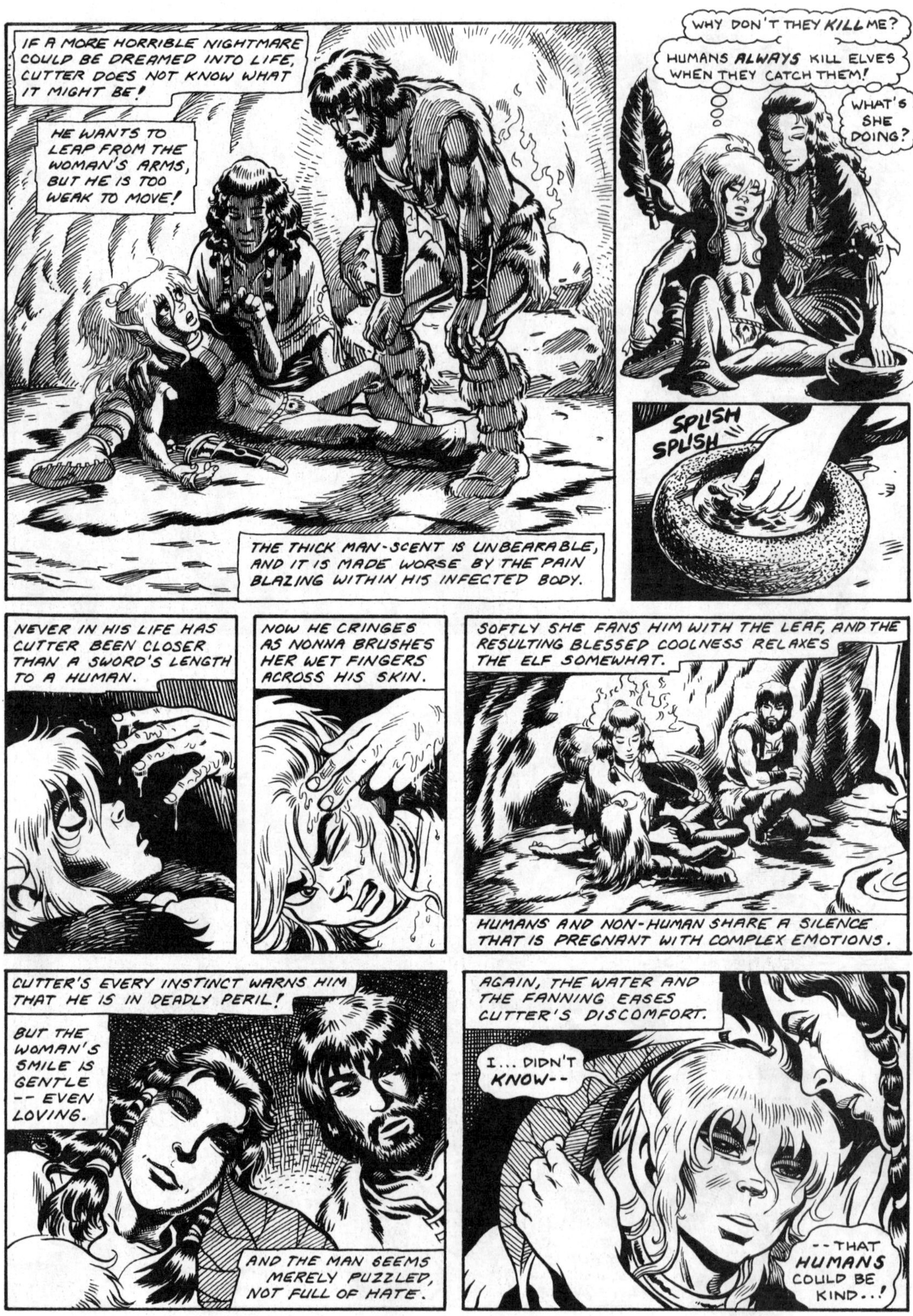
IF A MORE HORRIBLE NIGHTMARE COULD BE DREAMED INTO LIFE, CUTTER DOES NOT KNOW WHAT IT MIGHT BE!
HE WANTS TO LEAP FROM THE WOMAN'S ARMS, BUT HE IS TOO WEAK TO MOVE!
THE THICK MAN-SCENT IS UNBEARABLE, AND IT IS MADE WORSE BY THE PAIN BLAZING WITHIN HIS INFECTED BODY.
WHY DON'T THEY KILL ME?
HUMANS ALWAYS KILL ELVES WHEN THEY CATCH THEM!
WHAT'S SHE DOING?
SPLISH SPLISH
NEVER IN HIS LIFE HAS CUTTER BEEN CLOSER THAN A SWORD'S LENGTH TO A HUMAN.
NOW HE CRINGES AS NONNA BRUSHES HER WET FINGERS ACROSS HIS SKIN.
SOFTLY SHE FANS HIM WITH THE LEAF, AND THE RESULTING BLESSED COOLNESS RELAXES THE ELF SOMEWHAT.
HUMANS AND NON-HUMAN SHARE A SILENCE THAT IS PREGNANT WITH COMPLEX EMOTIONS.
CUTTER'S EVERY INSTINCT WARNS HIM THAT HE IS IN DEADLY PERIL!
BUT THE WOMAN'S SMILE IS GENTLE -- EVEN LOVING.
AND THE MAN SEEMS MERELY PUZZLED, NOT FULL OF HATE.
AGAIN, THE WATER AND THE FANNING EASES CUTTER'S DISCOMFORT.
I... DIDN'T KNOW--
--THAT HUMANS COULD BE KIND..!

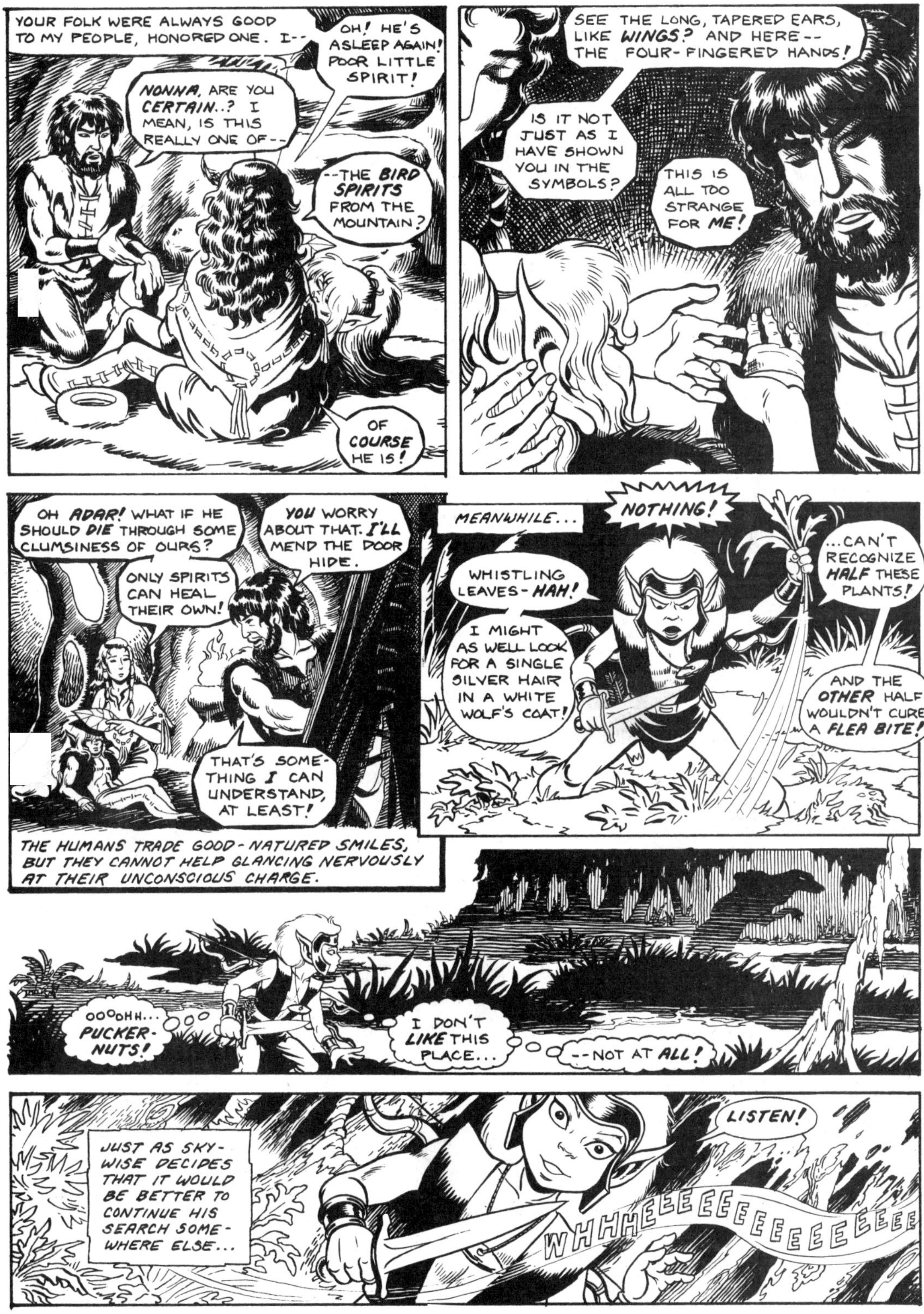

YOUR FOLK WERE ALWAYS GOOD TO MY PEOPLE, HONORED ONE. I--
OH! HE'S ASLEEP AGAIN! POOR LITTLE SPIRIT!
NONNA, ARE YOU CERTAIN..? I MEAN, IS THIS REALLY ONE OF--
--THE BIRD SPIRITS FROM THE MOUNTAIN?
OF COURSE HE IS!
SEE THE LONG, TAPERED EARS, LIKE WINGS? AND HERE-- THE FOUR-FINGERED HANDS!
IS IT NOT JUST AS I HAVE SHOWN YOU IN THE SYMBOLS?
THIS IS ALL TOO STRANGE FOR ME!
OH ADAR! WHAT IF HE SHOULD DIE THROUGH SOME CLUMSINESS OF OURS?
YOU WORRY ABOUT THAT. I'LL MEND THE DOOR HIDE.
ONLY SPIRITS CAN HEAL THEIR OWN!
THAT'S SOMETHING I CAN UNDERSTAND, AT LEAST!
THE HUMANS TRADE GOOD-NATURED SMILES, BUT THEY CANNOT HELP GLANCING NERVOUSLY AT THEIR UNCONSCIOUS CHARGE.
MEANWHILE...
NOTHING!
WHISTLING LEAVES-HAH!
I MIGHT AS WELL LOOK FOR A SINGLE SILVER HAIR IN A WHITE WOLF'S COAT!
...CAN'T RECOGNIZE HALF THESE PLANTS!
AND THE OTHER HALF WOULDN'T CURE A FLEA BITE!
OOOOHH... PUCKER-NUTS!
I DON'T LIKE THIS PLACE...
--NOT AT ALL!
JUST AS SKYWISE DECIDES THAT IT WOULD BE BETTER TO CONTINUE HIS SEARCH SOMEWHERE ELSE...
LISTEN!
WHHHEEEEEEEEEEEEEEEEE

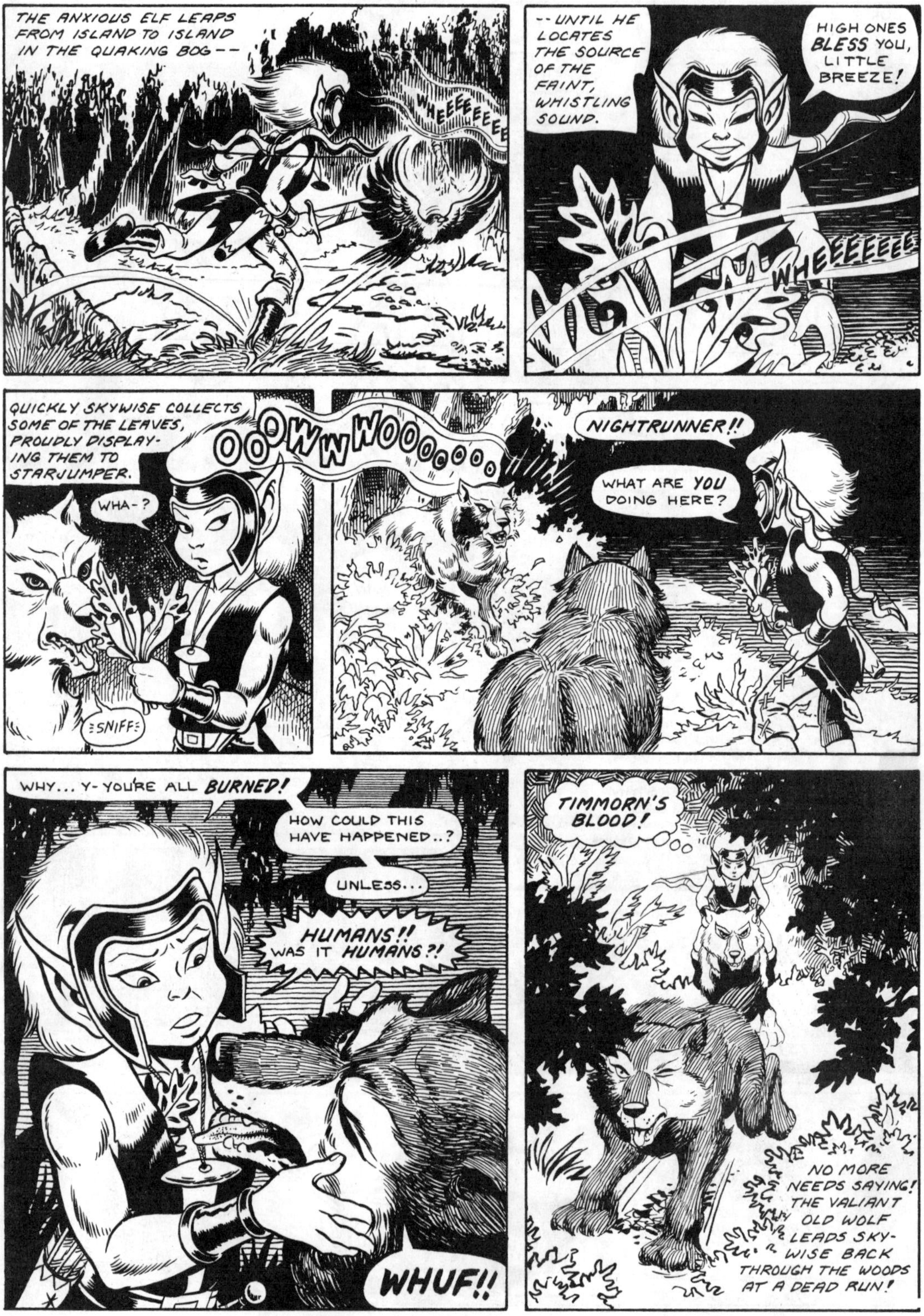
THE ANXIOUS ELF LEAPS FROM ISLAND TO ISLAND IN THE QUAKING BOG--
WHEEEEEEEEE
--UNTIL HE LOCATES THE SOURCE OF THE FAINT, WHISTLING SOUND.
HIGH ONES BLESS YOU, LITTLE BREEZE!
WHEEEEEEEE
QUICKLY SKYWISE COLLECTS SOME OF THE LEAVES, PROUDLY DISPLAYING THEM TO STARJUMPER.
WHA-?
SNIFF
OOOWWWOOOOoooo
NIGHTRUNNER!!
WHAT ARE YOU DOING HERE?
WHY... Y-YOU'RE ALL BURNED!
HOW COULD THIS HAVE HAPPENED..?
UNLESS...
HUMANS!! WAS IT HUMANS?!
WHUF!!
TIMMORN'S BLOOD!
NO MORE NEEDS SAYING! THE VALIANT OLD WOLF LEADS SKYWISE BACK THROUGH THE WOODS AT A DEAD RUN!

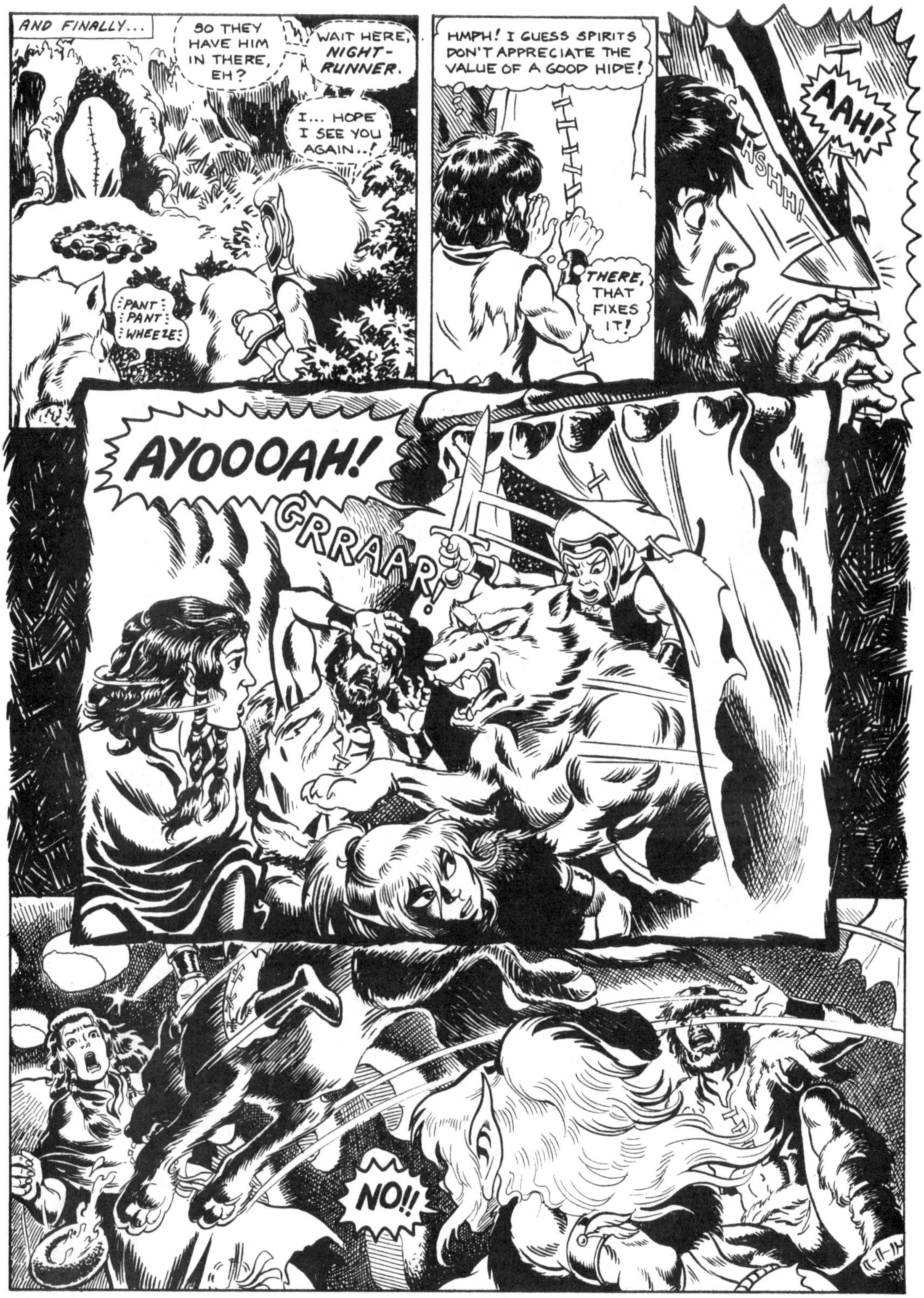
AND FINALLY...
SO THEY HAVE HIM IN THERE, EH?
WAIT HERE, NIGHT-RUNNER.
I... HOPE I SEE YOU AGAIN..!
PANT PANT WHEEZE
HMPH! I GUESS SPIRITS DON'T APPRECIATE THE VALUE OF A GOOD HIDE!
THERE, THAT FIXES IT!
SLASHHH!
AAH!
AYOOOAH!
GRRRAAAR!
NO!!

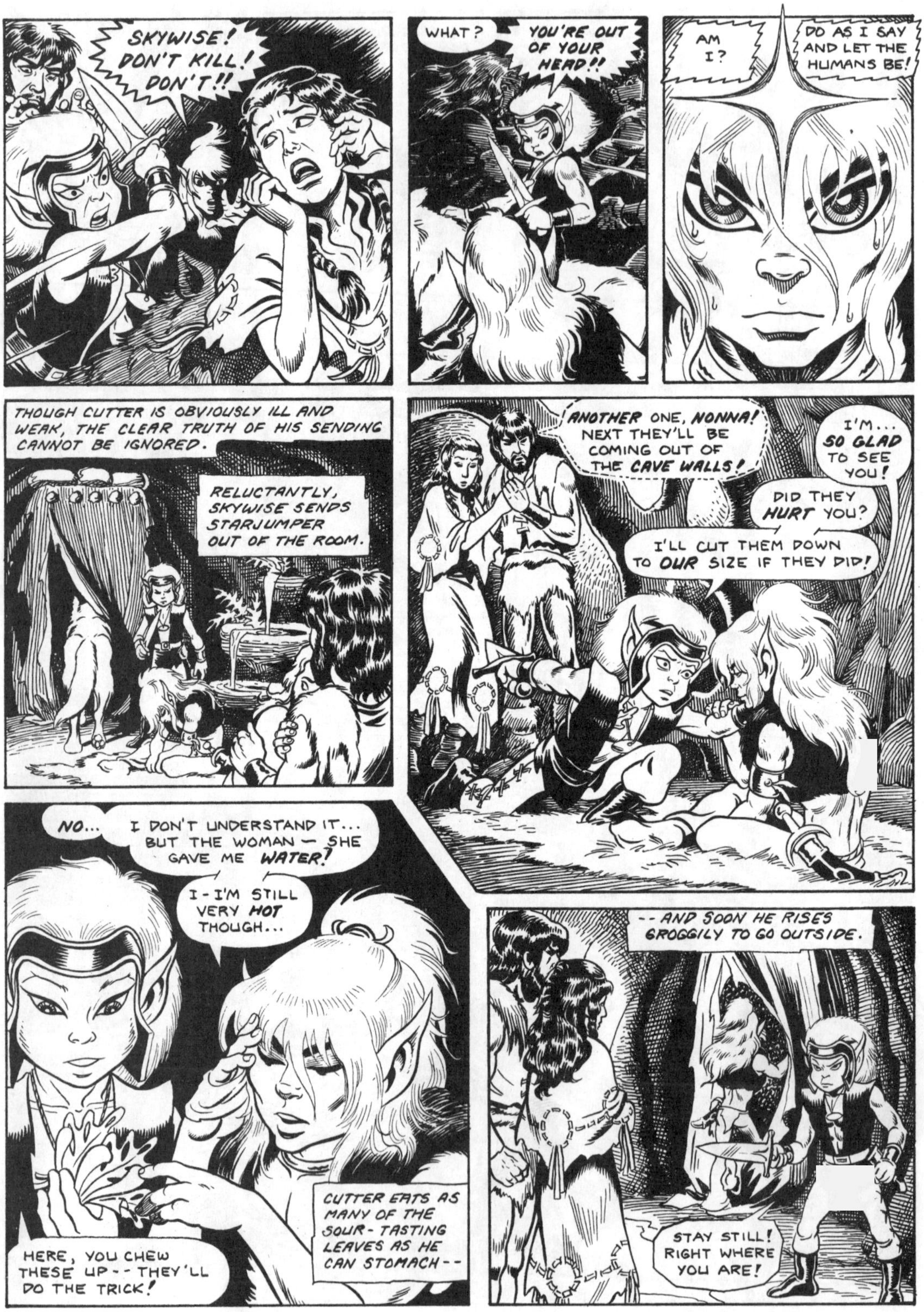
SKYWISE! DON'T KILL! DON'T!!
WHAT?
YOU'RE OUT OF YOUR HEAD!!
AM I?
DO AS I SAY AND LET THE HUMANS BE!
THOUGH CUTTER IS OBVIOUSLY ILL AND WEAK, THE CLEAR TRUTH OF HIS SENDING CANNOT BE IGNORED.
RELUCTANTLY, SKYWISE SENDS STARJUMPER OUT OF THE ROOM.
ANOTHER ONE, NONNA! NEXT THEY'LL BE COMING OUT OF THE CAVE WALLS!
I'M... SO GLAD TO SEE YOU!
DID THEY HURT YOU?
I'LL CUT THEM DOWN TO OUR SIZE IF THEY DID!
NO...
I DON'T UNDERSTAND IT... BUT THE WOMAN — SHE GAVE ME WATER!
I-I'M STILL VERY HOT THOUGH...
HERE, YOU CHEW THESE UP--THEY'LL DO THE TRICK!
CUTTER EATS AS MANY OF THE SOUR-TASTING LEAVES AS HE CAN STOMACH--
--AND SOON HE RISES GROGGILY TO GO OUTSIDE.
STAY STILL! RIGHT WHERE YOU ARE!

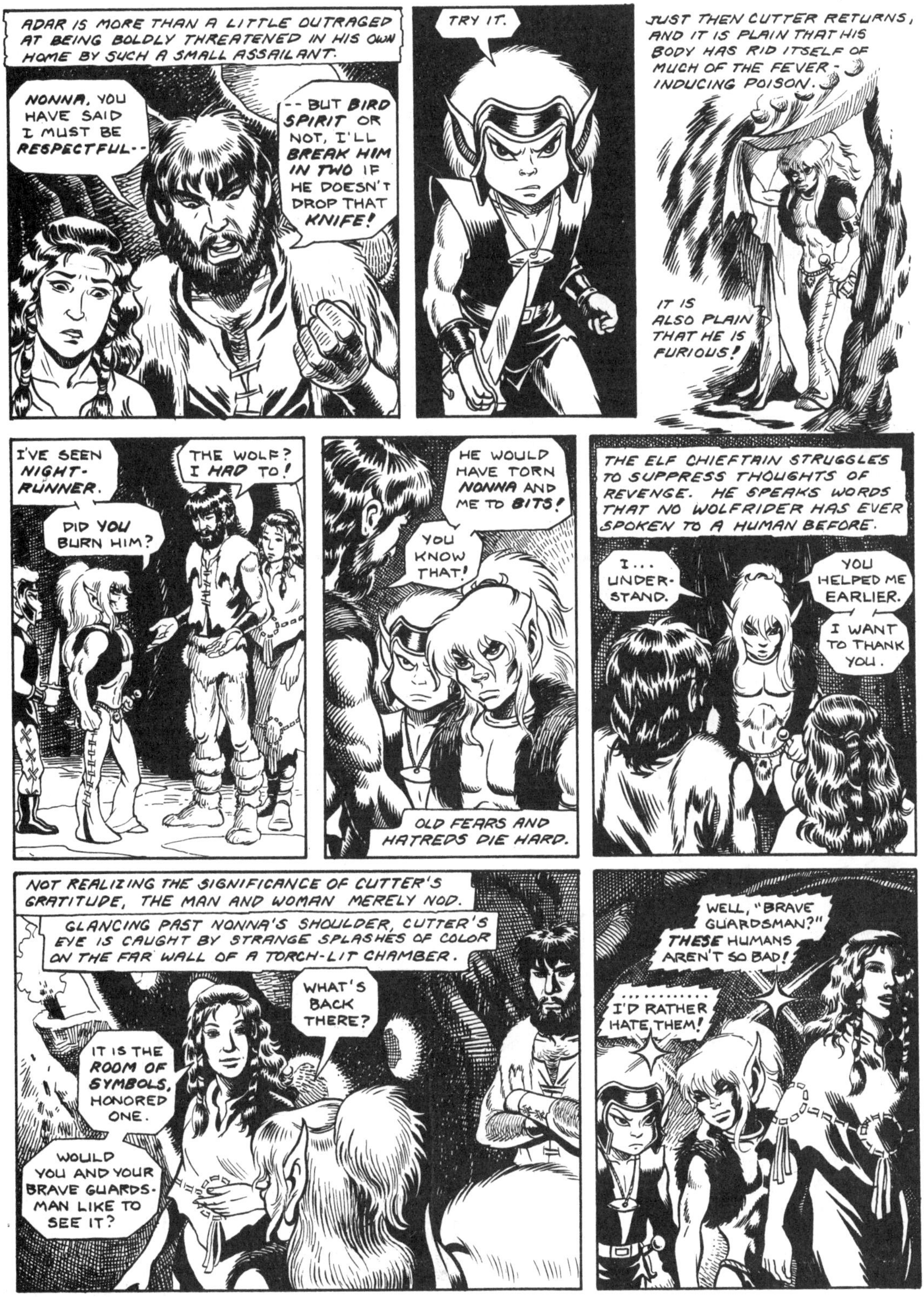
ADAR IS MORE THAN A LITTLE OUTRAGED AT BEING BOLDLY THREATENED IN HIS OWN HOME BY SUCH A SMALL ASSAILANT.
NONNA, YOU HAVE SAID I MUST BE RESPECTFUL--
--BUT BIRD SPIRIT OR NOT, I'LL BREAK HIM IN TWO IF HE DOESN'T DROP THAT KNIFE!
TRY IT.
JUST THEN CUTTER RETURNS, AND IT IS PLAIN THAT HIS BODY HAS RID ITSELF OF MUCH OF THE FEVER-INDUCING POISON.
IT IS ALSO PLAIN THAT HE IS FURIOUS!
I'VE SEEN NIGHT-RUNNER.
DID YOU BURN HIM?
THE WOLF? I HAD TO!
HE WOULD HAVE TORN NONNA AND ME TO BITS!
YOU KNOW THAT!
OLD FEARS AND HATREDS DIE HARD.
THE ELF CHIEFTAIN STRUGGLES TO SUPPRESS THOUGHTS OF REVENGE. HE SPEAKS WORDS THAT NO WOLFRIDER HAS EVER SPOKEN TO A HUMAN BEFORE.
I... UNDER-STAND.
YOU HELPED ME EARLIER.
I WANT TO THANK YOU.
NOT REALIZING THE SIGNIFICANCE OF CUTTER'S GRATITUDE, THE MAN AND WOMAN MERELY NOD.
GLANCING PAST NONNA'S SHOULDER, CUTTER'S EYE IS CAUGHT BY STRANGE SPLASHES OF COLOR ON THE FAR WALL OF A TORCH-LIT CHAMBER.
WHAT'S BACK THERE?
IT IS THE ROOM OF SYMBOLS, HONORED ONE.
WOULD YOU AND YOUR BRAVE GUARDS-MAN LIKE TO SEE IT?
WELL, "BRAVE GUARDSMAN?" THESE HUMANS AREN'T SO BAD!
.... I'D RATHER HATE THEM!

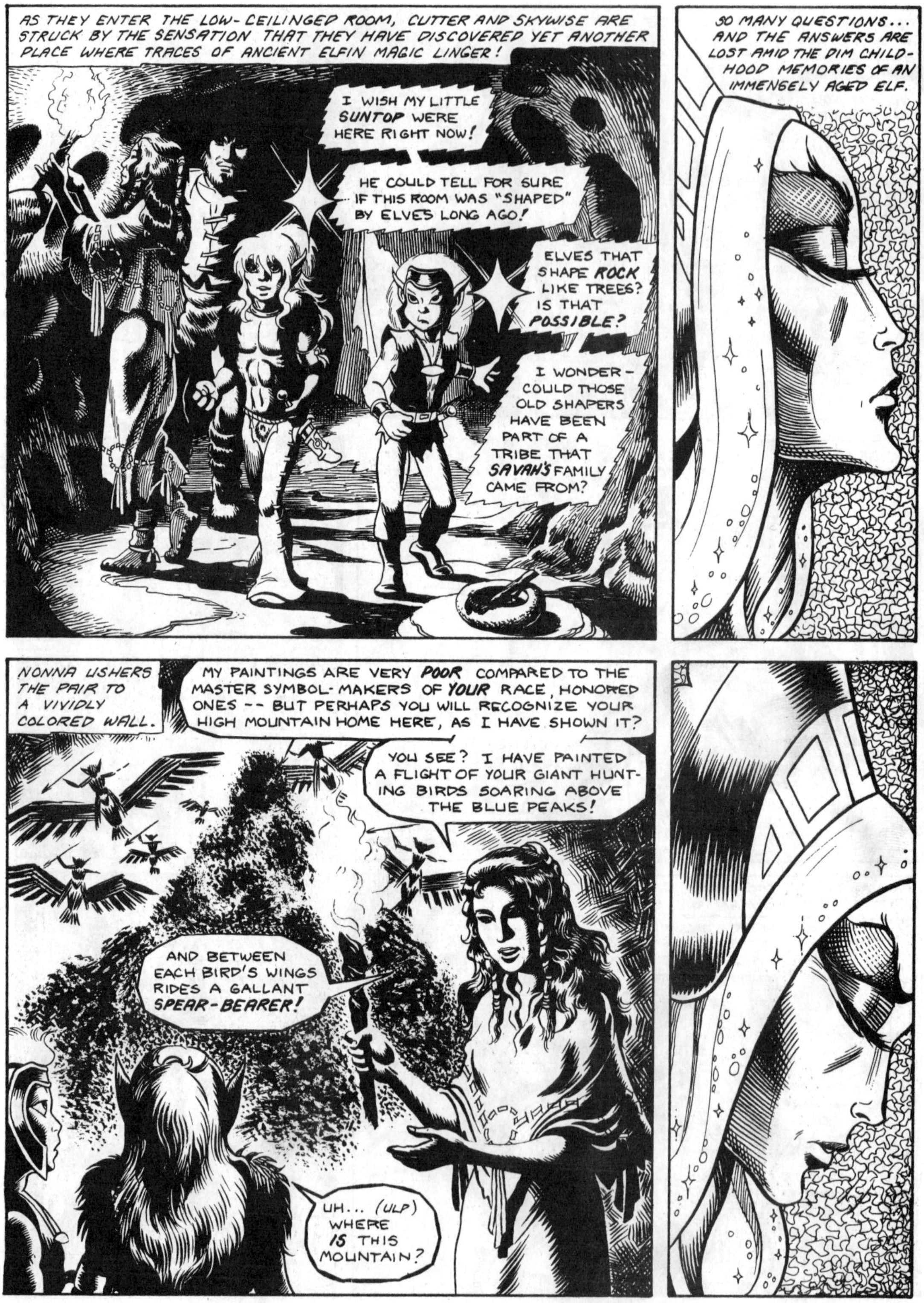
AS THEY ENTER THE LOW-CEILINGED ROOM, CUTTER AND SKYWISE ARE STRUCK BY THE SENSATION THAT THEY HAVE DISCOVERED YET ANOTHER PLACE WHERE TRACES OF ANCIENT ELFIN MAGIC LINGER!
I WISH MY LITTLE SUNTOP WERE HERE RIGHT NOW!
HE COULD TELL FOR SURE IF THIS ROOM WAS "SHAPED" BY ELVES LONG AGO!
ELVES THAT SHAPE ROCK LIKE TREES? IS THAT POSSIBLE?
I WONDER - COULD THOSE OLD SHAPERS HAVE BEEN PART OF A TRIBE THAT SAVAH'S FAMILY CAME FROM?
SO MANY QUESTIONS... AND THE ANSWERS ARE LOST AMID THE DIM CHILDHOOD MEMORIES OF AN IMMENSELY AGED ELF.
NONNA USHERS THE PAIR TO A VIVIDLY COLORED WALL.
MY PAINTINGS ARE VERY POOR COMPARED TO THE MASTER SYMBOL-MAKERS OF YOUR RACE, HONORED ONES -- BUT PERHAPS YOU WILL RECOGNIZE YOUR HIGH MOUNTAIN HOME HERE, AS I HAVE SHOWN IT?
YOU SEE? I HAVE PAINTED A FLIGHT OF YOUR GIANT HUNTING BIRDS SOARING ABOVE THE BLUE PEAKS!
AND BETWEEN EACH BIRD'S WINGS RIDES A GALLANT SPEAR-BEARER!
UH... (ULP) WHERE IS THIS MOUNTAIN?

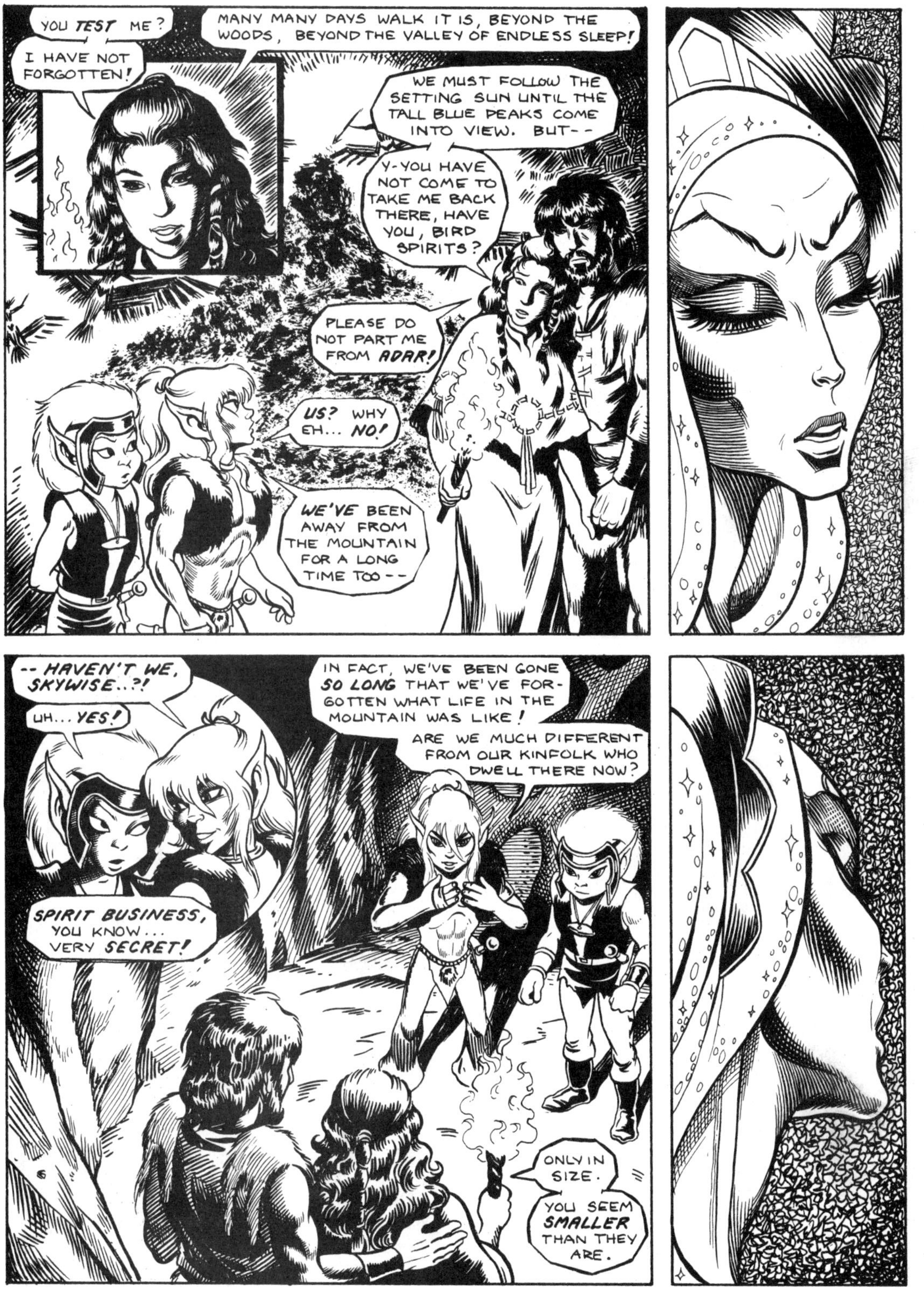
YOU TEST ME?
I HAVE NOT FORGOTTEN!
MANY MANY DAYS WALK IT IS, BEYOND THE WOODS, BEYOND THE VALLEY OF ENDLESS SLEEP!
WE MUST FOLLOW THE SETTING SUN UNTIL THE TALL BLUE PEAKS COME INTO VIEW. BUT--
Y-YOU HAVE NOT COME TO TAKE ME BACK THERE, HAVE YOU, BIRD SPIRITS?
PLEASE DO NOT PART ME FROM ADAR!
US? WHY EH... NO!
WE'VE BEEN AWAY FROM THE MOUNTAIN FOR A LONG TIME TOO--
--HAVEN'T WE, SKYWISE...?!
UH... YES!
SPIRIT BUSINESS, YOU KNOW... VERY SECRET!
IN FACT, WE'VE BEEN GONE SO LONG THAT WE'VE FOR-GOTTEN WHAT LIFE IN THE MOUNTAIN WAS LIKE!
ARE WE MUCH DIFFERENT FROM OUR KINFOLK WHO DWELL THERE NOW?
ONLY IN SIZE.
YOU SEEM SMALLER THAN THEY ARE.

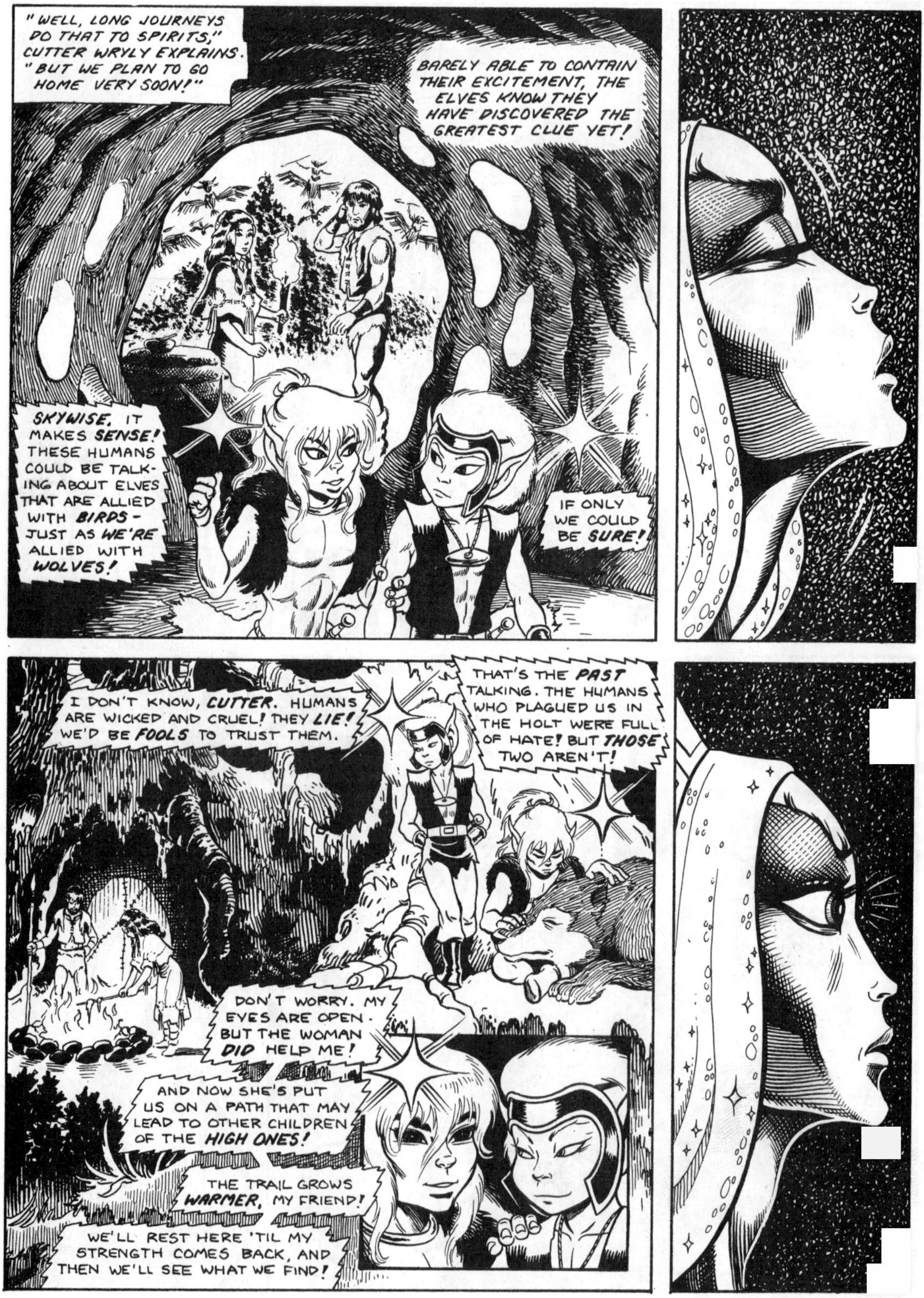
"WELL, LONG JOURNEYS DO THAT TO SPIRITS," CUTTER WRYLY EXPLAINS. "BUT WE PLAN TO GO HOME VERY SOON!"
BARELY ABLE TO CONTAIN THEIR EXCITEMENT, THE ELVES KNOW THEY HAVE DISCOVERED THE GREATEST CLUE YET!
SKYWISE, IT MAKES SENSE! THESE HUMANS COULD BE TALKING ABOUT ELVES THAT ARE ALLIED WITH BIRDS - JUST AS WE'RE ALLIED WITH WOLVES!
IF ONLY WE COULD BE SURE!
I DON'T KNOW, CUTTER. HUMANS ARE WICKED AND CRUEL! THEY LIE! WE'D BE FOOLS TO TRUST THEM.
THAT'S THE PAST TALKING. THE HUMANS WHO PLAGUED US IN THE HOLT WERE FULL OF HATE! BUT THOSE TWO AREN'T!
DON'T WORRY. MY EYES ARE OPEN. BUT THE WOMAN DID HELP ME!
AND NOW SHE'S PUT US ON A PATH THAT MAY LEAD TO OTHER CHILDREN OF THE HIGH ONES!
THE TRAIL GROWS WARMER, MY FRIEND!
WE'LL REST HERE 'TIL MY STRENGTH COMES BACK, AND THEN WE'LL SEE WHAT WE FIND!

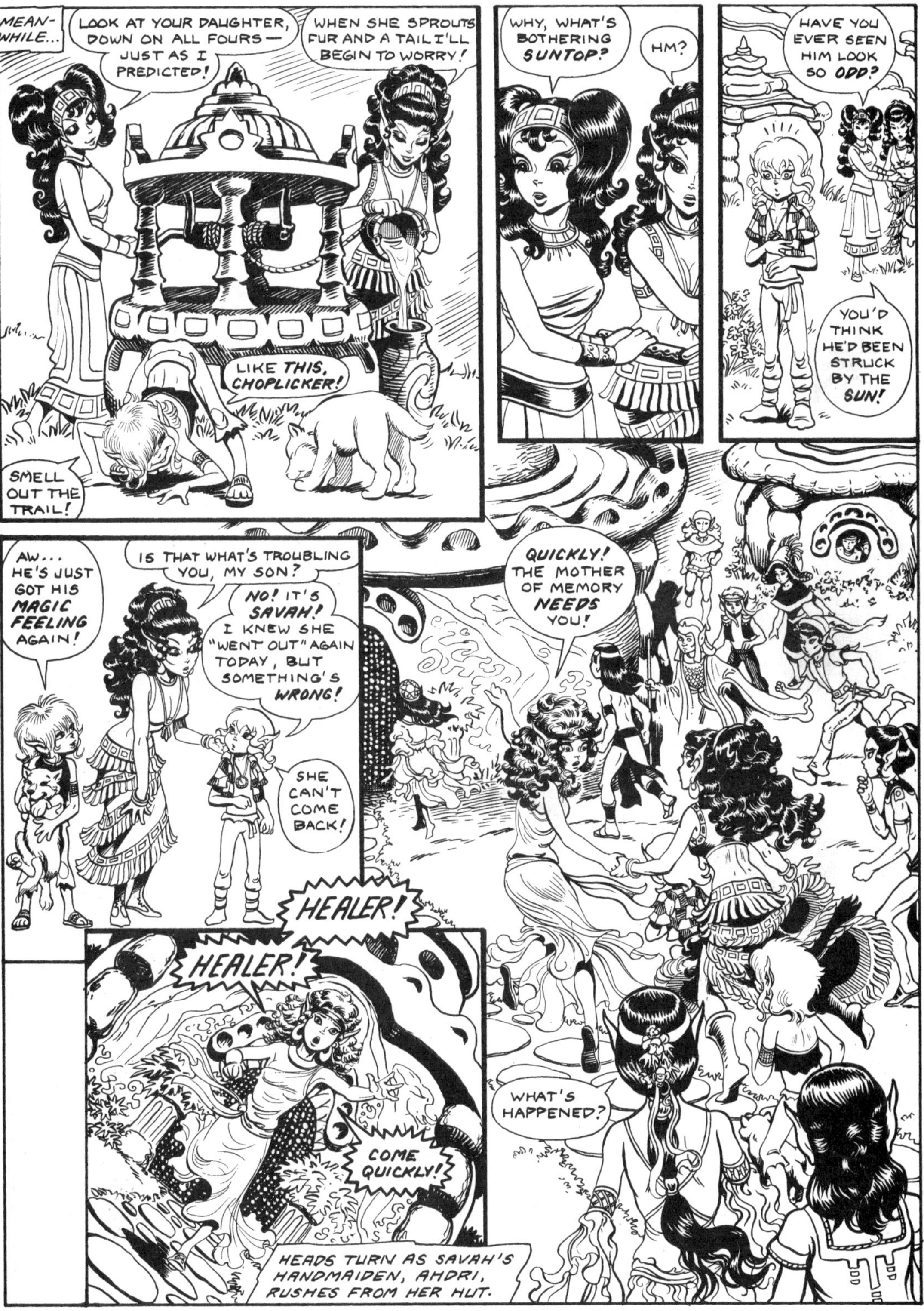
MEAN-WHILE...
LOOK AT YOUR DAUGHTER, DOWN ON ALL FOURS — JUST AS I PREDICTED!
WHEN SHE SPROUTS FUR AND A TAIL I'LL BEGIN TO WORRY!
LIKE THIS, CHOPLICKER!
SMELL OUT THE TRAIL!
WHY, WHAT'S BOTHERING SUNTOP?
HM?
HAVE YOU EVER SEEN HIM LOOK SO ODD?
YOU'D THINK HE'D BEEN STRUCK BY THE SUN!
AW... HE'S JUST GOT HIS MAGIC FEELING AGAIN!
IS THAT WHAT'S TROUBLING YOU, MY SON?
NO! IT'S SAVAH! I KNEW SHE "WENT OUT" AGAIN TODAY, BUT SOMETHING'S WRONG!
SHE CAN'T COME BACK!
QUICKLY! THE MOTHER OF MEMORY NEEDS YOU!
HEALER!
HEALER!
COME QUICKLY!
WHAT'S HAPPENED?
HEADS TURN AS SAVAH'S HANDMAIDEN, AMDRI, RUSHES FROM HER HUT.

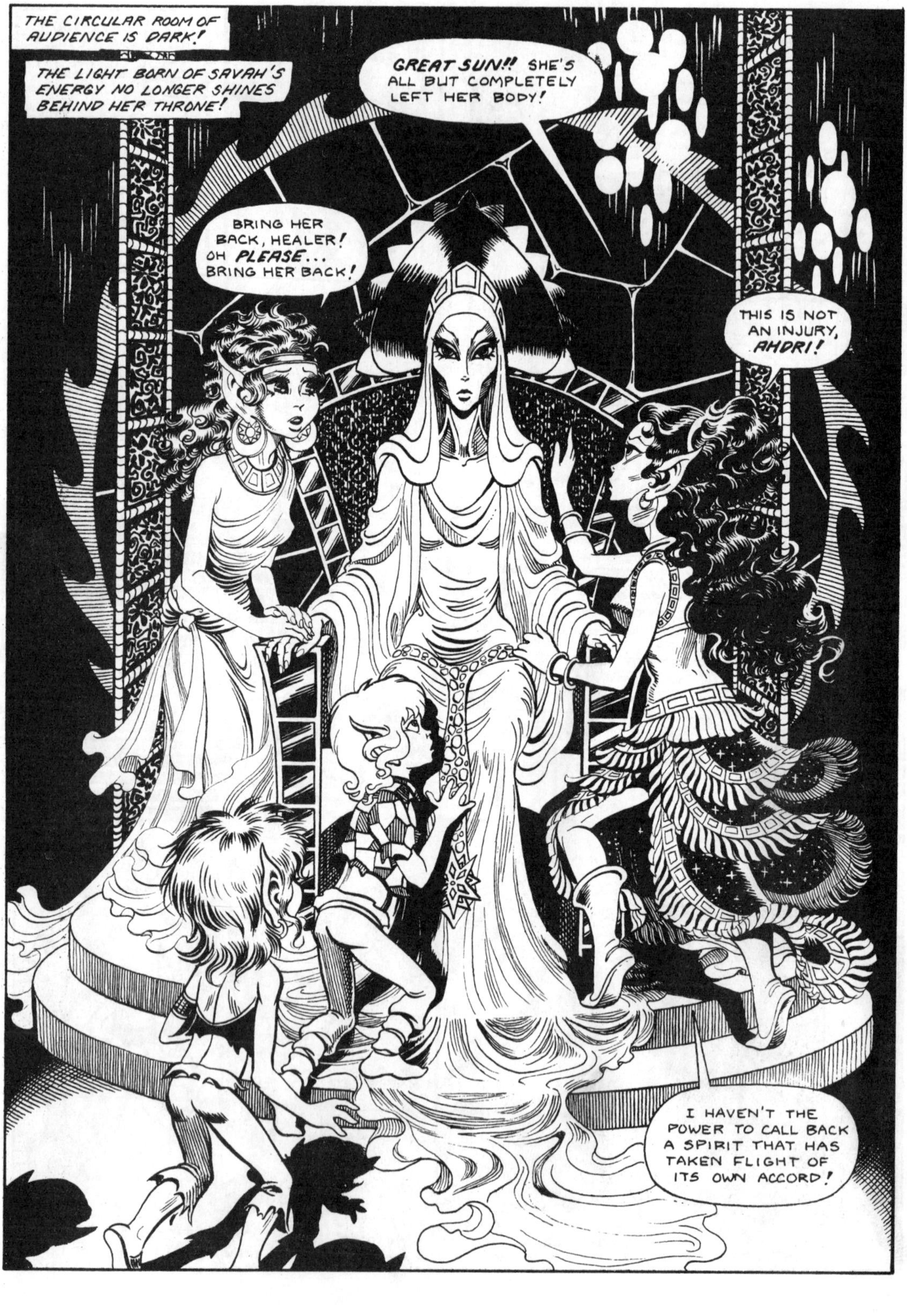
THE CIRCULAR ROOM OF AUDIENCE IS DARK!
THE LIGHT BORN OF SAVAH'S ENERGY NO LONGER SHINES BEHIND HER THRONE!
GREAT SUN!! SHE'S ALL BUT COMPLETELY LEFT HER BODY!
BRING HER BACK, HEALER! OH PLEASE... BRING HER BACK!
THIS IS NOT AN INJURY, AHDRI!
I HAVEN'T THE POWER TO CALL BACK A SPIRIT THAT HAS TAKEN FLIGHT OF ITS OWN ACCORD!

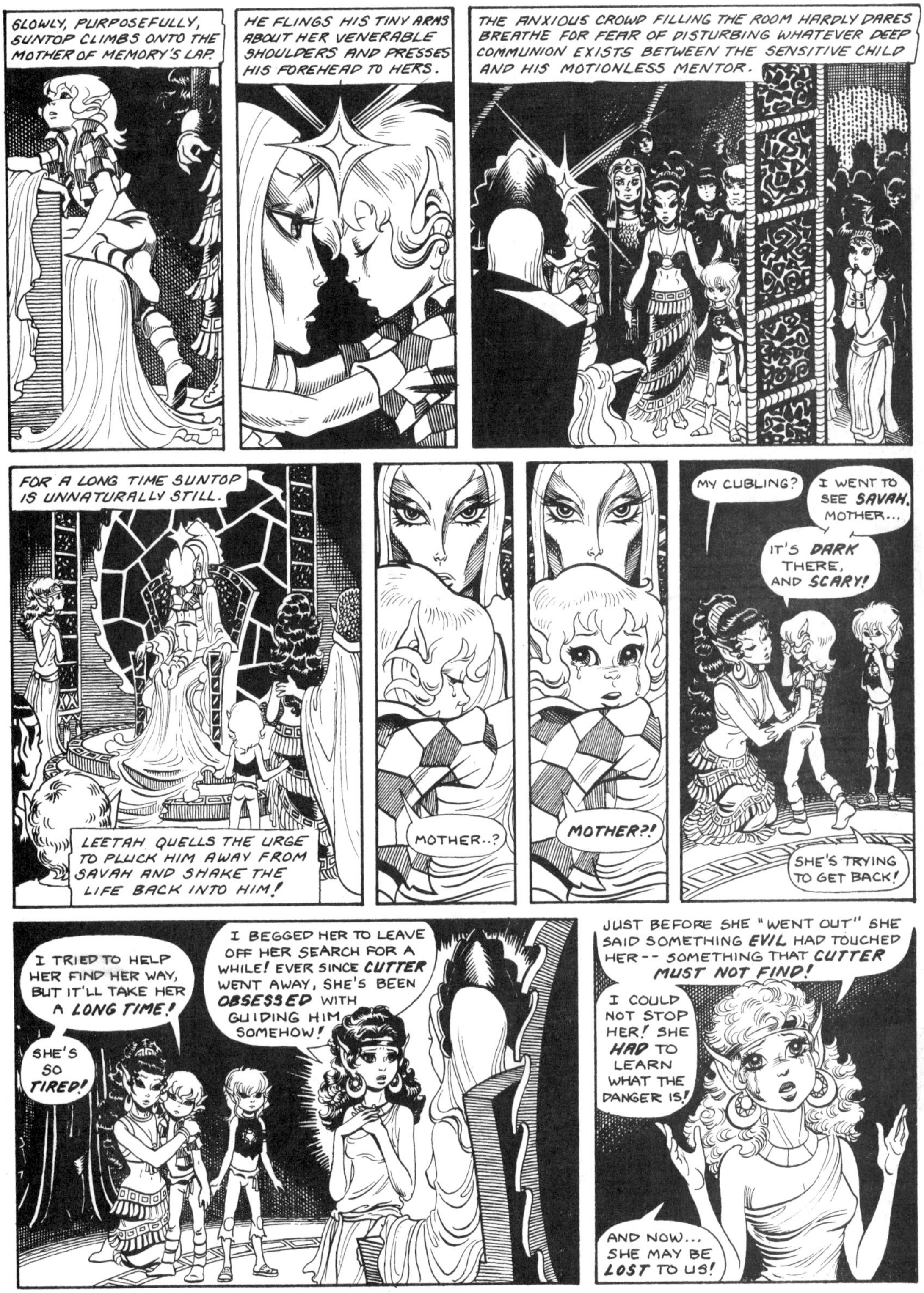
SLOWLY, PURPOSEFULLY, SUNTOP CLIMBS ONTO THE MOTHER OF MEMORY'S LAP.
HE FLINGS HIS TINY ARMS ABOUT HER VENERABLE SHOULDERS AND PRESSES HIS FOREHEAD TO HERS.
THE ANXIOUS CROWD FILLING THE ROOM HARDLY DARES BREATHE FOR FEAR OF DISTURBING WHATEVER DEEP COMMUNION EXISTS BETWEEN THE SENSITIVE CHILD AND HIS MOTIONLESS MENTOR.
FOR A LONG TIME SUNTOP IS UNNATURALLY STILL.
LEETAH QUELLS THE URGE TO PLUCK HIM AWAY FROM SAVAH AND SHAKE THE LIFE BACK INTO HIM!
MOTHER..?
MOTHER?!
MY CUBLING?
I WENT TO SEE SAVAH, MOTHER...
IT'S DARK THERE, AND SCARY!
SHE'S TRYING TO GET BACK!
I TRIED TO HELP HER FIND HER WAY, BUT IT'LL TAKE HER A LONG TIME!
SHE'S SO TIRED!
I BEGGED HER TO LEAVE OFF HER SEARCH FOR A WHILE! EVER SINCE CUTTER WENT AWAY, SHE'S BEEN OBSESSED WITH GUIDING HIM SOMEHOW!
JUST BEFORE SHE "WENT OUT" SHE SAID SOMETHING EVIL HAD TOUCHED HER-- SOMETHING THAT CUTTER MUST NOT FIND!
I COULD NOT STOP HER! SHE HAD TO LEARN WHAT THE DANGER IS!
AND NOW... SHE MAY BE LOST TO US!

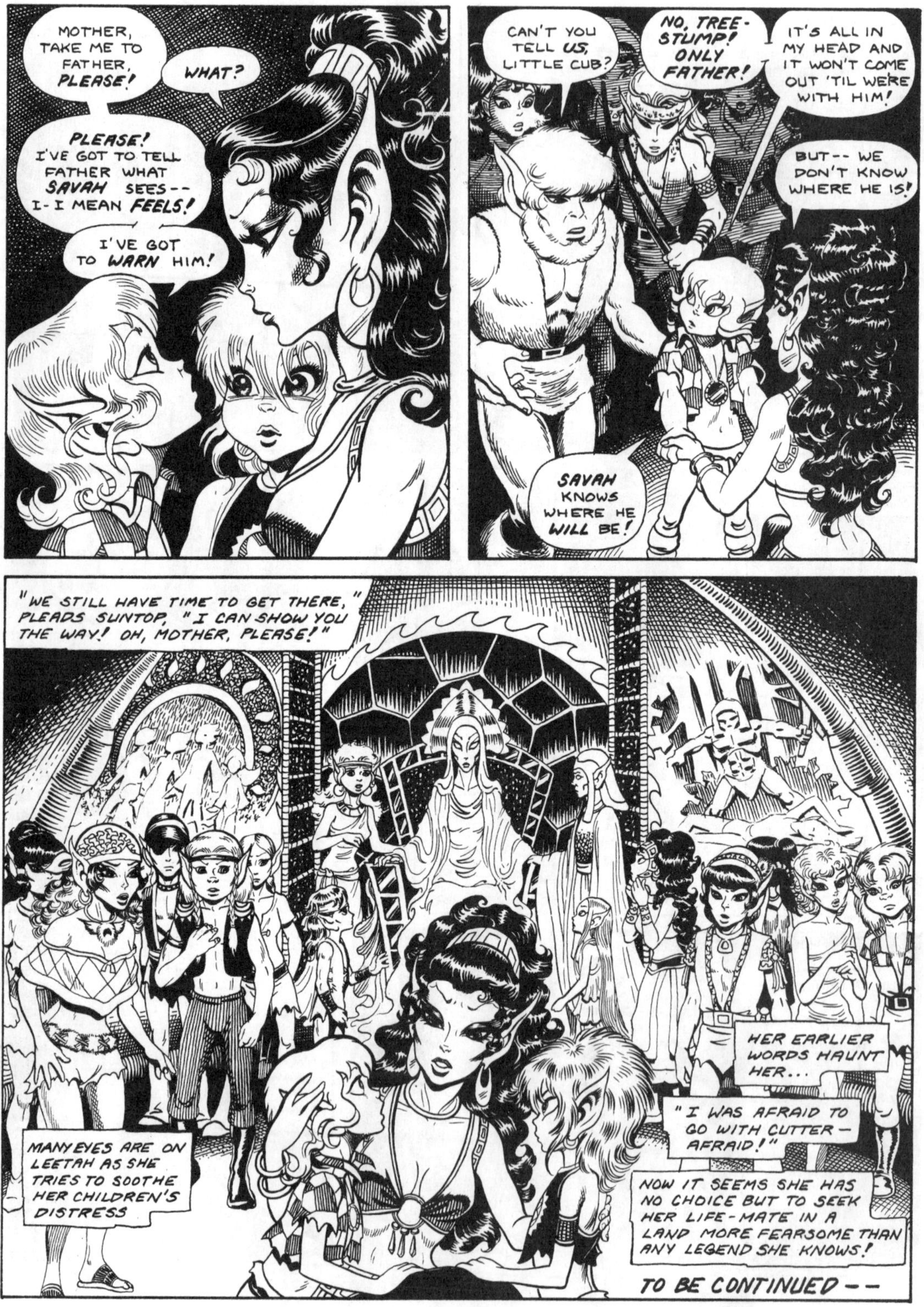
MOTHER, TAKE ME TO FATHER, PLEASE!
WHAT?
PLEASE! I'VE GOT TO TELL FATHER WHAT SAVAH SEES-- I- I MEAN FEELS!
I'VE GOT TO WARN HIM!
CAN'T YOU TELL US, LITTLE CUB?
NO, TREE-STUMP! ONLY FATHER!
IT'S ALL IN MY HEAD AND IT WON'T COME OUT 'TIL WE'RE WITH HIM!
BUT-- WE DON'T KNOW WHERE HE IS!
SAVAH KNOWS WHERE HE WILL BE!
"WE STILL HAVE TIME TO GET THERE," PLEADS SUNTOP, "I CAN SHOW YOU THE WAY! OH, MOTHER, PLEASE!"
MANY EYES ARE ON LEETAH AS SHE TRIES TO SOOTHE HER CHILDREN'S DISTRESS
HER EARLIER WORDS HAUNT HER...
"I WAS AFRAID TO GO WITH CUTTER-AFRAID!"
NOW IT SEEMS SHE HAS NO CHOICE BUT TO SEEK HER LIFE-MATE IN A LAND MORE FEARSOME THAN ANY LEGEND SHE KNOWS!
TO BE CONTINUED --

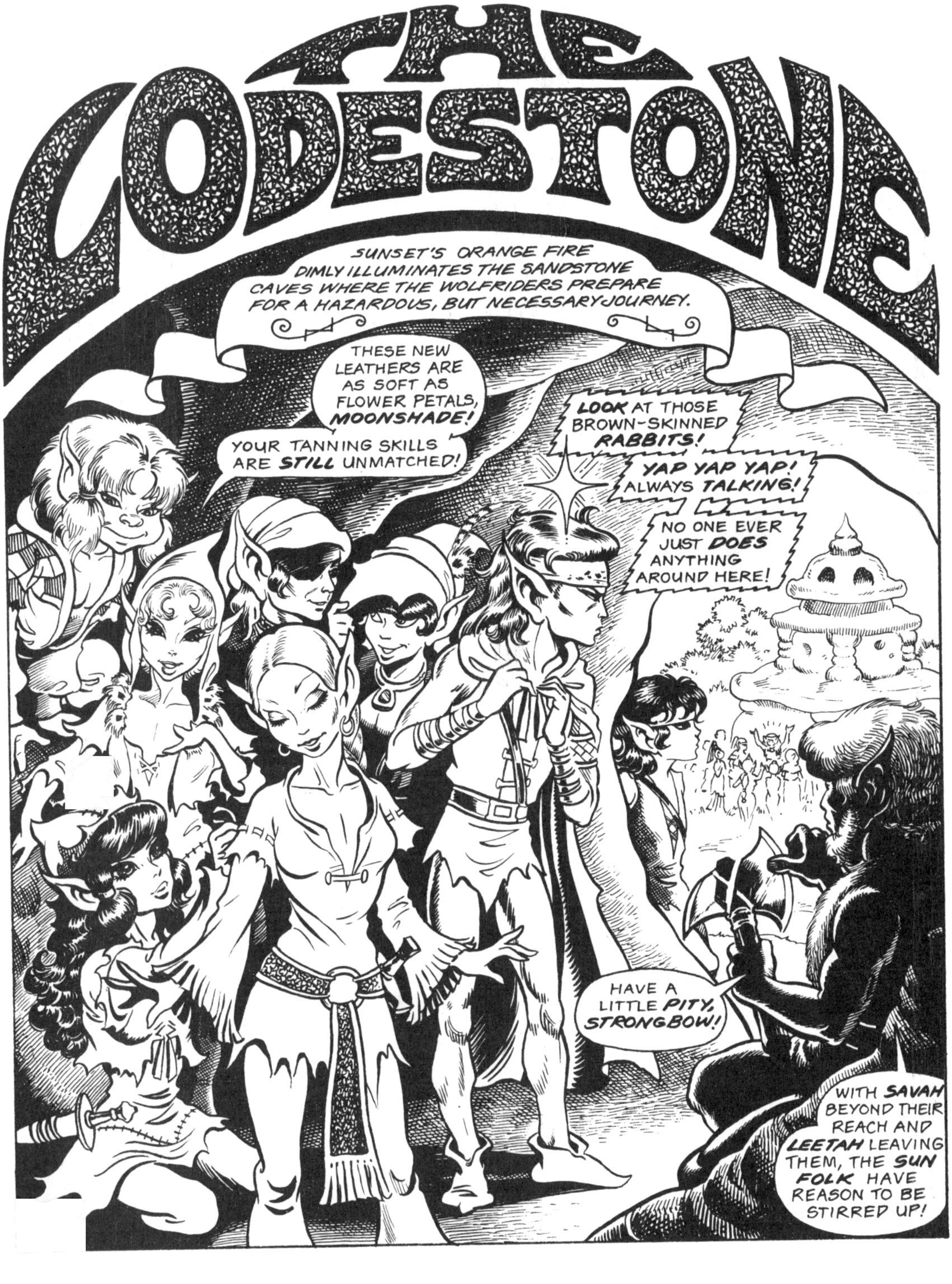
THE LODESTONE
SUNSET'S ORANGE FIRE DIMLY ILLUMINATES THE SANDSTONE CAVES WHERE THE WOLFRIDERS PREPARE FOR A HAZARDOUS, BUT NECESSARY JOURNEY.
THESE NEW LEATHERS ARE AS SOFT AS FLOWER PETALS, MOONSHADE!
YOUR TANNING SKILLS ARE STILL UNMATCHED!
LOOK AT THOSE BROWN-SKINNED RABBITS!
YAP YAP YAP! ALWAYS TALKING!
NO ONE EVER JUST DOES ANYTHING AROUND HERE!
HAVE A LITTLE PITY, STRONGBOW!
WITH SAVAH BEYOND THEIR REACH AND LEETAH LEAVING THEM, THE SUN FOLK HAVE REASON TO BE STIRRED UP!

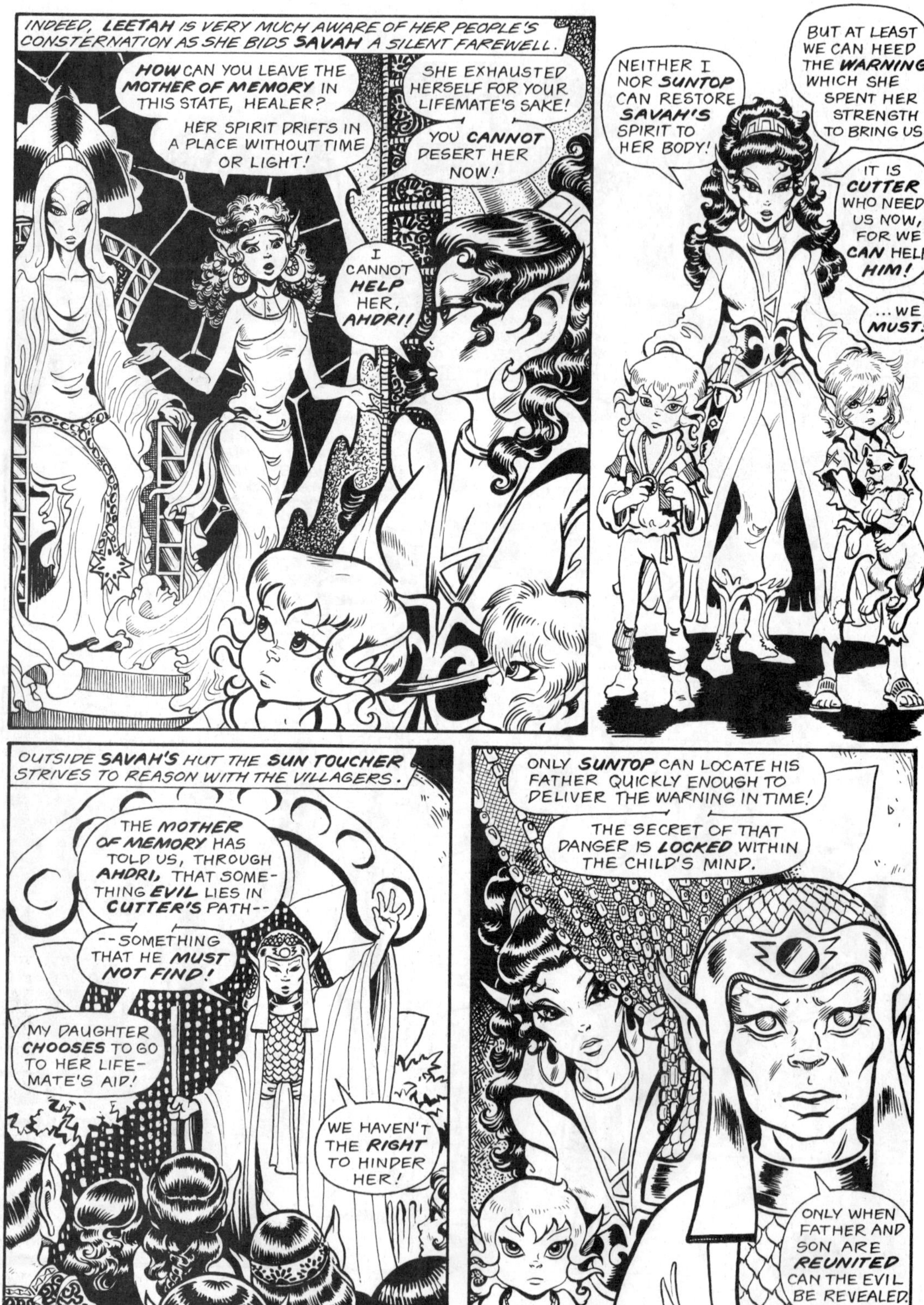
INDEED, LEETAH IS VERY MUCH AWARE OF HER PEOPLE'S CONSTERNATION AS SHE BIDS SAVAH A SILENT FAREWELL.
HOW CAN YOU LEAVE THE MOTHER OF MEMORY IN THIS STATE, HEALER?
HER SPIRIT DRIFTS IN A PLACE WITHOUT TIME OR LIGHT!
SHE EXHAUSTED HERSELF FOR YOUR LIFEMATE'S SAKE!
YOU CANNOT DESERT HER NOW!
I CANNOT HELP HER, AHDRI!
NEITHER I NOR SUNTOP CAN RESTORE SAVAH'S SPIRIT TO HER BODY!
BUT AT LEAST WE CAN HEED THE WARNING WHICH SHE SPENT HER STRENGTH TO BRING US.
IT IS CUTTER WHO NEEDS US NOW, FOR WE CAN HELP HIM!
...WE MUST!
OUTSIDE SAVAH'S HUT THE SUN TOUCHER STRIVES TO REASON WITH THE VILLAGERS.
THE MOTHER OF MEMORY HAS TOLD US, THROUGH AHDRI, THAT SOMETHING EVIL LIES IN CUTTER'S PATH--
--SOMETHING THAT HE MUST NOT FIND!
MY DAUGHTER CHOOSES TO GO TO HER LIFE-MATE'S AID!
WE HAVEN'T THE RIGHT TO HINDER HER!
ONLY SUNTOP CAN LOCATE HIS FATHER QUICKLY ENOUGH TO DELIVER THE WARNING IN TIME!
THE SECRET OF THAT DANGER IS LOCKED WITHIN THE CHILD'S MIND.
ONLY WHEN FATHER AND SON ARE REUNITED CAN THE EVIL BE REVEALED.

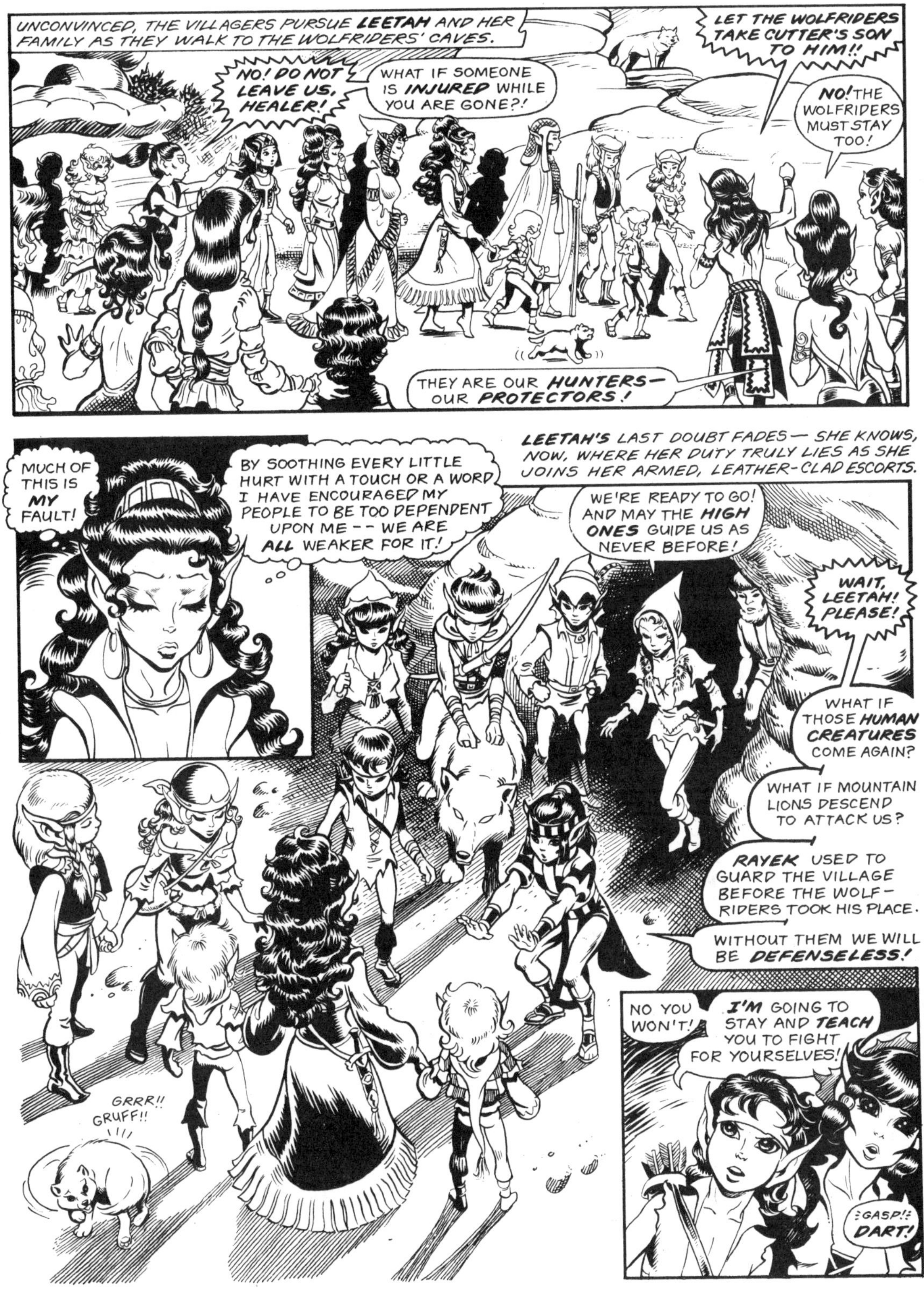

UNCONVINCED, THE VILLAGERS PURSUE LEETAH AND HER FAMILY AS THEY WALK TO THE WOLFRIDERS' CAVES.
NO! DO NOT LEAVE US, HEALER!
WHAT IF SOMEONE IS INJURED WHILE YOU ARE GONE?!
LET THE WOLFRIDERS TAKE CUTTER'S SON TO HIM!!
NO! THE WOLFRIDERS MUST STAY TOO!
THEY ARE OUR HUNTERS— OUR PROTECTORS!
MUCH OF THIS IS MY FAULT!
BY SOOTHING EVERY LITTLE HURT WITH A TOUCH OR A WORD I HAVE ENCOURAGED MY PEOPLE TO BE TOO DEPENDENT UPON ME -- WE ARE ALL WEAKER FOR IT!
LEETAH'S LAST DOUBT FADES— SHE KNOWS, NOW, WHERE HER DUTY TRULY LIES AS SHE JOINS HER ARMED, LEATHER-CLAD ESCORTS.
WE'RE READY TO GO! AND MAY THE HIGH ONES GUIDE US AS NEVER BEFORE!
WAIT, LEETAH! PLEASE!
WHAT IF THOSE HUMAN CREATURES COME AGAIN?
WHAT IF MOUNTAIN LIONS DESCEND TO ATTACK US?
RAYEK USED TO GUARD THE VILLAGE BEFORE THE WOLF-RIDERS TOOK HIS PLACE.
WITHOUT THEM WE WILL BE DEFENSELESS!
GRRR!! GRUFF!!
NO YOU WON'T!
I'M GOING TO STAY AND TEACH YOU TO FIGHT FOR YOURSELVES!
GASP! DART!

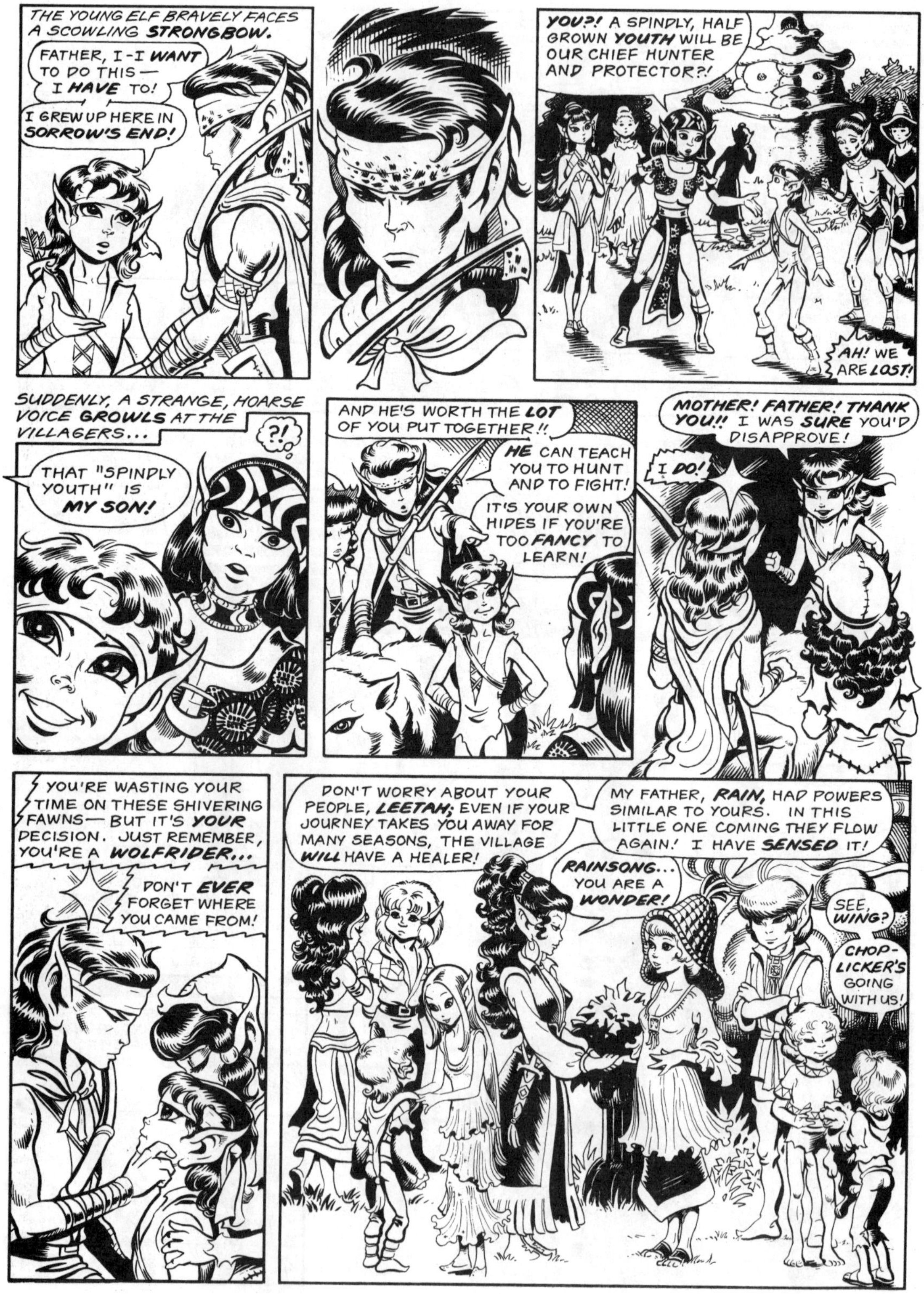
THE YOUNG ELF BRAVELY FACES A SCOWLING STRONGBOW.
FATHER, I-I WANT TO DO THIS— I HAVE TO!
I GREW UP HERE IN SORROW'S END!
YOU?! A SPINDLY, HALF GROWN YOUTH WILL BE OUR CHIEF HUNTER AND PROTECTOR?!
AH! WE ARE LOST!
SUDDENLY, A STRANGE, HOARSE VOICE GROWLS AT THE VILLAGERS...
?!
THAT "SPINDLY YOUTH" IS MY SON!
AND HE'S WORTH THE LOT OF YOU PUT TOGETHER!!
HE CAN TEACH YOU TO HUNT AND TO FIGHT!
IT'S YOUR OWN HIDES IF YOU'RE TOO FANCY TO LEARN!
MOTHER! FATHER! THANK YOU!! I WAS SURE YOU'D DISAPPROVE!
I DO!
YOU'RE WASTING YOUR TIME ON THESE SHIVERING FAWNS— BUT IT'S YOUR DECISION. JUST REMEMBER, YOU'RE A WOLFRIDER...
DON'T EVER FORGET WHERE YOU CAME FROM!
DON'T WORRY ABOUT YOUR PEOPLE, LEETAH; EVEN IF YOUR JOURNEY TAKES YOU AWAY FOR MANY SEASONS, THE VILLAGE WILL HAVE A HEALER!
MY FATHER, RAIN, HAD POWERS SIMILAR TO YOURS. IN THIS LITTLE ONE COMING THEY FLOW AGAIN! I HAVE SENSED IT!
RAINSONG... YOU ARE A WONDER!
SEE, WING?
CHOP-LICKER'S GOING WITH US!

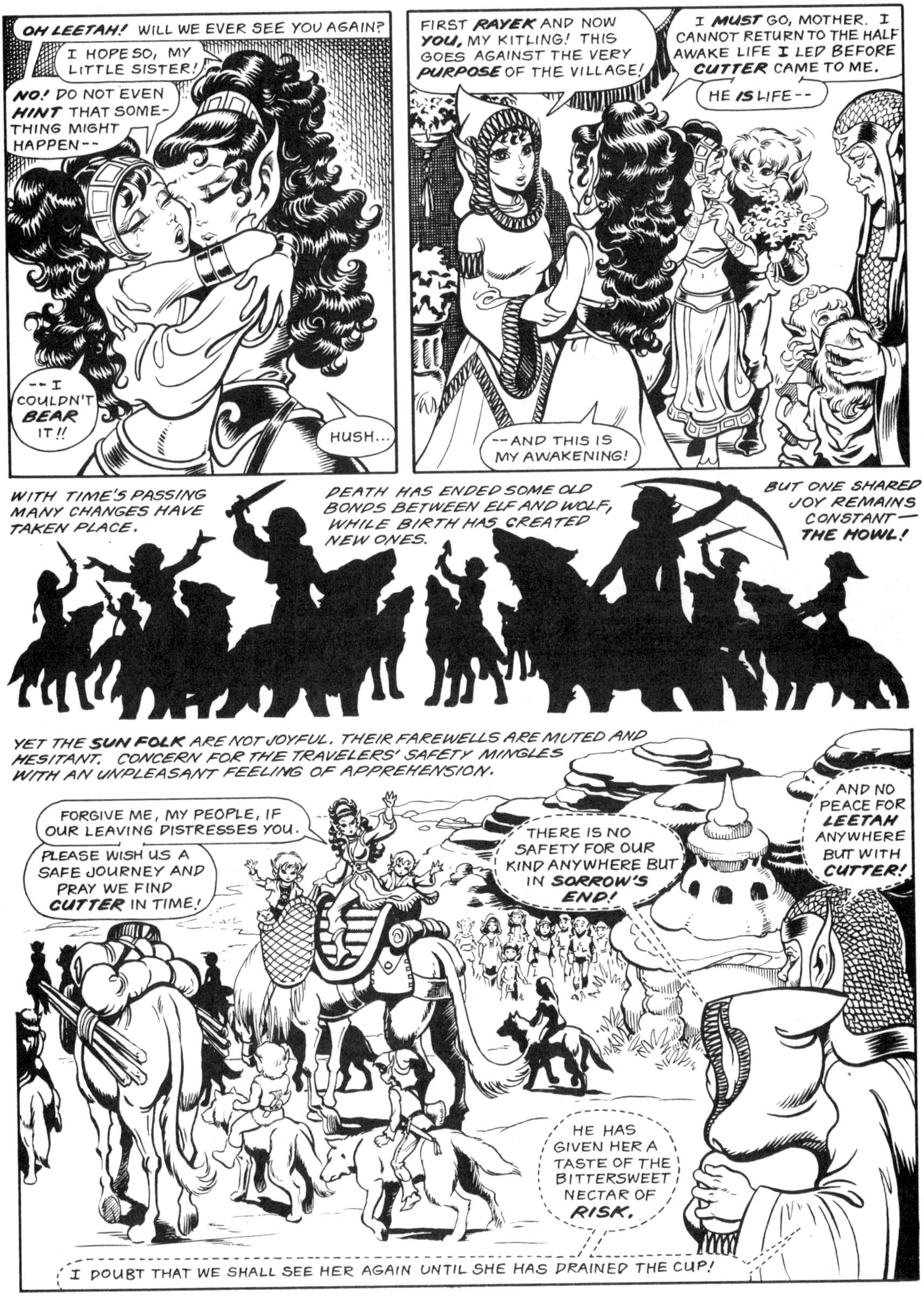
OH LEETAH! WILL WE EVER SEE YOU AGAIN?
I HOPE SO, MY LITTLE SISTER!
NO! DO NOT EVEN HINT THAT SOMETHING MIGHT HAPPEN--
--I COULDN'T BEAR IT!!
HUSH...
FIRST RAYEK AND NOW YOU, MY KITLING! THIS GOES AGAINST THE VERY PURPOSE OF THE VILLAGE!
I MUST GO, MOTHER. I CANNOT RETURN TO THE HALF AWAKE LIFE I LED BEFORE CUTTER CAME TO ME.
HE IS LIFE--
--AND THIS IS MY AWAKENING!
WITH TIME'S PASSING MANY CHANGES HAVE TAKEN PLACE.
DEATH HAS ENDED SOME OLD BONDS BETWEEN ELF AND WOLF, WHILE BIRTH HAS CREATED NEW ONES.
BUT ONE SHARED JOY REMAINS CONSTANT— THE HOWL!
YET THE SUN FOLK ARE NOT JOYFUL. THEIR FAREWELLS ARE MUTED AND HESITANT. CONCERN FOR THE TRAVELERS' SAFETY MINGLES WITH AN UNPLEASANT FEELING OF APPREHENSION.
FORGIVE ME, MY PEOPLE, IF OUR LEAVING DISTRESSES YOU.
PLEASE WISH US A SAFE JOURNEY AND PRAY WE FIND CUTTER IN TIME!
THERE IS NO SAFETY FOR OUR KIND ANYWHERE BUT IN SORROW'S END!
AND NO PEACE FOR LEETAH ANYWHERE BUT WITH CUTTER!
HE HAS GIVEN HER A TASTE OF THE BITTERSWEET NECTAR OF RISK.
I DOUBT THAT WE SHALL SEE HER AGAIN UNTIL SHE HAS DRAINED THE CUP!

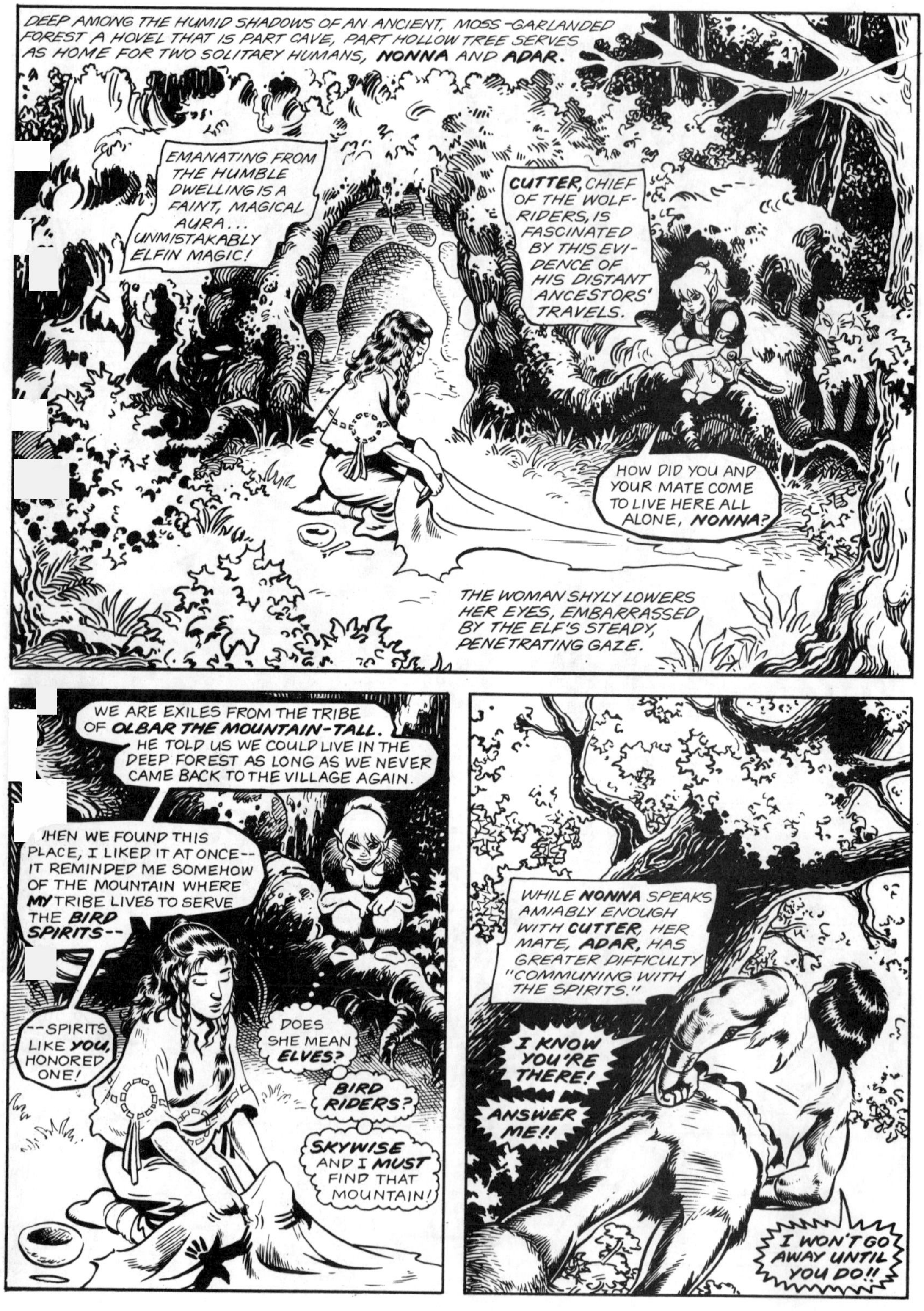
DEEP AMONG THE HUMID SHADOWS OF AN ANCIENT, MOSS-GARLANDED FOREST A HOVEL THAT IS PART CAVE, PART HOLLOW TREE SERVES AS HOME FOR TWO SOLITARY HUMANS, NONNA AND ADAR.
EMANATING FROM THE HUMBLE DWELLING IS A FAINT, MAGICAL AURA... UNMISTAKABLY ELFIN MAGIC!
CUTTER, CHIEF OF THE WOLF-RIDERS, IS FASCINATED BY THIS EVIDENCE OF HIS DISTANT ANCESTORS' TRAVELS.
HOW DID YOU AND YOUR MATE COME TO LIVE HERE ALL ALONE, NONNA?
THE WOMAN SHYLY LOWERS HER EYES, EMBARRASSED BY THE ELF'S STEADY, PENETRATING GAZE.
WE ARE EXILES FROM THE TRIBE OF OLBAR THE MOUNTAIN-TALL. HE TOLD US WE COULD LIVE IN THE DEEP FOREST AS LONG AS WE NEVER CAME BACK TO THE VILLAGE AGAIN.
WHEN WE FOUND THIS PLACE, I LIKED IT AT ONCE-- IT REMINDED ME SOMEHOW OF THE MOUNTAIN WHERE MY TRIBE LIVES TO SERVE THE BIRD SPIRITS--
--SPIRITS LIKE YOU, HONORED ONE!
DOES SHE MEAN ELVES?
BIRD RIDERS?
SKYWISE AND I MUST FIND THAT MOUNTAIN!
WHILE NONNA SPEAKS AMIABLY ENOUGH WITH CUTTER, HER MATE, ADAR, HAS GREATER DIFFICULTY "COMMUNING WITH THE SPIRITS."
I KNOW YOU'RE THERE!
ANSWER ME!!
I WON'T GO AWAY UNTIL YOU DO!!

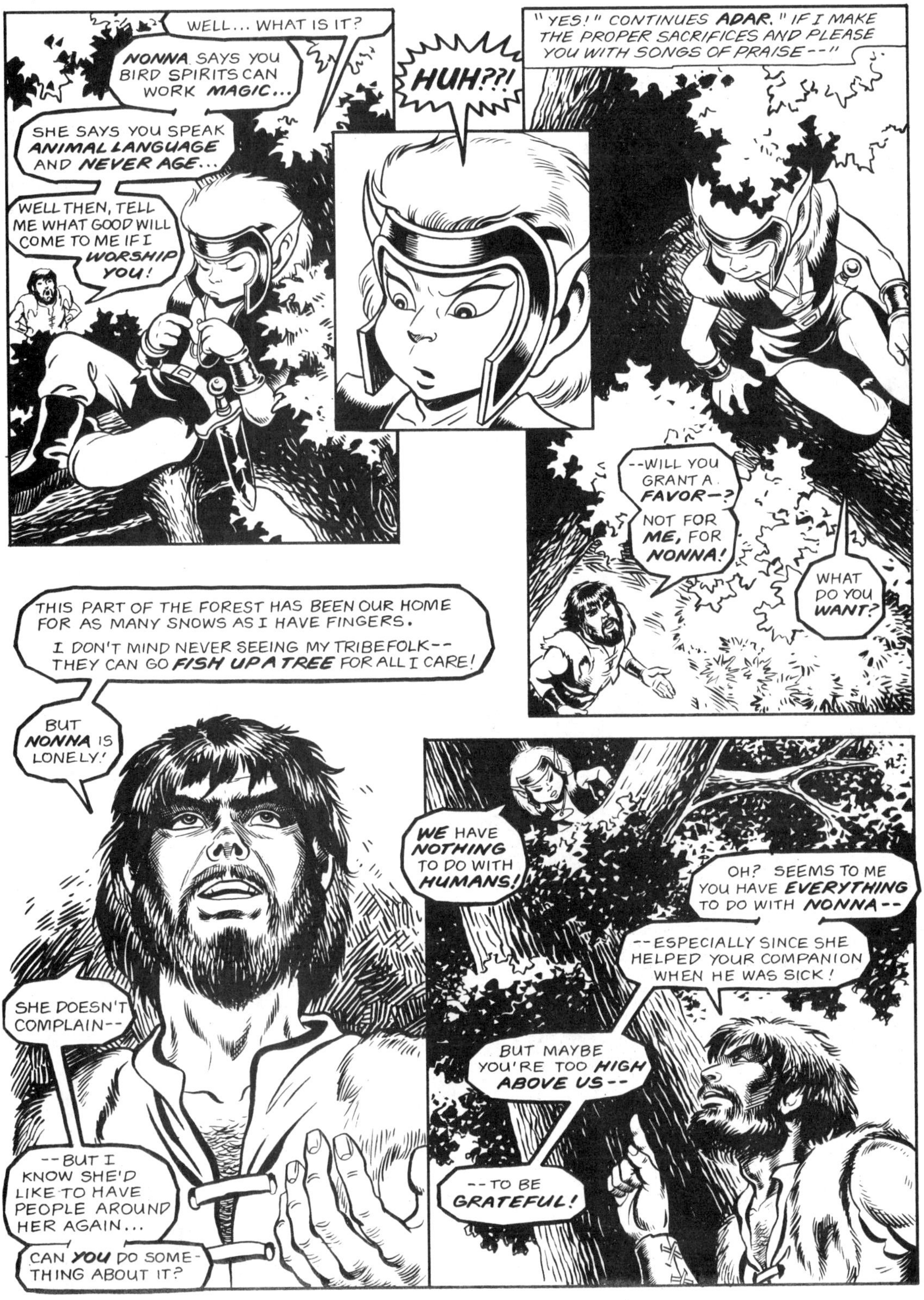

WELL... WHAT IS IT?
NONNA SAYS YOU BIRD SPIRITS CAN WORK MAGIC...
SHE SAYS YOU SPEAK ANIMAL LANGUAGE AND NEVER AGE...
WELL THEN, TELL ME WHAT GOOD WILL COME TO ME IF I WORSHIP YOU!
HUH??!
"YES!" CONTINUES ADAR. "IF I MAKE THE PROPER SACRIFICES AND PLEASE YOU WITH SONGS OF PRAISE--"
--WILL YOU GRANT A FAVOR--?
NOT FOR ME, FOR NONNA!
WHAT DO YOU WANT?
THIS PART OF THE FOREST HAS BEEN OUR HOME FOR AS MANY SNOWS AS I HAVE FINGERS.
I DON'T MIND NEVER SEEING MY TRIBEFOLK-- THEY CAN GO FISH UP A TREE FOR ALL I CARE!
BUT NONNA IS LONELY!
SHE DOESN'T COMPLAIN--
--BUT I KNOW SHE'D LIKE TO HAVE PEOPLE AROUND HER AGAIN...
CAN YOU DO SOMETHING ABOUT IT?
WE HAVE NOTHING TO DO WITH HUMANS!
OH? SEEMS TO ME YOU HAVE EVERYTHING TO DO WITH NONNA--
--ESPECIALLY SINCE SHE HELPED YOUR COMPANION WHEN HE WAS SICK!
BUT MAYBE YOU'RE TOO HIGH ABOVE US--
--TO BE GRATEFUL!

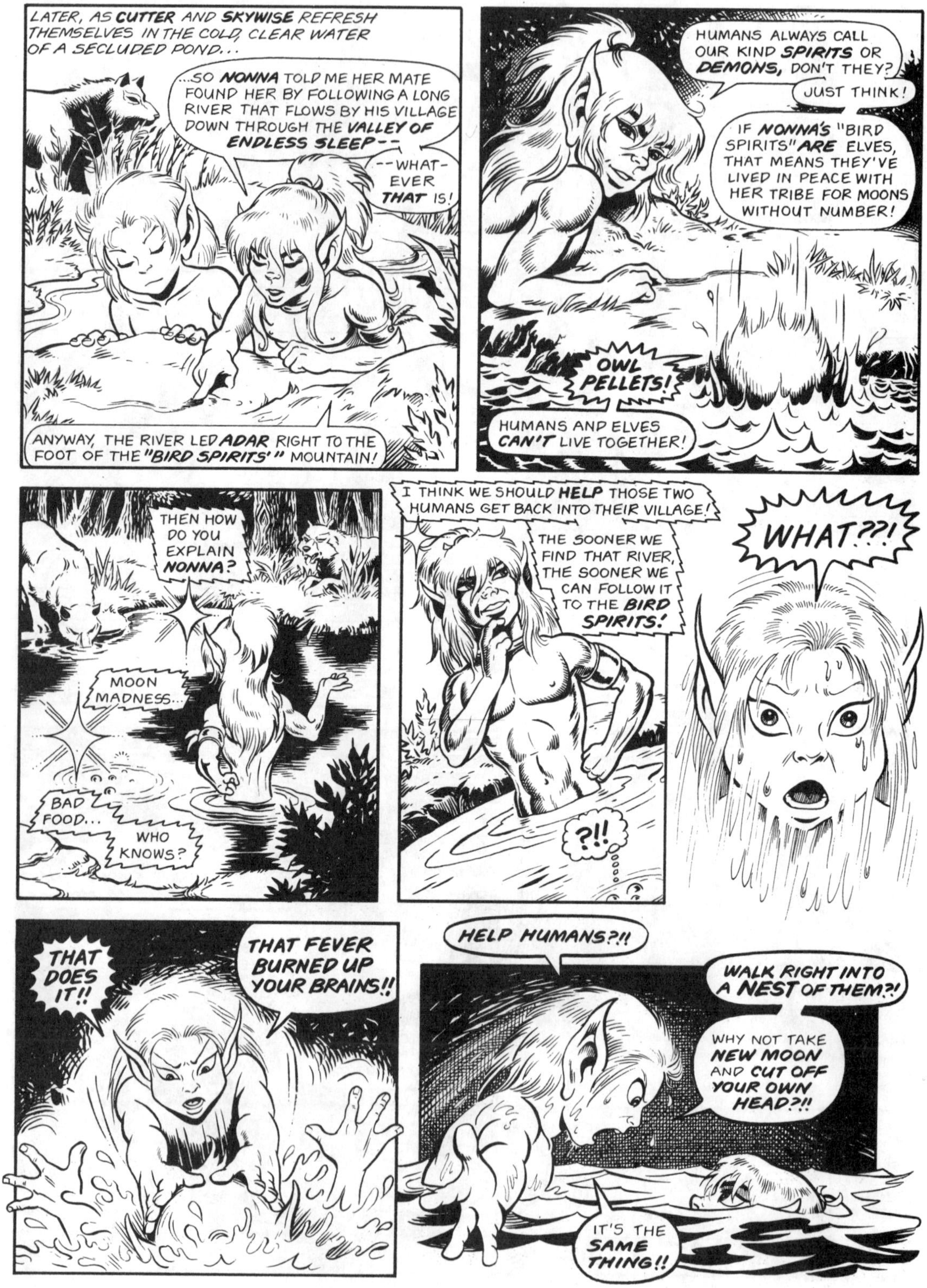
LATER, AS CUTTER AND SKYWISE REFRESH THEMSELVES IN THE COLD, CLEAR WATER OF A SECLUDED POND...
...SO NONNA TOLD ME HER MATE FOUND HER BY FOLLOWING A LONG RIVER THAT FLOWS BY HIS VILLAGE DOWN THROUGH THE VALLEY OF ENDLESS SLEEP--
--WHAT-EVER THAT IS!
ANYWAY, THE RIVER LED ADAR RIGHT TO THE FOOT OF THE "BIRD SPIRITS'" MOUNTAIN!
HUMANS ALWAYS CALL OUR KIND SPIRITS OR DEMONS, DON'T THEY?
JUST THINK!
IF NONNA'S "BIRD SPIRITS" ARE ELVES, THAT MEANS THEY'VE LIVED IN PEACE WITH HER TRIBE FOR MOONS WITHOUT NUMBER!
OWL PELLETS!
HUMANS AND ELVES CAN'T LIVE TOGETHER!
THEN HOW DO YOU EXPLAIN NONNA?
MOON MADNESS...
BAD FOOD...
WHO KNOWS?
I THINK WE SHOULD HELP THOSE TWO HUMANS GET BACK INTO THEIR VILLAGE!
THE SOONER WE FIND THAT RIVER, THE SOONER WE CAN FOLLOW IT TO THE BIRD SPIRITS!
?!!
WHAT??!
THAT DOES IT!!
THAT FEVER BURNED UP YOUR BRAINS!!
HELP HUMANS?!!
WALK RIGHT INTO A NEST OF THEM?!
WHY NOT TAKE NEW MOON AND CUT OFF YOUR OWN HEAD?!!
IT'S THE SAME THING!!

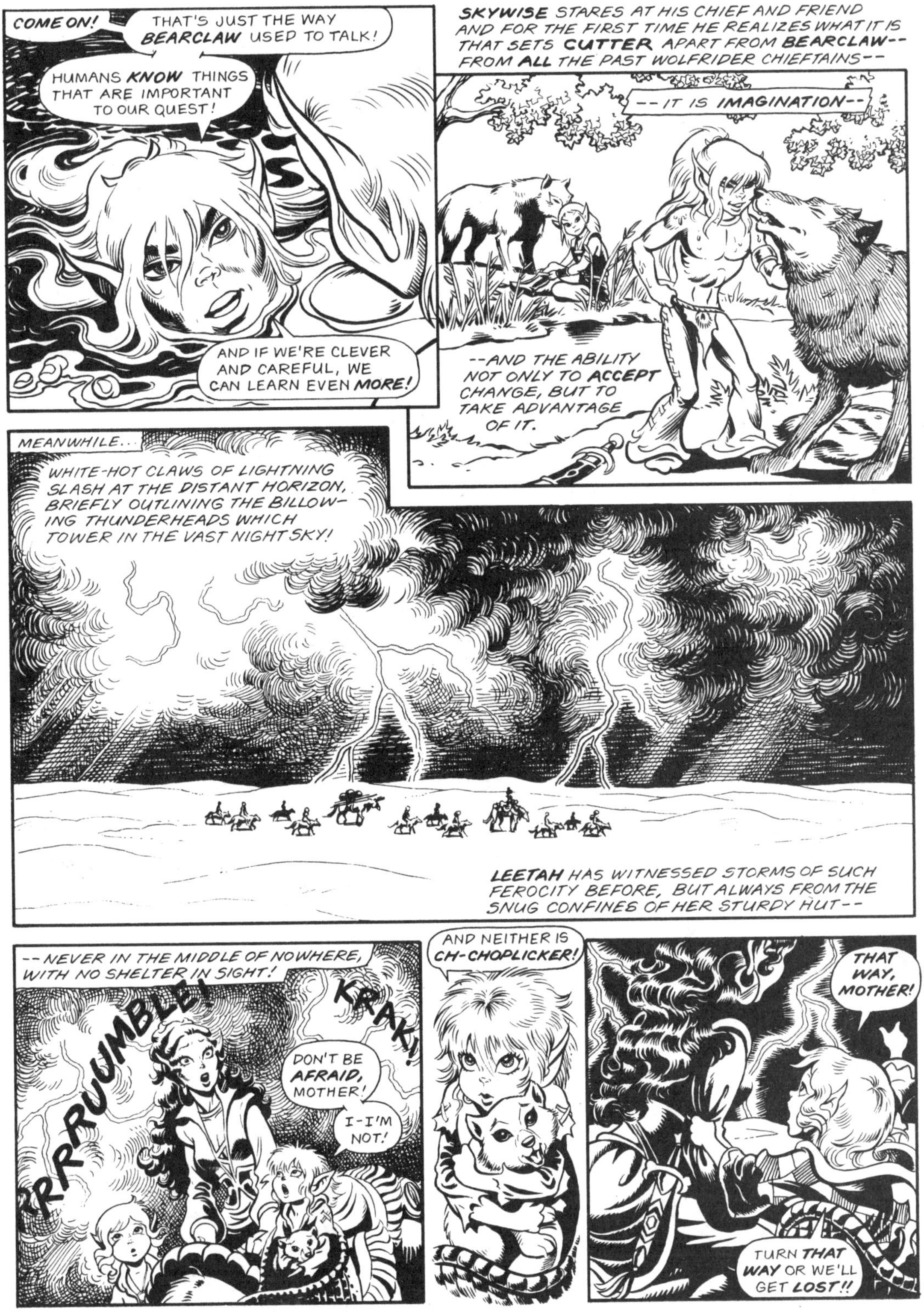
COME ON!
THAT'S JUST THE WAY BEARCLAW USED TO TALK!
HUMANS KNOW THINGS THAT ARE IMPORTANT TO OUR QUEST!
AND IF WE'RE CLEVER AND CAREFUL, WE CAN LEARN EVEN MORE!
SKYWISE STARES AT HIS CHIEF AND FRIEND AND FOR THE FIRST TIME HE REALIZES WHAT IT IS THAT SETS CUTTER APART FROM BEARCLAW-- FROM ALL THE PAST WOLFRIDER CHIEFTAINS--
--IT IS IMAGINATION--
--AND THE ABILITY NOT ONLY TO ACCEPT CHANGE, BUT TO TAKE ADVANTAGE OF IT.
MEANWHILE...
WHITE-HOT CLAWS OF LIGHTNING SLASH AT THE DISTANT HORIZON, BRIEFLY OUTLINING THE BILLOWING THUNDERHEADS WHICH TOWER IN THE VAST NIGHT SKY!
LEETAH HAS WITNESSED STORMS OF SUCH FEROCITY BEFORE, BUT ALWAYS FROM THE SNUG CONFINES OF HER STURDY HUT--
--NEVER IN THE MIDDLE OF NOWHERE, WITH NO SHELTER IN SIGHT!
RRRRUUMBLE!
KRAK!
DON'T BE AFRAID, MOTHER!
I-I'M NOT!
AND NEITHER IS CH-CHOPLICKER!
THAT WAY, MOTHER!
TURN THAT WAY OR WE'LL GET LOST!!

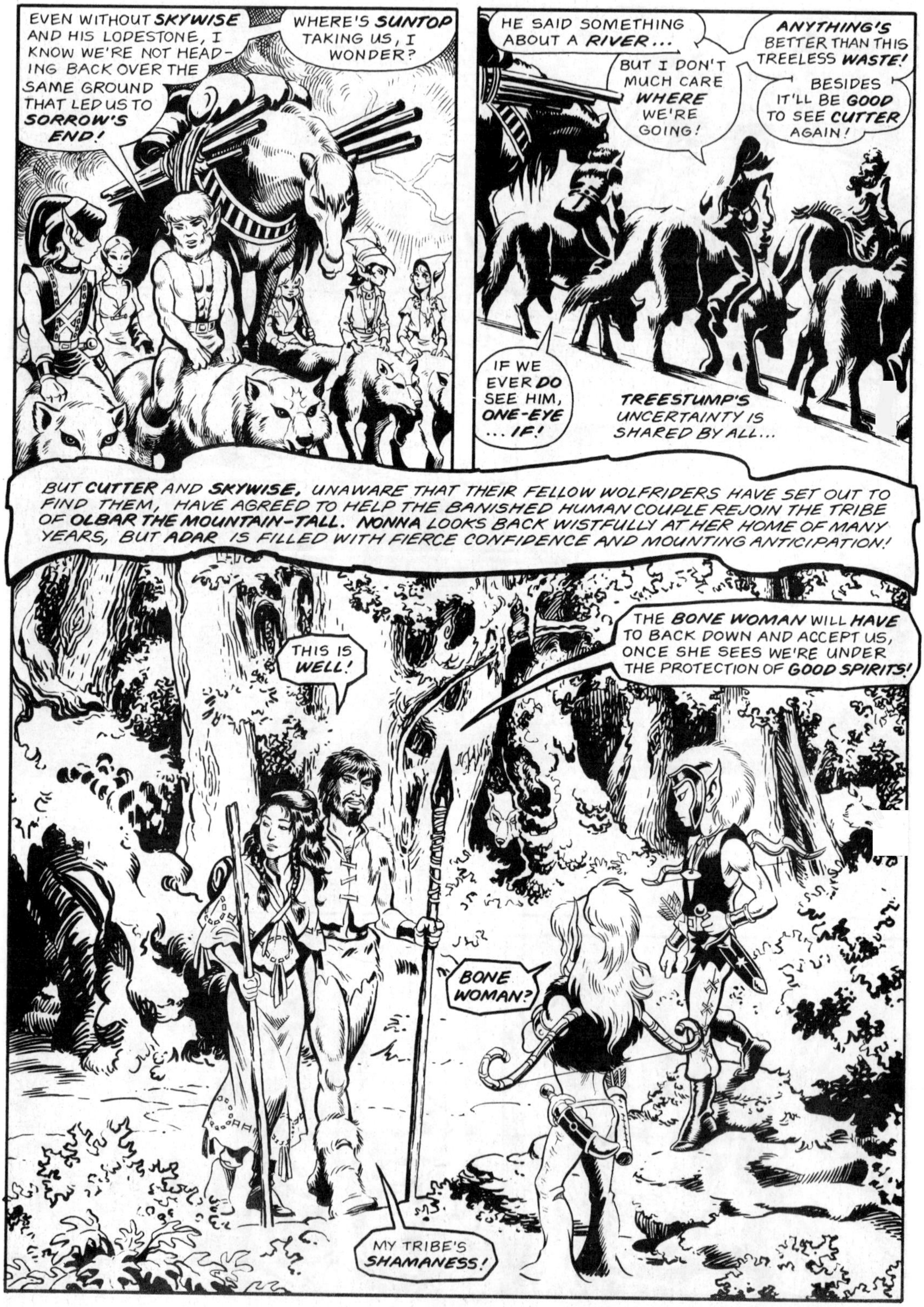
EVEN WITHOUT SKYWISE AND HIS LODESTONE, I KNOW WE'RE NOT HEADING BACK OVER THE SAME GROUND THAT LED US TO SORROW'S END!
WHERE'S SUNTOP TAKING US, I WONDER?
HE SAID SOMETHING ABOUT A RIVER...
BUT I DON'T MUCH CARE WHERE WE'RE GOING!
ANYTHING'S BETTER THAN THIS TREELESS WASTE!
BESIDES IT'LL BE GOOD TO SEE CUTTER AGAIN!
IF WE EVER DO SEE HIM, ONE-EYE ...IF!
TREESTUMP'S UNCERTAINTY IS SHARED BY ALL...
BUT CUTTER AND SKYWISE, UNAWARE THAT THEIR FELLOW WOLFRIDERS HAVE SET OUT TO FIND THEM, HAVE AGREED TO HELP THE BANISHED HUMAN COUPLE REJOIN THE TRIBE OF OLBAR THE MOUNTAIN-TALL. NONNA LOOKS BACK WISTFULLY AT HER HOME OF MANY YEARS, BUT ADAR IS FILLED WITH FIERCE CONFIDENCE AND MOUNTING ANTICIPATION!
THIS IS WELL!
THE BONE WOMAN WILL HAVE TO BACK DOWN AND ACCEPT US, ONCE SHE SEES WE'RE UNDER THE PROTECTION OF GOOD SPIRITS!
BONE WOMAN?
MY TRIBE'S SHAMANESS!

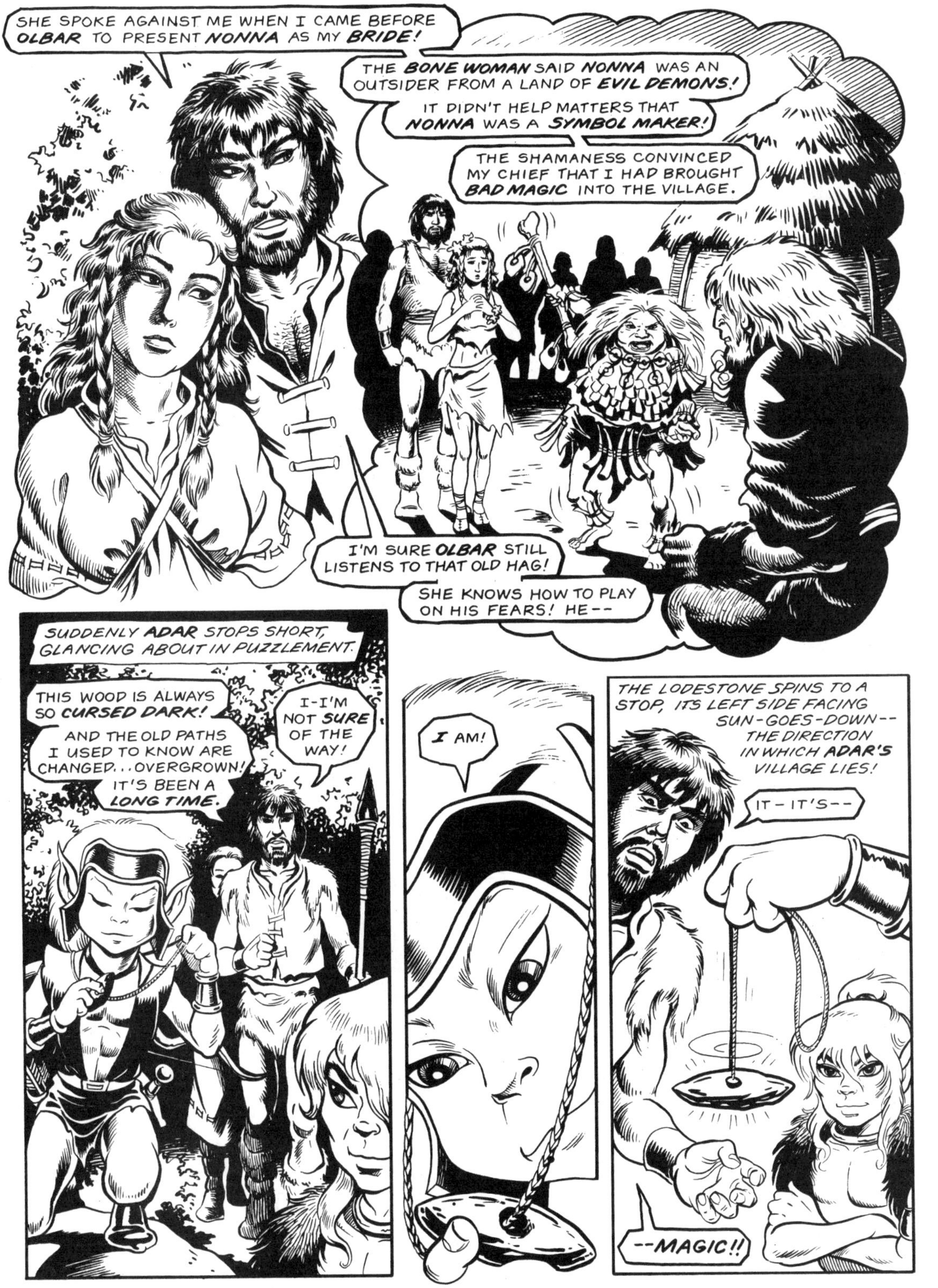
SHE SPOKE AGAINST ME WHEN I CAME BEFORE OLBAR TO PRESENT NONNA AS MY BRIDE!
THE BONE WOMAN SAID NONNA WAS AN OUTSIDER FROM A LAND OF EVIL DEMONS!
IT DIDN'T HELP MATTERS THAT NONNA WAS A SYMBOL MAKER!
THE SHAMANESS CONVINCED MY CHIEF THAT I HAD BROUGHT BAD MAGIC INTO THE VILLAGE.
I'M SURE OLBAR STILL LISTENS TO THAT OLD HAG!
SHE KNOWS HOW TO PLAY ON HIS FEARS! HE--
SUDDENLY ADAR STOPS SHORT, GLANCING ABOUT IN PUZZLEMENT.
THIS WOOD IS ALWAYS SO CURSED DARK!
AND THE OLD PATHS I USED TO KNOW ARE CHANGED...OVERGROWN!
IT'S BEEN A LONG TIME.
I-I'M NOT SURE OF THE WAY!
I AM!
THE LODESTONE SPINS TO A STOP, ITS LEFT SIDE FACING SUN-GOES-DOWN-- THE DIRECTION IN WHICH ADAR'S VILLAGE LIES!
IT-IT'S--
--MAGIC!!

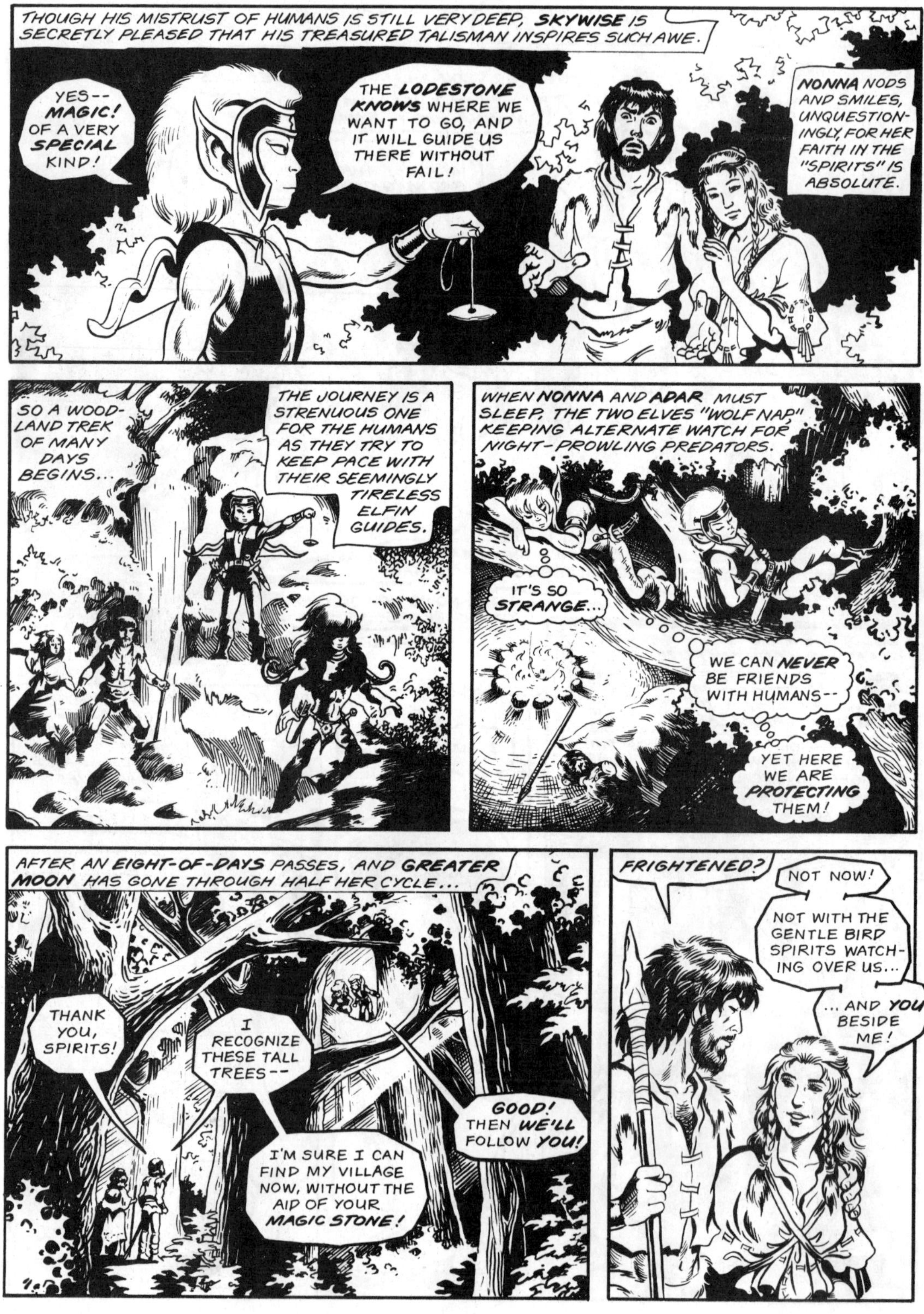
THOUGH HIS MISTRUST OF HUMANS IS STILL VERY DEEP, SKYWISE IS SECRETLY PLEASED THAT HIS TREASURED TALISMAN INSPIRES SUCH AWE.
YES-- MAGIC! OF A VERY SPECIAL KIND!
THE LODESTONE KNOWS WHERE WE WANT TO GO, AND IT WILL GUIDE US THERE WITHOUT FAIL!
NONNA NODS AND SMILES, UNQUESTIONINGLY, FOR HER FAITH IN THE "SPIRITS" IS ABSOLUTE.
SO A WOODLAND TREK OF MANY DAYS BEGINS...
THE JOURNEY IS A STRENUOUS ONE FOR THE HUMANS AS THEY TRY TO KEEP PACE WITH THEIR SEEMINGLY TIRELESS ELFIN GUIDES.
WHEN NONNA AND ADAR MUST SLEEP, THE TWO ELVES "WOLF NAP," KEEPING ALTERNATE WATCH FOR NIGHT-PROWLING PREDATORS.
IT'S SO STRANGE...
WE CAN NEVER BE FRIENDS WITH HUMANS--
YET HERE WE ARE PROTECTING THEM!
AFTER AN EIGHT-OF-DAYS PASSES, AND GREATER MOON HAS GONE THROUGH HALF HER CYCLE...
THANK YOU, SPIRITS!
I RECOGNIZE THESE TALL TREES--
I'M SURE I CAN FIND MY VILLAGE NOW, WITHOUT THE AID OF YOUR MAGIC STONE!
GOOD! THEN WE'LL FOLLOW YOU!
FRIGHTENED?
NOT NOW!
NOT WITH THE GENTLE BIRD SPIRITS WATCHING OVER US...
... AND YOU BESIDE ME!

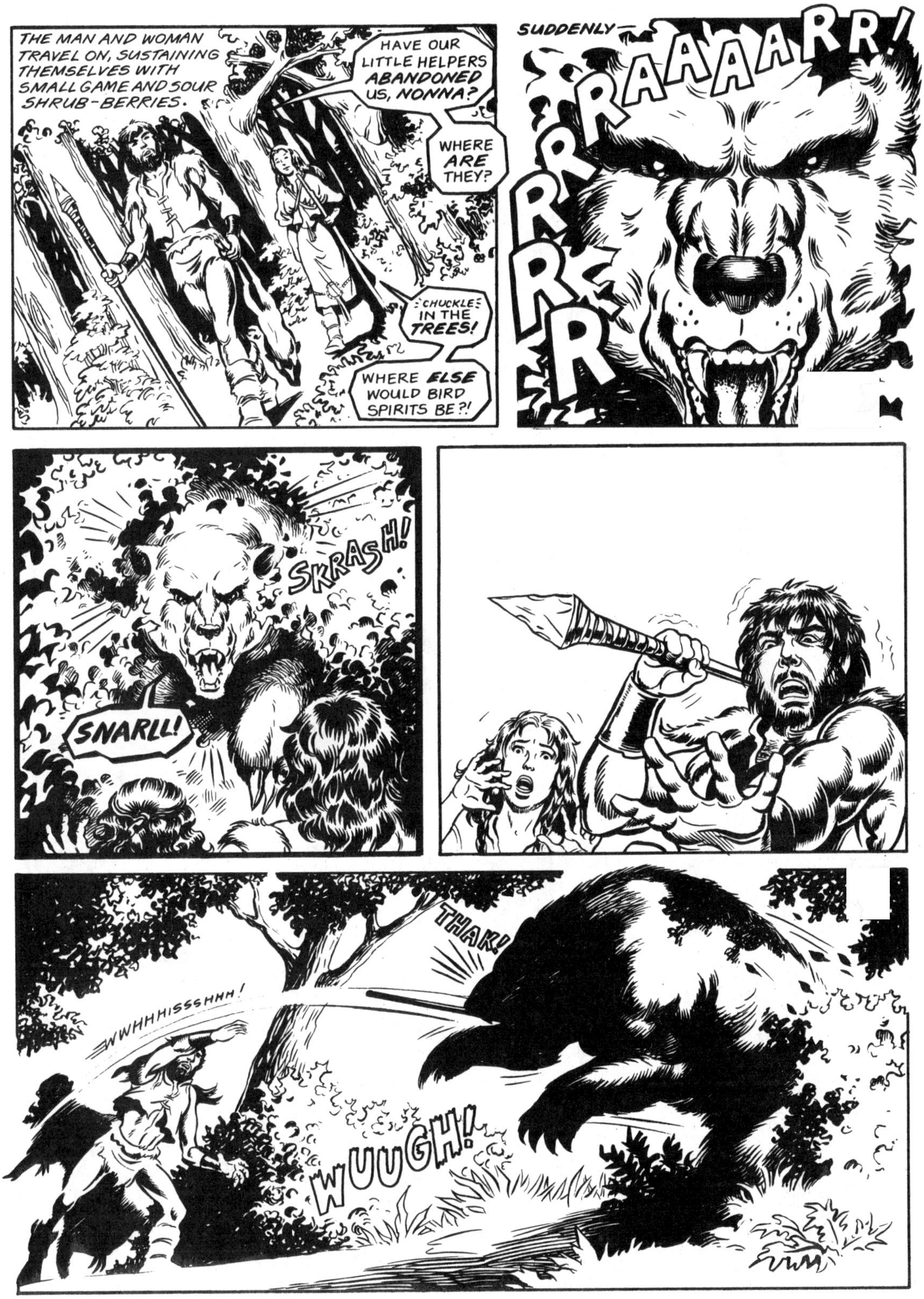
THE MAN AND WOMAN TRAVEL ON, SUSTAINING THEMSELVES WITH SMALL GAME AND SOUR SHRUB-BERRIES.
HAVE OUR LITTLE HELPERS ABANDONED US, NONNA?
WHERE ARE THEY?
CHUCKLE IN THE TREES!
WHERE ELSE WOULD BIRD SPIRITS BE?!
SUDDENLY—
RRRRRAAAAARR!
SKRASH!
SNARLL!
THAK!
WWHHHISSSHHH!
WUUGH!

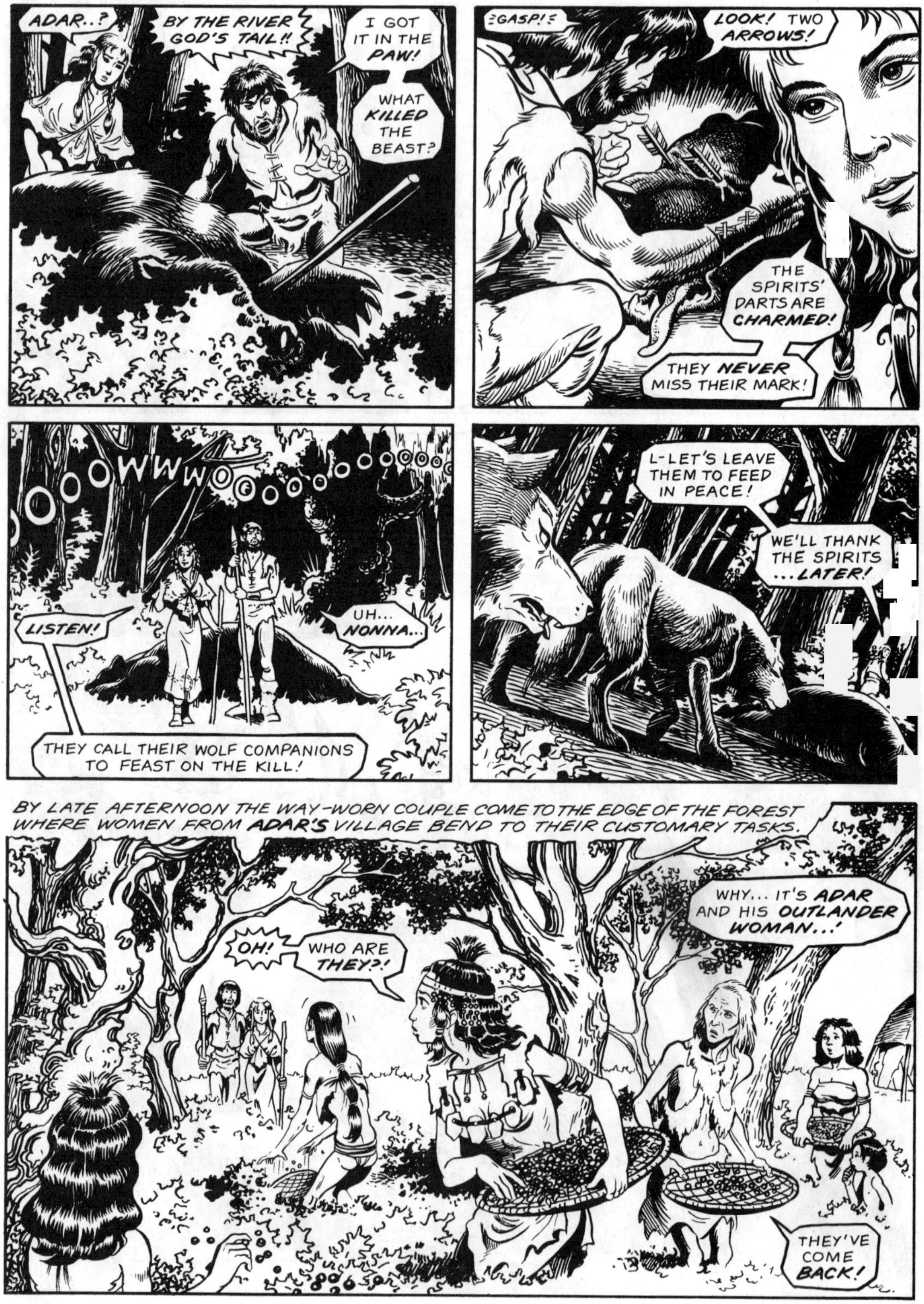

ADAR..?
BY THE RIVER GOD'S TAIL!!
I GOT IT IN THE PAW!
WHAT KILLED THE BEAST?
GASP!
LOOK! TWO ARROWS!
THE SPIRITS' DARTS ARE CHARMED!
THEY NEVER MISS THEIR MARK!
OOOOWWWOOOOOOOOOOOO
LISTEN!
UH... NONNA...
THEY CALL THEIR WOLF COMPANIONS TO FEAST ON THE KILL!
L-LET'S LEAVE THEM TO FEED IN PEACE!
WE'LL THANK THE SPIRITS ...LATER!
BY LATE AFTERNOON THE WAY-WORN COUPLE COME TO THE EDGE OF THE FOREST WHERE WOMEN FROM ADAR'S VILLAGE BEND TO THEIR CUSTOMARY TASKS.
OH!
WHO ARE THEY?!
WHY... IT'S ADAR AND HIS OUTLANDER WOMAN...!
THEY'VE COME BACK!

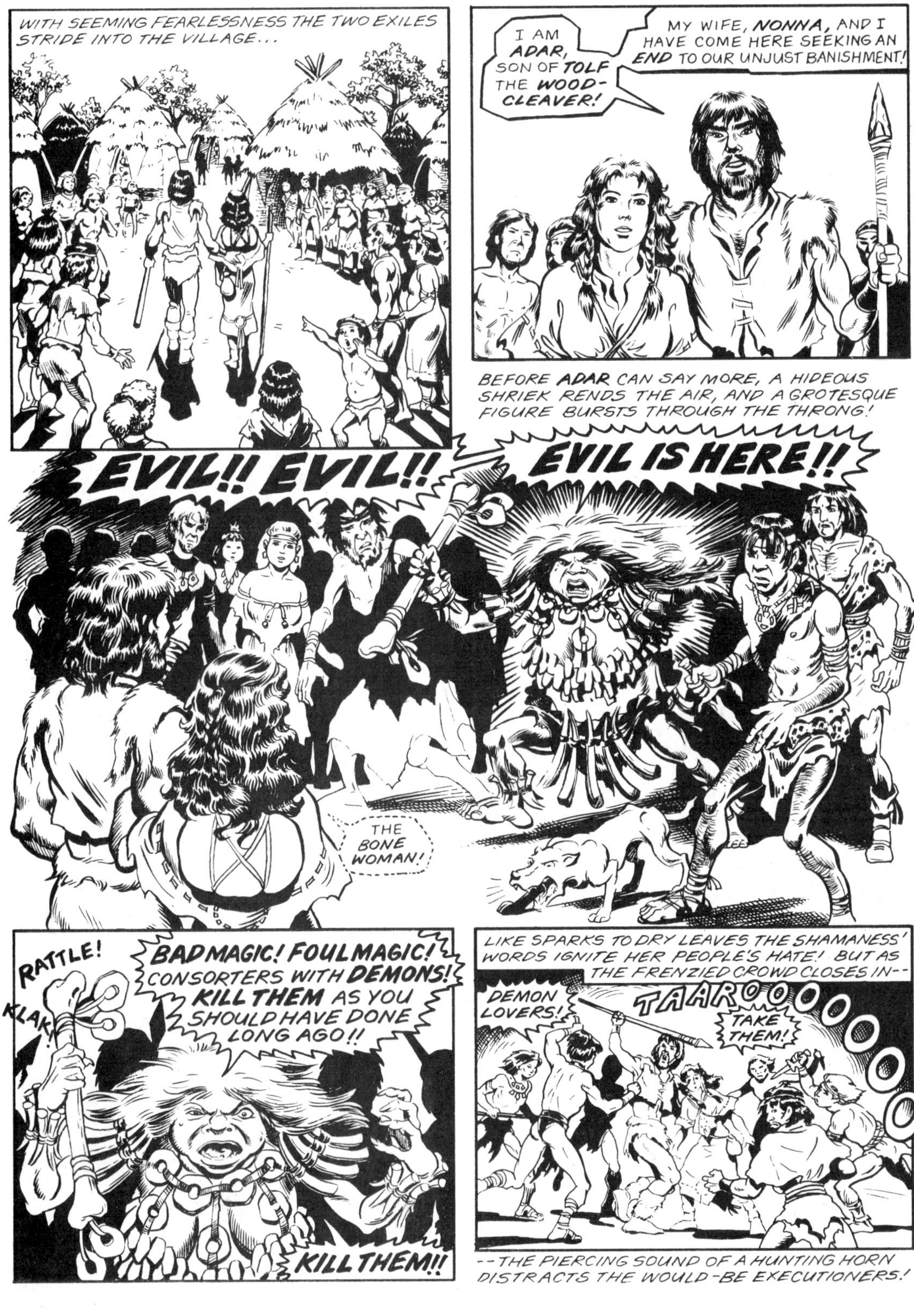
WITH SEEMING FEARLESSNESS THE TWO EXILES STRIDE INTO THE VILLAGE...
I AM ADAR, SON OF TOLF THE WOOD-CLEAVER!
MY WIFE, NONNA, AND I HAVE COME HERE SEEKING AN END TO OUR UNJUST BANISHMENT!
BEFORE ADAR CAN SAY MORE, A HIDEOUS SHRIEK RENDS THE AIR, AND A GROTESQUE FIGURE BURSTS THROUGH THE THRONG!
EVIL!! EVIL!!
EVIL IS HERE!!
THE BONE WOMAN!
RATTLE!
KLAK
BAD MAGIC! FOUL MAGIC! CONSORTERS WITH DEMONS! KILL THEM AS YOU SHOULD HAVE DONE LONG AGO!!
KILL THEM!!
LIKE SPARKS TO DRY LEAVES THE SHAMANESS' WORDS IGNITE HER PEOPLE'S HATE! BUT AS THE FRENZIED CROWD CLOSES IN--
DEMON LOVERS!
TAAROOOOOOOOO
TAKE THEM!
--THE PIERCING SOUND OF A HUNTING HORN DISTRACTS THE WOULD-BE EXECUTIONERS!

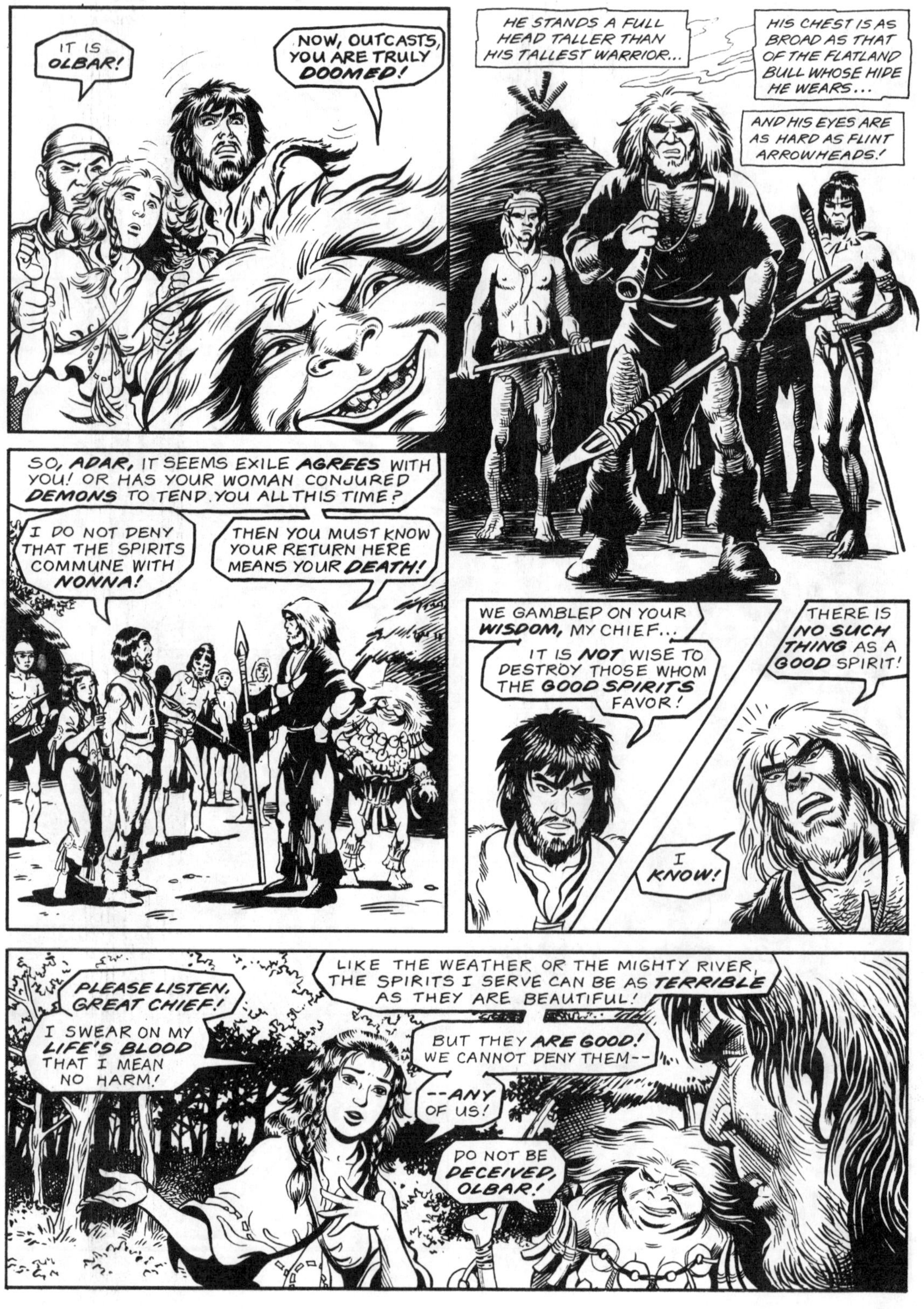
IT IS OLBAR!
NOW, OUTCASTS, YOU ARE TRULY DOOMED!
HE STANDS A FULL HEAD TALLER THAN HIS TALLEST WARRIOR...
HIS CHEST IS AS BROAD AS THAT OF THE FLATLAND BULL WHOSE HIDE HE WEARS...
AND HIS EYES ARE AS HARD AS FLINT ARROWHEADS!
SO, ADAR, IT SEEMS EXILE AGREES WITH YOU! OR HAS YOUR WOMAN CONJURED DEMONS TO TEND YOU ALL THIS TIME?
I DO NOT DENY THAT THE SPIRITS COMMUNE WITH NONNA!
THEN YOU MUST KNOW YOUR RETURN HERE MEANS YOUR DEATH!
WE GAMBLED ON YOUR WISDOM, MY CHIEF...
IT IS NOT WISE TO DESTROY THOSE WHOM THE GOOD SPIRITS FAVOR!
THERE IS NO SUCH THING AS A GOOD SPIRIT!
I KNOW!
PLEASE LISTEN, GREAT CHIEF!
I SWEAR ON MY LIFE'S BLOOD THAT I MEAN NO HARM!
LIKE THE WEATHER OR THE MIGHTY RIVER, THE SPIRITS I SERVE CAN BE AS TERRIBLE AS THEY ARE BEAUTIFUL!
BUT THEY ARE GOOD! WE CANNOT DENY THEM--
--ANY OF US!
DO NOT BE DECEIVED, OLBAR!

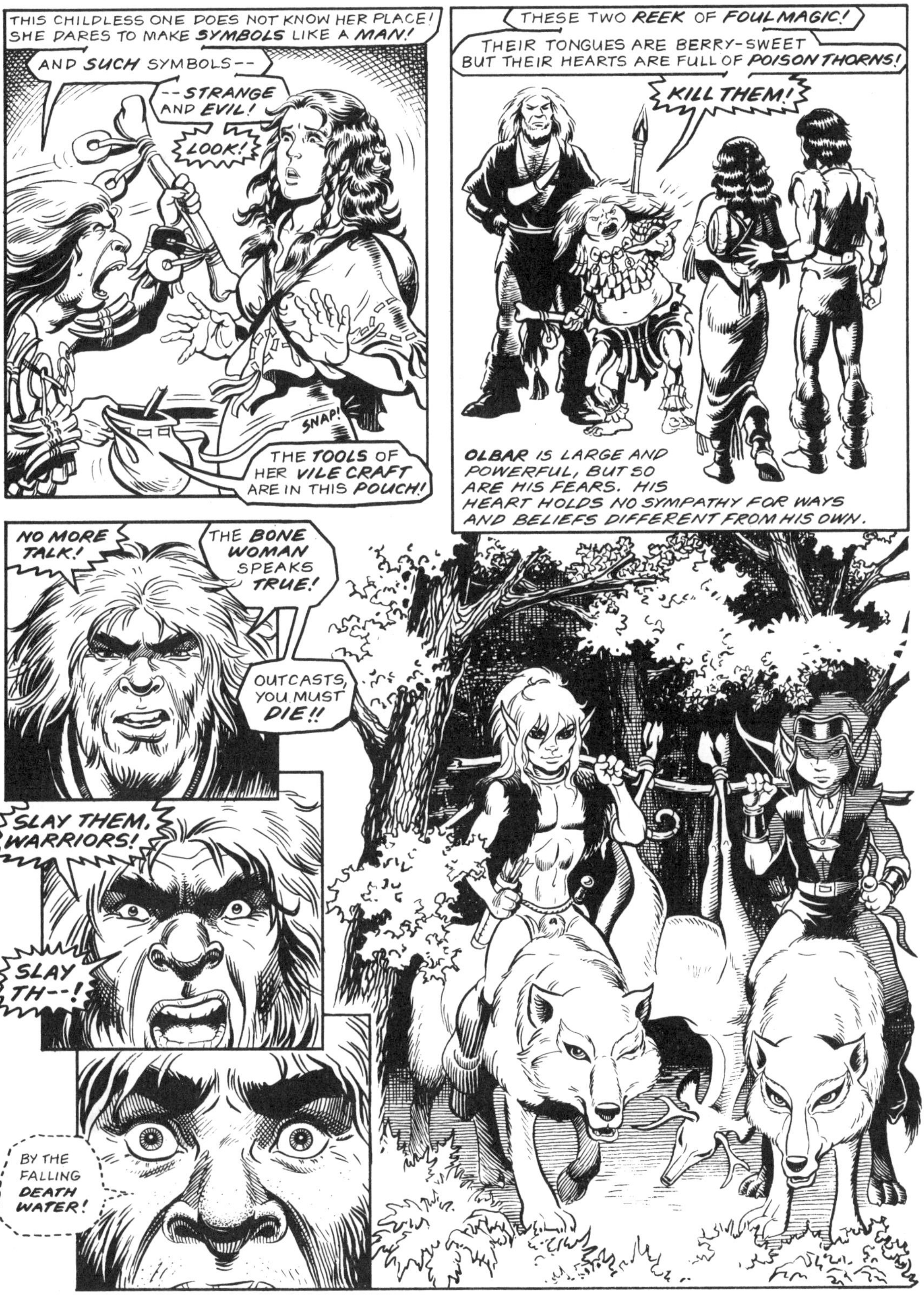
THIS CHILDLESS ONE DOES NOT KNOW HER PLACE! SHE DARES TO MAKE SYMBOLS LIKE A MAN!
AND SUCH SYMBOLS--
--STRANGE AND EVIL!
LOOK!
SNAP!
THE TOOLS OF HER VILE CRAFT ARE IN THIS POUCH!
THESE TWO REEK OF FOUL MAGIC!
THEIR TONGUES ARE BERRY-SWEET BUT THEIR HEARTS ARE FULL OF POISON THORNS!
KILL THEM!
OLBAR IS LARGE AND POWERFUL, BUT SO ARE HIS FEARS. HIS HEART HOLDS NO SYMPATHY FOR WAYS AND BELIEFS DIFFERENT FROM HIS OWN.
NO MORE TALK!
THE BONE WOMAN SPEAKS TRUE!
OUTCASTS, YOU MUST DIE!!
SLAY THEM, WARRIORS!
SLAY TH--!
BY THE FALLING DEATH WATER!

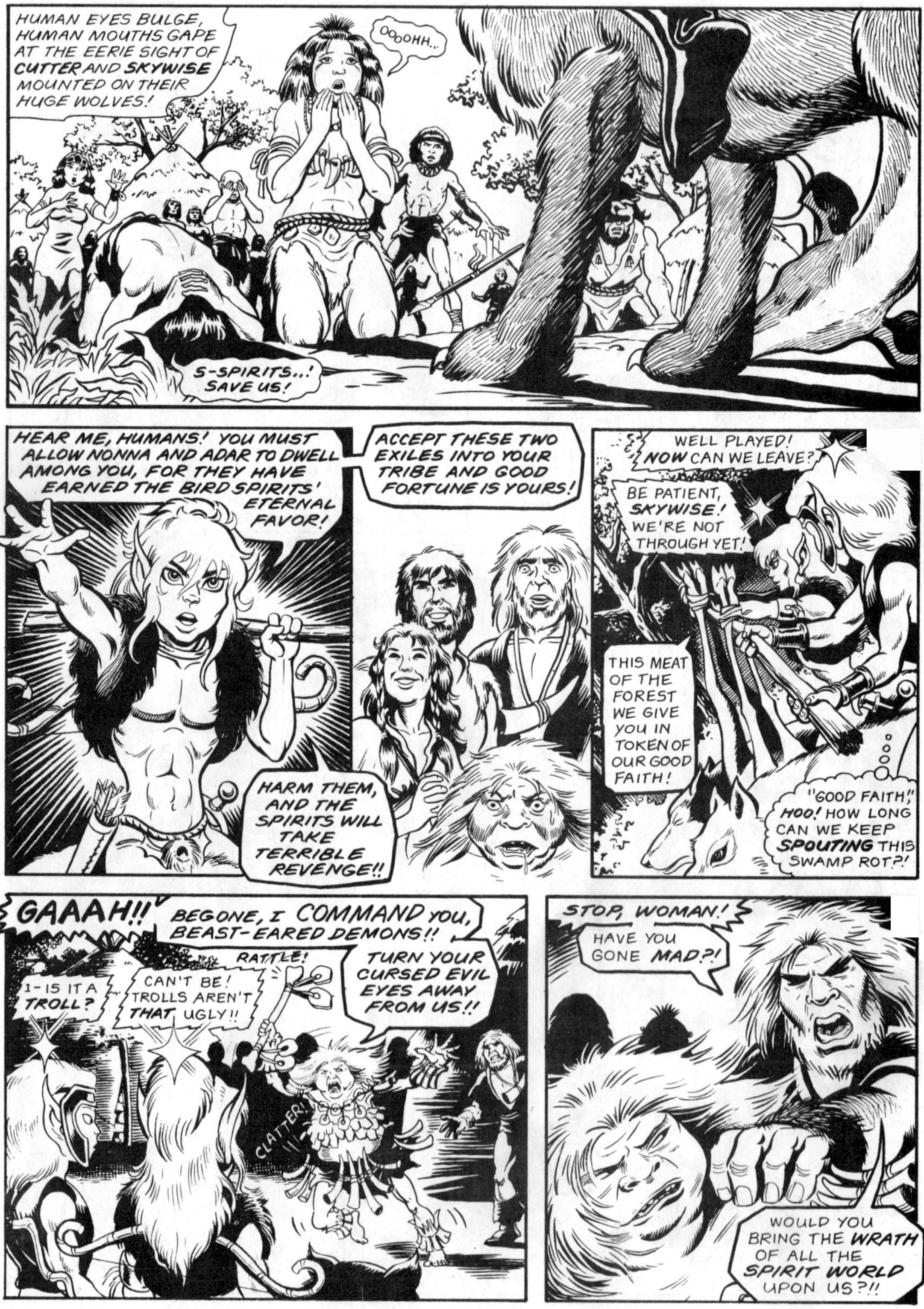

HUMAN EYES BULGE, HUMAN MOUTHS GAPE AT THE EERIE SIGHT OF CUTTER AND SKYWISE MOUNTED ON THEIR HUGE WOLVES!
OOOOHH...
S-SPIRITS...! SAVE US!
HEAR ME, HUMANS! YOU MUST ALLOW NONNA AND ADAR TO DWELL AMONG YOU, FOR THEY HAVE EARNED THE BIRD SPIRITS' ETERNAL FAVOR!
ACCEPT THESE TWO EXILES INTO YOUR TRIBE AND GOOD FORTUNE IS YOURS!
HARM THEM, AND THE SPIRITS WILL TAKE TERRIBLE REVENGE!!
WELL PLAYED! NOW CAN WE LEAVE?
BE PATIENT, SKYWISE! WE'RE NOT THROUGH YET!
THIS MEAT OF THE FOREST WE GIVE YOU IN TOKEN OF OUR GOOD FAITH!
"GOOD FAITH," HOO! HOW LONG CAN WE KEEP SPOUTING THIS SWAMP ROT?!
GAAAH!!
BEGONE, I COMMAND YOU, BEAST-EARED DEMONS!!
RATTLE!
I-IS IT A TROLL?
CAN'T BE! TROLLS AREN'T THAT UGLY!!
TURN YOUR CURSED EVIL EYES AWAY FROM US!!
CLATTER!
STOP, WOMAN!
HAVE YOU GONE MAD?!
WOULD YOU BRING THE WRATH OF ALL THE SPIRIT WORLD UPON US?!!

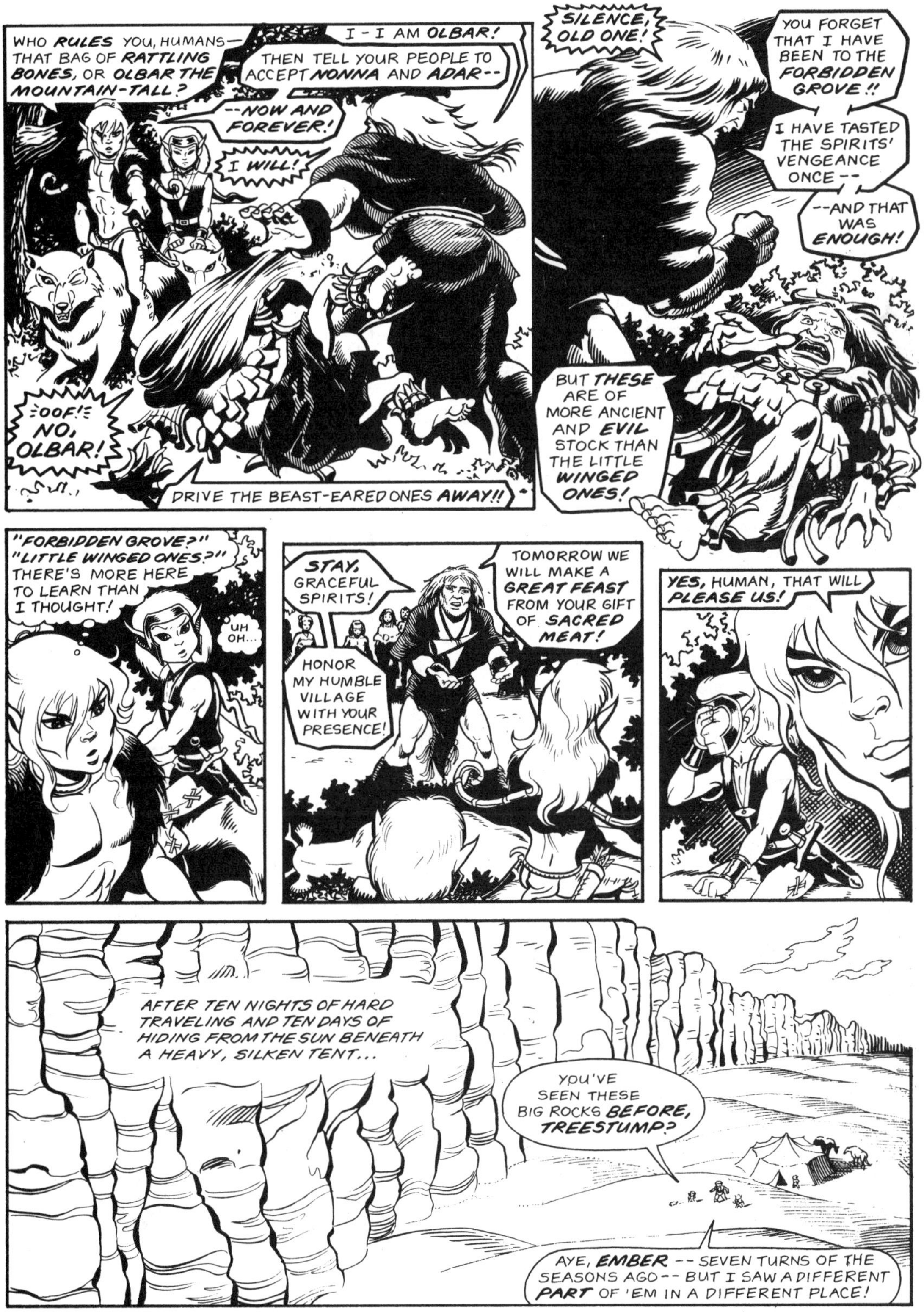
WHO RULES YOU, HUMANS— THAT BAG OF RATTLING BONES, OR OLBAR THE MOUNTAIN-TALL?
I-I AM OLBAR!
THEN TELL YOUR PEOPLE TO ACCEPT NONNA AND ADAR--
--NOW AND FOREVER!
I WILL!
OOF! NO, OLBAR!
DRIVE THE BEAST-EARED ONES AWAY!!
SILENCE, OLD ONE!
YOU FORGET THAT I HAVE BEEN TO THE FORBIDDEN GROVE!!
I HAVE TASTED THE SPIRITS' VENGEANCE ONCE--
--AND THAT WAS ENOUGH!
BUT THESE ARE OF MORE ANCIENT AND EVIL STOCK THAN THE LITTLE WINGED ONES!
"FORBIDDEN GROVE?" "LITTLE WINGED ONES?" THERE'S MORE HERE TO LEARN THAN I THOUGHT!
UH OH...
STAY, GRACEFUL SPIRITS!
HONOR MY HUMBLE VILLAGE WITH YOUR PRESENCE!
TOMORROW WE WILL MAKE A GREAT FEAST FROM YOUR GIFT OF SACRED MEAT!
YES, HUMAN, THAT WILL PLEASE US!
AFTER TEN NIGHTS OF HARD TRAVELING AND TEN DAYS OF HIDING FROM THE SUN BENEATH A HEAVY, SILKEN TENT...
YOU'VE SEEN THESE BIG ROCKS BEFORE, TREESTUMP?
AYE, EMBER -- SEVEN TURNS OF THE SEASONS AGO-- BUT I SAW A DIFFERENT PART OF 'EM IN A DIFFERENT PLACE!

INSIDE THE TENT THE WOLFRIDERS EAT AND DRINK SPARINGLY OF THEIR DWINDLING SUPPLIES.

IF ONLY *SUNTOP* COULD TELL US MORE ABOUT WHERE WE'RE GOING.

WE'VE *GOT* TO GET OUT OF THIS DESERT SOON!

THE CUB CAN'T REALLY UNDERSTAND WHAT IT'S LIKE TO *SUFFER* IN THIS WILDERNESS.

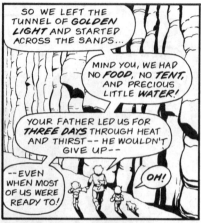

SO WE LEFT THE TUNNEL OF *GOLDEN LIGHT* AND STARTED ACROSS THE SANDS...

MIND YOU, WE HAD NO *FOOD*, NO *TENT*, AND PRECIOUS LITTLE *WATER*!

YOUR FATHER LED US FOR *THREE DAYS* THROUGH HEAT AND THIRST-- HE WOULDN'T GIVE UP--

--EVEN WHEN MOST OF US WERE READY TO!

OH!

LOOK! OVER THERE!

"THERE'S A LITTLE *CAVE* IN THE CLIFF SIDE!" CRIES *EMBER*.

CAREFUL, SHE-CUB!

WATCH OUT FOR SNAKES!

OOO!

THERE'S NO SNAKES IN HERE, *TREESTUMP*--

BUT I SURE SMELL SOME-THING!

TREESTUMP SENDS FOR THE OTHERS TO SHARE IN *EMBER'S* DISCOVERY...

SUNTOP!

LOOK WHAT I FOUND!!

BONES!!

HERE'S A *FUNNY* LOOKING ONE!

SEE?

R-RRUFF! YAP!

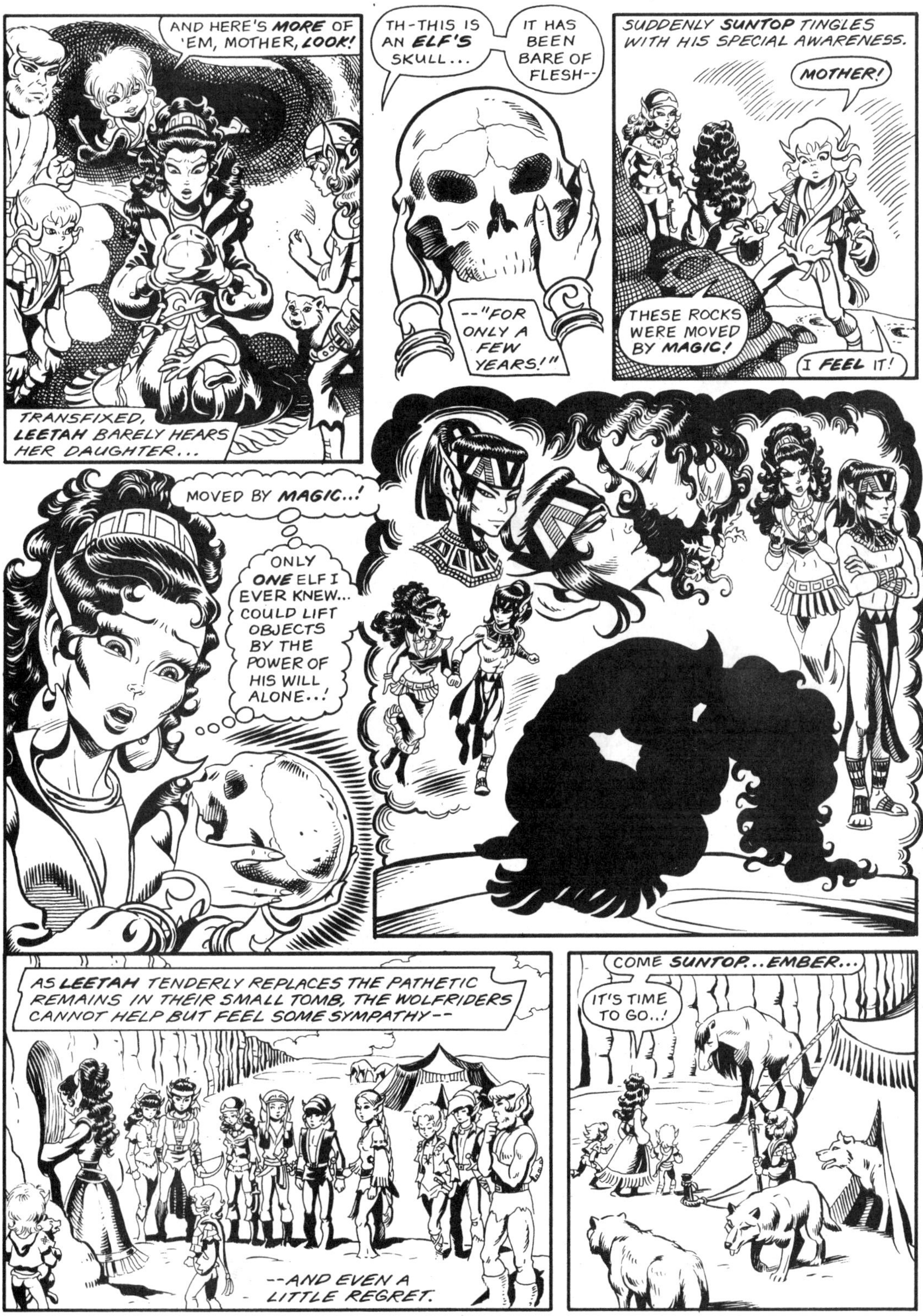
AND HERE'S MORE OF 'EM, MOTHER, LOOK!
TRANSFIXED, LEETAH BARELY HEARS HER DAUGHTER...
TH-THIS IS AN ELF'S SKULL...
IT HAS BEEN BARE OF FLESH--
--"FOR ONLY A FEW YEARS!"
SUDDENLY SUNTOP TINGLES WITH HIS SPECIAL AWARENESS.
MOTHER!
THESE ROCKS WERE MOVED BY MAGIC!
I FEEL IT!
MOVED BY MAGIC..!
ONLY ONE ELF I EVER KNEW... COULD LIFT OBJECTS BY THE POWER OF HIS WILL ALONE..!
AS LEETAH TENDERLY REPLACES THE PATHETIC REMAINS IN THEIR SMALL TOMB, THE WOLFRIDERS CANNOT HELP BUT FEEL SOME SYMPATHY--
--AND EVEN A LITTLE REGRET.
COME SUNTOP...EMBER...
IT'S TIME TO GO..!

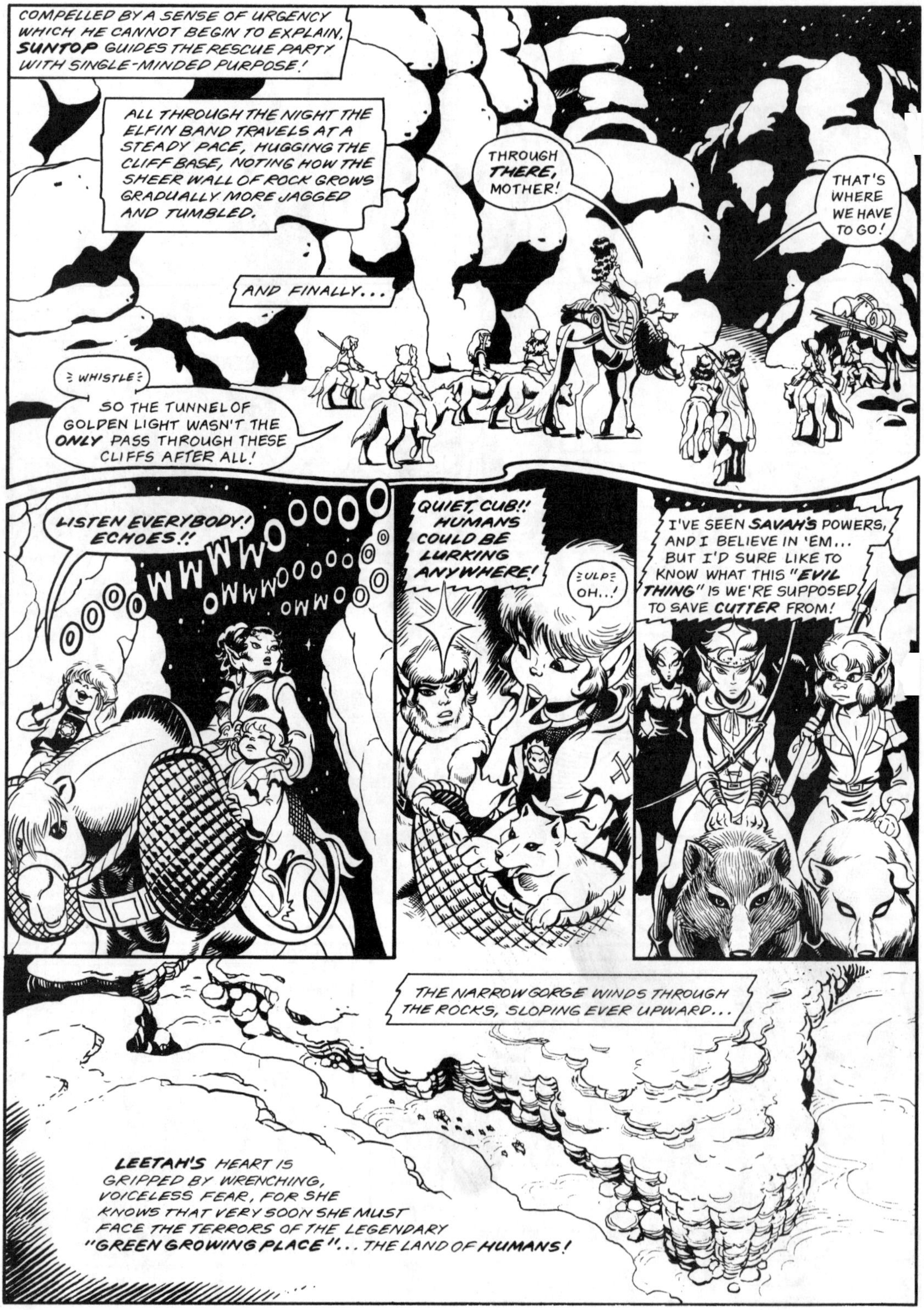

COMPELLED BY A SENSE OF URGENCY WHICH HE CANNOT BEGIN TO EXPLAIN, SUNTOP GUIDES THE RESCUE PARTY WITH SINGLE-MINDED PURPOSE!
ALL THROUGH THE NIGHT THE ELFIN BAND TRAVELS AT A STEADY PACE, HUGGING THE CLIFF BASE, NOTING HOW THE SHEER WALL OF ROCK GROWS GRADUALLY MORE JAGGED AND TUMBLED.
THROUGH THERE, MOTHER!
THAT'S WHERE WE HAVE TO GO!
AND FINALLY...
WHISTLE
SO THE TUNNEL OF GOLDEN LIGHT WASN'T THE ONLY PASS THROUGH THESE CLIFFS AFTER ALL!
LISTEN EVERYBODY! ECHOES!!
OOOOWWWWOOOOOO
OWWWOOOOOO
OWWOOOO
QUIET, CUB!! HUMANS COULD BE LURKING ANYWHERE!
ULP
OH...!
I'VE SEEN SAVAH'S POWERS, AND I BELIEVE IN 'EM... BUT I'D SURE LIKE TO KNOW WHAT THIS "EVIL THING" IS WE'RE SUPPOSED TO SAVE CUTTER FROM!
THE NARROW GORGE WINDS THROUGH THE ROCKS, SLOPING EVER UPWARD...
LEETAH'S HEART IS GRIPPED BY WRENCHING, VOICELESS FEAR, FOR SHE KNOWS THAT VERY SOON SHE MUST FACE THE TERRORS OF THE LEGENDARY "GREEN GROWING PLACE"... THE LAND OF HUMANS!

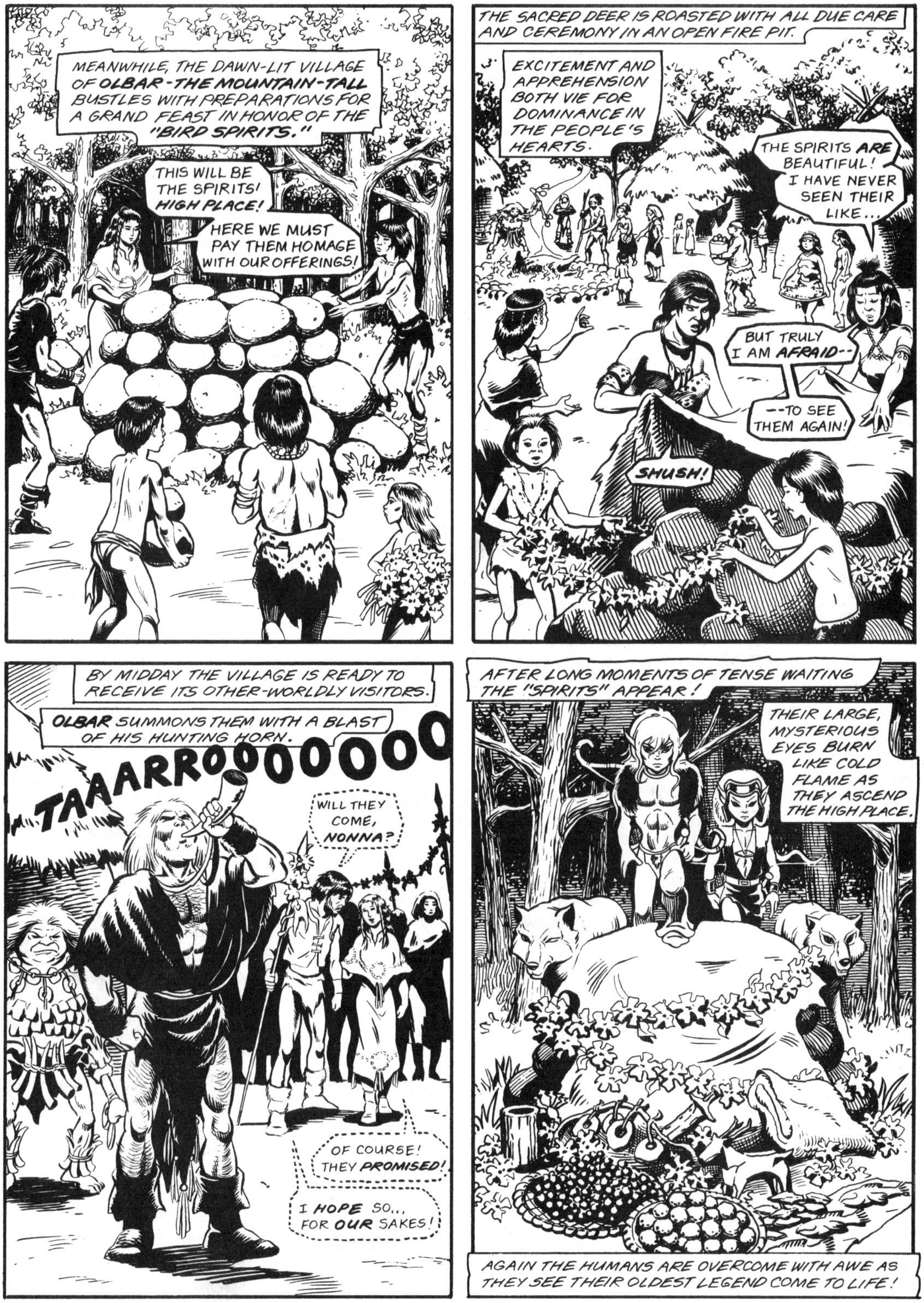
MEANWHILE, THE DAWN-LIT VILLAGE OF OLBAR-THE MOUNTAIN-TALL BUSTLES WITH PREPARATIONS FOR A GRAND FEAST IN HONOR OF THE "BIRD SPIRITS."
THIS WILL BE THE SPIRITS! HIGH PLACE!
HERE WE MUST PAY THEM HOMAGE WITH OUR OFFERINGS!
THE SACRED DEER IS ROASTED WITH ALL DUE CARE AND CEREMONY IN AN OPEN FIRE PIT.
EXCITEMENT AND APPREHENSION BOTH VIE FOR DOMINANCE IN THE PEOPLE'S HEARTS.
THE SPIRITS ARE BEAUTIFUL! I HAVE NEVER SEEN THEIR LIKE...
BUT TRULY I AM AFRAID--
--TO SEE THEM AGAIN!
SHUSH!
BY MIDDAY THE VILLAGE IS READY TO RECEIVE ITS OTHER-WORLDLY VISITORS.
OLBAR SUMMONS THEM WITH A BLAST OF HIS HUNTING HORN.
TAAARROOOOOOOO
WILL THEY COME, NONNA?
OF COURSE! THEY PROMISED!
I HOPE SO... FOR OUR SAKES!
AFTER LONG MOMENTS OF TENSE WAITING THE "SPIRITS" APPEAR!
THEIR LARGE, MYSTERIOUS EYES BURN LIKE COLD FLAME AS THEY ASCEND THE HIGH PLACE.
AGAIN THE HUMANS ARE OVERCOME WITH AWE AS THEY SEE THEIR OLDEST LEGEND COME TO LIFE!

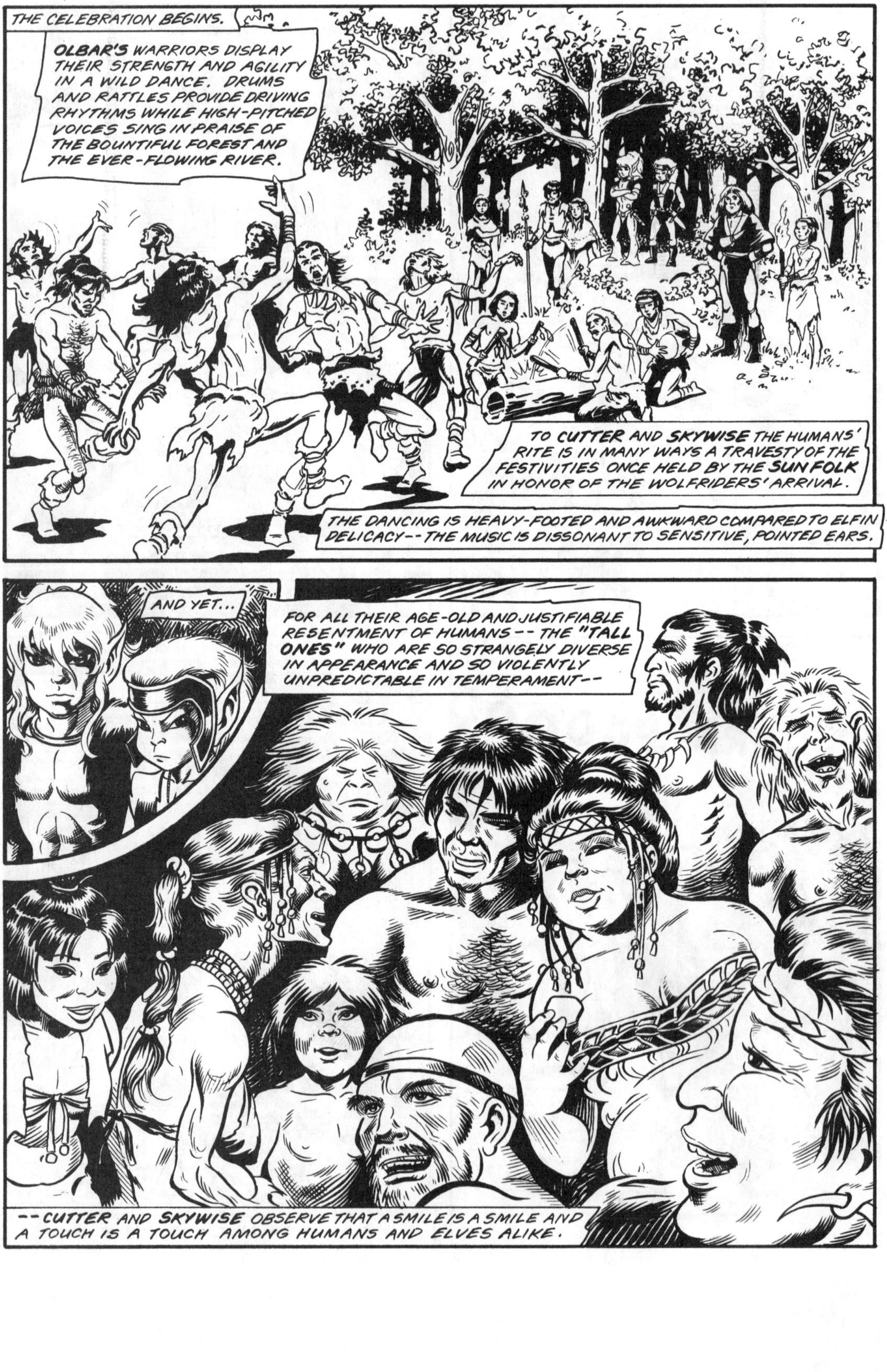
THE CELEBRATION BEGINS.
OLBAR'S WARRIORS DISPLAY THEIR STRENGTH AND AGILITY IN A WILD DANCE. DRUMS AND RATTLES PROVIDE DRIVING RHYTHMS WHILE HIGH-PITCHED VOICES SING IN PRAISE OF THE BOUNTIFUL FOREST AND THE EVER-FLOWING RIVER.
TO CUTTER AND SKYWISE THE HUMANS' RITE IS IN MANY WAYS A TRAVESTY OF THE FESTIVITIES ONCE HELD BY THE SUN FOLK IN HONOR OF THE WOLFRIDERS' ARRIVAL.
THE DANCING IS HEAVY-FOOTED AND AWKWARD COMPARED TO ELFIN DELICACY--THE MUSIC IS DISSONANT TO SENSITIVE, POINTED EARS.
AND YET...
FOR ALL THEIR AGE-OLD AND JUSTIFIABLE RESENTMENT OF HUMANS--THE "TALL ONES" WHO ARE SO STRANGELY DIVERSE IN APPEARANCE AND SO VIOLENTLY UNPREDICTABLE IN TEMPERAMENT--
--CUTTER AND SKYWISE OBSERVE THAT A SMILE IS A SMILE AND A TOUCH IS A TOUCH AMONG HUMANS AND ELVES ALIKE.

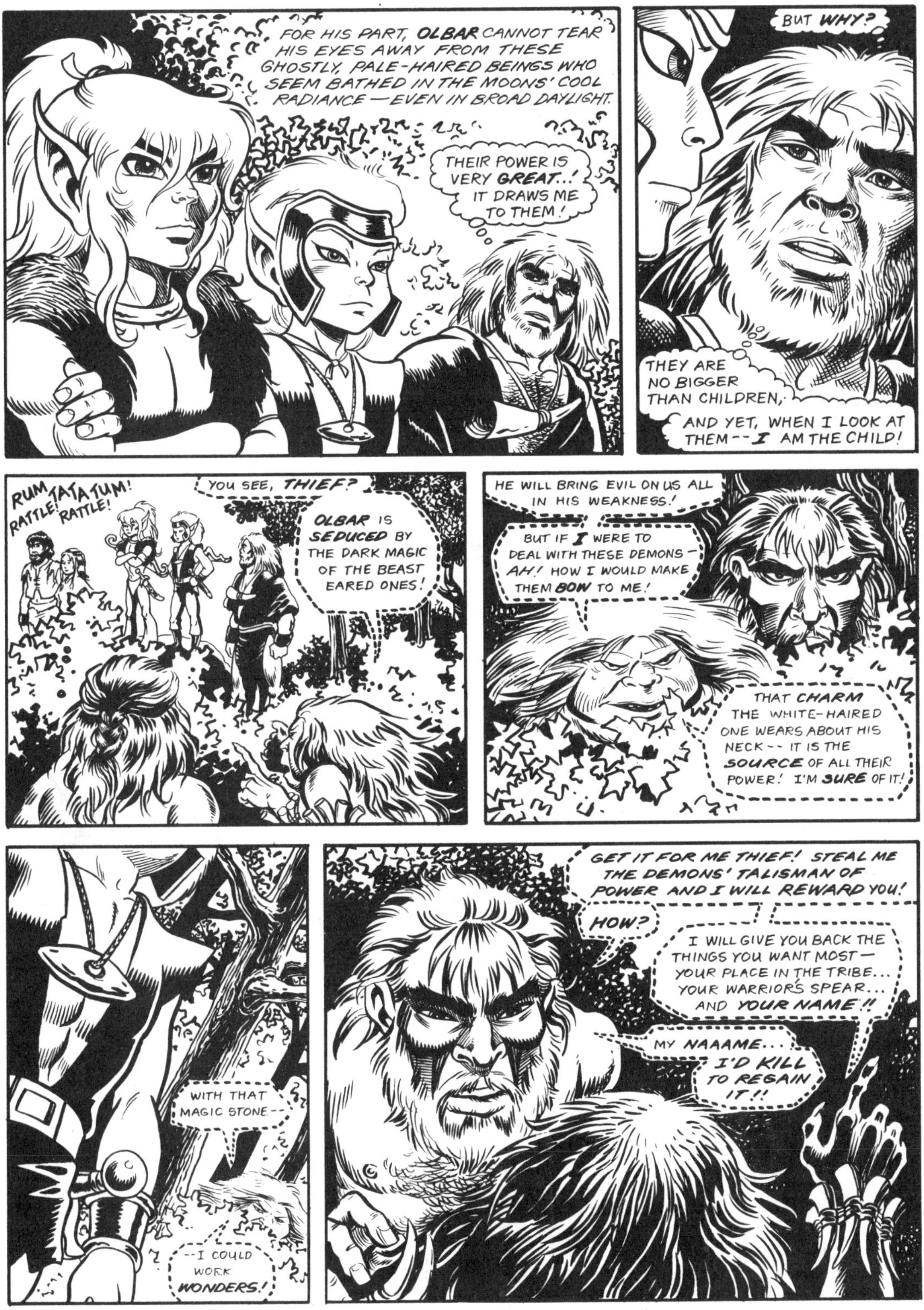
FOR HIS PART, OLBAR CANNOT TEAR HIS EYES AWAY FROM THESE GHOSTLY, PALE-HAIRED BEINGS WHO SEEM BATHED IN THE MOONS' COOL RADIANCE — EVEN IN BROAD DAYLIGHT.
THEIR POWER IS VERY GREAT...! IT DRAWS ME TO THEM!
BUT WHY?
THEY ARE NO BIGGER THAN CHILDREN,
AND YET, WHEN I LOOK AT THEM--I AM THE CHILD!
RUM TATATUM! RATTLE! RATTLE!
YOU SEE, THIEF?
OLBAR IS SEDUCED BY THE DARK MAGIC OF THE BEAST EARED ONES!
HE WILL BRING EVIL ON US ALL IN HIS WEAKNESS!
BUT IF I WERE TO DEAL WITH THESE DEMONS— AH! HOW I WOULD MAKE THEM BOW TO ME!
THAT CHARM THE WHITE-HAIRED ONE WEARS ABOUT HIS NECK-- IT IS THE SOURCE OF ALL THEIR POWER! I'M SURE OF IT!
WITH THAT MAGIC STONE--
--I COULD WORK WONDERS!
GET IT FOR ME THIEF! STEAL ME THE DEMONS' TALISMAN OF POWER AND I WILL REWARD YOU!
HOW?
I WILL GIVE YOU BACK THE THINGS YOU WANT MOST— YOUR PLACE IN THE TRIBE... YOUR WARRIOR'S SPEAR... AND YOUR NAME!!
MY NAAAME... I'D KILL TO REGAIN IT!!

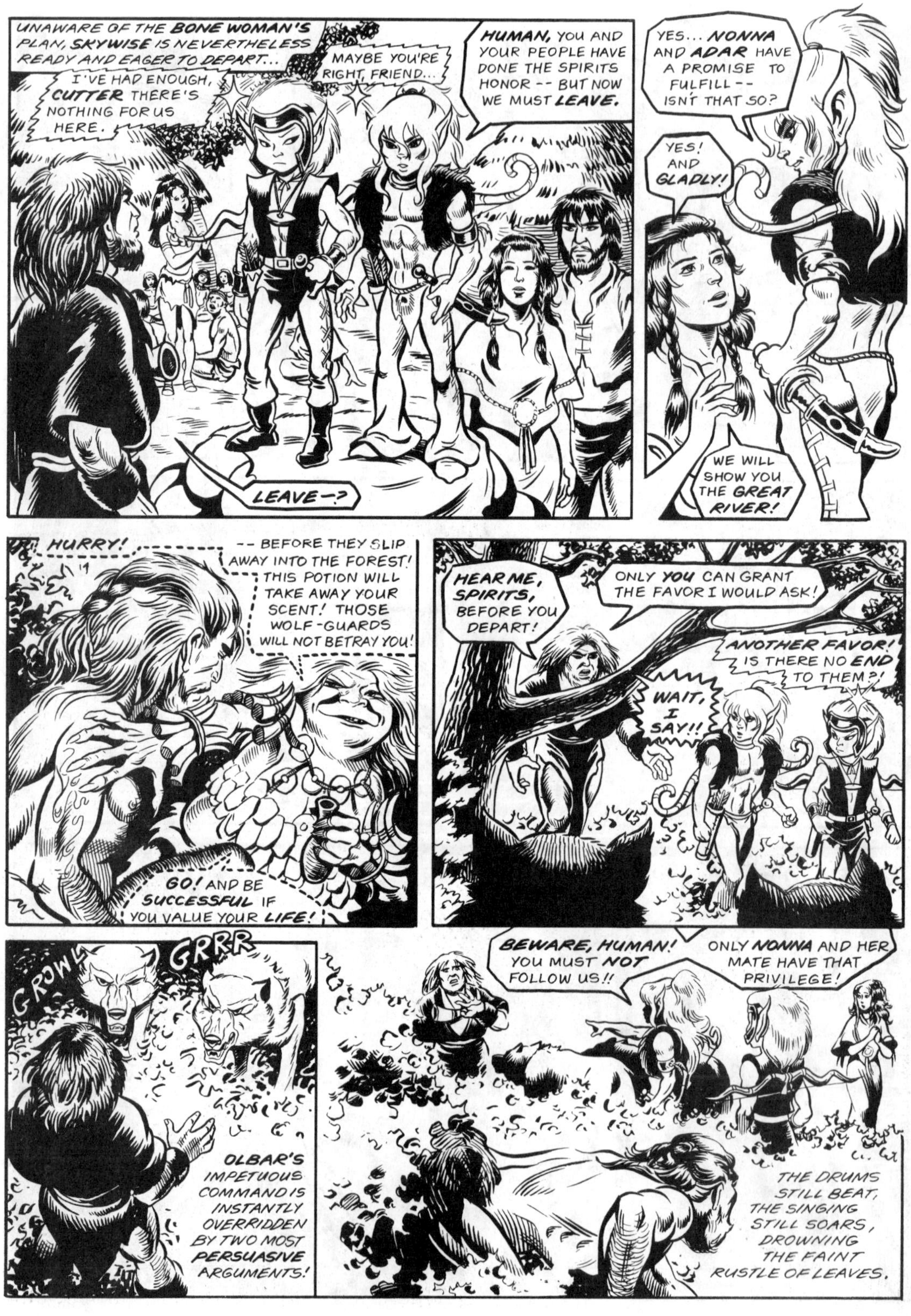
UNAWARE OF THE BONE WOMAN'S PLAN, SKYWISE IS NEVERTHELESS READY AND EAGER TO DEPART...
I'VE HAD ENOUGH, CUTTER THERE'S NOTHING FOR US HERE.
MAYBE YOU'RE RIGHT, FRIEND...
HUMAN, YOU AND YOUR PEOPLE HAVE DONE THE SPIRITS HONOR -- BUT NOW WE MUST LEAVE.
LEAVE -?
YES... NONNA AND ADAR HAVE A PROMISE TO FULFILL -- ISN'T THAT SO?
YES! AND GLADLY!
WE WILL SHOW YOU THE GREAT RIVER!
HURRY!
-- BEFORE THEY SLIP AWAY INTO THE FOREST! THIS POTION WILL TAKE AWAY YOUR SCENT! THOSE WOLF-GUARDS WILL NOT BETRAY YOU!
GO! AND BE SUCCESSFUL IF YOU VALUE YOUR LIFE!
HEAR ME, SPIRITS, BEFORE YOU DEPART!
ONLY YOU CAN GRANT THE FAVOR I WOULD ASK!
ANOTHER FAVOR! IS THERE NO END TO THEM?!
WAIT, I SAY!!
GROWL
GRRR
OLBAR'S IMPETUOUS COMMAND IS INSTANTLY OVERRIDDEN BY TWO MOST PERSUASIVE ARGUMENTS!
BEWARE, HUMAN! YOU MUST NOT FOLLOW US!!
ONLY NONNA AND HER MATE HAVE THAT PRIVILEGE!
THE DRUMS STILL BEAT, THE SINGING STILL SOARS, DROWNING THE FAINT RUSTLE OF LEAVES.

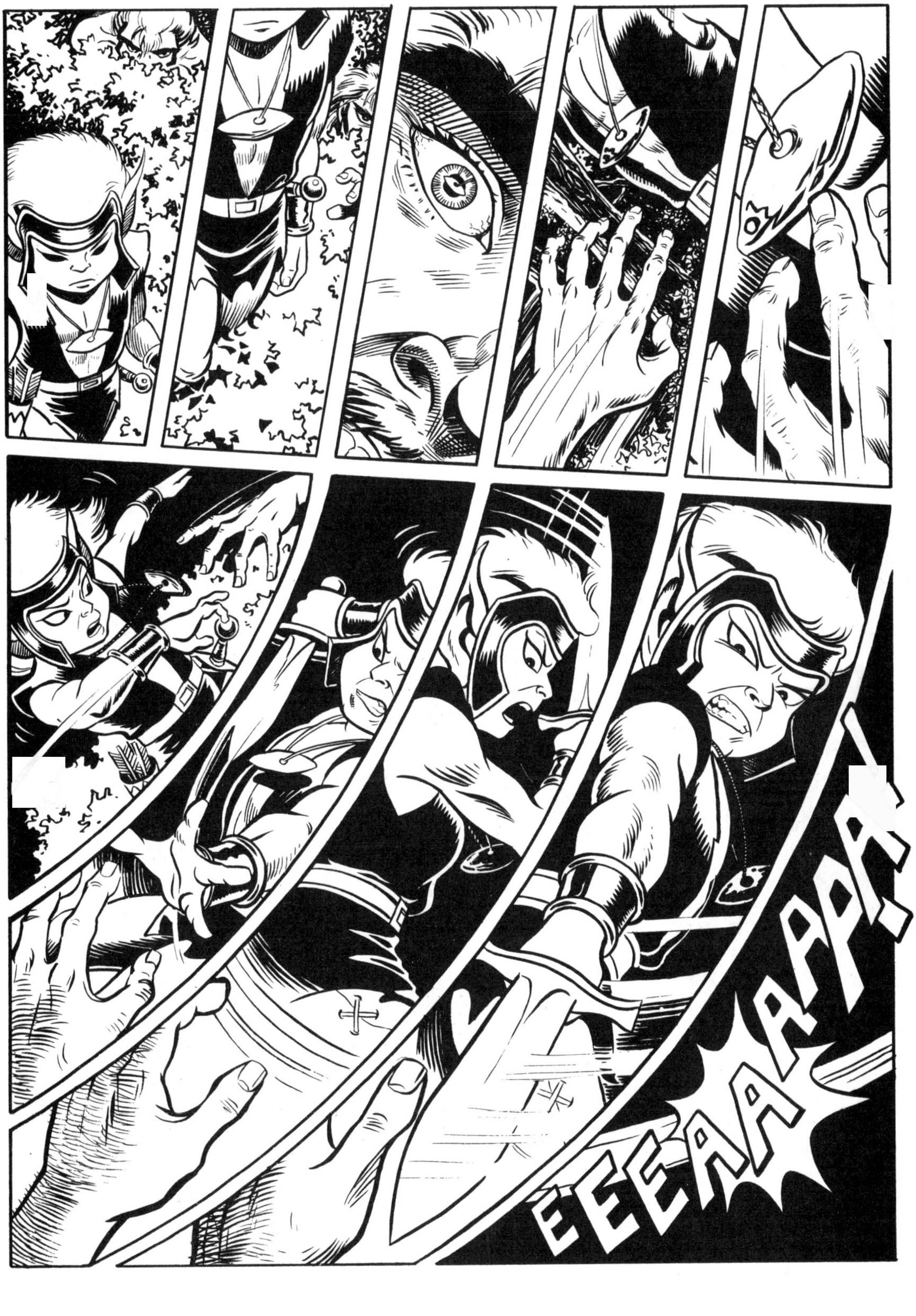
EEEAAAAAA!

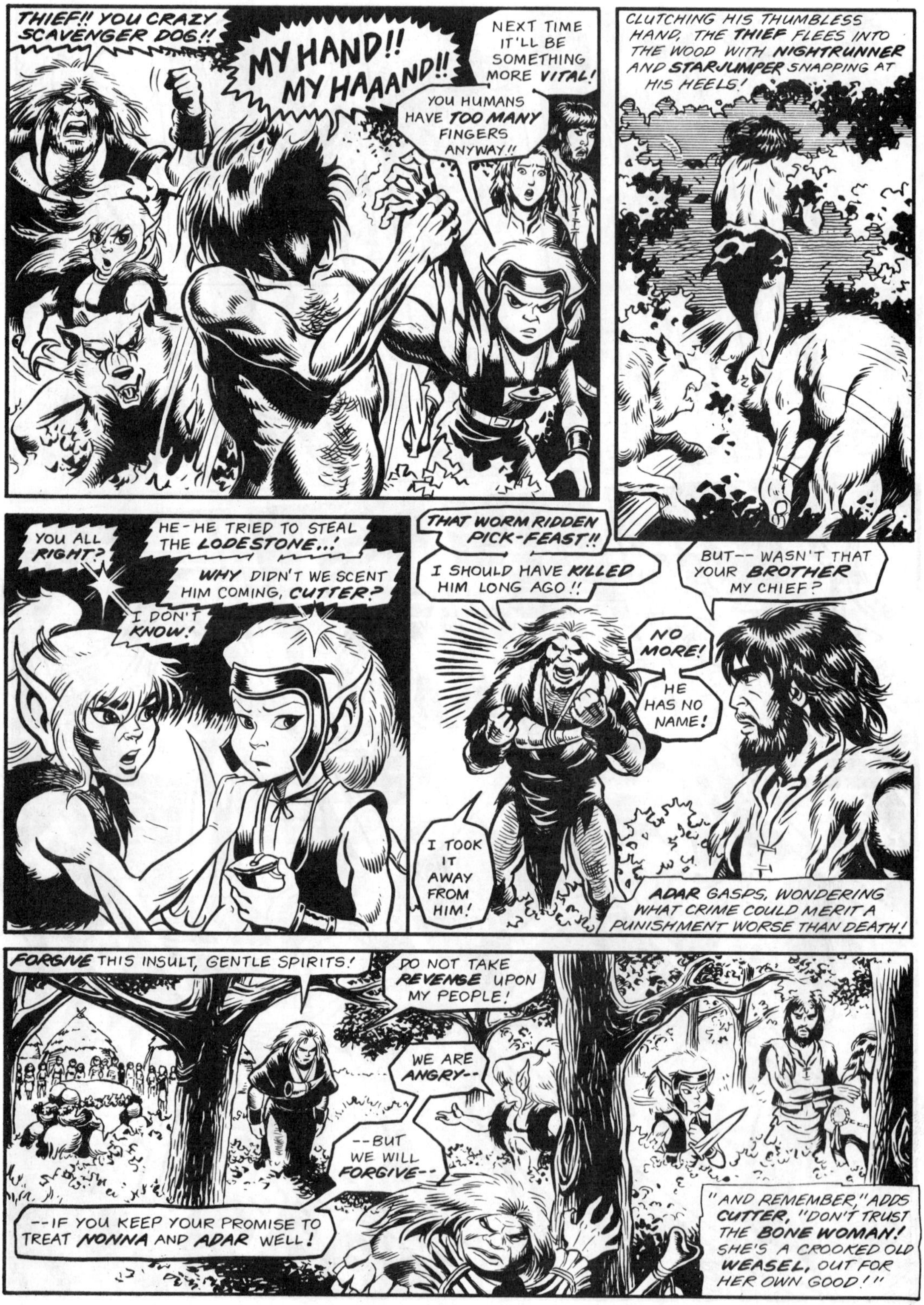

THIEF!! YOU CRAZY SCAVENGER DOG!!
MY HAND!! MY HAAAND!!
NEXT TIME IT'LL BE SOMETHING MORE VITAL!
YOU HUMANS HAVE TOO MANY FINGERS ANYWAY!!
CLUTCHING HIS THUMBLESS HAND, THE THIEF FLEES INTO THE WOOD WITH NIGHTRUNNER AND STARJUMPER SNAPPING AT HIS HEELS!
YOU ALL RIGHT?
HE-HE TRIED TO STEAL THE LODESTONE...!
WHY DIDN'T WE SCENT HIM COMING, CUTTER?
I DON'T KNOW!
THAT WORM RIDDEN PICK-FEAST!!
I SHOULD HAVE KILLED HIM LONG AGO!!
BUT-- WASN'T THAT YOUR BROTHER MY CHIEF?
NO MORE!
HE HAS NO NAME!
I TOOK IT AWAY FROM HIM!
ADAR GASPS, WONDERING WHAT CRIME COULD MERIT A PUNISHMENT WORSE THAN DEATH!
FORGIVE THIS INSULT, GENTLE SPIRITS!
DO NOT TAKE REVENGE UPON MY PEOPLE!
WE ARE ANGRY--
--BUT WE WILL FORGIVE--
--IF YOU KEEP YOUR PROMISE TO TREAT NONNA AND ADAR WELL!
"AND REMEMBER," ADDS CUTTER, "DON'T TRUST THE BONE WOMAN! SHE'S A CROOKED OLD WEASEL, OUT FOR HER OWN GOOD!"

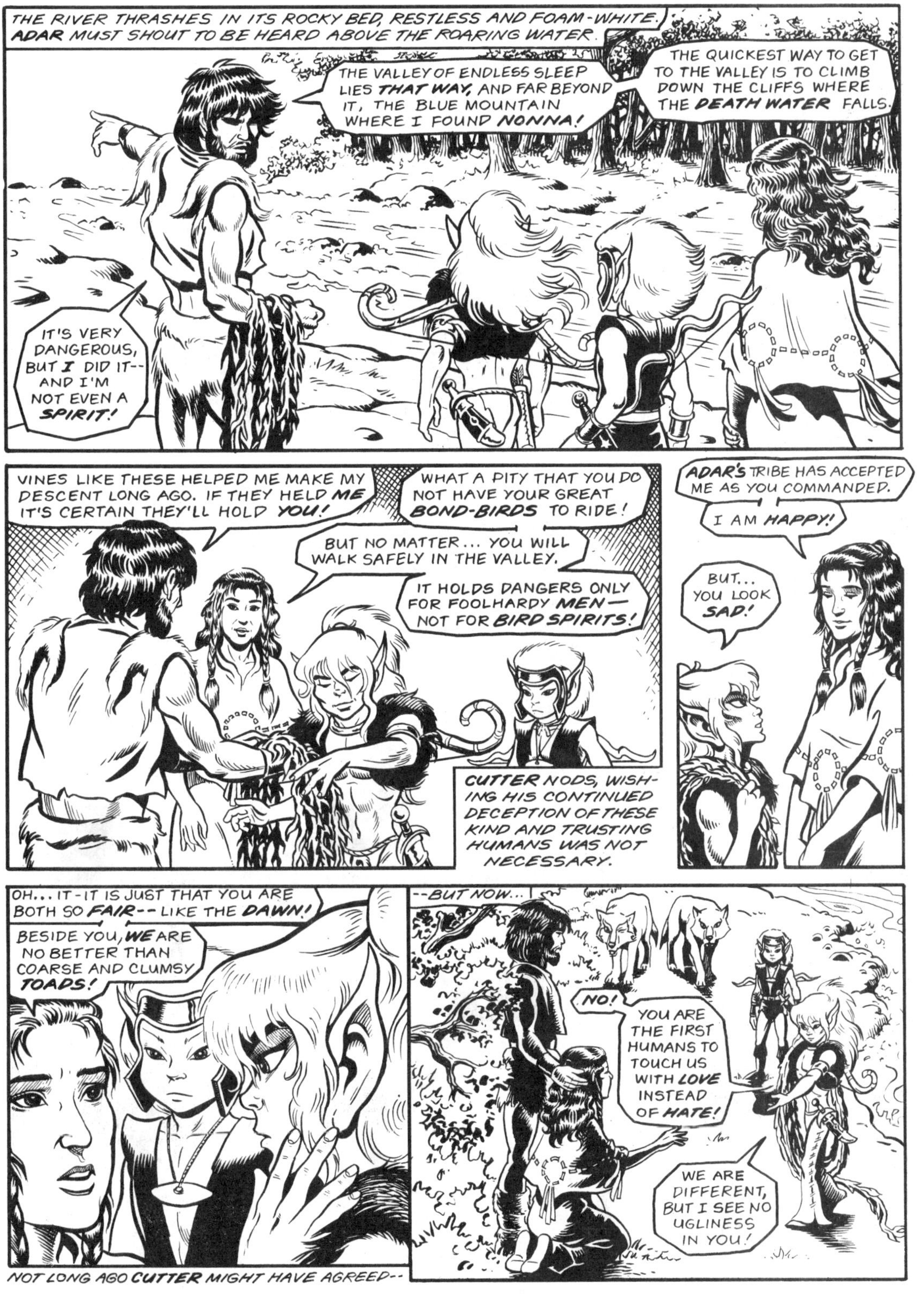
THE RIVER THRASHES IN ITS ROCKY BED, RESTLESS AND FOAM-WHITE. ADAR MUST SHOUT TO BE HEARD ABOVE THE ROARING WATER.
THE VALLEY OF ENDLESS SLEEP LIES THAT WAY, AND FAR BEYOND IT, THE BLUE MOUNTAIN WHERE I FOUND NONNA!
THE QUICKEST WAY TO GET TO THE VALLEY IS TO CLIMB DOWN THE CLIFFS WHERE THE DEATH WATER FALLS.
IT'S VERY DANGEROUS, BUT I DID IT-- AND I'M NOT EVEN A SPIRIT!
VINES LIKE THESE HELPED ME MAKE MY DESCENT LONG AGO. IF THEY HELD ME IT'S CERTAIN THEY'LL HOLD YOU!
WHAT A PITY THAT YOU DO NOT HAVE YOUR GREAT BOND-BIRDS TO RIDE!
BUT NO MATTER... YOU WILL WALK SAFELY IN THE VALLEY.
IT HOLDS DANGERS ONLY FOR FOOLHARDY MEN— NOT FOR BIRD SPIRITS!
CUTTER NODS, WISHING HIS CONTINUED DECEPTION OF THESE KIND AND TRUSTING HUMANS WAS NOT NECESSARY.
ADAR'S TRIBE HAS ACCEPTED ME AS YOU COMMANDED.
I AM HAPPY!
BUT... YOU LOOK SAD!
OH... IT-IT IS JUST THAT YOU ARE BOTH SO FAIR-- LIKE THE DAWN!
BESIDE YOU, WE ARE NO BETTER THAN COARSE AND CLUMSY TOADS!
NOT LONG AGO CUTTER MIGHT HAVE AGREED--
--BUT NOW...
NO!
YOU ARE THE FIRST HUMANS TO TOUCH US WITH LOVE INSTEAD OF HATE!
WE ARE DIFFERENT, BUT I SEE NO UGLINESS IN YOU!

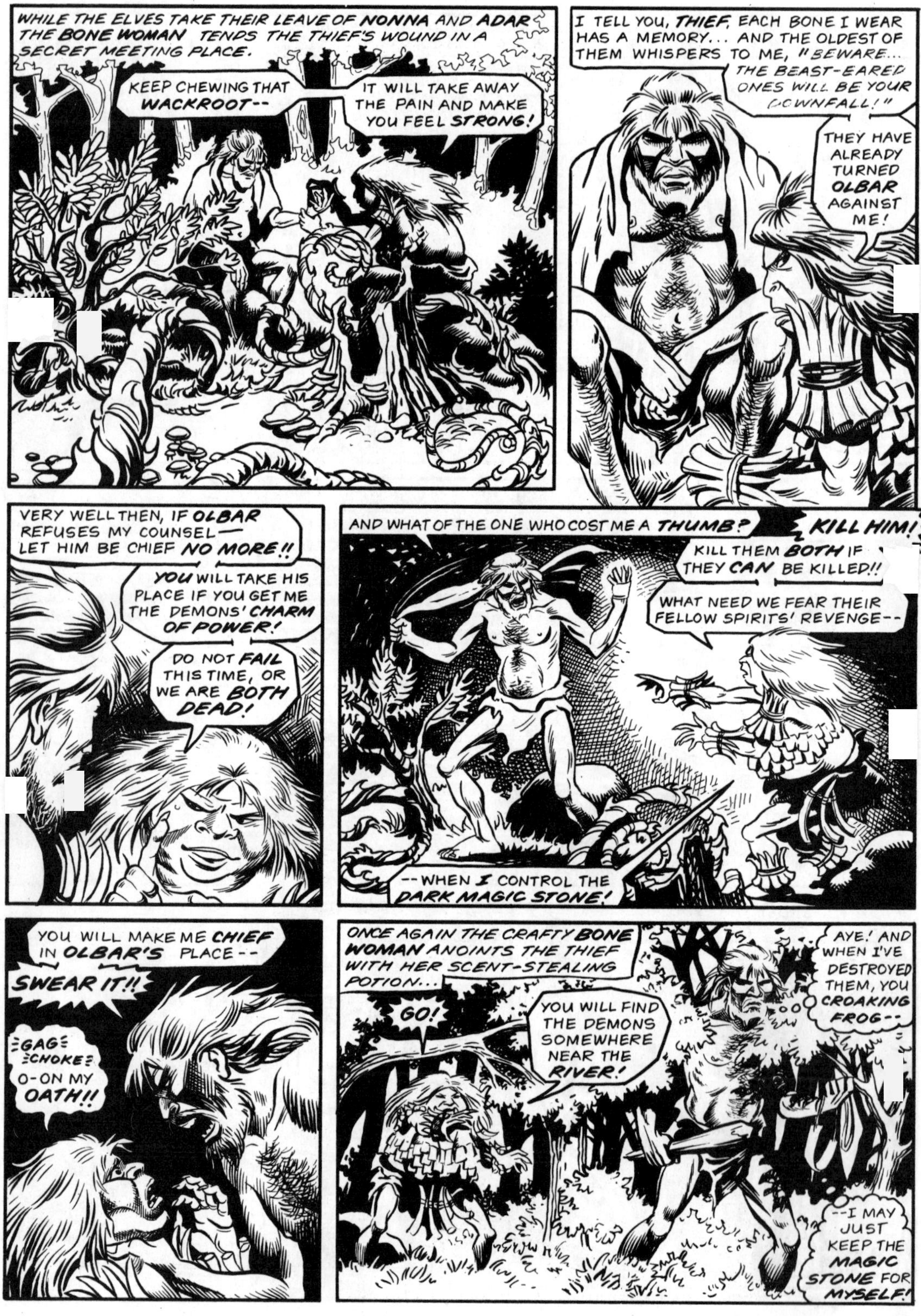
WHILE THE ELVES TAKE THEIR LEAVE OF NONNA AND ADAR THE BONE WOMAN TENDS THE THIEF'S WOUND IN A SECRET MEETING PLACE.
KEEP CHEWING THAT WACKROOT--
IT WILL TAKE AWAY THE PAIN AND MAKE YOU FEEL STRONG!
I TELL YOU, THIEF, EACH BONE I WEAR HAS A MEMORY... AND THE OLDEST OF THEM WHISPERS TO ME, "BEWARE... THE BEAST-EARED ONES WILL BE YOUR DOWNFALL!"
THEY HAVE ALREADY TURNED OLBAR AGAINST ME!
VERY WELL THEN, IF OLBAR REFUSES MY COUNSEL— LET HIM BE CHIEF NO MORE!!
YOU WILL TAKE HIS PLACE IF YOU GET ME THE DEMONS' CHARM OF POWER!
DO NOT FAIL THIS TIME, OR WE ARE BOTH DEAD!
AND WHAT OF THE ONE WHO COST ME A THUMB?
KILL HIM!
KILL THEM BOTH IF THEY CAN BE KILLED!!
WHAT NEED WE FEAR THEIR FELLOW SPIRITS' REVENGE--
--WHEN I CONTROL THE DARK MAGIC STONE!
YOU WILL MAKE ME CHIEF IN OLBAR'S PLACE--
SWEAR IT!!
GAG CHOKE O-ON MY OATH!!
ONCE AGAIN THE CRAFTY BONE WOMAN ANOINTS THE THIEF WITH HER SCENT-STEALING POTION...
GO!
YOU WILL FIND THE DEMONS SOMEWHERE NEAR THE RIVER!
AYE! AND WHEN I'VE DESTROYED THEM, YOU CROAKING FROG--
--I MAY JUST KEEP THE MAGIC STONE FOR MYSELF!

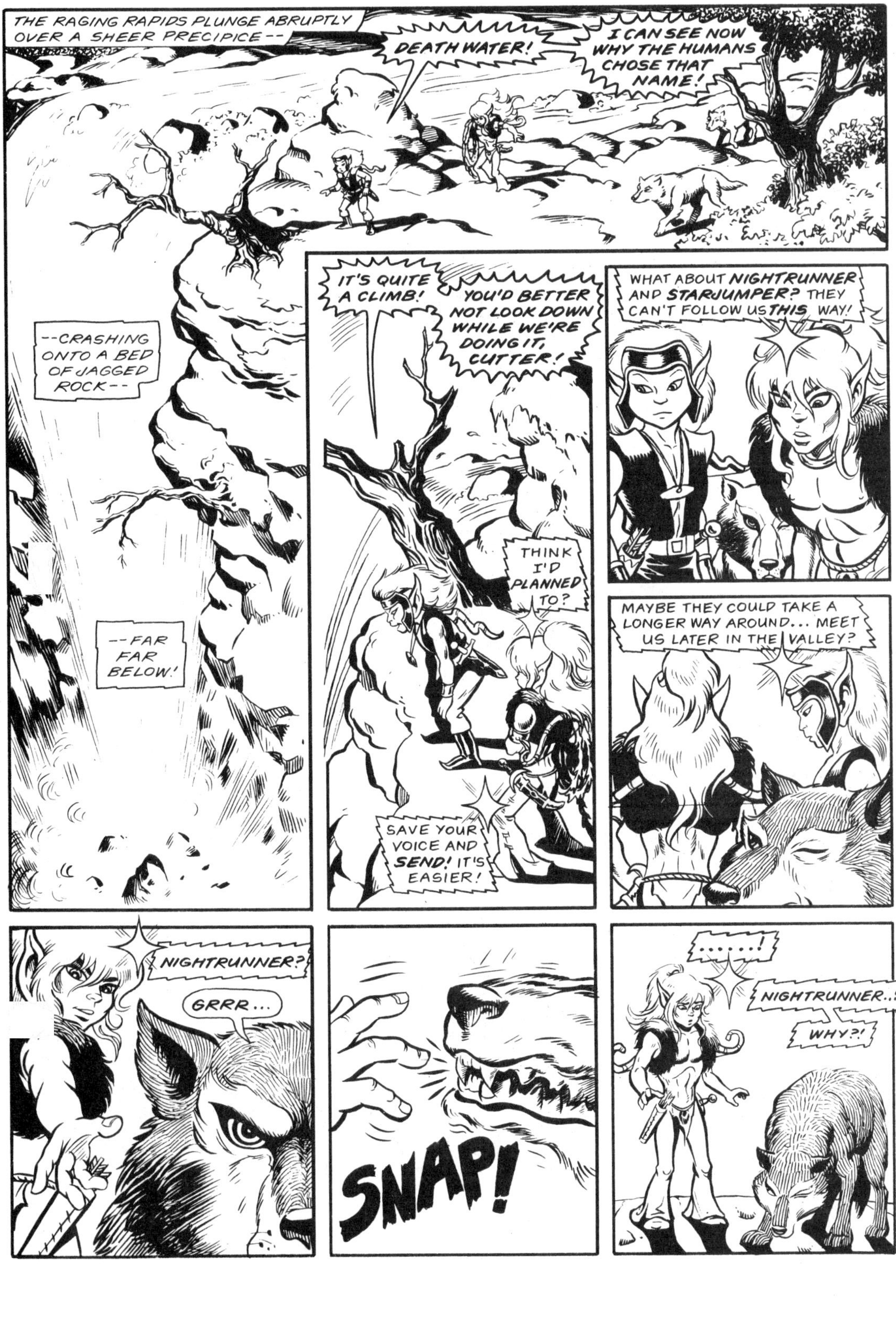
THE RAGING RAPIDS PLUNGE ABRUPTLY OVER A SHEER PRECIPICE--
DEATH WATER!
I CAN SEE NOW WHY THE HUMANS CHOSE THAT NAME!
--CRASHING ONTO A BED OF JAGGED ROCK--
--FAR FAR BELOW!
IT'S QUITE A CLIMB!
YOU'D BETTER NOT LOOK DOWN WHILE WE'RE DOING IT, CUTTER!
THINK I'D PLANNED TO?
SAVE YOUR VOICE AND SEND! IT'S EASIER!
WHAT ABOUT NIGHTRUNNER AND STARJUMPER? THEY CAN'T FOLLOW US THIS WAY!
MAYBE THEY COULD TAKE A LONGER WAY AROUND... MEET US LATER IN THE VALLEY?
NIGHTRUNNER?
GRRR...
SNAP!
......!
NIGHTRUNNER..!
WHY?!

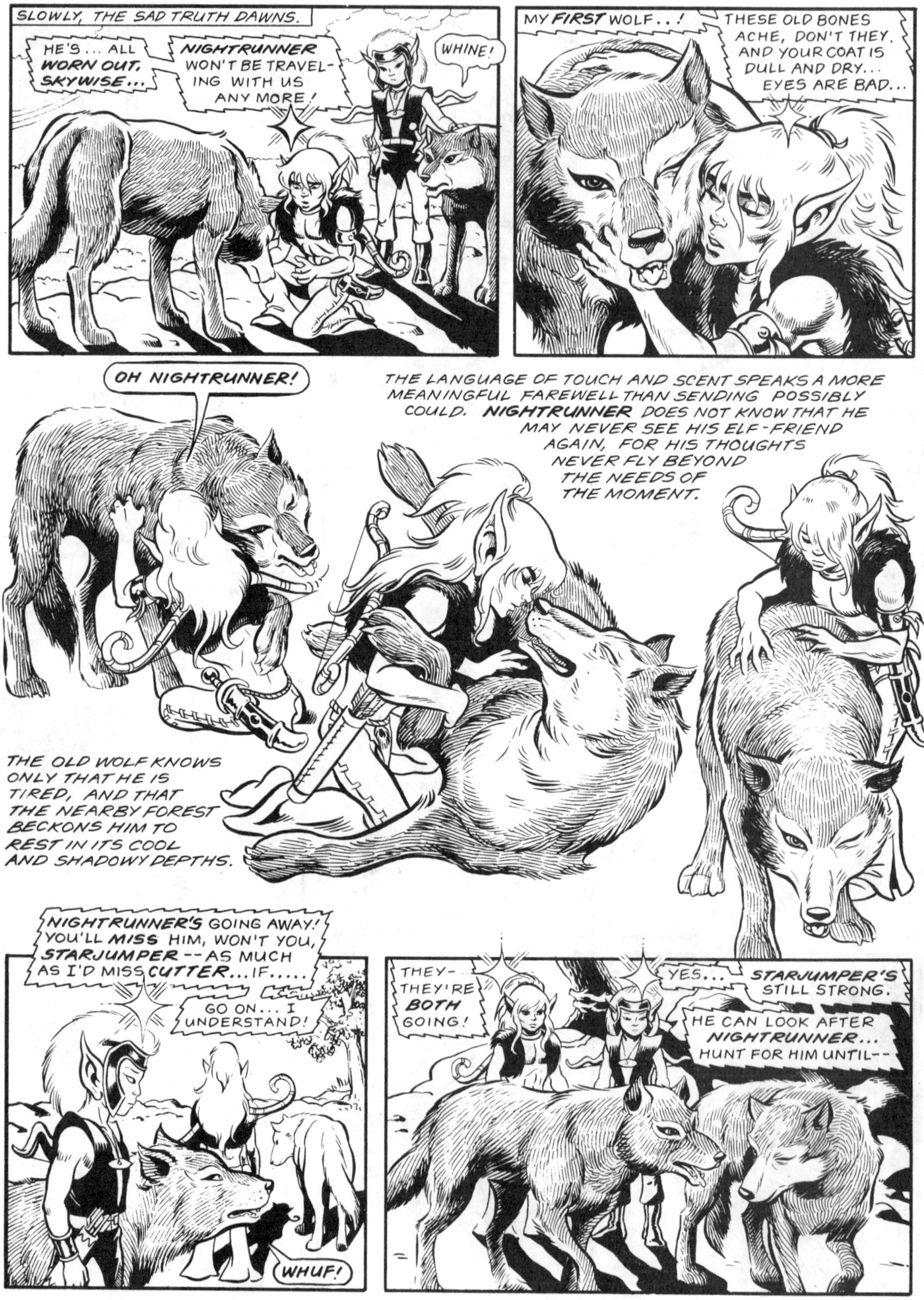
SLOWLY, THE SAD TRUTH DAWNS.
HE'S... ALL WORN OUT, SKYWISE...
NIGHTRUNNER WON'T BE TRAVELING WITH US ANY MORE!
WHINE!
MY FIRST WOLF..!
THESE OLD BONES ACHE, DON'T THEY. AND YOUR COAT IS DULL AND DRY... EYES ARE BAD...
OH NIGHTRUNNER!
THE LANGUAGE OF TOUCH AND SCENT SPEAKS A MORE MEANINGFUL FAREWELL THAN SENDING POSSIBLY COULD. NIGHTRUNNER DOES NOT KNOW THAT HE MAY NEVER SEE HIS ELF-FRIEND AGAIN, FOR HIS THOUGHTS NEVER FLY BEYOND THE NEEDS OF THE MOMENT.
THE OLD WOLF KNOWS ONLY THAT HE IS TIRED, AND THAT THE NEARBY FOREST BECKONS HIM TO REST IN ITS COOL AND SHADOWY DEPTHS.
NIGHTRUNNER'S GOING AWAY! YOU'LL MISS HIM, WON'T YOU, STARJUMPER--AS MUCH AS I'D MISS CUTTER...IF.....
GO ON... I UNDERSTAND!
WHUF!
THEY-THEY'RE BOTH GOING!
YES... STARJUMPER'S STILL STRONG.
HE CAN LOOK AFTER NIGHTRUNNER... HUNT FOR HIM UNTIL--

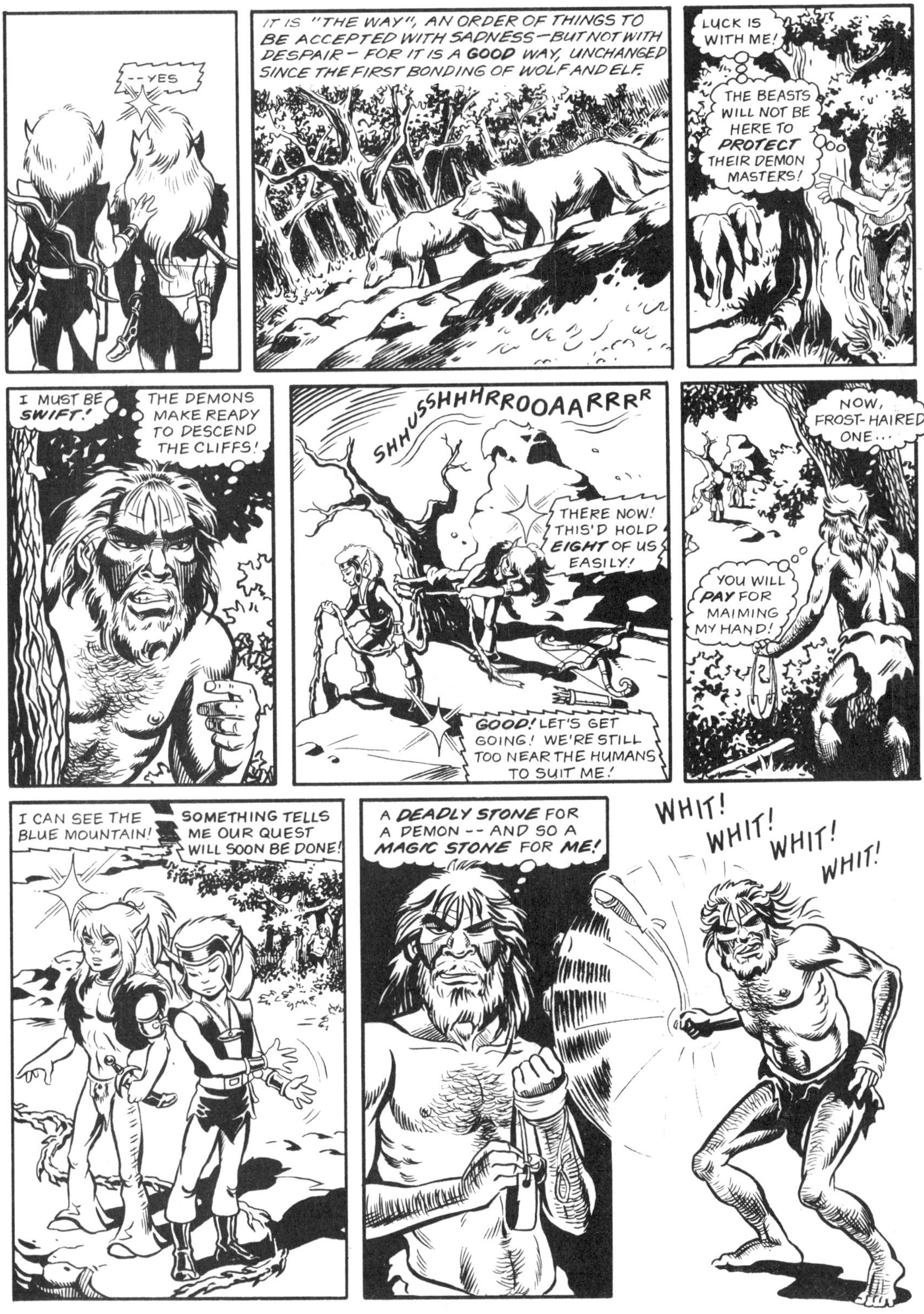

--YES
IT IS "THE WAY", AN ORDER OF THINGS TO BE ACCEPTED WITH SADNESS—BUT NOT WITH DESPAIR— FOR IT IS A GOOD WAY, UNCHANGED SINCE THE FIRST BONDING OF WOLF AND ELF.
LUCK IS WITH ME!
THE BEASTS WILL NOT BE HERE TO PROTECT THEIR DEMON MASTERS!
I MUST BE SWIFT!
THE DEMONS MAKE READY TO DESCEND THE CLIFFS!
SHHUSSHHHRROOAARRRR
THERE NOW! THIS'D HOLD EIGHT OF US EASILY!
GOOD! LET'S GET GOING! WE'RE STILL TOO NEAR THE HUMANS TO SUIT ME!
NOW, FROST-HAIRED ONE...
YOU WILL PAY FOR MAIMING MY HAND!
I CAN SEE THE BLUE MOUNTAIN!
SOMETHING TELLS ME OUR QUEST WILL SOON BE DONE!
A DEADLY STONE FOR A DEMON -- AND SO A MAGIC STONE FOR ME!
WHIT!
WHIT!
WHIT!
WHIT!

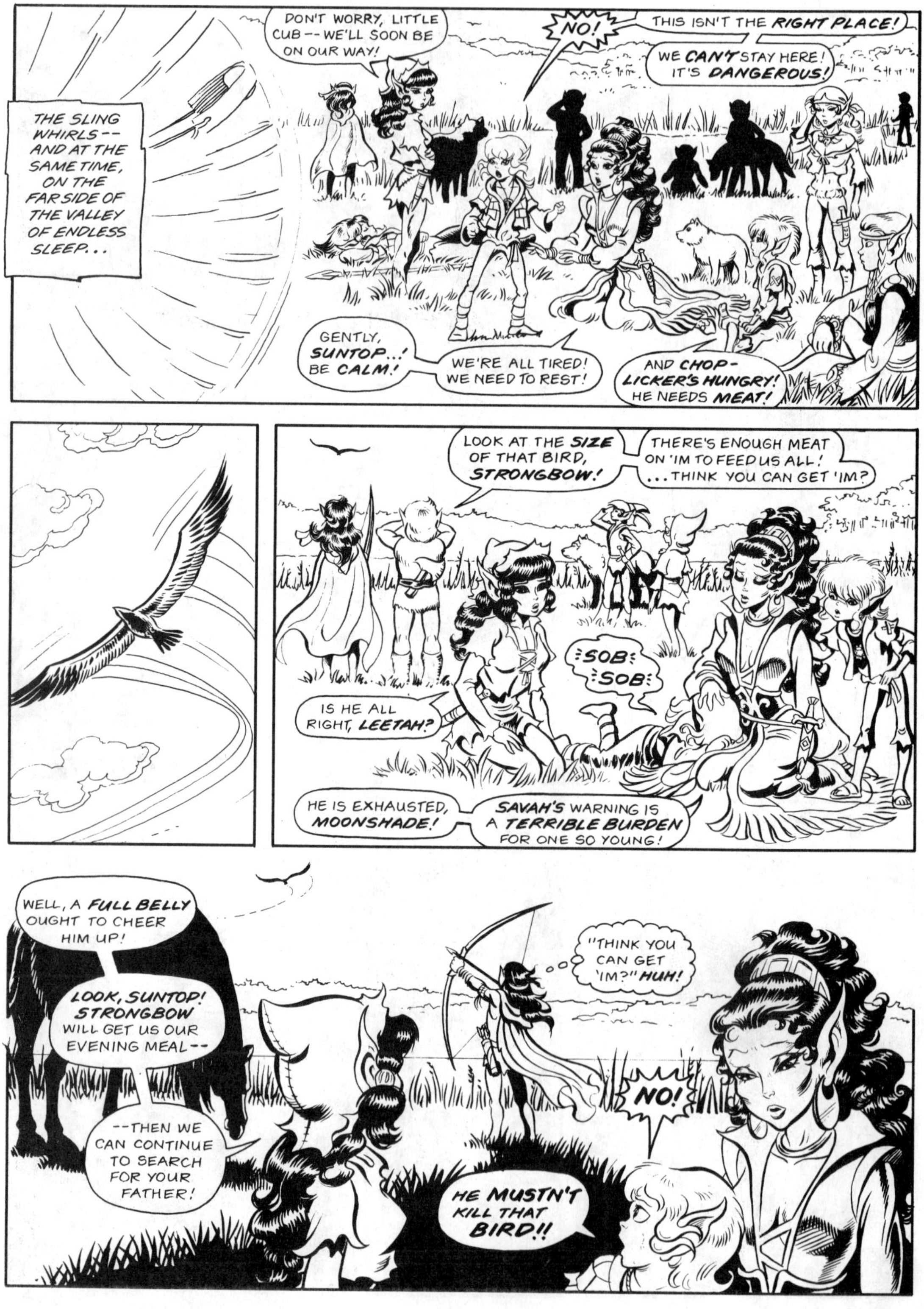
THE SLING WHIRLS -- AND AT THE SAME TIME, ON THE FAR SIDE OF THE VALLEY OF ENDLESS SLEEP...
DON'T WORRY, LITTLE CUB -- WE'LL SOON BE ON OUR WAY!
NO!
THIS ISN'T THE RIGHT PLACE!
WE CAN'T STAY HERE! IT'S DANGEROUS!
GENTLY, SUNTOP...! BE CALM!
WE'RE ALL TIRED! WE NEED TO REST!
AND CHOP-LICKER'S HUNGRY! HE NEEDS MEAT!
LOOK AT THE SIZE OF THAT BIRD, STRONGBOW!
THERE'S ENOUGH MEAT ON 'IM TO FEED US ALL! ...THINK YOU CAN GET 'IM?
SOB SOB
IS HE ALL RIGHT, LEETAH?
HE IS EXHAUSTED, MOONSHADE!
SAVAH'S WARNING IS A TERRIBLE BURDEN FOR ONE SO YOUNG!
WELL, A FULL BELLY OUGHT TO CHEER HIM UP!
LOOK, SUNTOP! STRONGBOW WILL GET US OUR EVENING MEAL --
-- THEN WE CAN CONTINUE TO SEARCH FOR YOUR FATHER!
"THINK YOU CAN GET 'IM?" HUH!
NO!
HE MUSTN'T KILL THAT BIRD!!

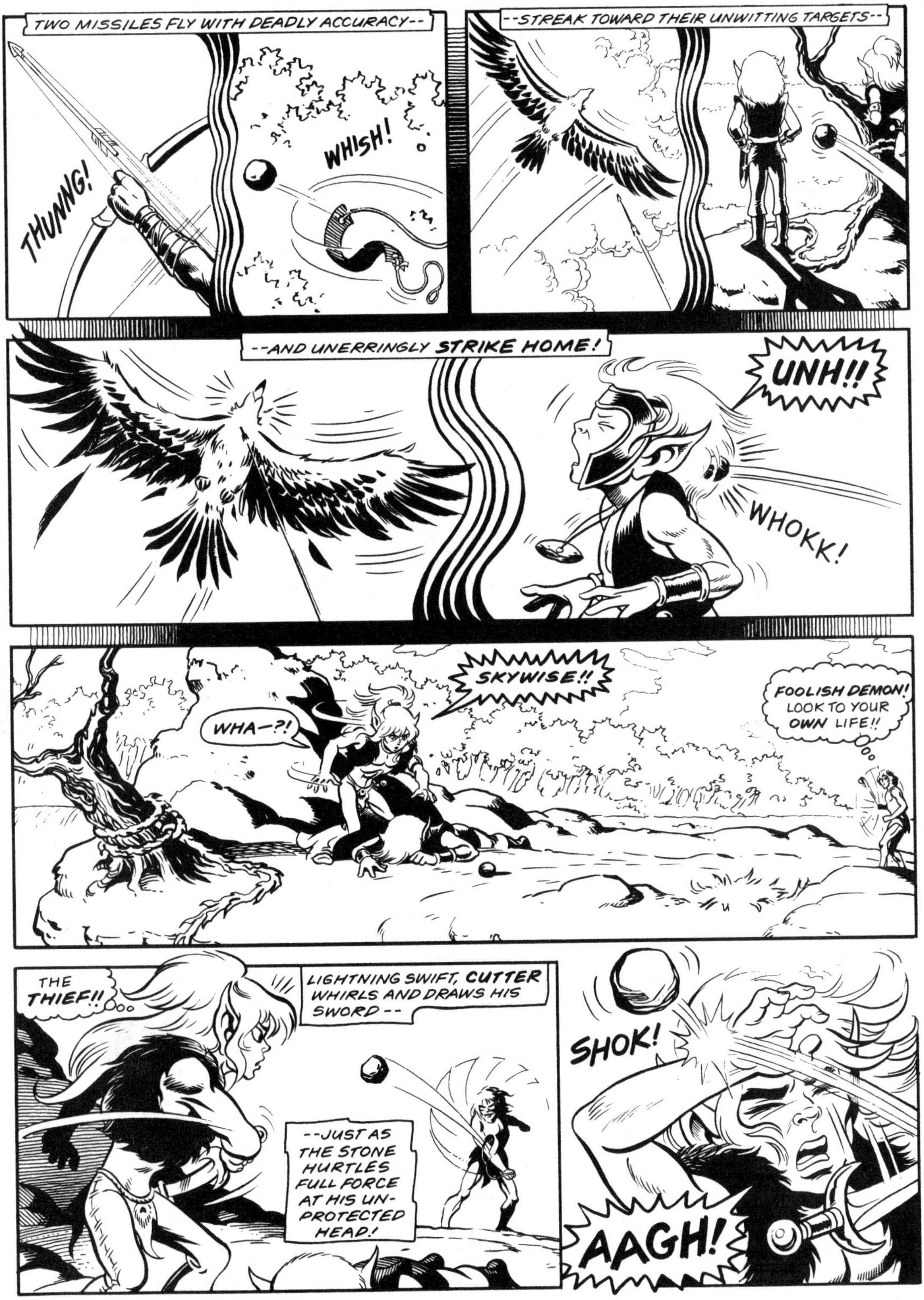
TWO MISSILES FLY WITH DEADLY ACCURACY--
THUNNG!
WHISH!
--STREAK TOWARD THEIR UNWITTING TARGETS--
--AND UNERRINGLY STRIKE HOME!
UNH!!
WHOKK!
SKYWISE!!
WHA--?!
FOOLISH DEMON! LOOK TO YOUR OWN LIFE!!
THE THIEF!!
LIGHTNING SWIFT, CUTTER WHIRLS AND DRAWS HIS SWORD --
--JUST AS THE STONE HURTLES FULL FORCE AT HIS UN-PROTECTED HEAD!
SHOK!
AAGH!

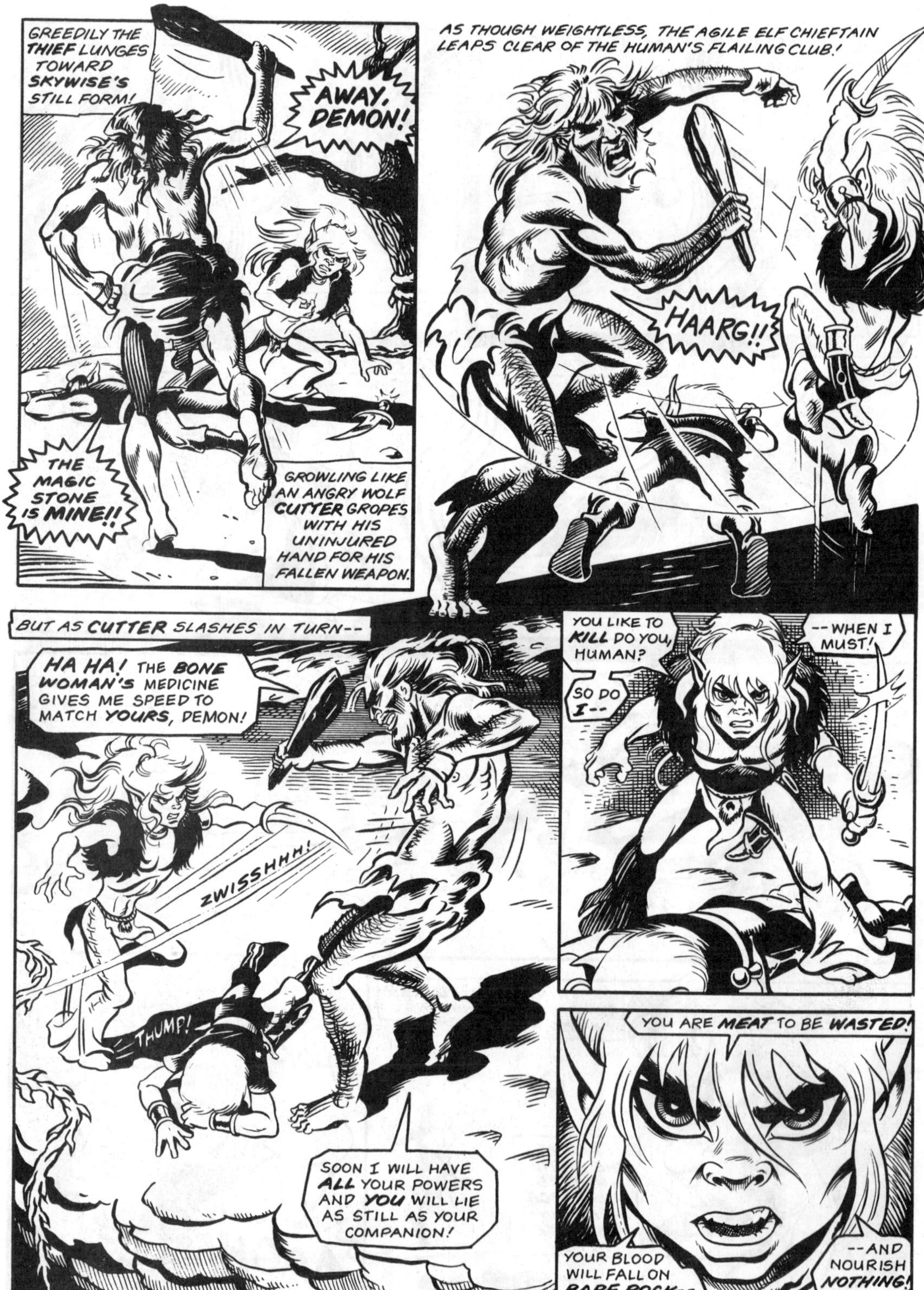
GREEDILY THE THIEF LUNGES TOWARD SKYWISE'S STILL FORM!
AWAY, DEMON!
THE MAGIC STONE IS MINE!!
GROWLING LIKE AN ANGRY WOLF CUTTER GROPES WITH HIS UNINJURED HAND FOR HIS FALLEN WEAPON.
AS THOUGH WEIGHTLESS, THE AGILE ELF CHIEFTAIN LEAPS CLEAR OF THE HUMAN'S FLAILING CLUB!
HAARG!!
BUT AS CUTTER SLASHES IN TURN--
HA HA! THE BONE WOMAN'S MEDICINE GIVES ME SPEED TO MATCH YOURS, DEMON!
ZWISSHHH!
THUMP!
SOON I WILL HAVE ALL YOUR POWERS AND YOU WILL LIE AS STILL AS YOUR COMPANION!
YOU LIKE TO KILL DO YOU, HUMAN?
SO DO I--
--WHEN I MUST!
YOU ARE MEAT TO BE WASTED!
YOUR BLOOD WILL FALL ON BARE ROCK--
--AND NOURISH NOTHING!

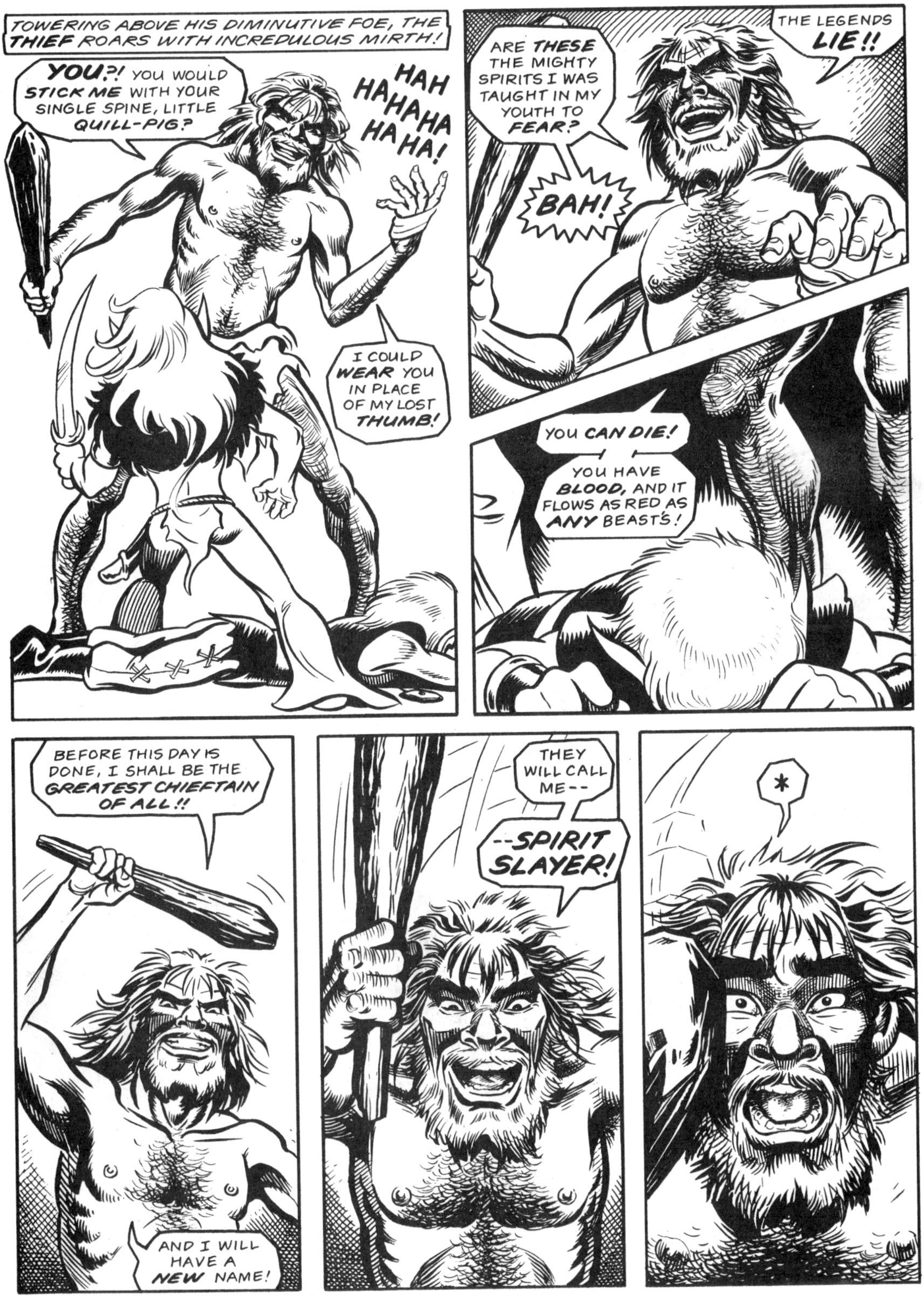
TOWERING ABOVE HIS DIMINUTIVE FOE, THE THIEF ROARS WITH INCREDULOUS MIRTH!
YOU?! YOU WOULD STICK ME WITH YOUR SINGLE SPINE, LITTLE QUILL-PIG?
HAH HAHAHAHA HA HA!
I COULD WEAR YOU IN PLACE OF MY LOST THUMB!
ARE THESE THE MIGHTY SPIRITS I WAS TAUGHT IN MY YOUTH TO FEAR?
BAH!
THE LEGENDS LIE!!
YOU CAN DIE!
YOU HAVE BLOOD, AND IT FLOWS AS RED AS ANY BEAST'S!
BEFORE THIS DAY IS DONE, I SHALL BE THE GREATEST CHIEFTAIN OF ALL!!
AND I WILL HAVE A NEW NAME!
THEY WILL CALL ME--
--SPIRIT SLAYER!
*

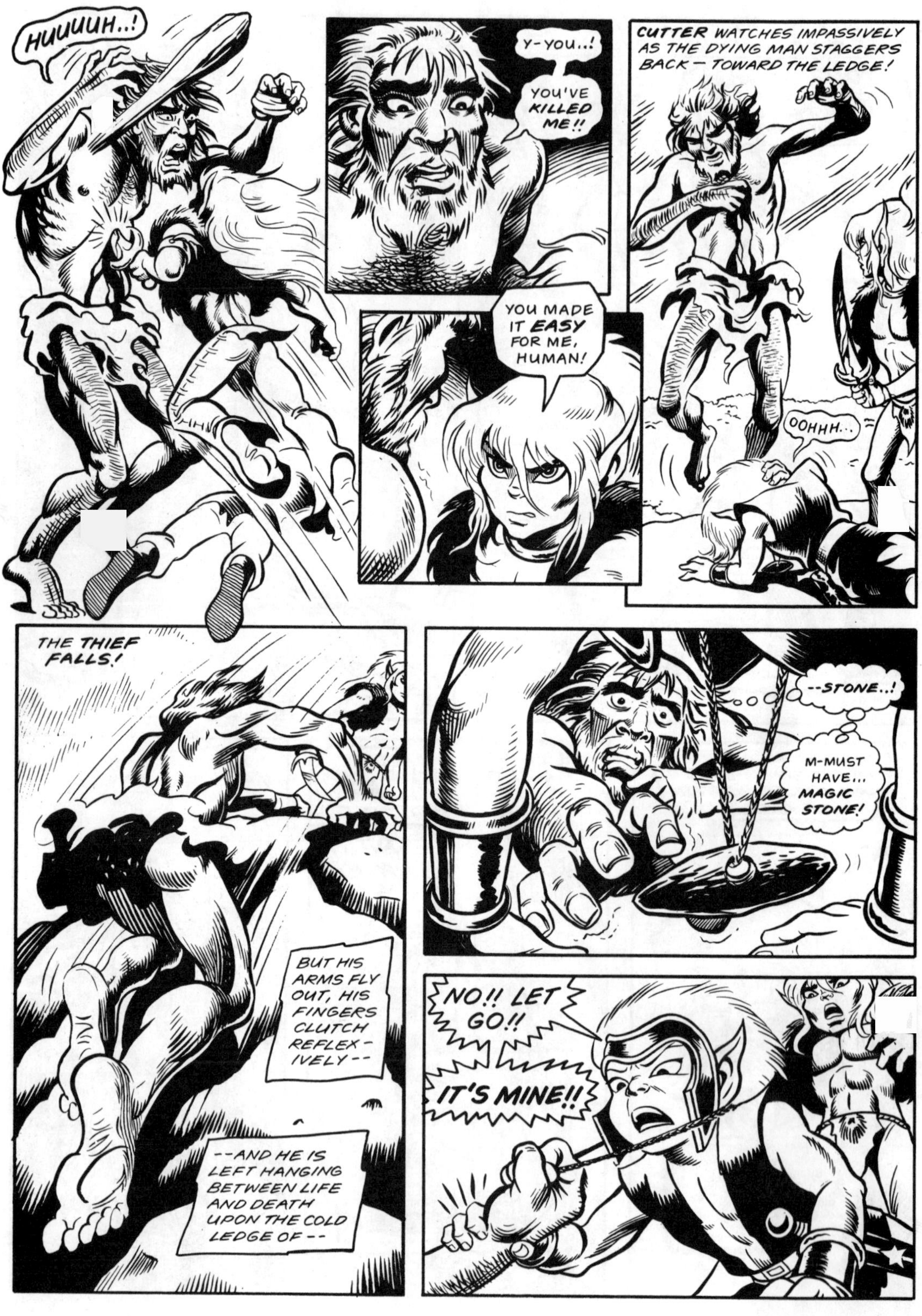
HUUUUH..!
Y-YOU..!
YOU'VE KILLED ME!!
YOU MADE IT EASY FOR ME, HUMAN!
CUTTER WATCHES IMPASSIVELY AS THE DYING MAN STAGGERS BACK — TOWARD THE LEDGE!
OOHHH...
THE THIEF FALLS!
BUT HIS ARMS FLY OUT, HIS FINGERS CLUTCH REFLEX-IVELY --
--AND HE IS LEFT HANGING BETWEEN LIFE AND DEATH UPON THE COLD LEDGE OF --
--STONE..!
M-MUST HAVE... MAGIC STONE!
NO!! LET GO!!
IT'S MINE!!

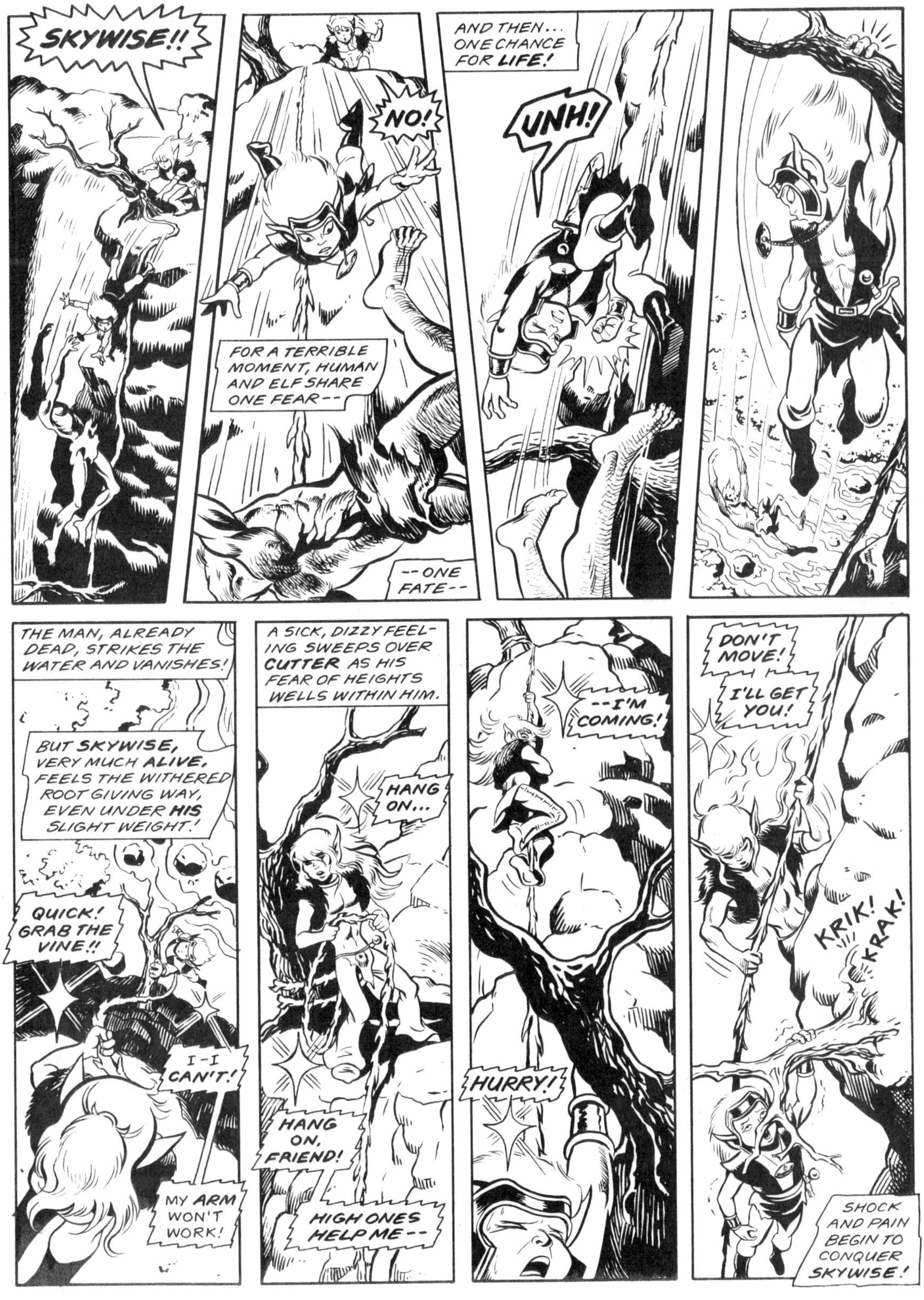
SKYWISE!!
NO!
FOR A TERRIBLE MOMENT, HUMAN AND ELF SHARE ONE FEAR--
--ONE FATE--
AND THEN... ONE CHANCE FOR LIFE!
UNH!
THE MAN, ALREADY DEAD, STRIKES THE WATER AND VANISHES!
BUT SKYWISE, VERY MUCH ALIVE, FEELS THE WITHERED ROOT GIVING WAY, EVEN UNDER HIS SLIGHT WEIGHT!
QUICK! GRAB THE VINE!!
I-I CAN'T!
MY ARM WON'T WORK!
A SICK, DIZZY FEELING SWEEPS OVER CUTTER AS HIS FEAR OF HEIGHTS WELLS WITHIN HIM.
HANG ON...
HANG ON, FRIEND!
HIGH ONES HELP ME--
--I'M COMING!
HURRY!
DON'T MOVE!
I'LL GET YOU!
KRIK! KRAK!
SHOCK AND PAIN BEGIN TO CONQUER SKYWISE!

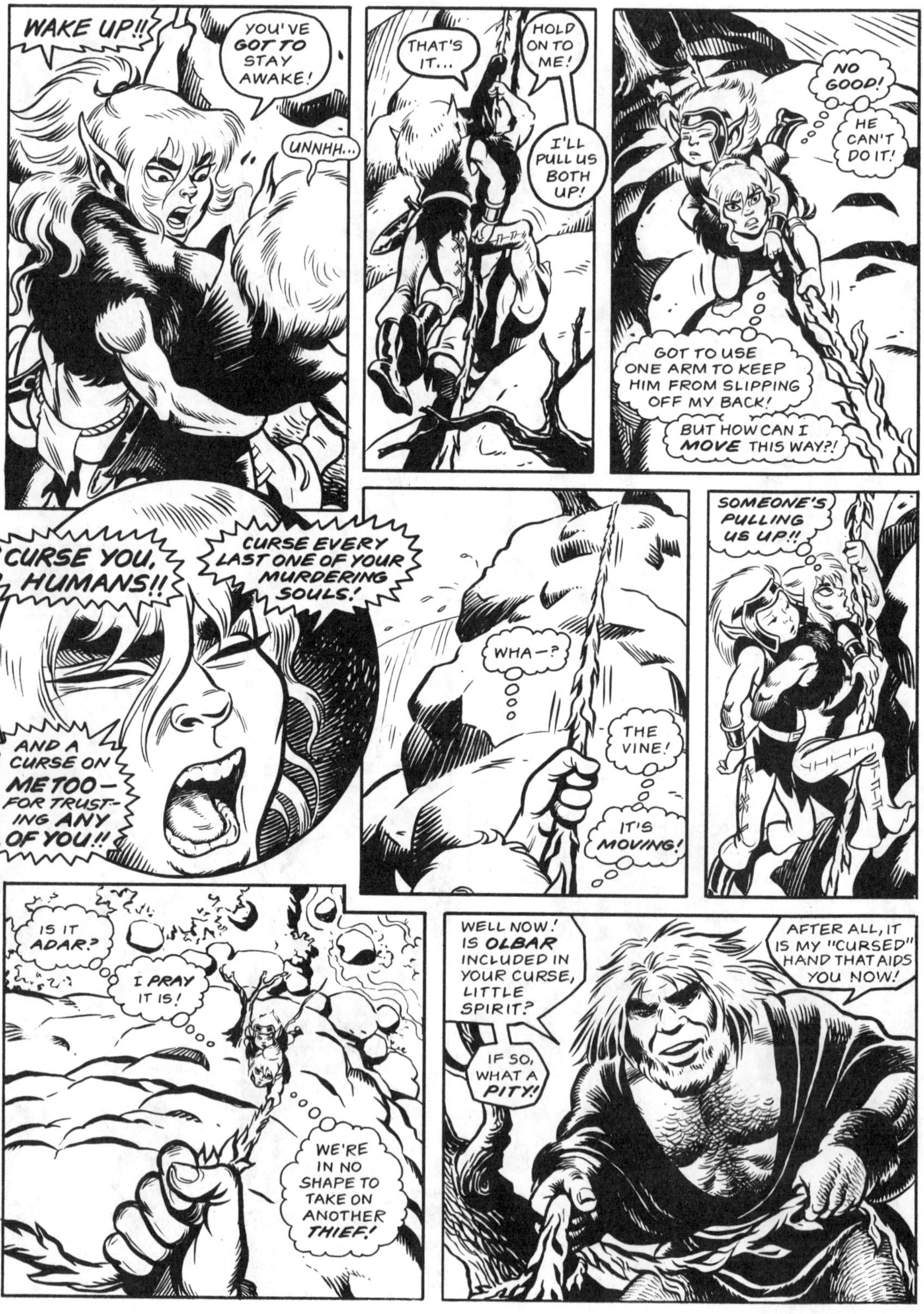
WAKE UP!!
YOU'VE GOT TO STAY AWAKE!
UNNHH...
THAT'S IT...
HOLD ON TO ME!
I'LL PULL US BOTH UP!
NO GOOD!
HE CAN'T DO IT!
GOT TO USE ONE ARM TO KEEP HIM FROM SLIPPING OFF MY BACK!
BUT HOW CAN I MOVE THIS WAY?!
CURSE YOU, HUMANS!!
CURSE EVERY LAST ONE OF YOUR MURDERING SOULS!
AND A CURSE ON ME TOO— FOR TRUSTING ANY OF YOU!!
WHA—?
THE VINE!
IT'S MOVING!
SOMEONE'S PULLING US UP!!
IS IT ADAR?
I PRAY IT IS!
WE'RE IN NO SHAPE TO TAKE ON ANOTHER THIEF!
WELL NOW! IS OLBAR INCLUDED IN YOUR CURSE, LITTLE SPIRIT?
IF SO, WHAT A PITY!
AFTER ALL, IT IS MY "CURSED" HAND THAT AIDS YOU NOW!

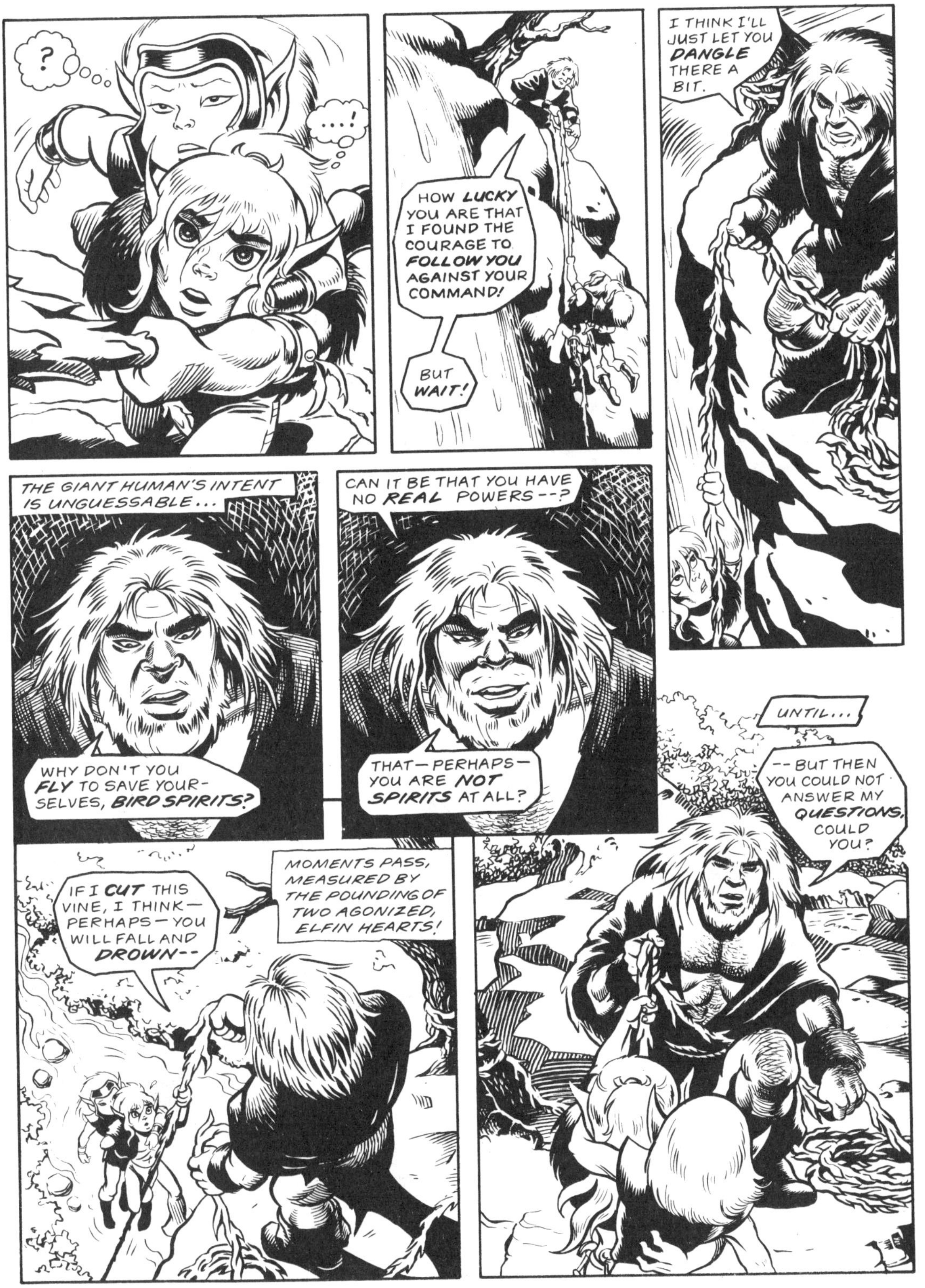
?
....!
HOW LUCKY YOU ARE THAT I FOUND THE COURAGE TO FOLLOW YOU AGAINST YOUR COMMAND!
BUT WAIT!
I THINK I'LL JUST LET YOU DANGLE THERE A BIT.
THE GIANT HUMAN'S INTENT IS UNGUESSABLE...
WHY DON'T YOU FLY TO SAVE YOURSELVES, BIRD SPIRITS?
CAN IT BE THAT YOU HAVE NO REAL POWERS--?
THAT—PERHAPS—YOU ARE NOT SPIRITS AT ALL?
IF I CUT THIS VINE, I THINK—PERHAPS—YOU WILL FALL AND DROWN--
MOMENTS PASS, MEASURED BY THE POUNDING OF TWO AGONIZED, ELFIN HEARTS!
UNTIL...
--BUT THEN YOU COULD NOT ANSWER MY QUESTIONS, COULD YOU?

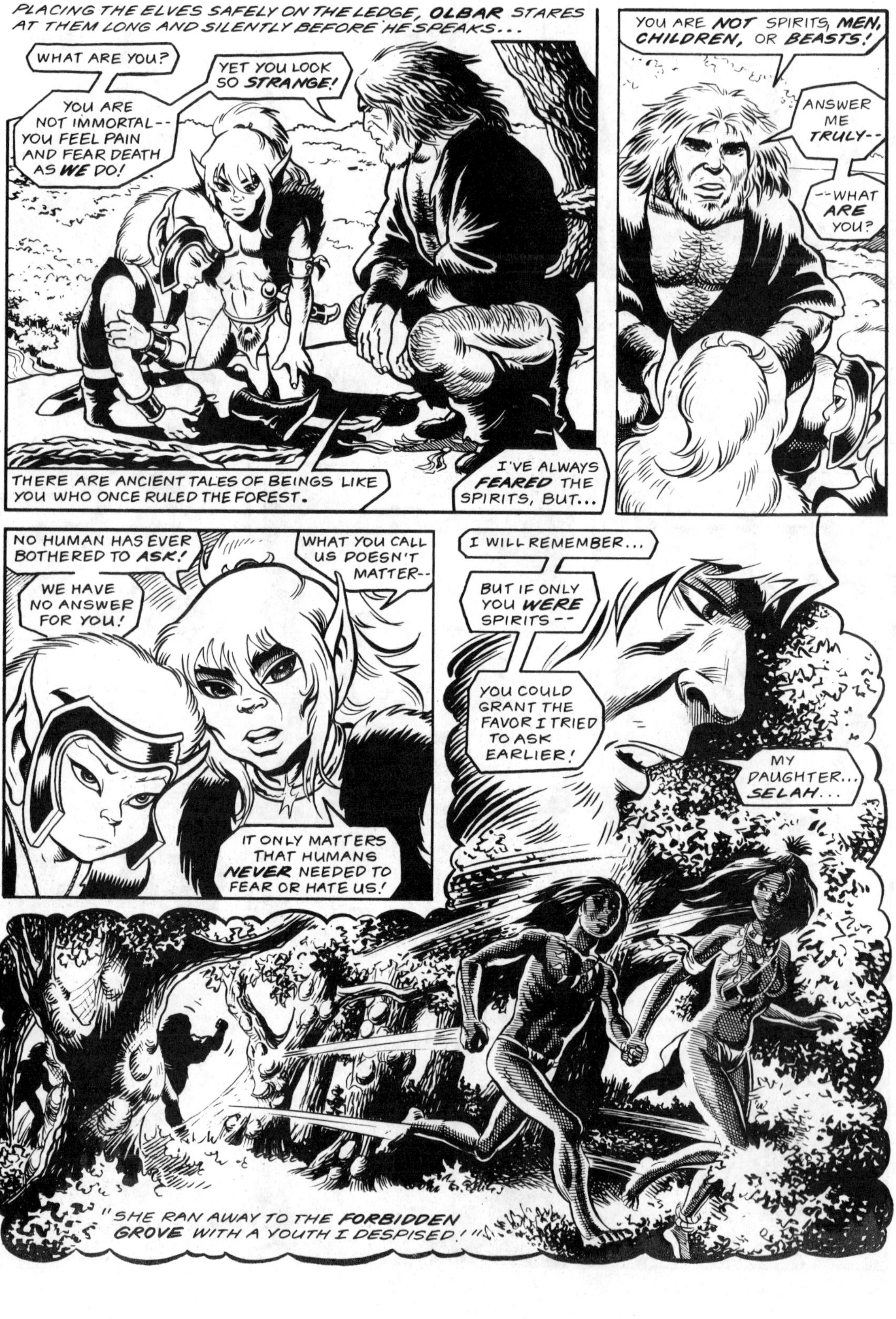
PLACING THE ELVES SAFELY ON THE LEDGE, OLBAR STARES AT THEM LONG AND SILENTLY BEFORE HE SPEAKS...
WHAT ARE YOU?
YOU ARE NOT IMMORTAL-- YOU FEEL PAIN AND FEAR DEATH AS WE DO!
YET YOU LOOK SO STRANGE!
THERE ARE ANCIENT TALES OF BEINGS LIKE YOU WHO ONCE RULED THE FOREST.
I'VE ALWAYS FEARED THE SPIRITS, BUT...
YOU ARE NOT SPIRITS, MEN, CHILDREN, OR BEASTS!
ANSWER ME TRULY--
--WHAT ARE YOU?
NO HUMAN HAS EVER BOTHERED TO ASK!
WE HAVE NO ANSWER FOR YOU!
WHAT YOU CALL US DOESN'T MATTER--
IT ONLY MATTERS THAT HUMANS NEVER NEEDED TO FEAR OR HATE US!
I WILL REMEMBER...
BUT IF ONLY YOU WERE SPIRITS--
YOU COULD GRANT THE FAVOR I TRIED TO ASK EARLIER!
MY DAUGHTER... SELAH...
"SHE RAN AWAY TO THE FORBIDDEN GROVE WITH A YOUTH I DESPISED!"

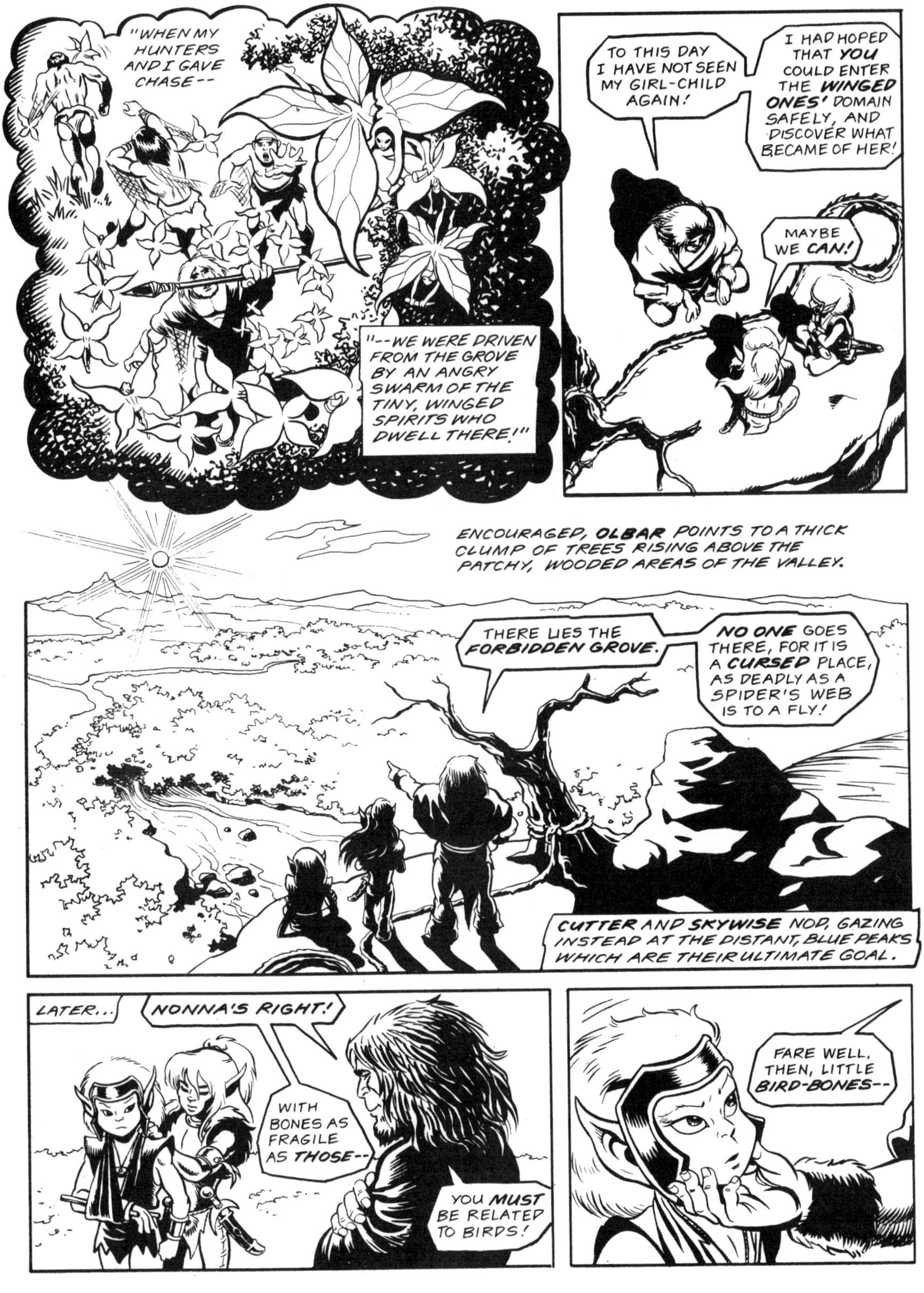
"WHEN MY HUNTERS AND I GAVE CHASE--
"--WE WERE DRIVEN FROM THE GROVE BY AN ANGRY SWARM OF THE TINY, WINGED SPIRITS WHO DWELL THERE!"
TO THIS DAY I HAVE NOT SEEN MY GIRL-CHILD AGAIN!
I HAD HOPED THAT YOU COULD ENTER THE WINGED ONES' DOMAIN SAFELY, AND DISCOVER WHAT BECAME OF HER!
MAYBE WE CAN!
ENCOURAGED, OLBAR POINTS TO A THICK CLUMP OF TREES RISING ABOVE THE PATCHY, WOODED AREAS OF THE VALLEY.
THERE LIES THE FORBIDDEN GROVE.
NO ONE GOES THERE, FOR IT IS A CURSED PLACE, AS DEADLY AS A SPIDER'S WEB IS TO A FLY!
CUTTER AND SKYWISE NOD, GAZING INSTEAD AT THE DISTANT, BLUE PEAKS WHICH ARE THEIR ULTIMATE GOAL.
LATER...
NONNA'S RIGHT!
WITH BONES AS FRAGILE AS THOSE--
YOU MUST BE RELATED TO BIRDS!
FARE WELL, THEN, LITTLE BIRD-BONES--

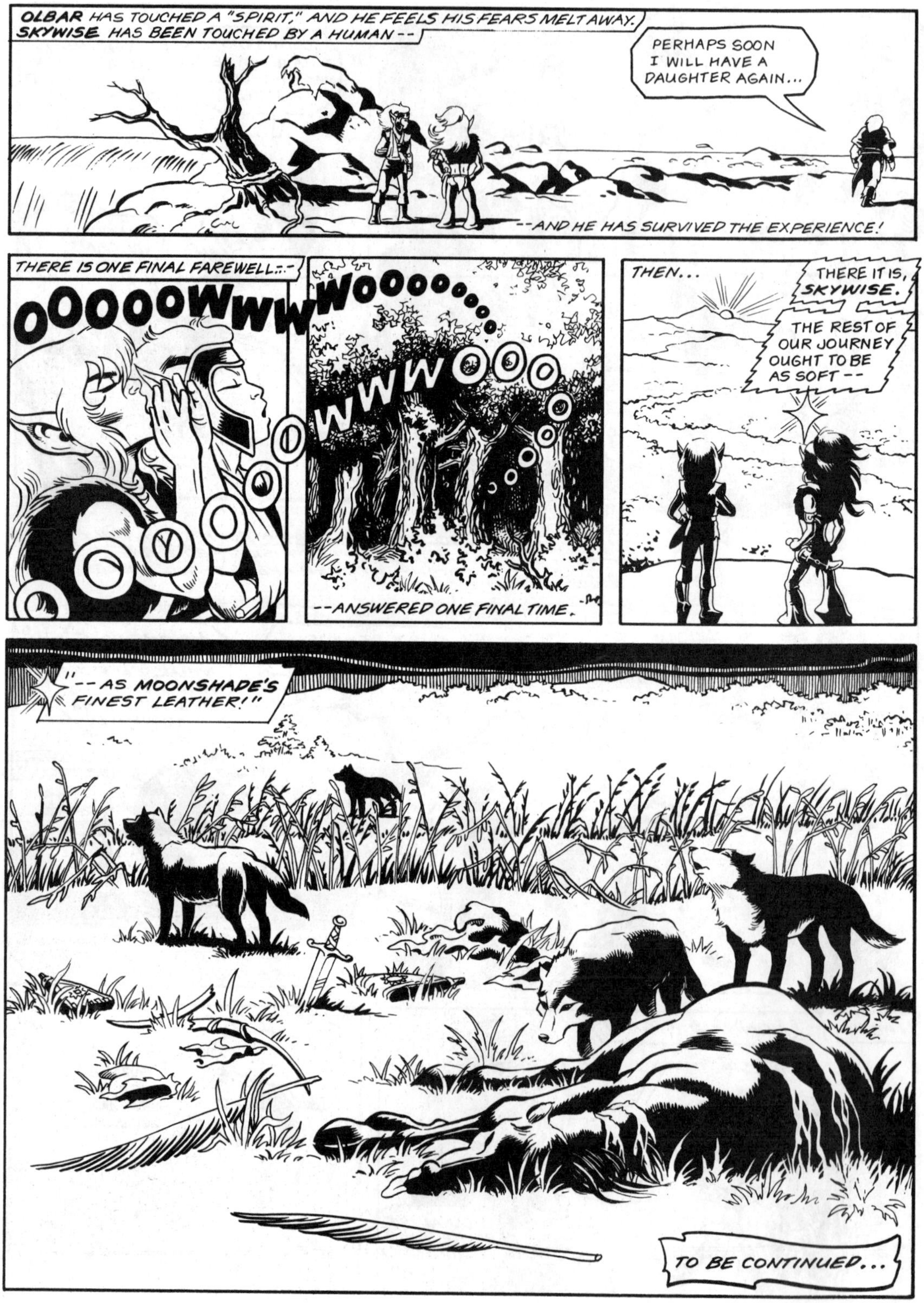
OLBAR HAS TOUCHED A "SPIRIT," AND HE FEELS HIS FEARS MELT AWAY. SKYWISE HAS BEEN TOUCHED BY A HUMAN --
PERHAPS SOON I WILL HAVE A DAUGHTER AGAIN...
--AND HE HAS SURVIVED THE EXPERIENCE!
THERE IS ONE FINAL FAREWELL...
OOOOOWWWWOOOOOOOOO
WWWOOOOOOO
--ANSWERED ONE FINAL TIME.
THEN...
THERE IT IS, SKYWISE.
THE REST OF OUR JOURNEY OUGHT TO BE AS SOFT --
"--AS MOONSHADE'S FINEST LEATHER!"
TO BE CONTINUED...

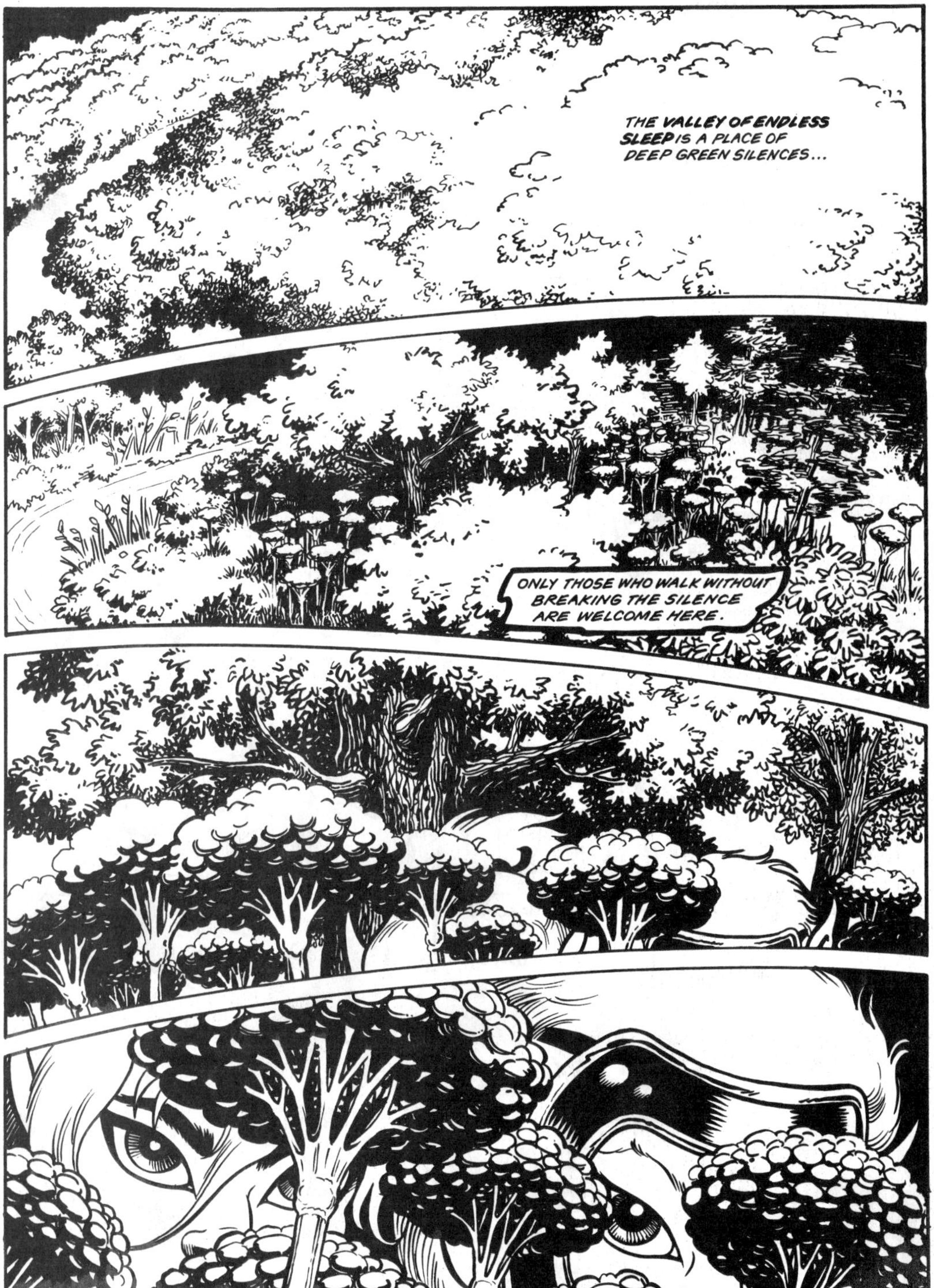
THE VALLEY OF ENDLESS SLEEP IS A PLACE OF DEEP GREEN SILENCES...
ONLY THOSE WHO WALK WITHOUT BREAKING THE SILENCE ARE WELCOME HERE.

WE'RE TWO NIGHTS CLOSER TO *BLUE MOUNTAIN*, BUT THE NEARER WE GET-- THE LESS *CUTTER* SEEMS TO CARE!

HE MISSES *NIGHTRUNNER* --BUT IT'S MORE THAN THAT.

STILL FAR AWAY, OBSCURRED BY THE TREES, LIES THE BLUE MOUNTAIN PEAK WHERE THE ELFIN PAIR HOPE TO FIND OTHERS OF THEIR KIND. THOUGH THERE HAS NEVER BEEN MUCH NEED FOR WORDS BETWEEN THEM, *SKYWISE* KNOWS THAT HIS FRIEND'S HEAVY HEART WANTS CHEERING.

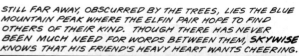

LOOK! THE TWO STARS I GAVE YOU AND *LEETAH* ON YOUR JOIN- ING NIGHT...

THEY'RE RIGHT OVERHEAD!

HMM... THEY SEEM FAR APART.

BUT ALWAYS TOGETHER!

YES... IT'S GOOD TO KNOW THAT *LEETAH* AND THE CUBS ARE SAFE IN *SORROW'S END.*

SHE WAS *WISE* NOT TO COME WITH ME ON THIS QUEST.

AND I SUPPOSE THAT MAKES *ME* A *FOOL!*

IF YOU HADN'T GRABBED THAT *ROOT* WHEN YOU FELL... IF YOU HAD *DROWNED* IN THE DEATHWATER...

I-I DON'T KNOW WHAT I--

YOU... WOULD HAVE MARCHED RIGHT UP TO THE *BIRD SPIRITS* AND ANNOUNCED YOURSELF WITH YOUR *SWORD!*

LUCKILY *I'M* STILL HERE TO MAKE APOLOGIES FOR MY CHIEF--

--WHO *STILL* HAS A FOUL DISPOSITION AND THE MANNERS OF A *TROLL!*

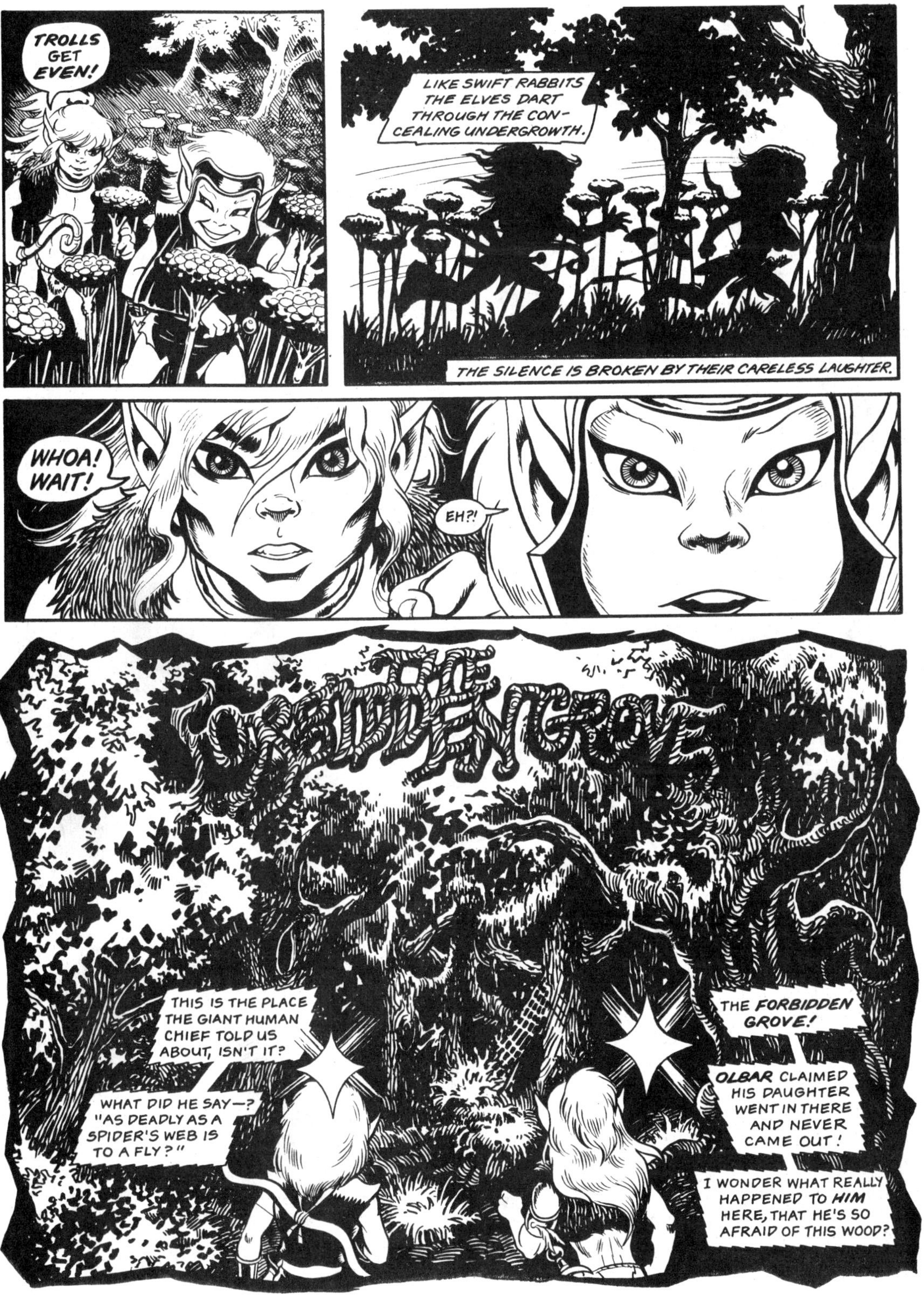
TROLLS GET EVEN!
LIKE SWIFT RABBITS THE ELVES DART THROUGH THE CONCEALING UNDERGROWTH.
THE SILENCE IS BROKEN BY THEIR CARELESS LAUGHTER.
WHOA! WAIT!
EH?!
THE FORBIDDEN GROVE
THIS IS THE PLACE THE GIANT HUMAN CHIEF TOLD US ABOUT, ISN'T IT?
WHAT DID HE SAY—? "AS DEADLY AS A SPIDER'S WEB IS TO A FLY?"
THE FORBIDDEN GROVE!
OLBAR CLAIMED HIS DAUGHTER WENT IN THERE AND NEVER CAME OUT!
I WONDER WHAT REALLY HAPPENED TO HIM HERE, THAT HE'S SO AFRAID OF THIS WOOD?

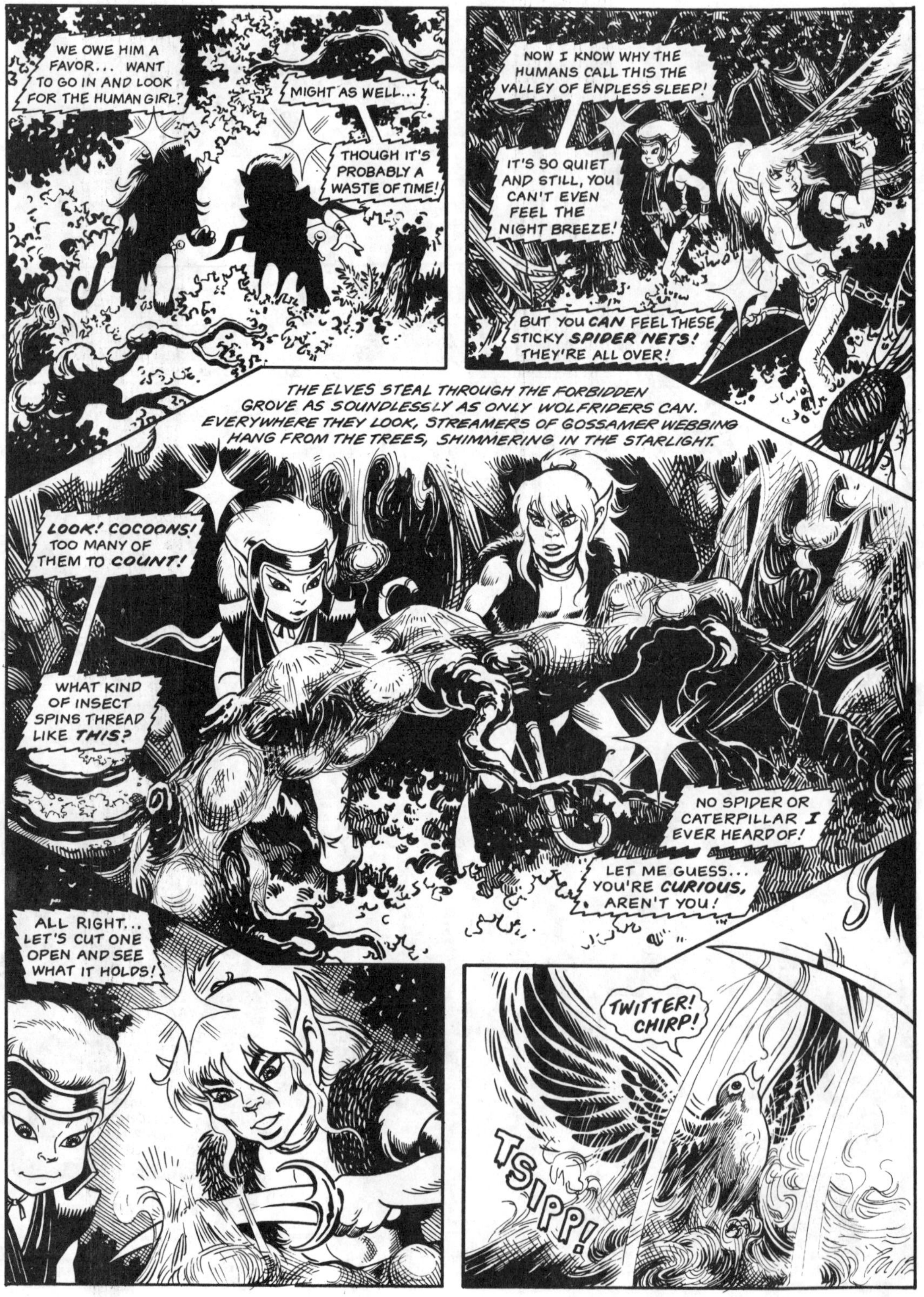

WE OWE HIM A FAVOR... WANT TO GO IN AND LOOK FOR THE HUMAN GIRL?
MIGHT AS WELL...
THOUGH IT'S PROBABLY A WASTE OF TIME!
NOW I KNOW WHY THE HUMANS CALL THIS THE VALLEY OF ENDLESS SLEEP!
IT'S SO QUIET AND STILL, YOU CAN'T EVEN FEEL THE NIGHT BREEZE!
BUT YOU CAN FEEL THESE STICKY SPIDER NETS! THEY'RE ALL OVER!
THE ELVES STEAL THROUGH THE FORBIDDEN GROVE AS SOUNDLESSLY AS ONLY WOLFRIDERS CAN. EVERYWHERE THEY LOOK, STREAMERS OF GOSSAMER WEBBING HANG FROM THE TREES, SHIMMERING IN THE STARLIGHT.
LOOK! COCOONS! TOO MANY OF THEM TO COUNT!
WHAT KIND OF INSECT SPINS THREAD LIKE THIS?
NO SPIDER OR CATERPILLAR I EVER HEARD OF!
LET ME GUESS... YOU'RE CURIOUS, AREN'T YOU!
ALL RIGHT... LET'S CUT ONE OPEN AND SEE WHAT IT HOLDS!
TWITTER! CHIRP!
TSIPP!

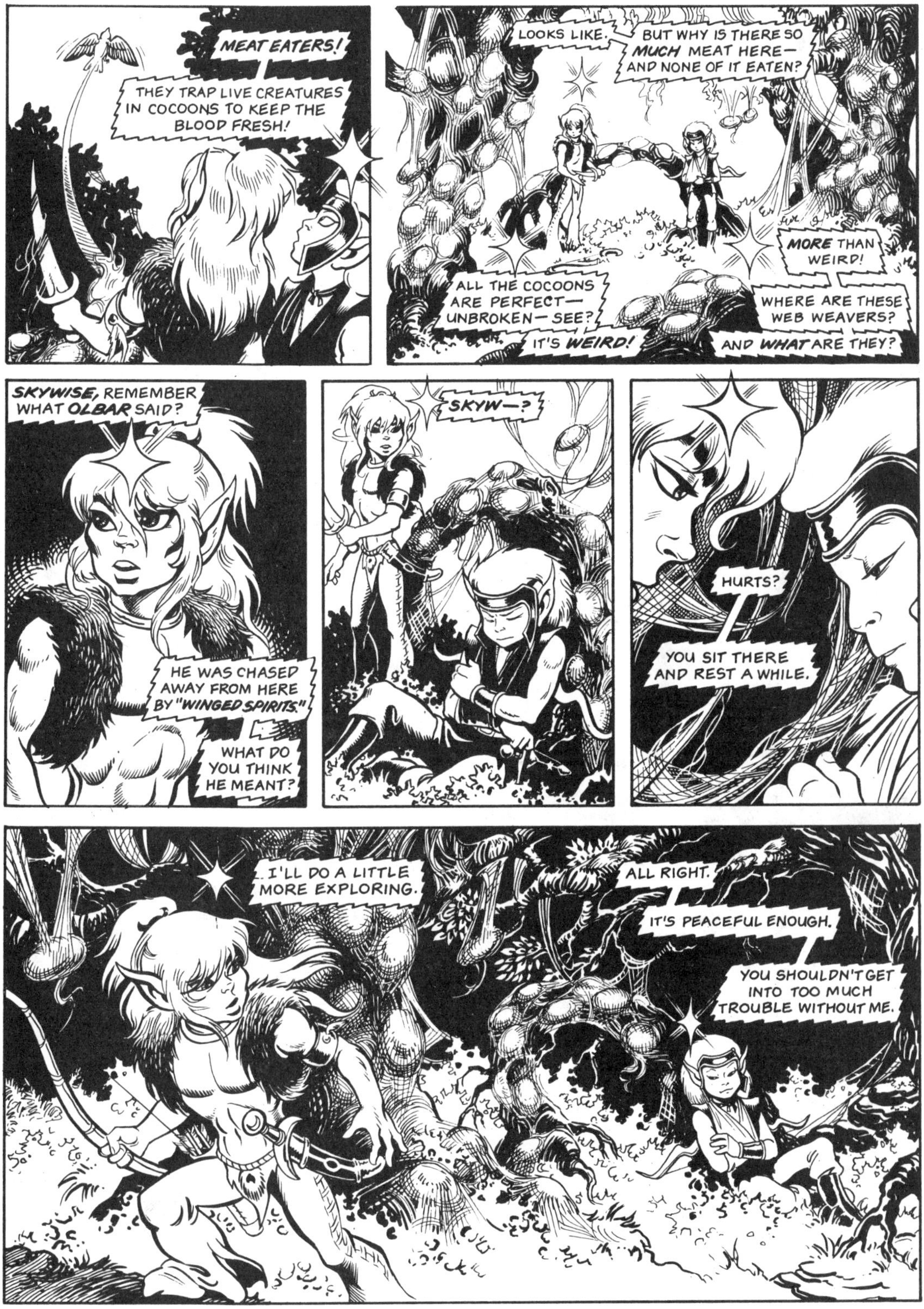
MEAT EATERS!
THEY TRAP LIVE CREATURES IN COCOONS TO KEEP THE BLOOD FRESH!
LOOKS LIKE.
BUT WHY IS THERE SO MUCH MEAT HERE— AND NONE OF IT EATEN?
ALL THE COCOONS ARE PERFECT— UNBROKEN— SEE?
IT'S WEIRD!
MORE THAN WEIRD!
WHERE ARE THESE WEB WEAVERS?
AND WHAT ARE THEY?
SKYWISE, REMEMBER WHAT OLBAR SAID?
HE WAS CHASED AWAY FROM HERE BY "WINGED SPIRITS."
WHAT DO YOU THINK HE MEANT?
SKYW—?
HURTS?
YOU SIT THERE AND REST A WHILE.
I'LL DO A LITTLE MORE EXPLORING.
ALL RIGHT.
IT'S PEACEFUL ENOUGH.
YOU SHOULDN'T GET INTO TOO MUCH TROUBLE WITHOUT ME.

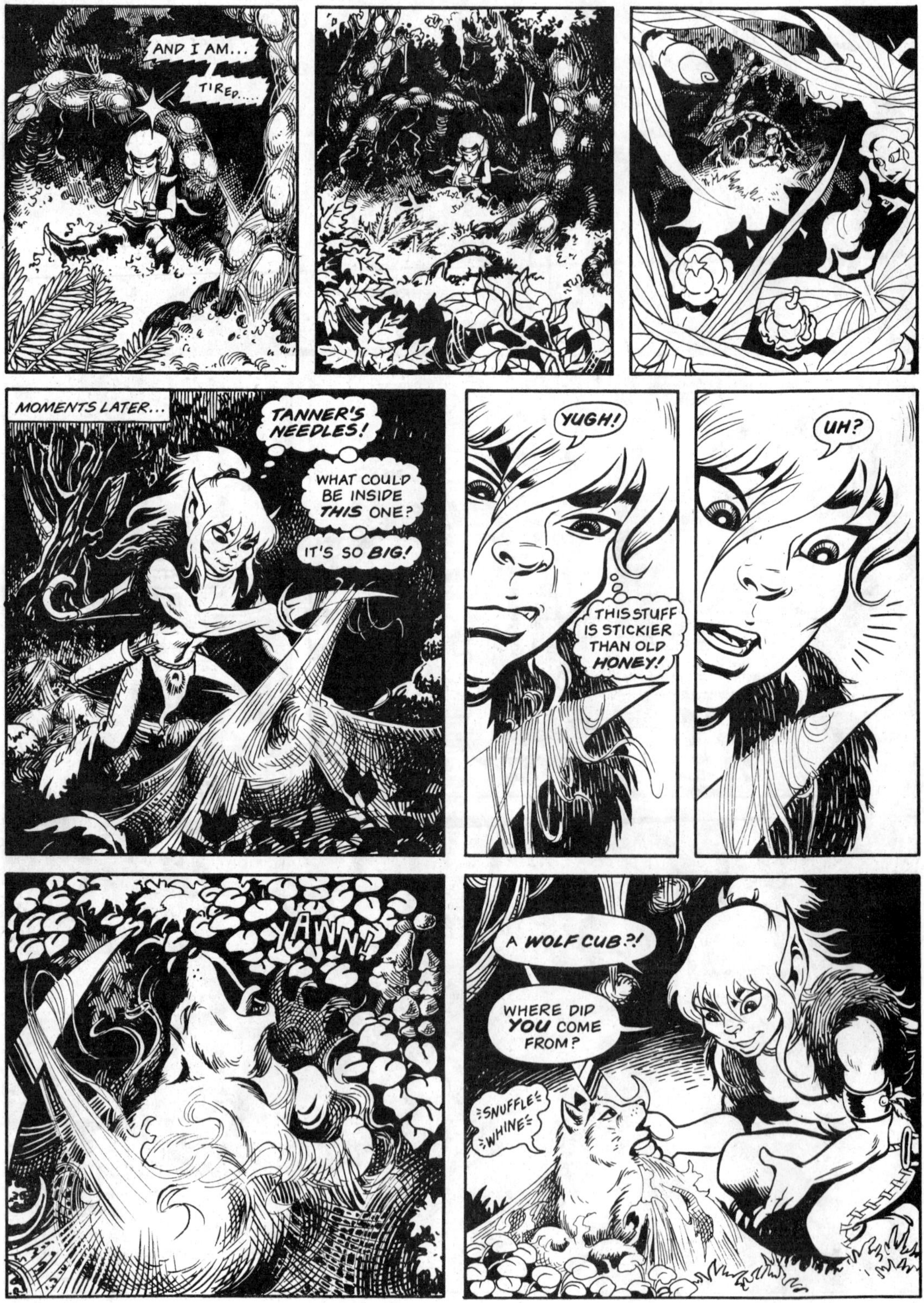
AND I AM...
TIRED.....
MOMENTS LATER...
TANNER'S NEEDLES!
WHAT COULD BE INSIDE THIS ONE?
IT'S SO BIG!
YUGH!
THIS STUFF IS STICKIER THAN OLD HONEY!
UH?
YAWN!
A WOLF CUB?!
WHERE DID YOU COME FROM?
SNUFFLE WHINE

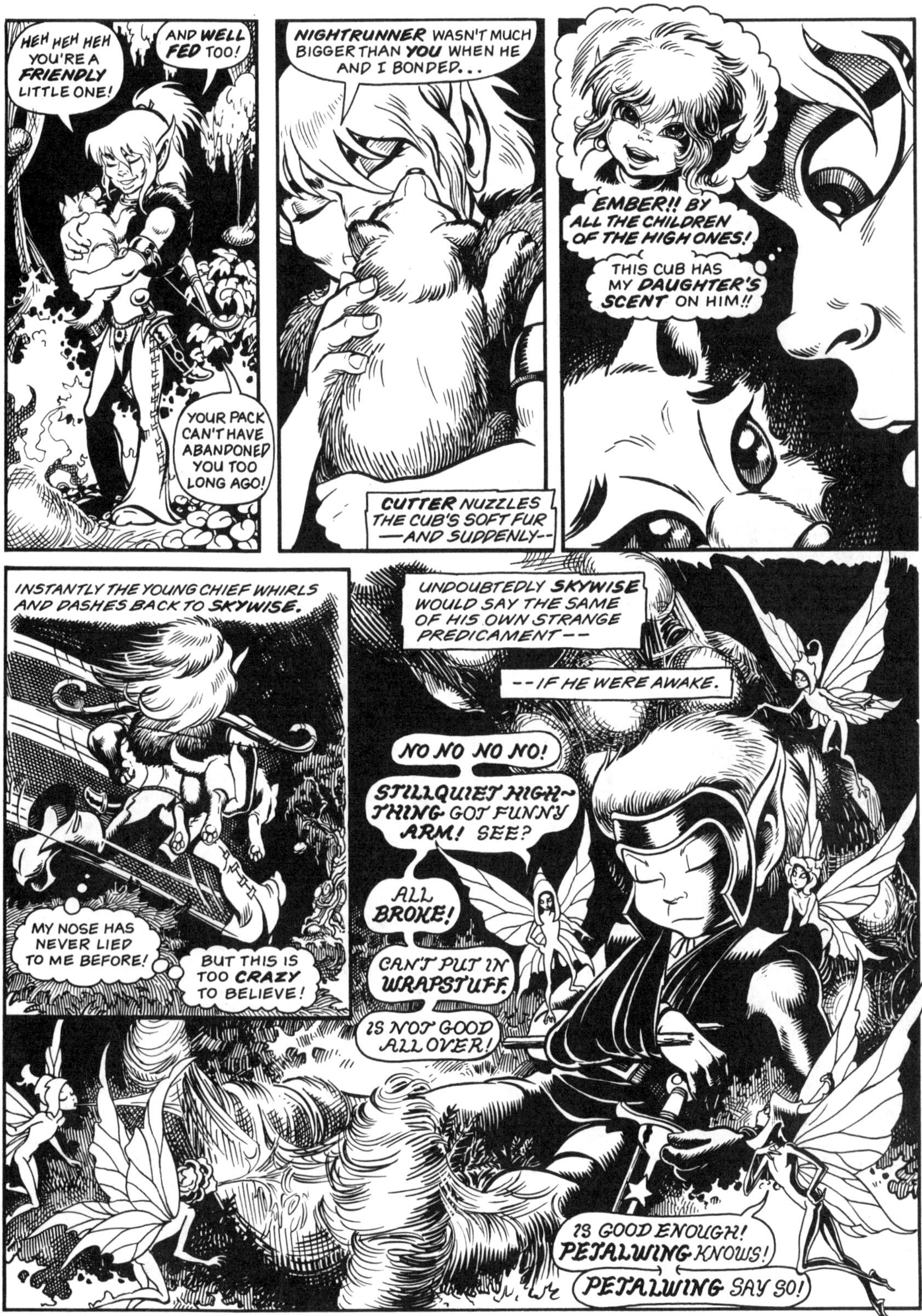
HEH HEH HEH YOU'RE A FRIENDLY LITTLE ONE!
AND WELL FED TOO!
YOUR PACK CAN'T HAVE ABANDONED YOU TOO LONG AGO!
NIGHTRUNNER WASN'T MUCH BIGGER THAN YOU WHEN HE AND I BONDED...
CUTTER NUZZLES THE CUB'S SOFT FUR —AND SUDDENLY--
EMBER!! BY ALL THE CHILDREN OF THE HIGH ONES!
THIS CUB HAS MY DAUGHTER'S SCENT ON HIM!!
INSTANTLY THE YOUNG CHIEF WHIRLS AND DASHES BACK TO SKYWISE.
MY NOSE HAS NEVER LIED TO ME BEFORE!
BUT THIS IS TOO CRAZY TO BELIEVE!
UNDOUBTEDLY SKYWISE WOULD SAY THE SAME OF HIS OWN STRANGE PREDICAMENT--
--IF HE WERE AWAKE.
NO NO NO NO!
STILLQUIET HIGH-THING GOT FUNNY ARM! SEE?
ALL BROKE!
CAN'T PUT IN WRAPSTUFF.
IS NOT GOOD ALL OVER!
IS GOOD ENOUGH! PETALWING KNOWS!
PETALWING SAY SO!

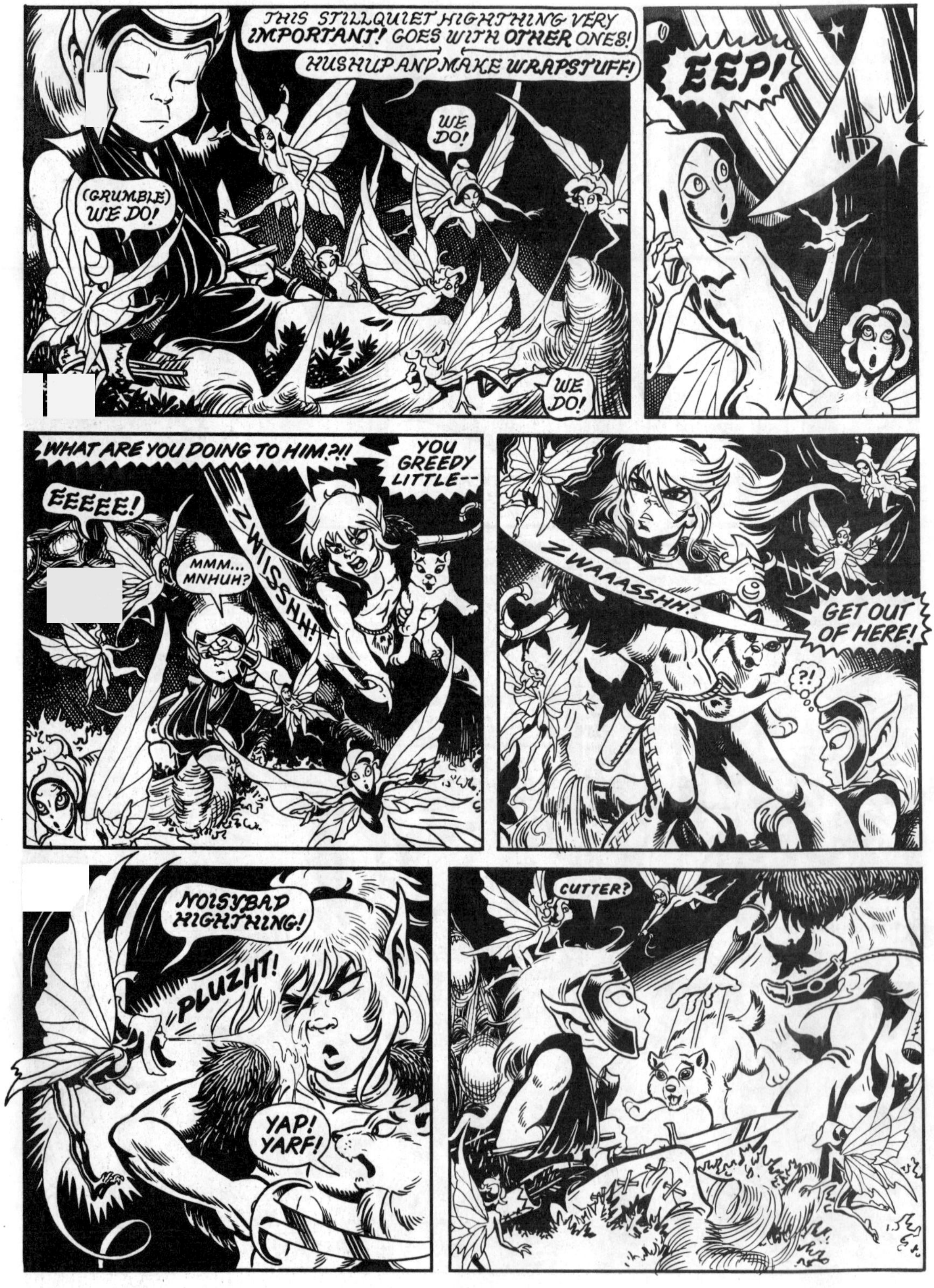
THIS STILLQUIET HIGHTHING VERY IMPORTANT! GOES WITH OTHER ONES!
HUSHUP AND MAKE WRAPSTUFF!
WE DO!
(GRUMBLE) WE DO!
WE DO!
EEP!
WHAT ARE YOU DOING TO HIM?!!
YOU GREEDY LITTLE--
EEEEE!
ZWIISSHH!
MMM... MNHUH?
ZWAAAASSHH!
GET OUT OF HERE!
?!
NOISYBAD HIGHTHING!
PLUZHT!
YAP! YARF!
CUTTER?

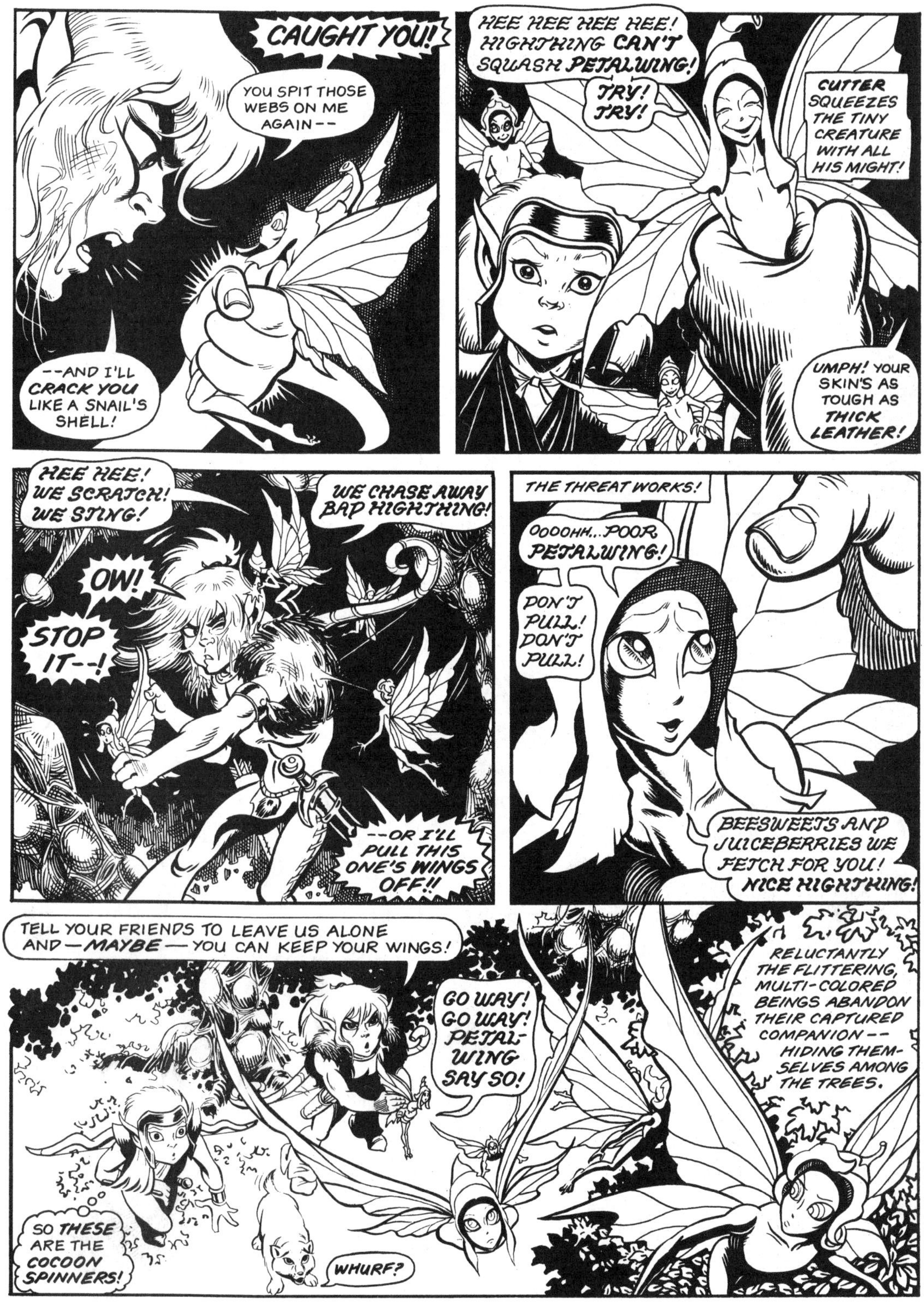
CAUGHT YOU!
YOU SPIT THOSE WEBS ON ME AGAIN--
--AND I'LL CRACK YOU LIKE A SNAIL'S SHELL!
HEE HEE HEE HEE! HIGHTHING CAN'T SQUASH PETALWING!
TRY! TRY!
CUTTER SQUEEZES THE TINY CREATURE WITH ALL HIS MIGHT!
UMPH! YOUR SKIN'S AS TOUGH AS THICK LEATHER!
HEE HEE! WE SCRATCH! WE STING!
WE CHASE AWAY BAD HIGHTHING!
OW!
STOP IT--!
--OR I'LL PULL THIS ONE'S WINGS OFF!!
THE THREAT WORKS!
OOOOHH... POOR PETALWING!
DON'T PULL! DON'T PULL!
BEESWEETS AND JUICEBERRIES WE FETCH FOR YOU! NICE HIGHTHING!
TELL YOUR FRIENDS TO LEAVE US ALONE AND—MAYBE—YOU CAN KEEP YOUR WINGS!
GO WAY! GO WAY! PETALWING SAY SO!
RELUCTANTLY THE FLITTERING, MULTI-COLORED BEINGS ABANDON THEIR CAPTURED COMPANION-- HIDING THEMSELVES AMONG THE TREES.
SO THESE ARE THE COCOON SPINNERS!
WHURF?

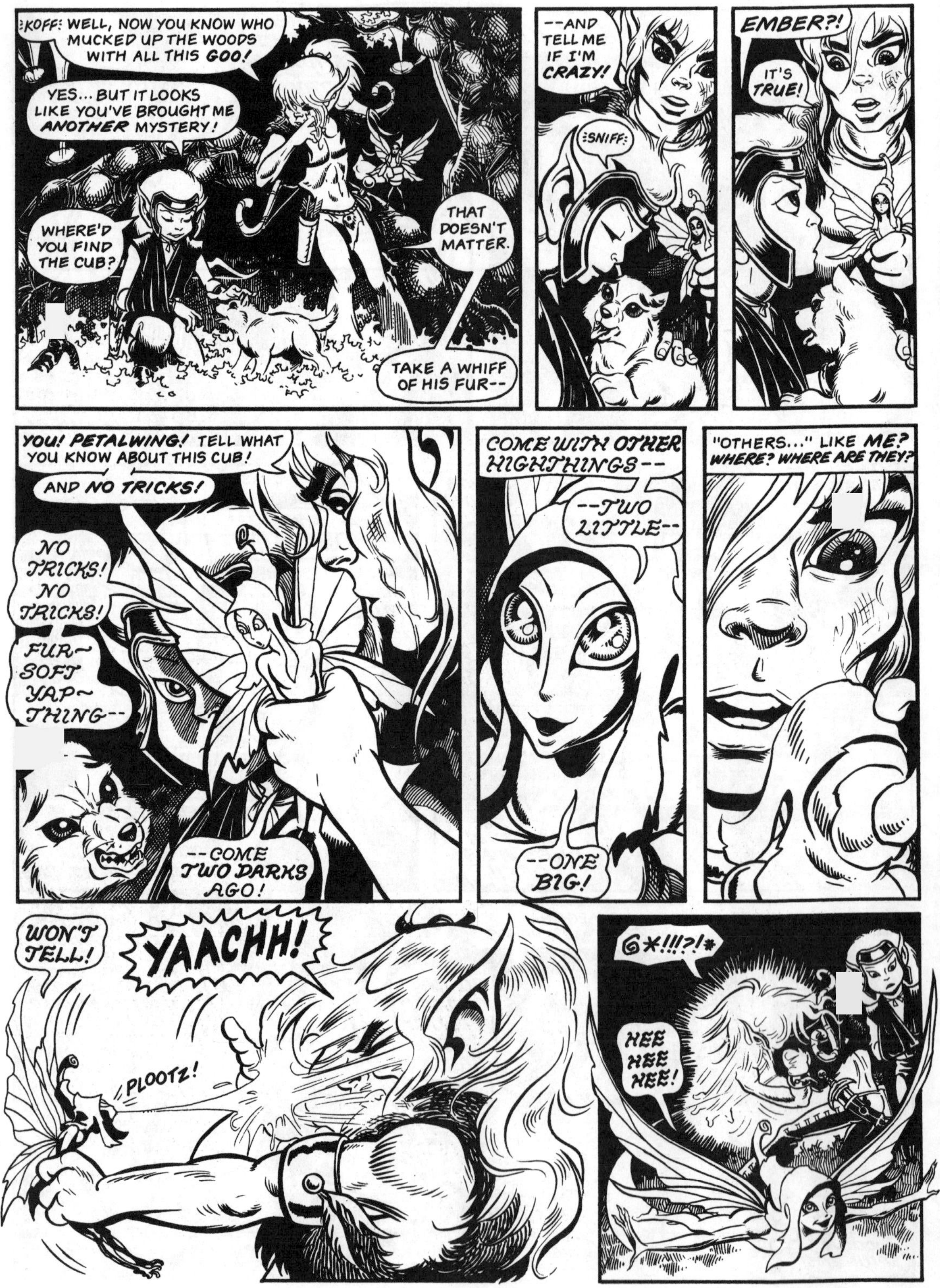
KOFF! WELL, NOW YOU KNOW WHO MUCKED UP THE WOODS WITH ALL THIS GOO!
YES... BUT IT LOOKS LIKE YOU'VE BROUGHT ME ANOTHER MYSTERY!
WHERE'D YOU FIND THE CUB?
THAT DOESN'T MATTER.
TAKE A WHIFF OF HIS FUR--
--AND TELL ME IF I'M CRAZY!
SNIFF
EMBER?!
IT'S TRUE!
YOU! PETALWING! TELL WHAT YOU KNOW ABOUT THIS CUB!
AND NO TRICKS!
NO TRICKS! NO TRICKS!
FUR-SOFT YAP-THING--
--COME TWO DARKS AGO!
COME WITH OTHER HIGHTHINGS--
--TWO LITTLE--
--ONE BIG!
"OTHERS..." LIKE ME? WHERE? WHERE ARE THEY?
WON'T TELL!
YAACHH!
PLOOTZ!
G*!!!?!*
HEE HEE HEE!

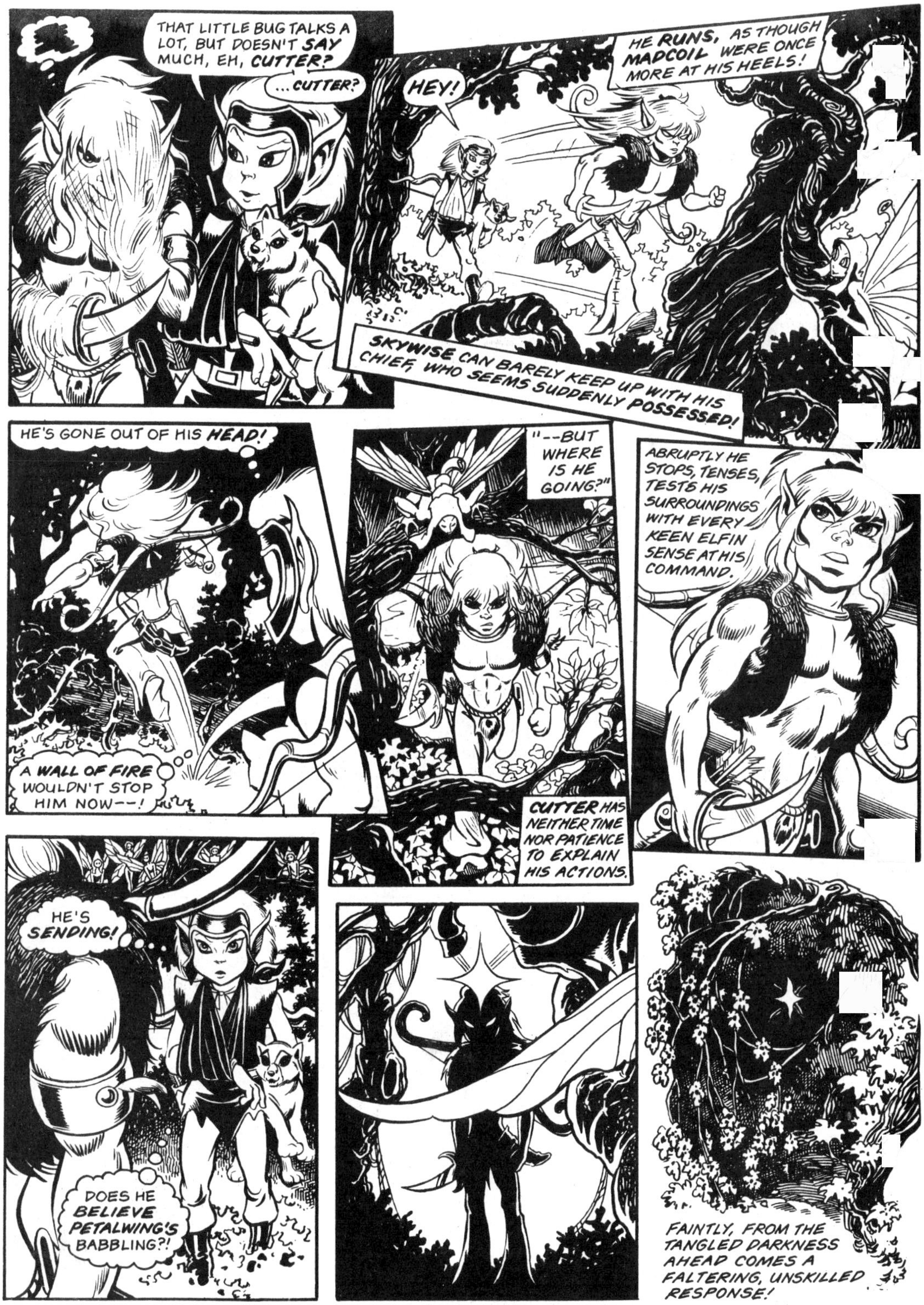

THAT LITTLE BUG TALKS A LOT, BUT DOESN'T SAY MUCH, EH, CUTTER?
...CUTTER?
HE RUNS, AS THOUGH MADCOIL WERE ONCE MORE AT HIS HEELS!
HEY!
SKYWISE CAN BARELY KEEP UP WITH HIS CHIEF, WHO SEEMS SUDDENLY POSSESSED!
HE'S GONE OUT OF HIS HEAD!
A WALL OF FIRE WOULDN'T STOP HIM NOW--!
"--BUT WHERE IS HE GOING?"
CUTTER HAS NEITHER TIME NOR PATIENCE TO EXPLAIN HIS ACTIONS.
ABRUPTLY HE STOPS, TENSES, TESTS HIS SURROUNDINGS WITH EVERY KEEN ELFIN SENSE AT HIS COMMAND.
HE'S SENDING!
DOES HE BELIEVE PETALWING'S BABBLING?!
FAINTLY, FROM THE TANGLED DARKNESS AHEAD COMES A FALTERING, UNSKILLED RESPONSE!

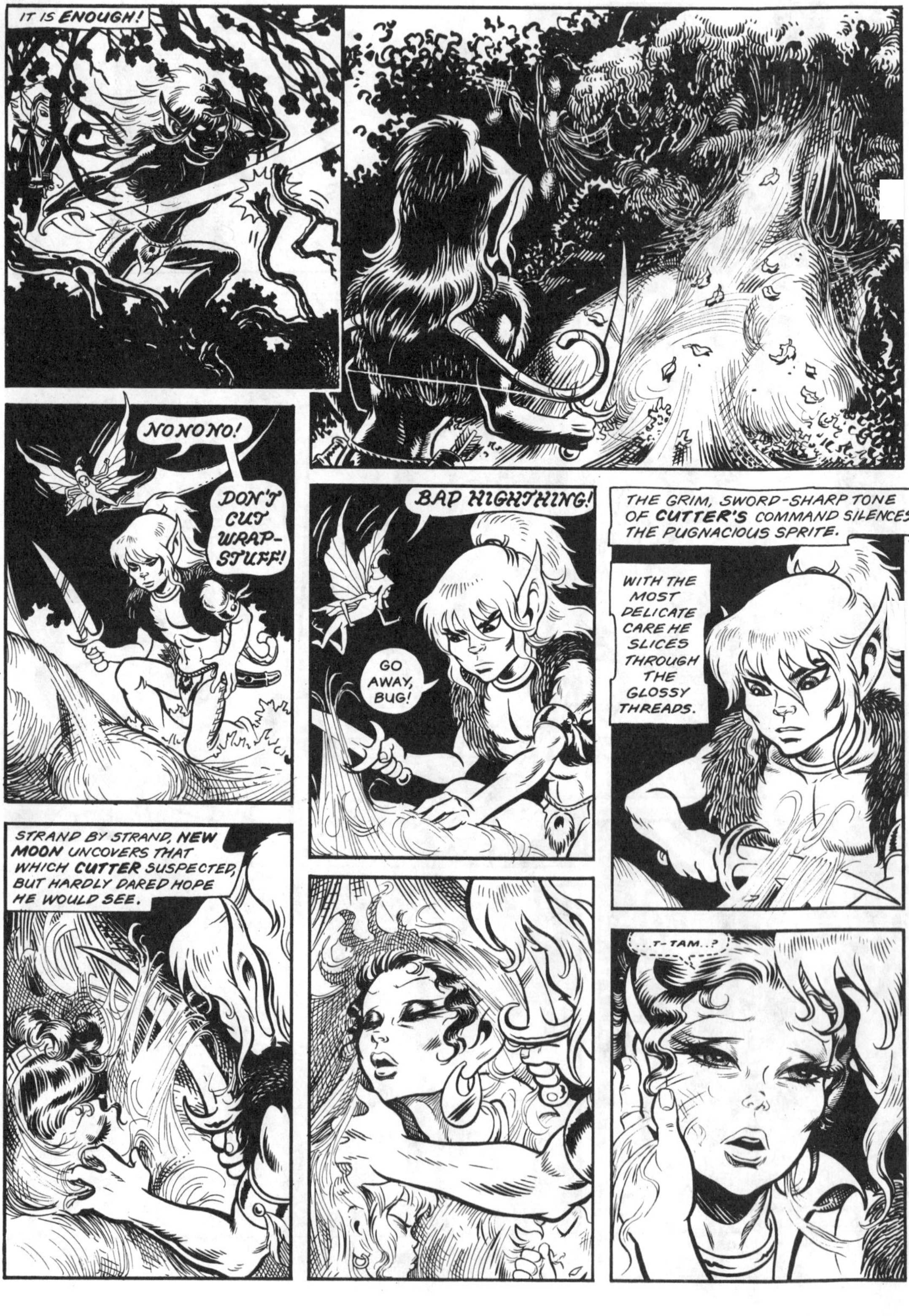
IT IS ENOUGH!
NONONO!
DON'T CUT WRAP-STUFF!
BAD HIGHTHING!
GO AWAY, BUG!
THE GRIM, SWORD-SHARP TONE OF CUTTER'S COMMAND SILENCES THE PUGNACIOUS SPRITE.
WITH THE MOST DELICATE CARE HE SLICES THROUGH THE GLOSSY THREADS.
STRAND BY STRAND, NEW MOON UNCOVERS THAT WHICH CUTTER SUSPECTED, BUT HARDLY DARED HOPE HE WOULD SEE.
...T-TAM..?

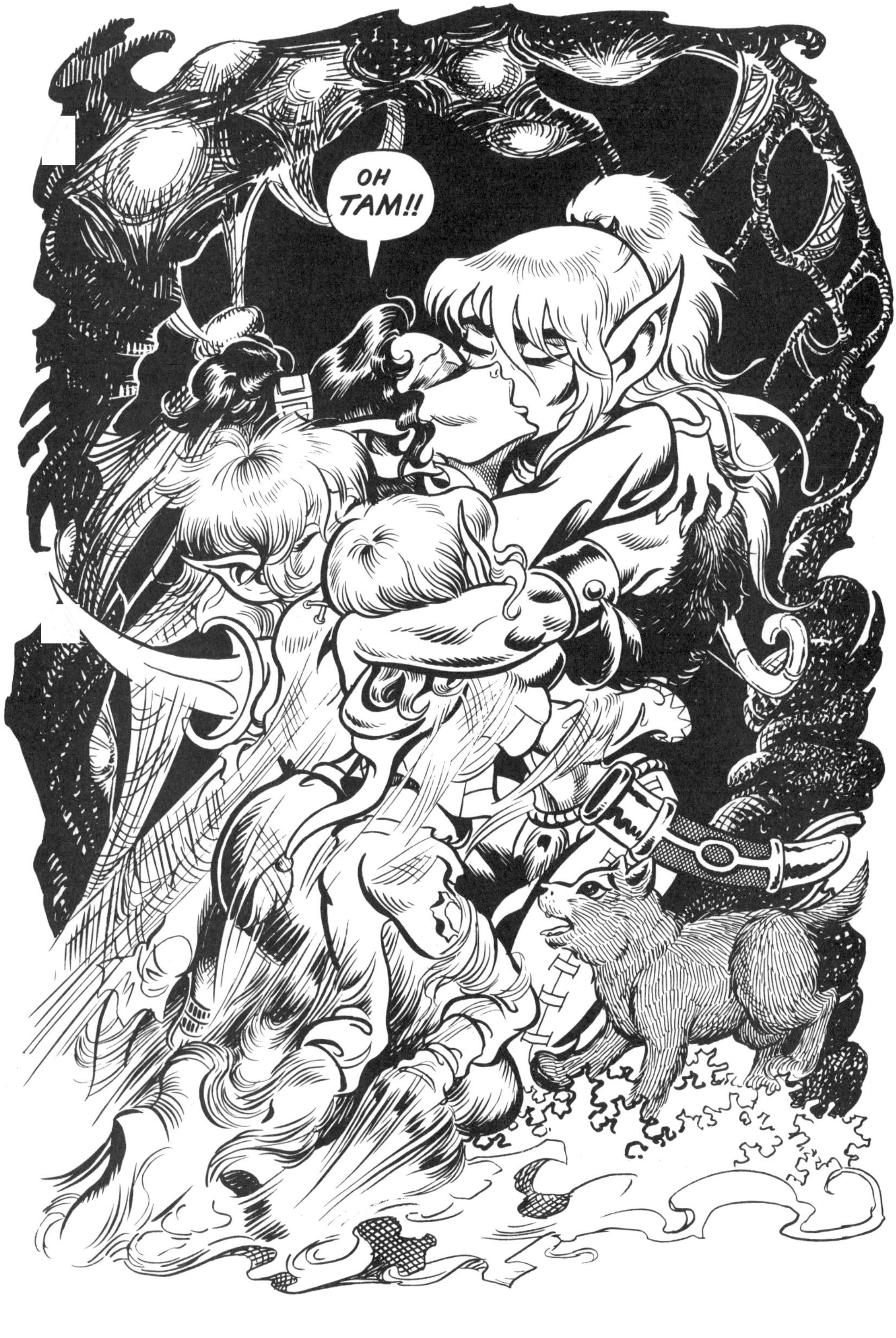
OH TAM!!

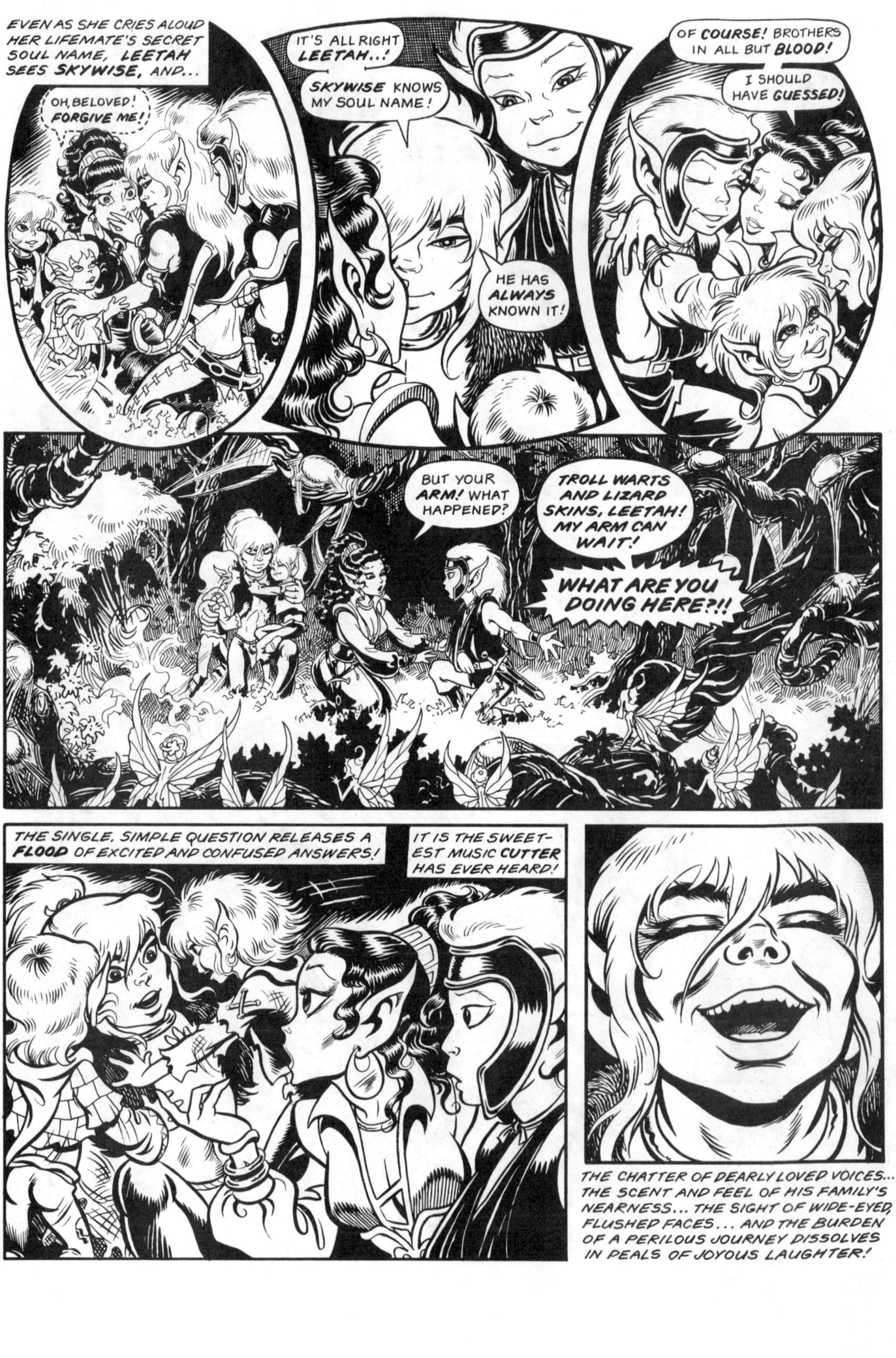
EVEN AS SHE CRIES ALOUD HER LIFEMATE'S SECRET SOUL NAME, LEETAH SEES SKYWISE, AND...
OH, BELOVED! FORGIVE ME!
IT'S ALL RIGHT LEETAH..!
SKYWISE KNOWS MY SOUL NAME!
HE HAS ALWAYS KNOWN IT!
OF COURSE! BROTHERS IN ALL BUT BLOOD!
I SHOULD HAVE GUESSED!
BUT YOUR ARM! WHAT HAPPENED?
TROLL WARTS AND LIZARD SKINS, LEETAH! MY ARM CAN WAIT!
WHAT ARE YOU DOING HERE?!!
THE SINGLE, SIMPLE QUESTION RELEASES A FLOOD OF EXCITED AND CONFUSED ANSWERS!
IT IS THE SWEETEST MUSIC CUTTER HAS EVER HEARD!
THE CHATTER OF DEARLY LOVED VOICES... THE SCENT AND FEEL OF HIS FAMILY'S NEARNESS... THE SIGHT OF WIDE-EYED, FLUSHED FACES... AND THE BURDEN OF A PERILOUS JOURNEY DISSOLVES IN PEALS OF JOYOUS LAUGHTER!

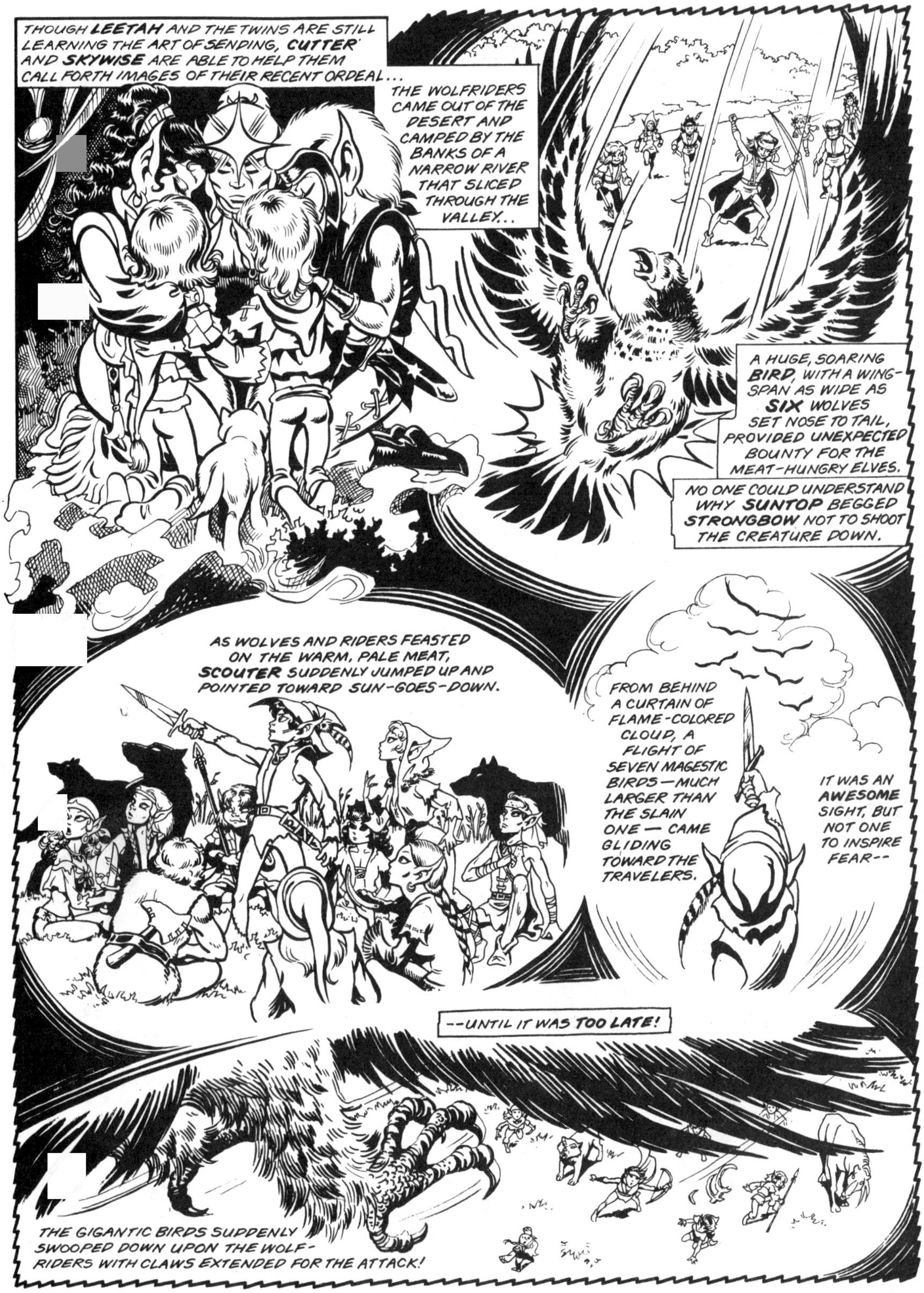
THOUGH LEETAH AND THE TWINS ARE STILL LEARNING THE ART OF SENDING, CUTTER AND SKYWISE ARE ABLE TO HELP THEM CALL FORTH IMAGES OF THEIR RECENT ORDEAL...
THE WOLFRIDERS CAME OUT OF THE DESERT AND CAMPED BY THE BANKS OF A NARROW RIVER THAT SLICED THROUGH THE VALLEY...
A HUGE, SOARING BIRD, WITH A WING-SPAN AS WIDE AS SIX WOLVES SET NOSE TO TAIL, PROVIDED UNEXPECTED BOUNTY FOR THE MEAT-HUNGRY ELVES.
NO ONE COULD UNDERSTAND WHY SUNTOP BEGGED STRONGBOW NOT TO SHOOT THE CREATURE DOWN.
AS WOLVES AND RIDERS FEASTED ON THE WARM, PALE MEAT, SCOUTER SUDDENLY JUMPED UP AND POINTED TOWARD SUN-GOES-DOWN.
FROM BEHIND A CURTAIN OF FLAME-COLORED CLOUD, A FLIGHT OF SEVEN MAGESTIC BIRDS—MUCH LARGER THAN THE SLAIN ONE — CAME GLIDING TOWARD THE TRAVELERS.
IT WAS AN AWESOME SIGHT, BUT NOT ONE TO INSPIRE FEAR--
--UNTIL IT WAS TOO LATE!
THE GIGANTIC BIRDS SUDDENLY SWOOPED DOWN UPON THE WOLF-RIDERS WITH CLAWS EXTENDED FOR THE ATTACK!

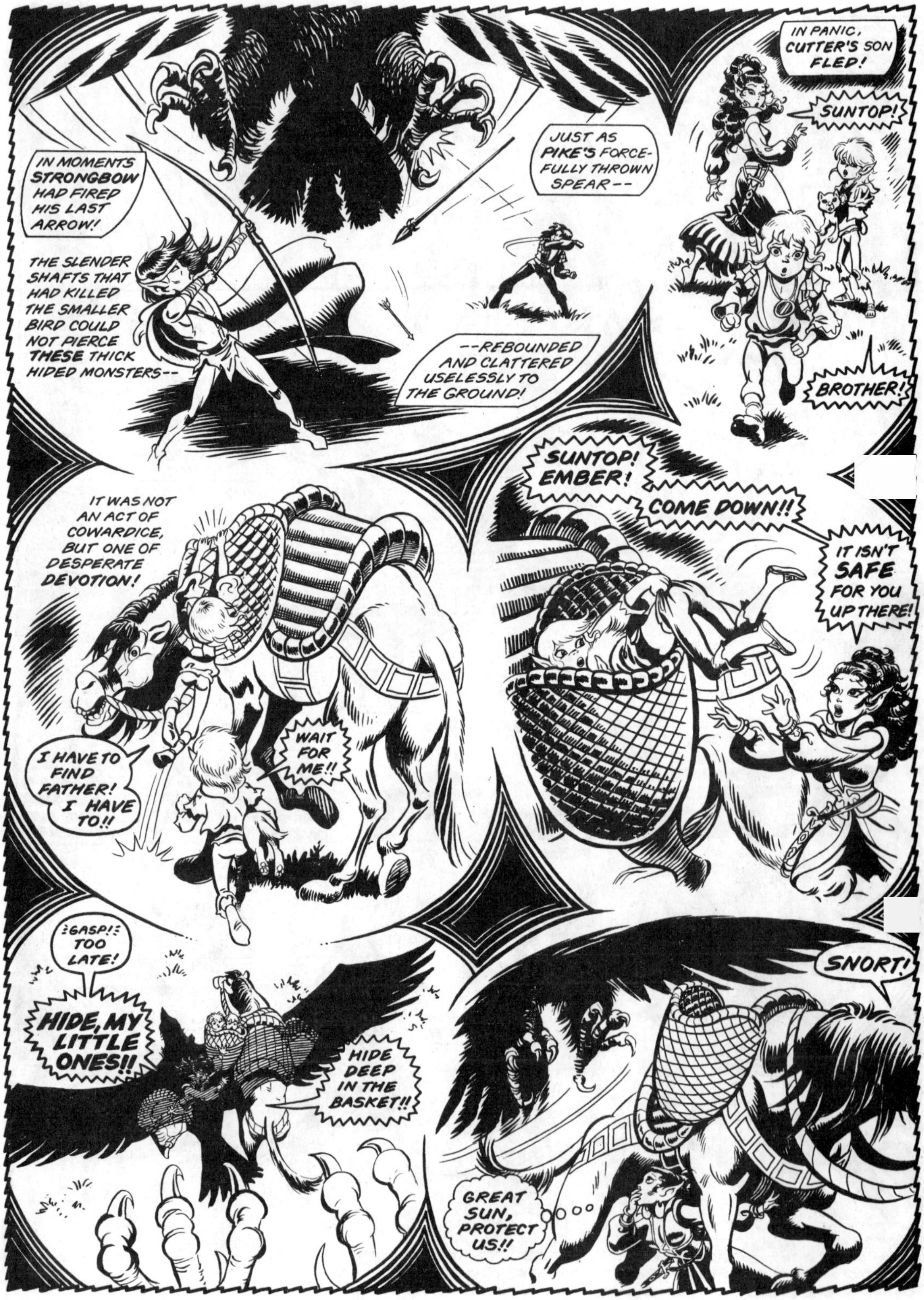
IN MOMENTS STRONGBOW HAD FIRED HIS LAST ARROW!
THE SLENDER SHAFTS THAT HAD KILLED THE SMALLER BIRD COULD NOT PIERCE THESE THICK HIDED MONSTERS--
JUST AS PIKE'S FORCE-FULLY THROWN SPEAR--
--REBOUNDED AND CLATTERED USELESSLY TO THE GROUND!
IN PANIC, CUTTER'S SON FLED!
SUNTOP!
BROTHER!
IT WAS NOT AN ACT OF COWARDICE, BUT ONE OF DESPERATE DEVOTION!
I HAVE TO FIND FATHER! I HAVE TO!!
WAIT FOR ME!!
SUNTOP! EMBER!
COME DOWN!!
IT ISN'T SAFE FOR YOU UP THERE!
GASP! TOO LATE!
HIDE, MY LITTLE ONES!!
HIDE DEEP IN THE BASKET!!
SNORT!
GREAT SUN, PROTECT US!!

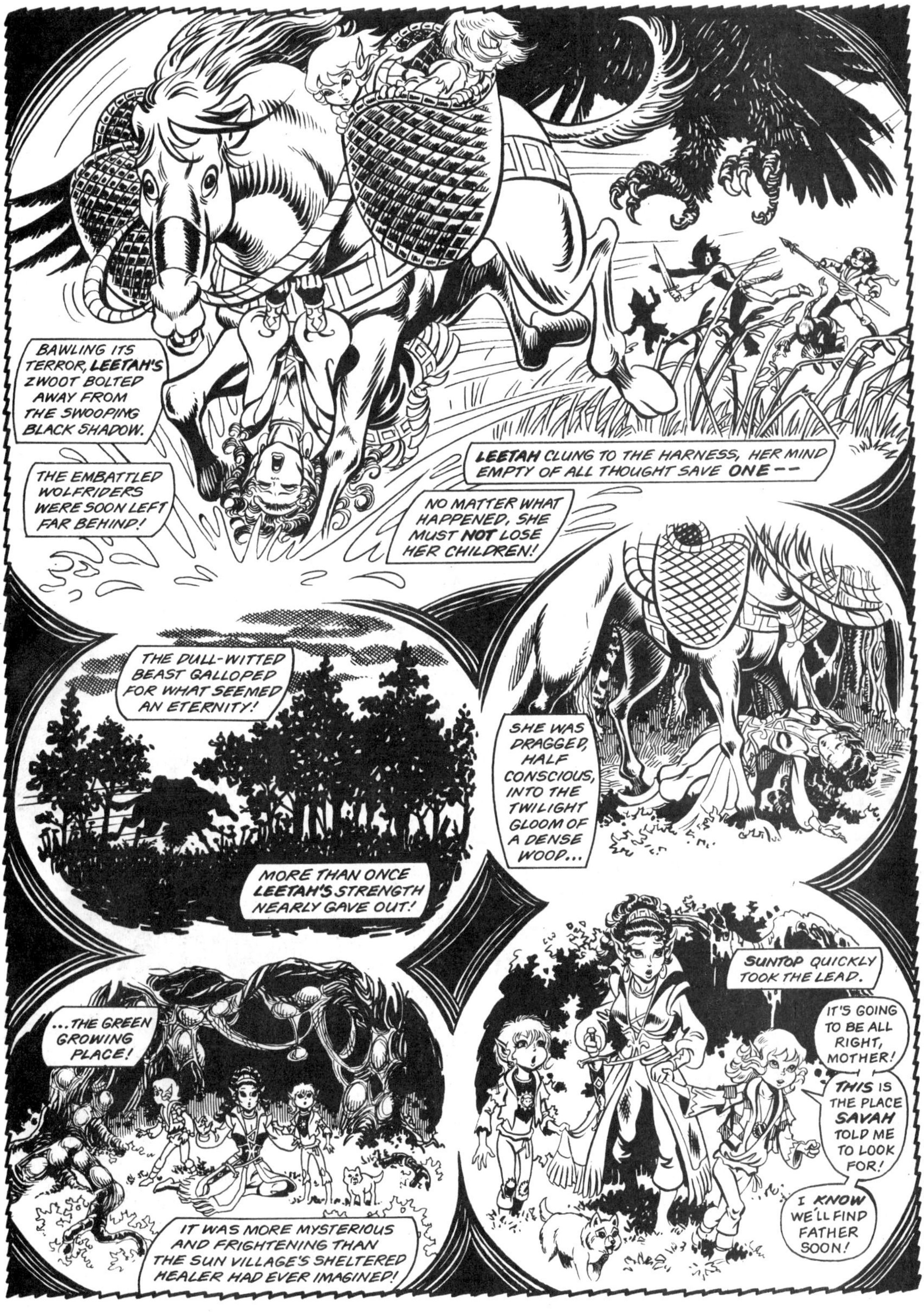
BAWLING ITS TERROR, LEETAH'S ZWOOT BOLTED AWAY FROM THE SWOOPING BLACK SHADOW.
THE EMBATTLED WOLFRIDERS WERE SOON LEFT FAR BEHIND!
LEETAH CLUNG TO THE HARNESS, HER MIND EMPTY OF ALL THOUGHT SAVE ONE--
NO MATTER WHAT HAPPENED, SHE MUST NOT LOSE HER CHILDREN!
THE DULL-WITTED BEAST GALLOPED FOR WHAT SEEMED AN ETERNITY!
MORE THAN ONCE LEETAH'S STRENGTH NEARLY GAVE OUT!
SHE WAS DRAGGED, HALF CONSCIOUS, INTO THE TWILIGHT GLOOM OF A DENSE WOOD...
...THE GREEN GROWING PLACE!
IT WAS MORE MYSTERIOUS AND FRIGHTENING THAN THE SUN VILLAGE'S SHELTERED HEALER HAD EVER IMAGINED!
SUNTOP QUICKLY TOOK THE LEAD.
IT'S GOING TO BE ALL RIGHT, MOTHER!
THIS IS THE PLACE SAVAH TOLD ME TO LOOK FOR!
I KNOW WE'LL FIND FATHER SOON!

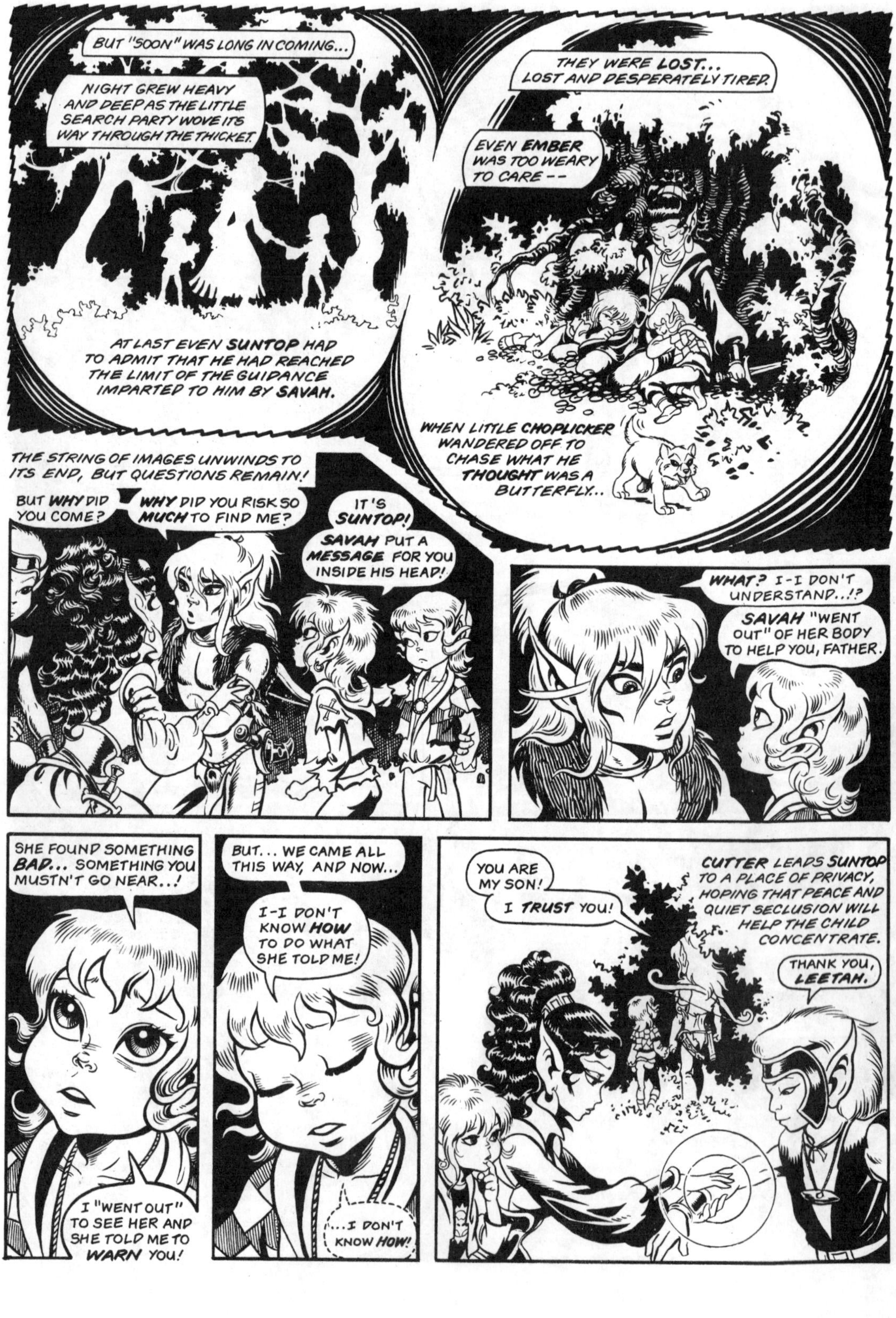
BUT "SOON" WAS LONG IN COMING...
NIGHT GREW HEAVY AND DEEP AS THE LITTLE SEARCH PARTY WOVE ITS WAY THROUGH THE THICKET.
AT LAST EVEN SUNTOP HAD TO ADMIT THAT HE HAD REACHED THE LIMIT OF THE GUIDANCE IMPARTED TO HIM BY SAVAH.
THEY WERE LOST... LOST AND DESPERATELY TIRED.
EVEN EMBER WAS TOO WEARY TO CARE --
WHEN LITTLE CHOPLICKER WANDERED OFF TO CHASE WHAT HE THOUGHT WAS A BUTTERFLY...
THE STRING OF IMAGES UNWINDS TO ITS END, BUT QUESTIONS REMAIN!
BUT WHY DID YOU COME?
WHY DID YOU RISK SO MUCH TO FIND ME?
IT'S SUNTOP! SAVAH PUT A MESSAGE FOR YOU INSIDE HIS HEAD!
WHAT? I-I DON'T UNDERSTAND..!?
SAVAH "WENT OUT" OF HER BODY TO HELP YOU, FATHER.
SHE FOUND SOMETHING BAD... SOMETHING YOU MUSTN'T GO NEAR..!
I "WENT OUT" TO SEE HER AND SHE TOLD ME TO WARN YOU!
BUT... WE CAME ALL THIS WAY, AND NOW...
I-I DON'T KNOW HOW TO DO WHAT SHE TOLD ME!
...I DON'T KNOW HOW!
YOU ARE MY SON!
I TRUST YOU!
CUTTER LEADS SUNTOP TO A PLACE OF PRIVACY, HOPING THAT PEACE AND QUIET SECLUSION WILL HELP THE CHILD CONCENTRATE.
THANK YOU, LEETAH.

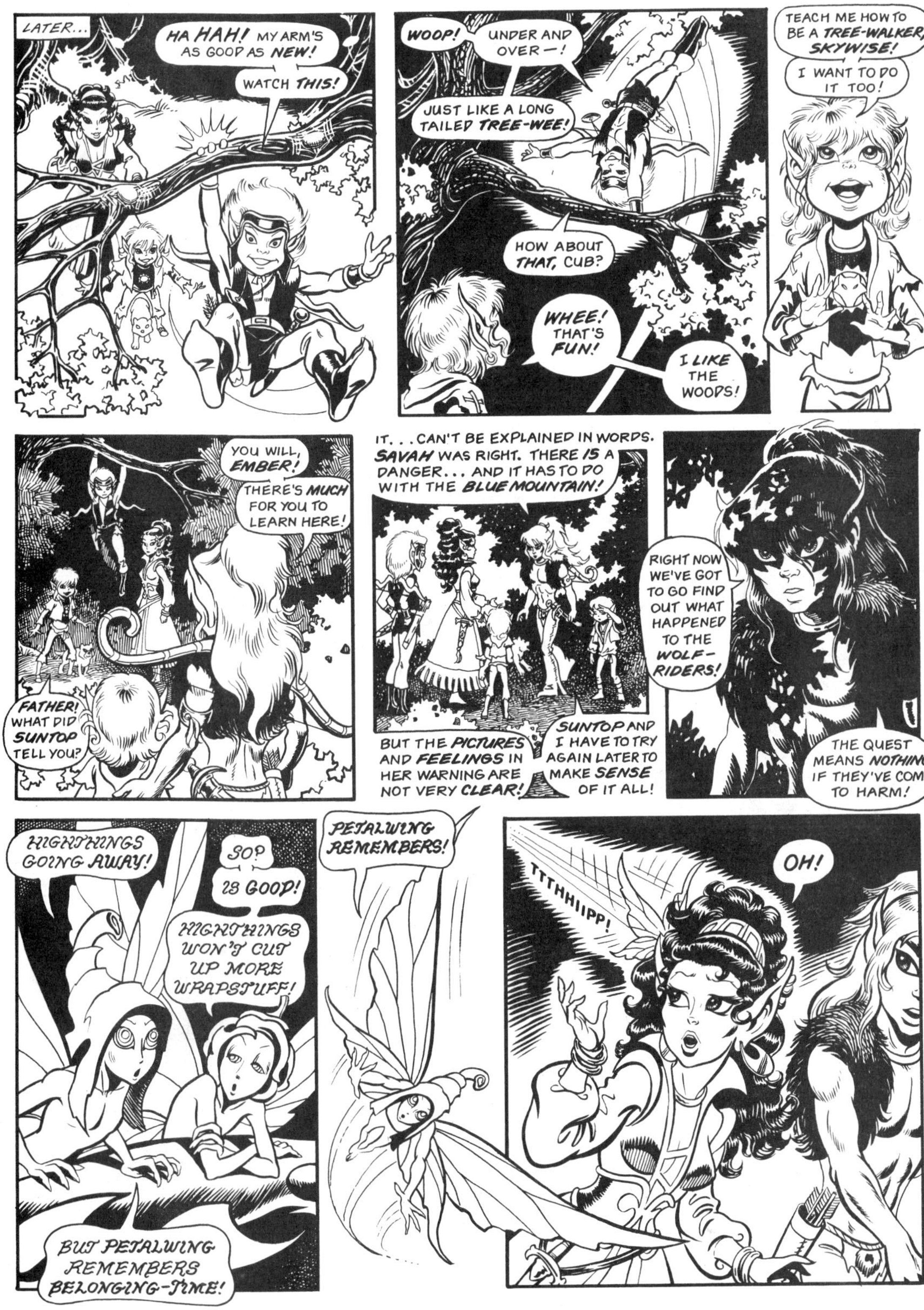
LATER...
HA HAH! MY ARM'S AS GOOD AS NEW!
WATCH THIS!
WOOP!
UNDER AND OVER—!
JUST LIKE A LONG TAILED TREE-WEE!
HOW ABOUT THAT, CUB?
WHEE! THAT'S FUN!
I LIKE THE WOODS!
TEACH ME HOW TO BE A TREE-WALKER, SKYWISE!
I WANT TO DO IT TOO!
YOU WILL, EMBER!
THERE'S MUCH FOR YOU TO LEARN HERE!
FATHER! WHAT DID SUNTOP TELL YOU?
IT... CAN'T BE EXPLAINED IN WORDS. SAVAH WAS RIGHT. THERE IS A DANGER... AND IT HAS TO DO WITH THE BLUE MOUNTAIN!
BUT THE PICTURES AND FEELINGS IN HER WARNING ARE NOT VERY CLEAR!
SUNTOP AND I HAVE TO TRY AGAIN LATER TO MAKE SENSE OF IT ALL!
RIGHT NOW WE'VE GOT TO GO FIND OUT WHAT HAPPENED TO THE WOLF-RIDERS!
THE QUEST MEANS NOTHING IF THEY'VE COME TO HARM!
HIGHTHINGS GOING AWAY!
SO?
IS GOOD!
HIGHTHINGS WON'T CUT UP MORE WRAPSTUFF!
BUT PETALWING REMEMBERS BELONGING-TIME!
PETALWING REMEMBERS!
TTTHHIIPP!
OH!

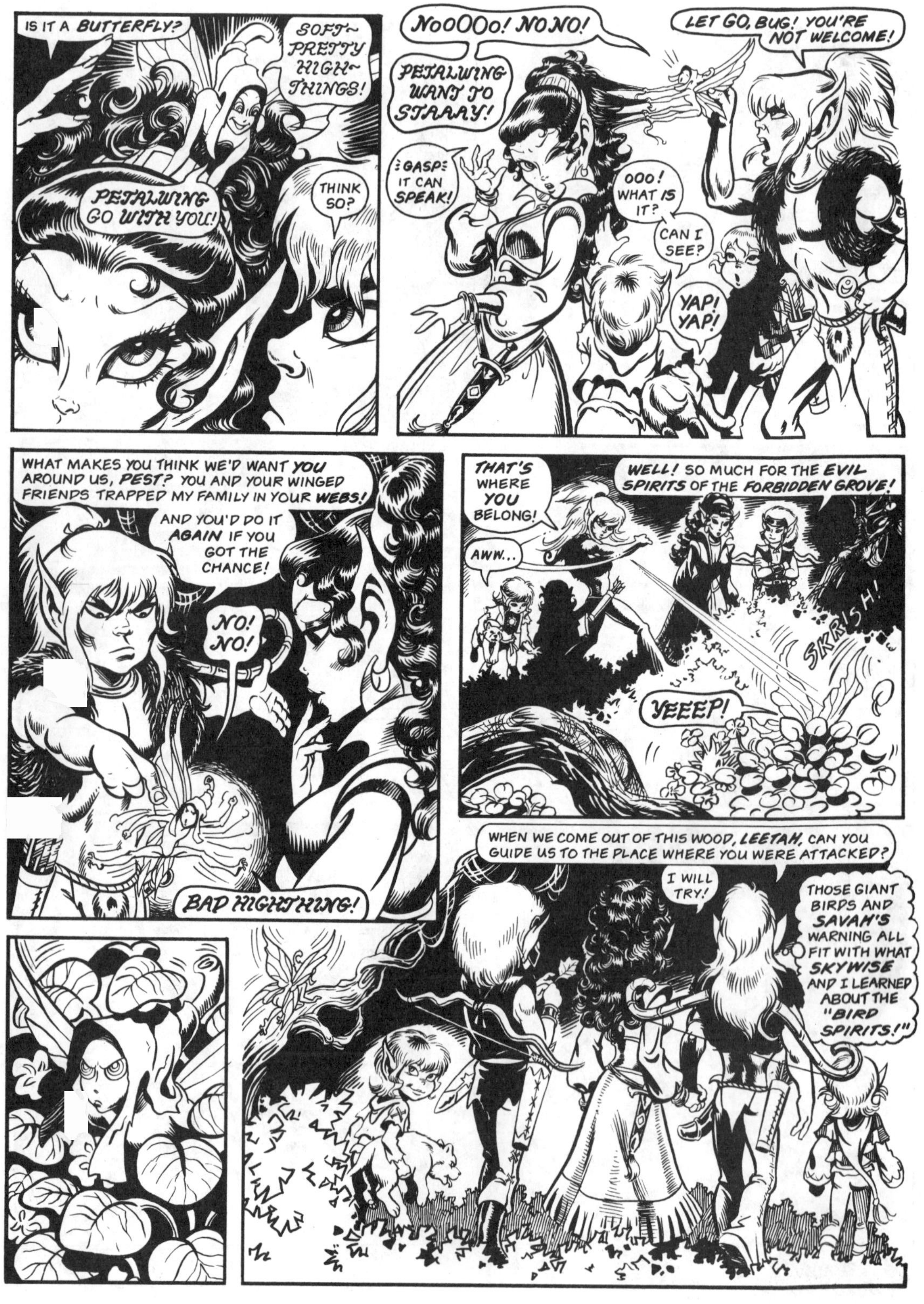

IS IT A BUTTERFLY?
SOFT~ PRETTY HIGH~ THINGS!
PETALWING GO WITH YOU!
THINK SO?
NoOOOo! NO NO!
PETALWING WANT TO STAAAY!
LET GO, BUG! YOU'RE NOT WELCOME!
GASP IT CAN SPEAK!
OOO! WHAT IS IT?
CAN I SEE?
YAP! YAP!
WHAT MAKES YOU THINK WE'D WANT YOU AROUND US, PEST? YOU AND YOUR WINGED FRIENDS TRAPPED MY FAMILY IN YOUR WEBS!
AND YOU'D DO IT AGAIN IF YOU GOT THE CHANCE!
NO! NO!
BAD HIGHTHING!
THAT'S WHERE YOU BELONG!
WELL! SO MUCH FOR THE EVIL SPIRITS OF THE FORBIDDEN GROVE!
AWW...
SKRISH!
YEEEP!
WHEN WE COME OUT OF THIS WOOD, LEETAH, CAN YOU GUIDE US TO THE PLACE WHERE YOU WERE ATTACKED?
I WILL TRY!
THOSE GIANT BIRDS AND SAVAH'S WARNING ALL FIT WITH WHAT SKYWISE AND I LEARNED ABOUT THE "BIRD SPIRITS!"

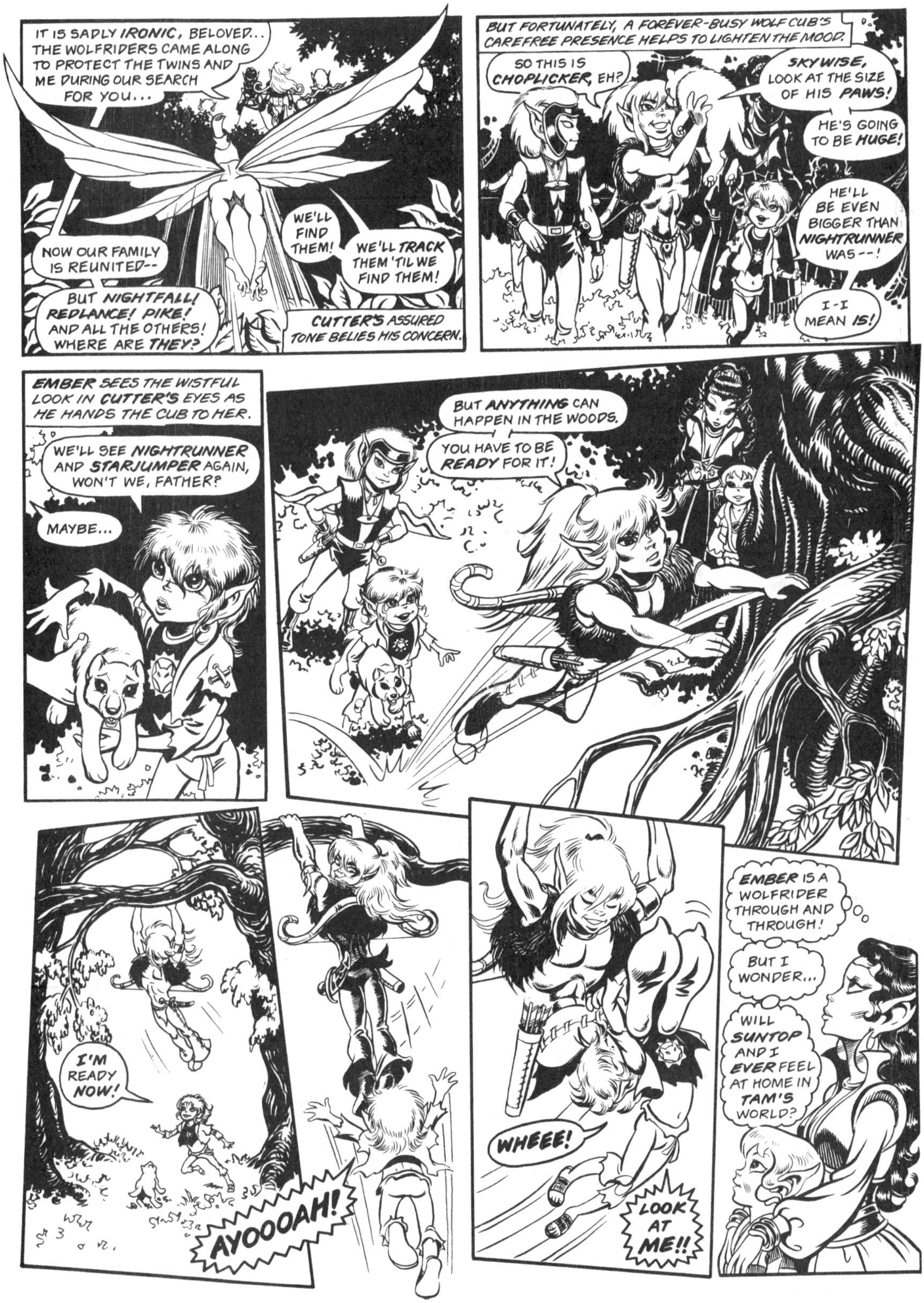
IT IS SADLY IRONIC, BELOVED... THE WOLFRIDERS CAME ALONG TO PROTECT THE TWINS AND ME DURING OUR SEARCH FOR YOU...
NOW OUR FAMILY IS REUNITED--
BUT NIGHTFALL! REDLANCE! PIKE! AND ALL THE OTHERS! WHERE ARE THEY?
WE'LL FIND THEM!
WE'LL TRACK THEM 'TIL WE FIND THEM!
CUTTER'S ASSURED TONE BELIES HIS CONCERN.
BUT FORTUNATELY, A FOREVER-BUSY WOLF CUB'S CAREFREE PRESENCE HELPS TO LIGHTEN THE MOOD.
SO THIS IS CHOPLICKER, EH?
SKYWISE, LOOK AT THE SIZE OF HIS PAWS!
HE'S GOING TO BE HUGE!
HE'LL BE EVEN BIGGER THAN NIGHTRUNNER WAS--!
I-I MEAN IS!
EMBER SEES THE WISTFUL LOOK IN CUTTER'S EYES AS HE HANDS THE CUB TO HER.
WE'LL SEE NIGHTRUNNER AND STARJUMPER AGAIN, WON'T WE, FATHER?
MAYBE...
BUT ANYTHING CAN HAPPEN IN THE WOODS.
YOU HAVE TO BE READY FOR IT!
I'M READY NOW!
AYOOOAH!
WHEEE!
LOOK AT ME!!
EMBER IS A WOLFRIDER THROUGH AND THROUGH!
BUT I WONDER...
WILL SUNTOP AND I EVER FEEL AT HOME IN TAM'S WORLD?

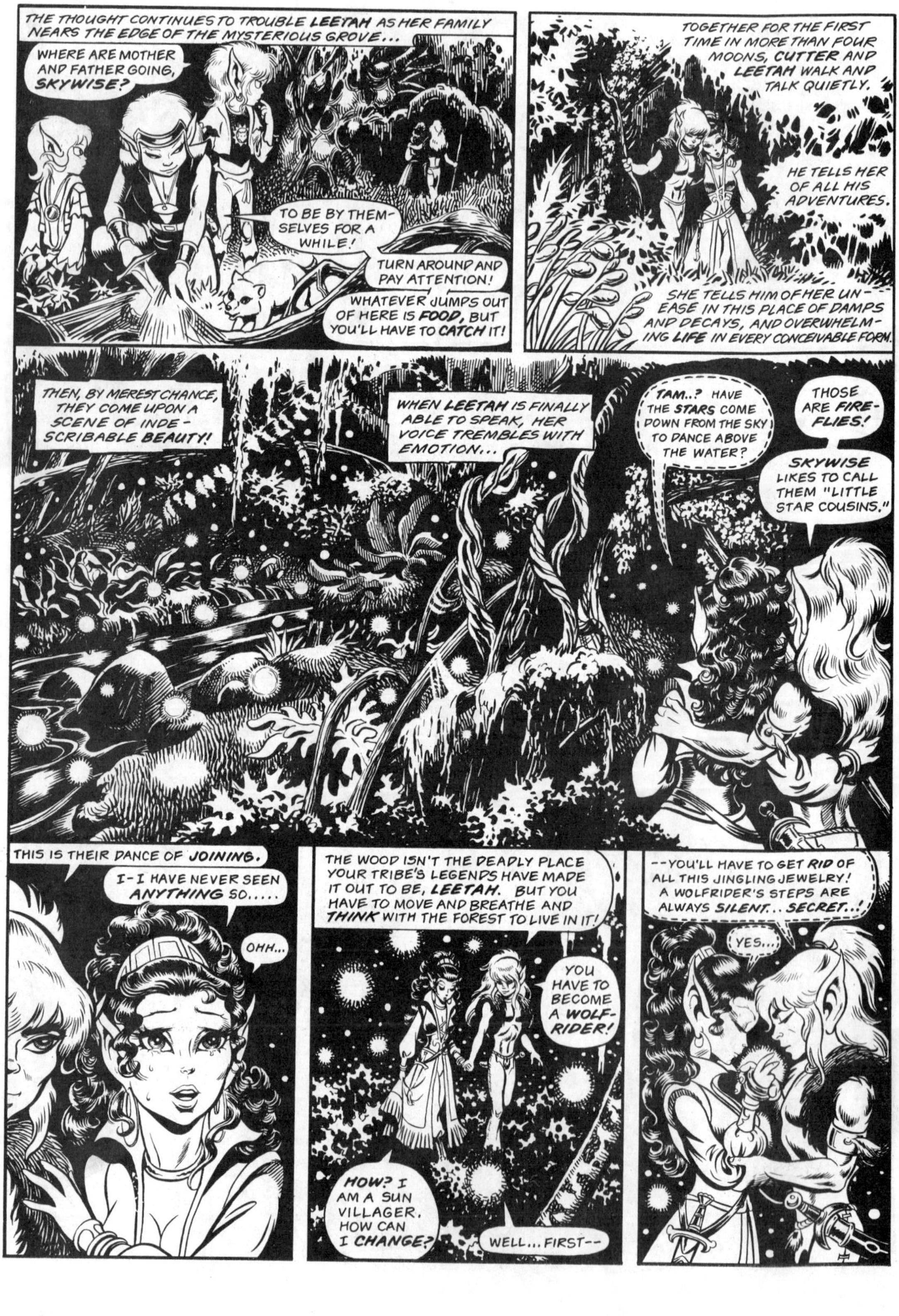
THE THOUGHT CONTINUES TO TROUBLE LEETAH AS HER FAMILY NEARS THE EDGE OF THE MYSTERIOUS GROVE...
WHERE ARE MOTHER AND FATHER GOING, SKYWISE?
TO BE BY THEMSELVES FOR A WHILE!
TURN AROUND AND PAY ATTENTION!
WHATEVER JUMPS OUT OF HERE IS FOOD, BUT YOU'LL HAVE TO CATCH IT!
TOGETHER FOR THE FIRST TIME IN MORE THAN FOUR MOONS, CUTTER AND LEETAH WALK AND TALK QUIETLY.
HE TELLS HER OF ALL HIS ADVENTURES.
SHE TELLS HIM OF HER UNEASE IN THIS PLACE OF DAMPS AND DECAYS, AND OVERWHELMING LIFE IN EVERY CONCEIVABLE FORM.
THEN, BY MEREST CHANCE, THEY COME UPON A SCENE OF INDESCRIBABLE BEAUTY!
WHEN LEETAH IS FINALLY ABLE TO SPEAK, HER VOICE TREMBLES WITH EMOTION...
TAM..? HAVE THE STARS COME DOWN FROM THE SKY TO DANCE ABOVE THE WATER?
THOSE ARE FIREFLIES!
SKYWISE LIKES TO CALL THEM "LITTLE STAR COUSINS."
THIS IS THEIR DANCE OF JOINING.
I-I HAVE NEVER SEEN ANYTHING SO.....
OHH...
THE WOOD ISN'T THE DEADLY PLACE YOUR TRIBE'S LEGENDS HAVE MADE IT OUT TO BE, LEETAH. BUT YOU HAVE TO MOVE AND BREATHE AND THINK WITH THE FOREST TO LIVE IN IT!
YOU HAVE TO BECOME A WOLFRIDER!
HOW? I AM A SUN VILLAGER. HOW CAN I CHANGE?
WELL... FIRST--
--YOU'LL HAVE TO GET RID OF ALL THIS JINGLING JEWELRY! A WOLFRIDER'S STEPS ARE ALWAYS SILENT... SECRET...!
YES...

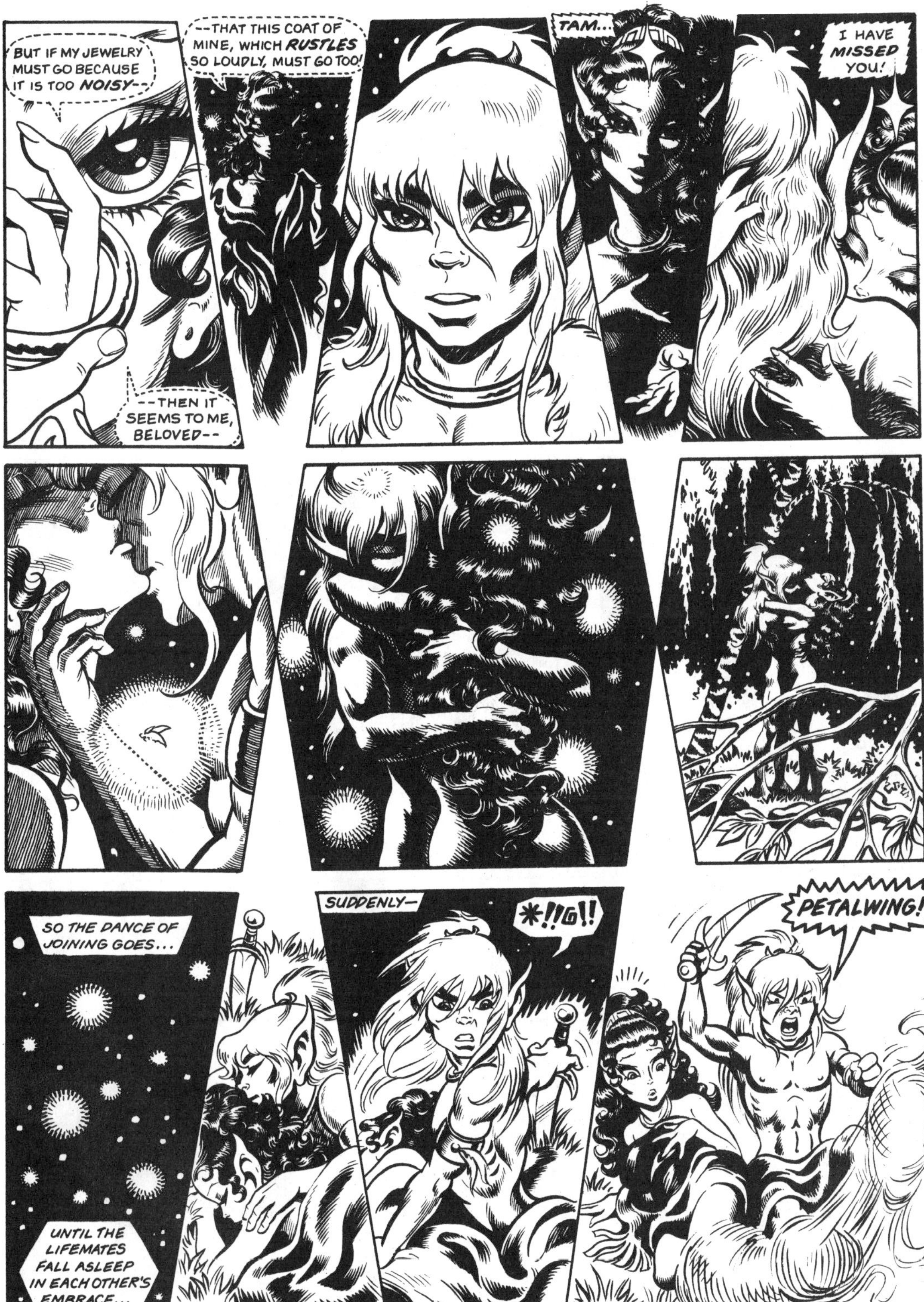
BUT IF MY JEWELRY MUST GO BECAUSE IT IS TOO NOISY--
--THEN IT SEEMS TO ME, BELOVED--
--THAT THIS COAT OF MINE, WHICH RUSTLES SO LOUDLY, MUST GO TOO!
TAM...
I HAVE MISSED YOU!
SO THE DANCE OF JOINING GOES...
UNTIL THE LIFEMATES FALL ASLEEP IN EACH OTHER'S EMBRACE...
SUDDENLY--
*!!G!!
PETALWING!

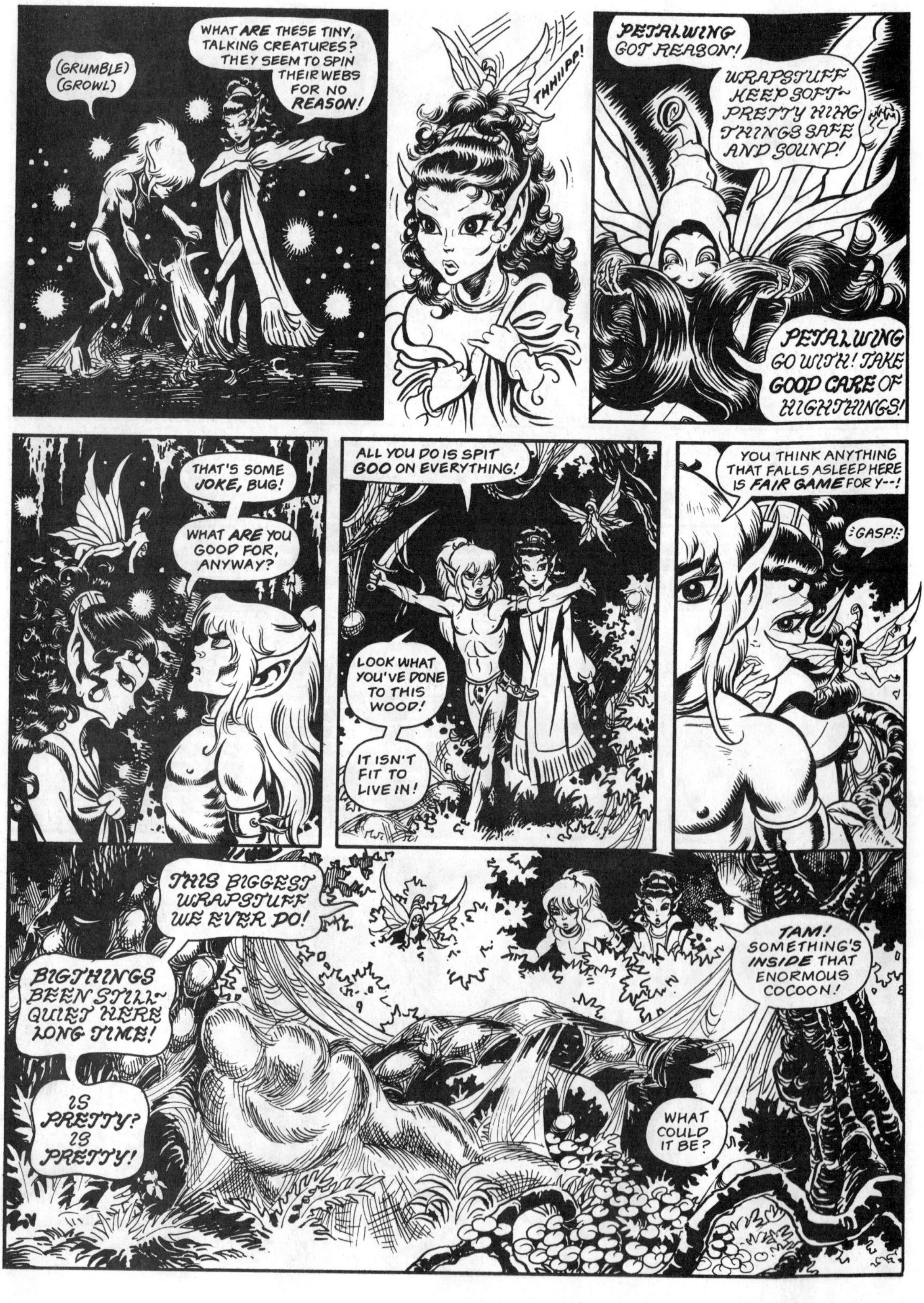
(GRUMBLE) (GROWL)
WHAT ARE THESE TINY, TALKING CREATURES? THEY SEEM TO SPIN THEIR WEBS FOR NO REASON!
THHIIPP!
PETALWING GOT REASON!
WRAPSTUFF KEEP SOFT-PRETTY HIHG THINGS SAFE AND SOUND!
PETALWING GO WITH! TAKE GOOD CARE OF HIGHTHINGS!
THAT'S SOME JOKE, BUG!
WHAT ARE YOU GOOD FOR, ANYWAY?
ALL YOU DO IS SPIT GOO ON EVERYTHING!
LOOK WHAT YOU'VE DONE TO THIS WOOD!
IT ISN'T FIT TO LIVE IN!
YOU THINK ANYTHING THAT FALLS ASLEEP HERE IS FAIR GAME FOR Y--!
GASP!
THIS BIGGEST WRAPSTUFF WE EVER DO!
BIGTHINGS BEEN STILL-QUIET HERE LONG TIME!
IS PRETTY? IS PRETTY!
TAM! SOMETHING'S INSIDE THAT ENORMOUS COCOON!
WHAT COULD IT BE?

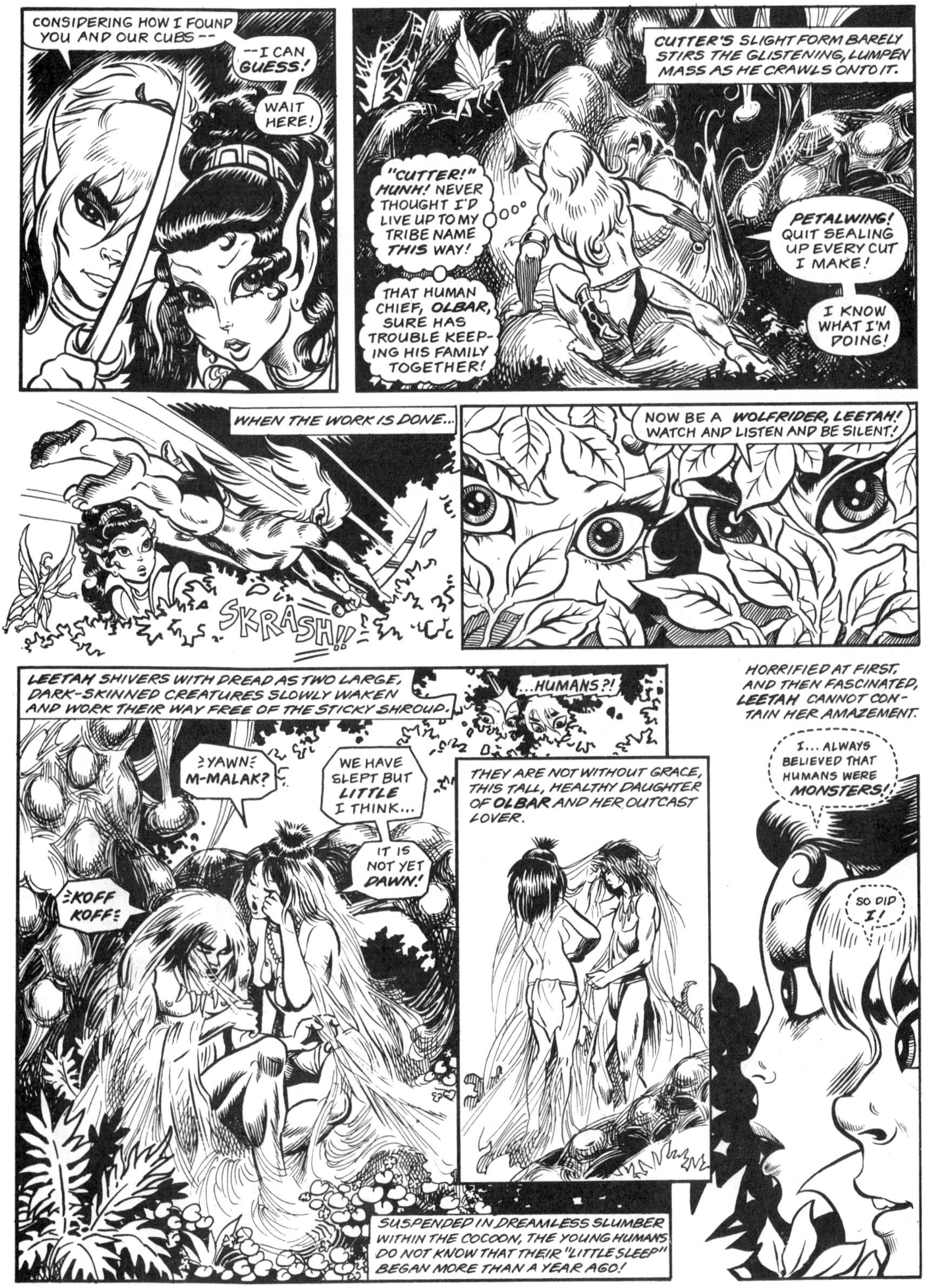
CONSIDERING HOW I FOUND YOU AND OUR CUBS --
--I CAN GUESS!
WAIT HERE!
CUTTER'S SLIGHT FORM BARELY STIRS THE GLISTENING, LUMPEN MASS AS HE CRAWLS ONTO IT.
"CUTTER!" HUNH! NEVER THOUGHT I'D LIVE UP TO MY TRIBE NAME THIS WAY!
THAT HUMAN CHIEF, OLBAR, SURE HAS TROUBLE KEEPING HIS FAMILY TOGETHER!
PETALWING! QUIT SEALING UP EVERY CUT I MAKE!
I KNOW WHAT I'M DOING!
WHEN THE WORK IS DONE...
SKRASH!!
NOW BE A WOLFRIDER, LEETAH! WATCH AND LISTEN AND BE SILENT!
LEETAH SHIVERS WITH DREAD AS TWO LARGE, DARK-SKINNED CREATURES SLOWLY WAKEN AND WORK THEIR WAY FREE OF THE STICKY SHROUD.
...HUMANS?!
YAWN? M-MALAK?
WE HAVE SLEPT BUT LITTLE I THINK...
IT IS NOT YET DAWN!
KOFF KOFF
THEY ARE NOT WITHOUT GRACE, THIS TALL, HEALTHY DAUGHTER OF OLBAR AND HER OUTCAST LOVER.
HORRIFIED AT FIRST, AND THEN FASCINATED, LEETAH CANNOT CONTAIN HER AMAZEMENT.
I... ALWAYS BELIEVED THAT HUMANS WERE MONSTERS!
SO DID I!
SUSPENDED IN DREAMLESS SLUMBER WITHIN THE COCOON, THE YOUNG HUMANS DO NOT KNOW THAT THEIR "LITTLE SLEEP" BEGAN MORE THAN A YEAR AGO!

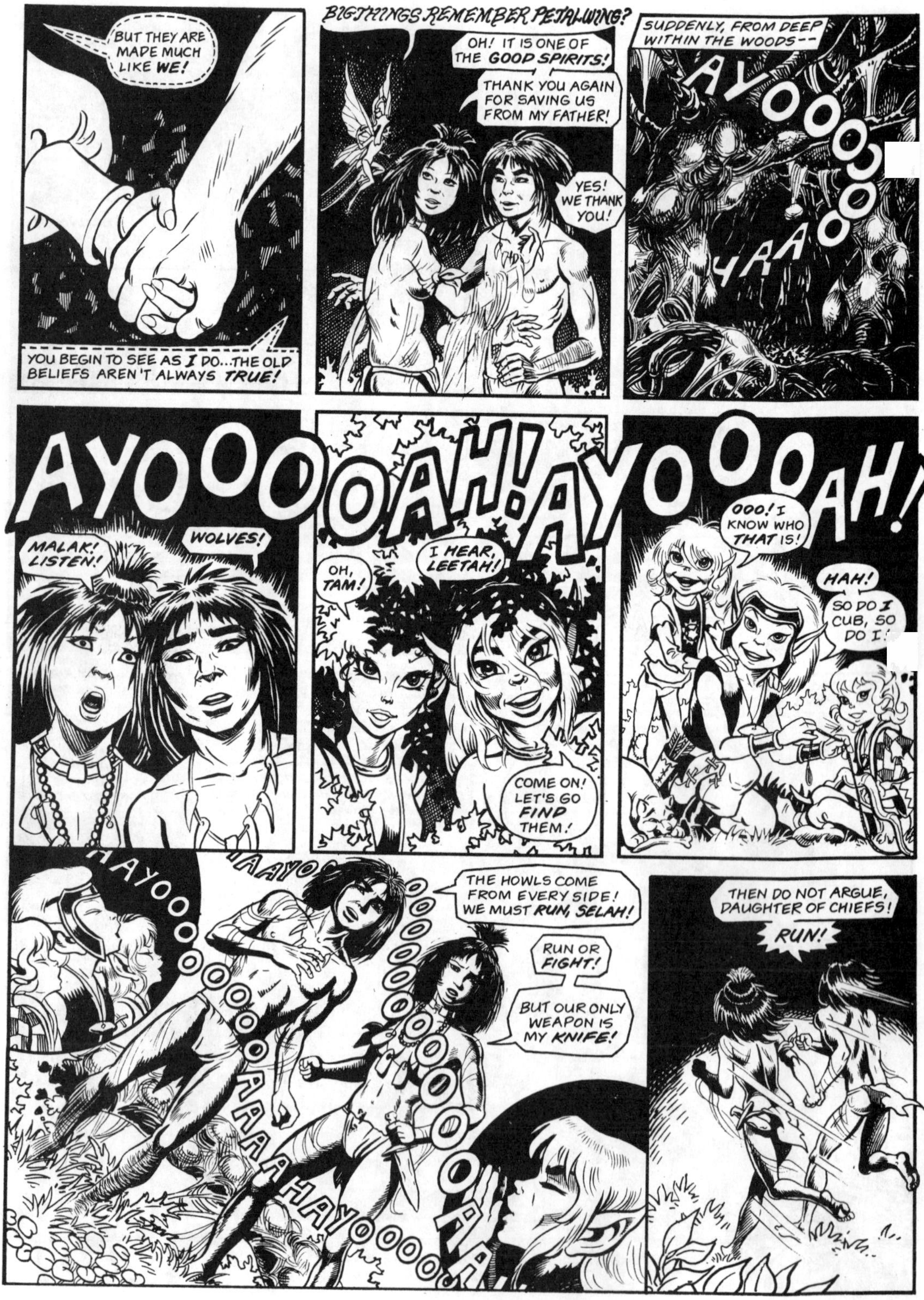
BUT THEY ARE MADE MUCH LIKE WE!
YOU BEGIN TO SEE AS I DO...THE OLD BELIEFS AREN'T ALWAYS TRUE!
BIGTHINGS REMEMBER PETALWING?
OH! IT IS ONE OF THE GOOD SPIRITS!
THANK YOU AGAIN FOR SAVING US FROM MY FATHER!
YES! WE THANK YOU!
SUDDENLY, FROM DEEP WITHIN THE WOODS--
AYOOOOOOO YAA
AYOOOOOAH! AYOOOAH!
MALAK! LISTEN!
WOLVES!
OH, TAM!
I HEAR, LEETAH!
COME ON! LET'S GO FIND THEM!
OOO! I KNOW WHO THAT IS!
HAH! SO DO I CUB, SO DO I!
HAYOOO
HAAYOOOOOOOOOOOOOOOOOAAAAH
THE HOWLS COME FROM EVERY SIDE! WE MUST RUN, SELAH!
RUN OR FIGHT!
BUT OUR ONLY WEAPON IS MY KNIFE!
HAYOOOOOAA
THEN DO NOT ARGUE, DAUGHTER OF CHIEFS!
RUN!

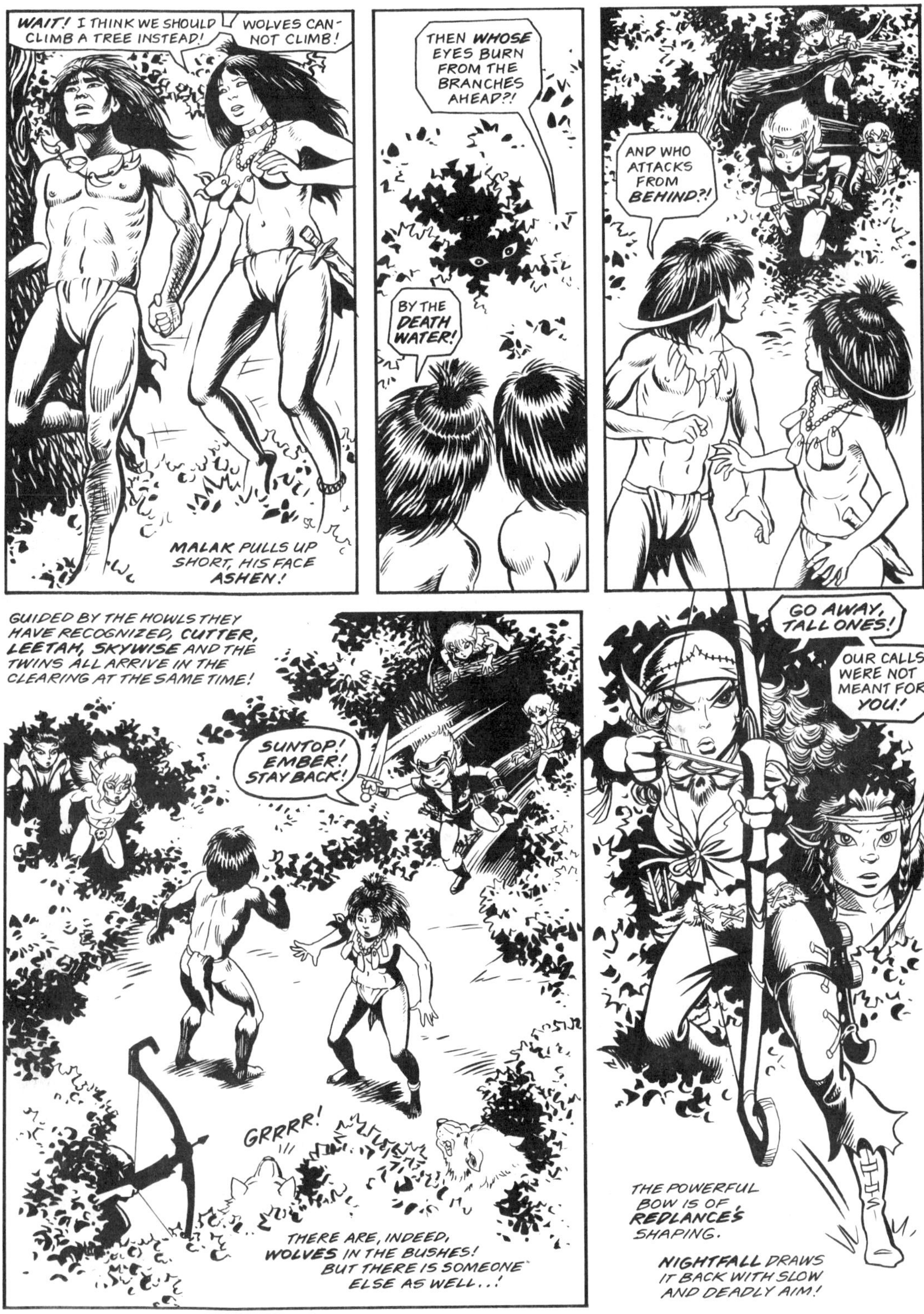
WAIT! I THINK WE SHOULD CLIMB A TREE INSTEAD!
WOLVES CAN-NOT CLIMB!
MALAK PULLS UP SHORT, HIS FACE ASHEN!
THEN WHOSE EYES BURN FROM THE BRANCHES AHEAD?!
BY THE DEATH WATER!
AND WHO ATTACKS FROM BEHIND?!
GUIDED BY THE HOWLS THEY HAVE RECOGNIZED, CUTTER, LEETAH, SKYWISE AND THE TWINS ALL ARRIVE IN THE CLEARING AT THE SAME TIME!
SUNTOP! EMBER! STAY BACK!
GRRRR!
THERE ARE, INDEED, WOLVES IN THE BUSHES! BUT THERE IS SOMEONE ELSE AS WELL..!
GO AWAY, TALL ONES!
OUR CALLS WERE NOT MEANT FOR YOU!
THE POWERFUL BOW IS OF REDLANCE'S SHAPING.
NIGHTFALL DRAWS IT BACK WITH SLOW AND DEADLY AIM!

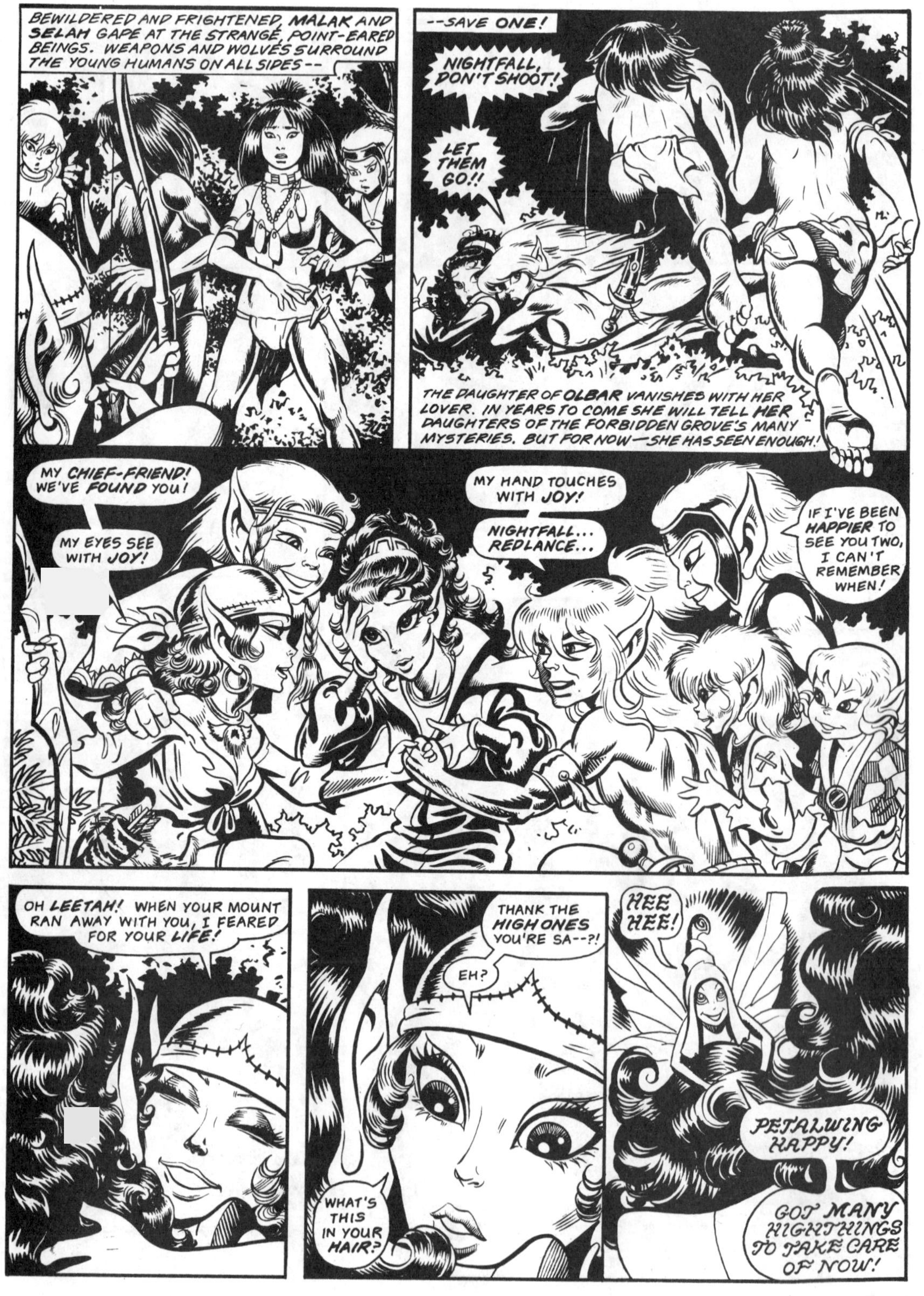
BEWILDERED AND FRIGHTENED, MALAK AND SELAH GAPE AT THE STRANGE, POINT-EARED BEINGS. WEAPONS AND WOLVES SURROUND THE YOUNG HUMANS ON ALL SIDES--
--SAVE ONE!
NIGHTFALL, DON'T SHOOT!
LET THEM GO!!
THE DAUGHTER OF OLBAR VANISHES WITH HER LOVER. IN YEARS TO COME SHE WILL TELL HER DAUGHTERS OF THE FORBIDDEN GROVE'S MANY MYSTERIES. BUT FOR NOW—SHE HAS SEEN ENOUGH!
MY CHIEF-FRIEND! WE'VE FOUND YOU!
MY EYES SEE WITH JOY!
MY HAND TOUCHES WITH JOY!
NIGHTFALL... REDLANCE...
IF I'VE BEEN HAPPIER TO SEE YOU TWO, I CAN'T REMEMBER WHEN!
OH LEETAH! WHEN YOUR MOUNT RAN AWAY WITH YOU, I FEARED FOR YOUR LIFE!
THANK THE HIGH ONES YOU'RE SA--?!
EH?
WHAT'S THIS IN YOUR HAIR?
HEE HEE!
PETALWING HAPPY!
GOT MANY HIGHTHINGS TO TAKE CARE OF NOW!

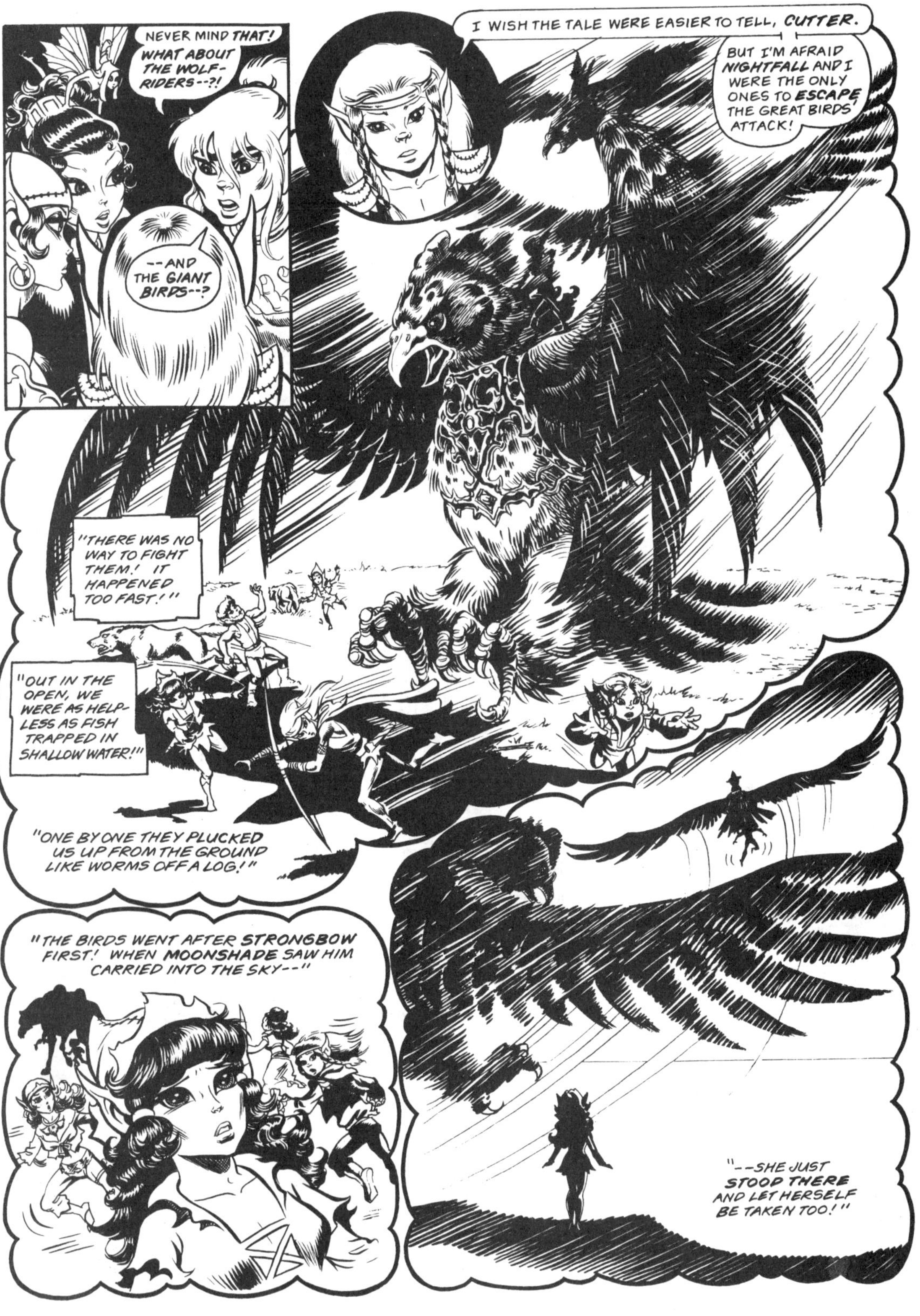
NEVER MIND THAT! WHAT ABOUT THE WOLF-RIDERS--?!
--AND THE GIANT BIRDS--?
I WISH THE TALE WERE EASIER TO TELL, CUTTER.
BUT I'M AFRAID NIGHTFALL AND I WERE THE ONLY ONES TO ESCAPE THE GREAT BIRDS' ATTACK!
"THERE WAS NO WAY TO FIGHT THEM! IT HAPPENED TOO FAST!"
"OUT IN THE OPEN, WE WERE AS HELPLESS AS FISH TRAPPED IN SHALLOW WATER!"
"ONE BY ONE THEY PLUCKED US UP FROM THE GROUND LIKE WORMS OFF A LOG!"
"THE BIRDS WENT AFTER STRONGBOW FIRST! WHEN MOONSHADE SAW HIM CARRIED INTO THE SKY--"
"--SHE JUST STOOD THERE AND LET HERSELF BE TAKEN TOO!"

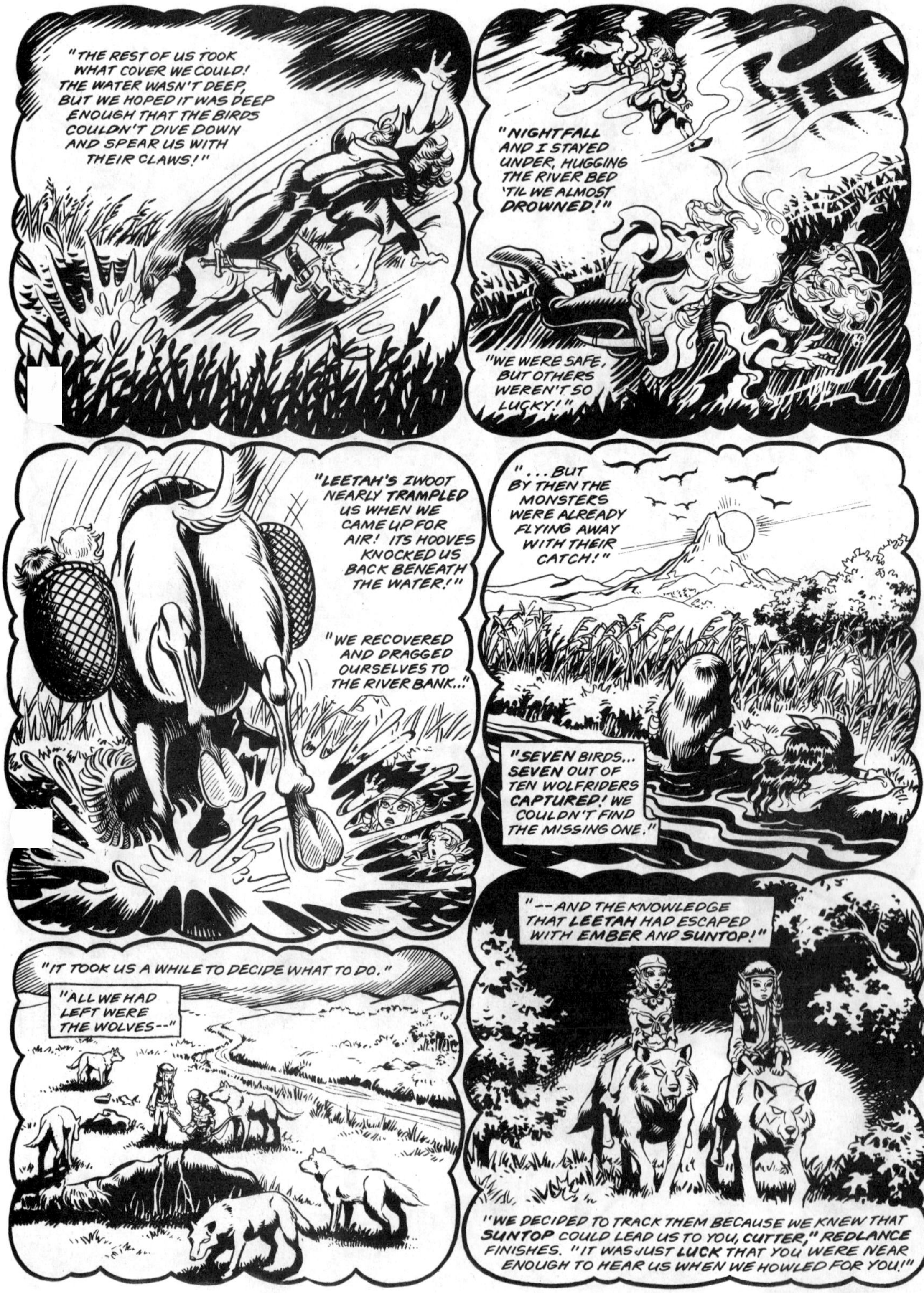
"THE REST OF US TOOK WHAT COVER WE COULD! THE WATER WASN'T DEEP, BUT WE HOPED IT WAS DEEP ENOUGH THAT THE BIRDS COULDN'T DIVE DOWN AND SPEAR US WITH THEIR CLAWS!"
"NIGHTFALL AND I STAYED UNDER, HUGGING THE RIVER BED 'TIL WE ALMOST DROWNED!"
"WE WERE SAFE, BUT OTHERS WEREN'T SO LUCKY!"
"LEETAH'S ZWOOT NEARLY TRAMPLED US WHEN WE CAME UP FOR AIR! ITS HOOVES KNOCKED US BACK BENEATH THE WATER!"
"WE RECOVERED AND DRAGGED OURSELVES TO THE RIVER BANK..."
"...BUT BY THEN THE MONSTERS WERE ALREADY FLYING AWAY WITH THEIR CATCH!"
"SEVEN BIRDS... SEVEN OUT OF TEN WOLFRIDERS CAPTURED! WE COULDN'T FIND THE MISSING ONE."
"IT TOOK US A WHILE TO DECIDE WHAT TO DO."
"ALL WE HAD LEFT WERE THE WOLVES--"
"--AND THE KNOWLEDGE THAT LEETAH HAD ESCAPED WITH EMBER AND SUNTOP!"
"WE DECIDED TO TRACK THEM BECAUSE WE KNEW THAT SUNTOP COULD LEAD US TO YOU, CUTTER," REDLANCE FINISHES. "IT WAS JUST LUCK THAT YOU WERE NEAR ENOUGH TO HEAR US WHEN WE HOWLED FOR YOU!"

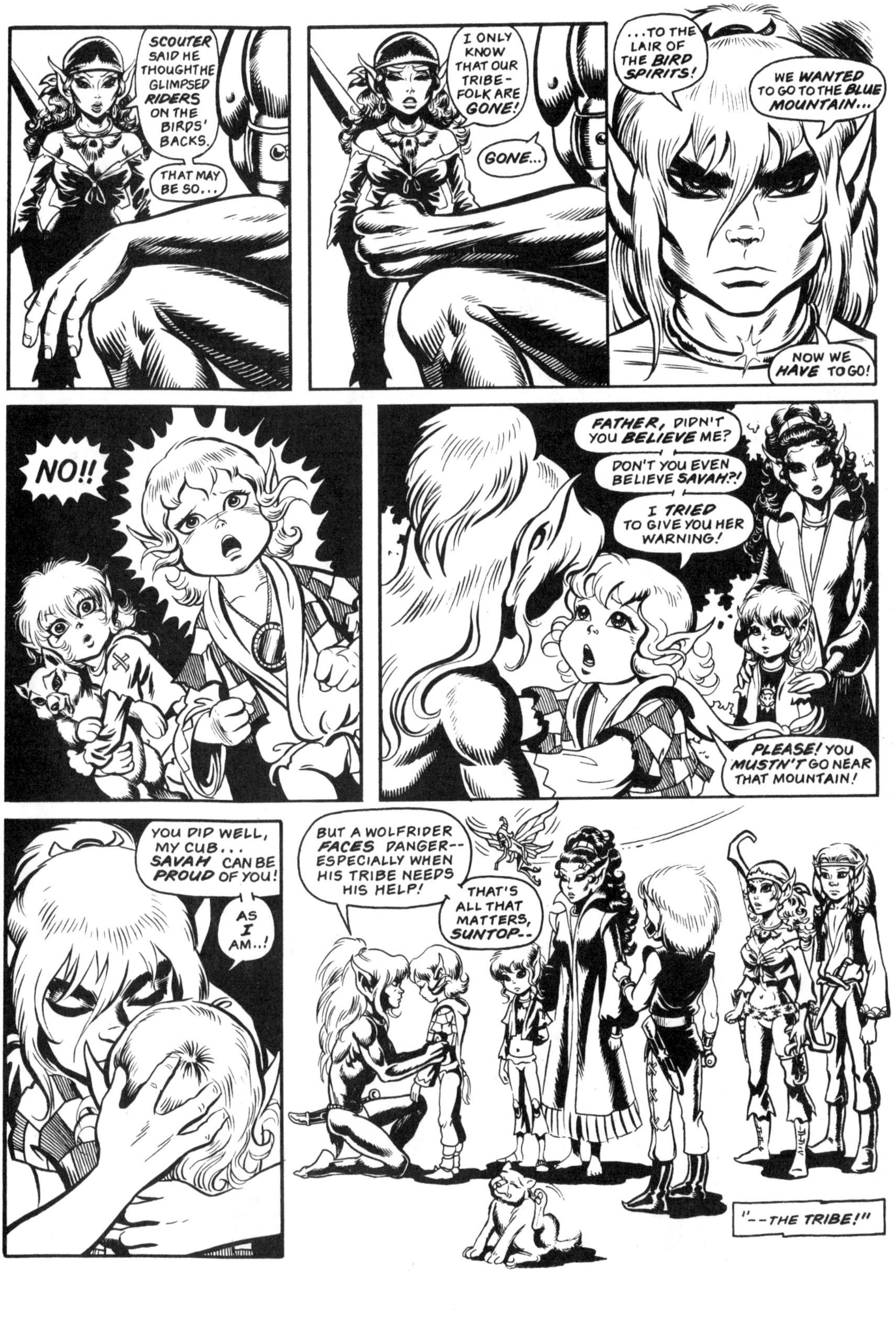
SCOUTER SAID HE THOUGHT HE GLIMPSED RIDERS ON THE BIRDS' BACKS.
THAT MAY BE SO...
I ONLY KNOW THAT OUR TRIBE-FOLK ARE GONE!
GONE...
...TO THE LAIR OF THE BIRD SPIRITS!
WE WANTED TO GO TO THE BLUE MOUNTAIN...
NOW WE HAVE TO GO!
NO!!
FATHER, DIDN'T YOU BELIEVE ME?
DON'T YOU EVEN BELIEVE SAVAH?!
I TRIED TO GIVE YOU HER WARNING!
PLEASE! YOU MUSTN'T GO NEAR THAT MOUNTAIN!
YOU DID WELL, MY CUB... SAVAH CAN BE PROUD OF YOU!
AS I AM..!
BUT A WOLFRIDER FACES DANGER-- ESPECIALLY WHEN HIS TRIBE NEEDS HIS HELP!
THAT'S ALL THAT MATTERS, SUNTOP--
"--THE TRIBE!"

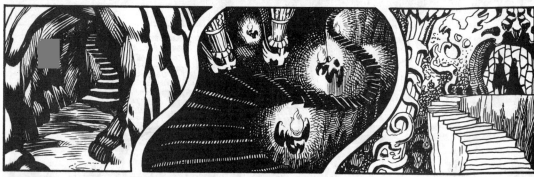

HAS HE CRIED OUT YET, *WINNOWILL?*

NOT YET... HE PLAYS THE GAME *WELL*-- BUT I SHALL WIN!

I ALWAYS DO!

TO BE CONTINUED...

What is the dark
and forbidding power that
holds the Wolfriders prisoner?

Cutter must pit his "wolf spirit"
against the ages-old magic of
the Gliders in volume 3,
"Captives of Blue Mountain."

no.6
WARP graphics
$1.50
$1.75 in Canada
ELFQUEST
The QUEST BEGINS

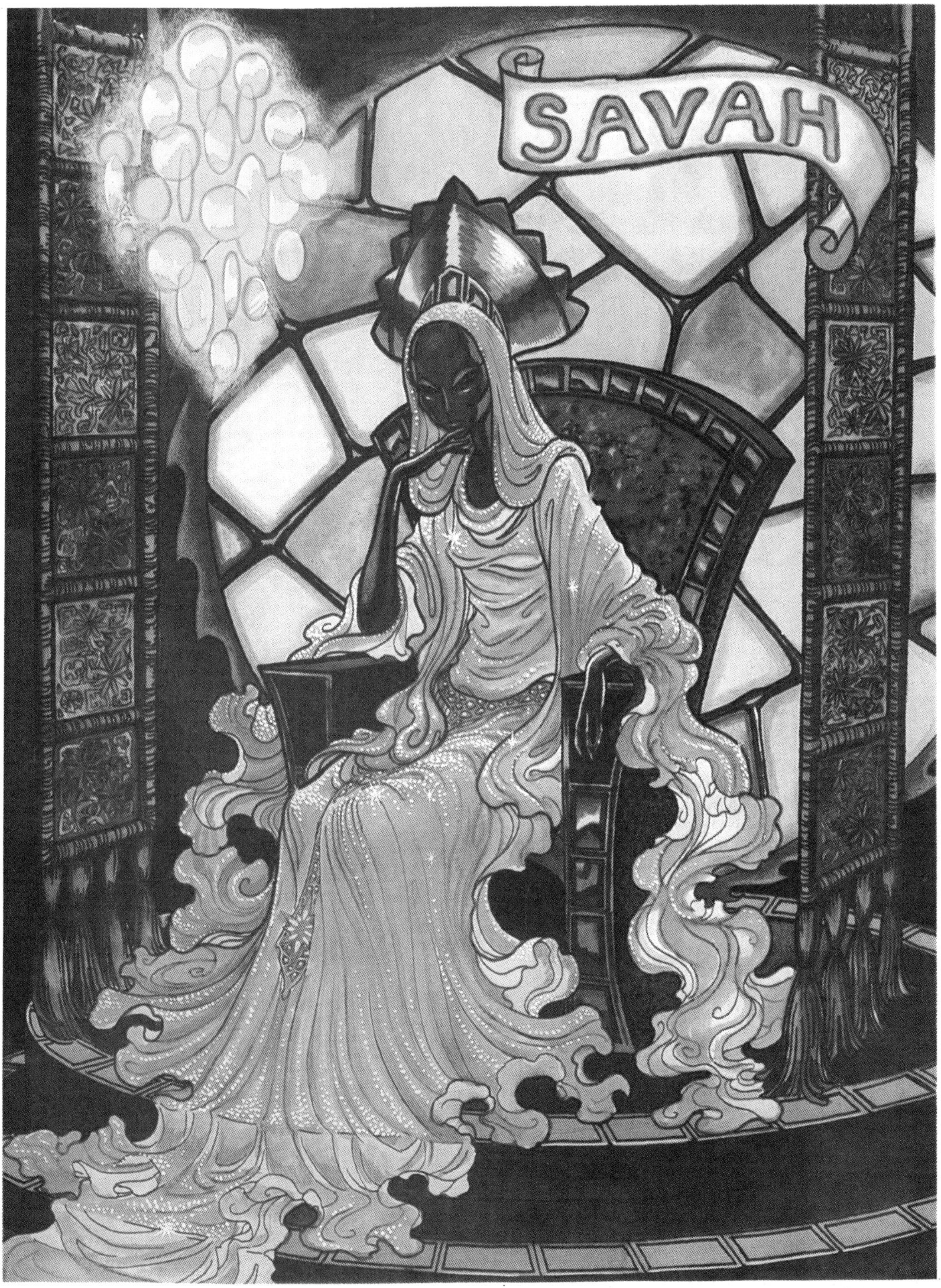
SAVAH

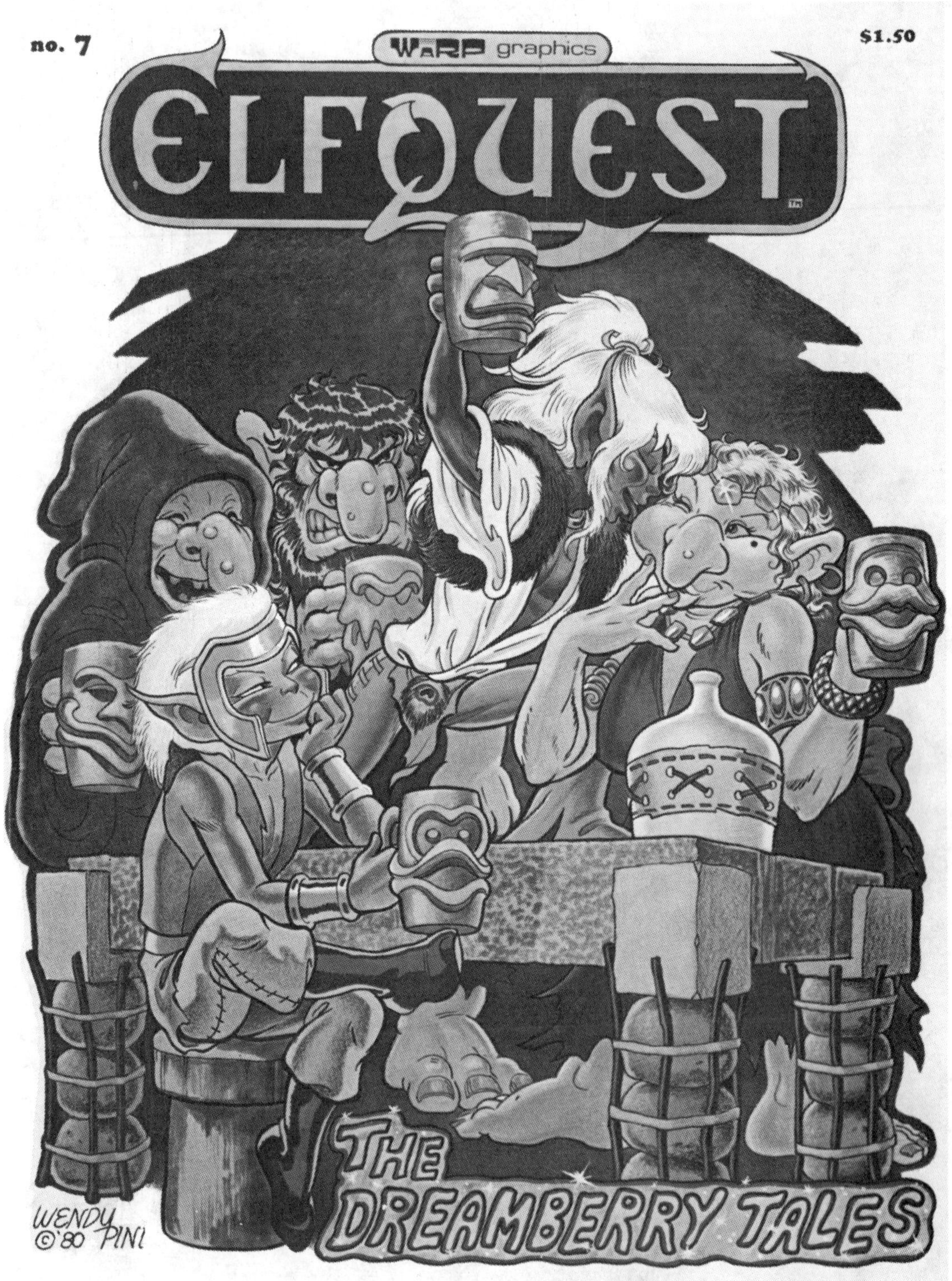

no. 7
WaRP graphics
$1.50
ELFQUEST
THE DREAMBERRY TALES
WENDY PINI ©'80

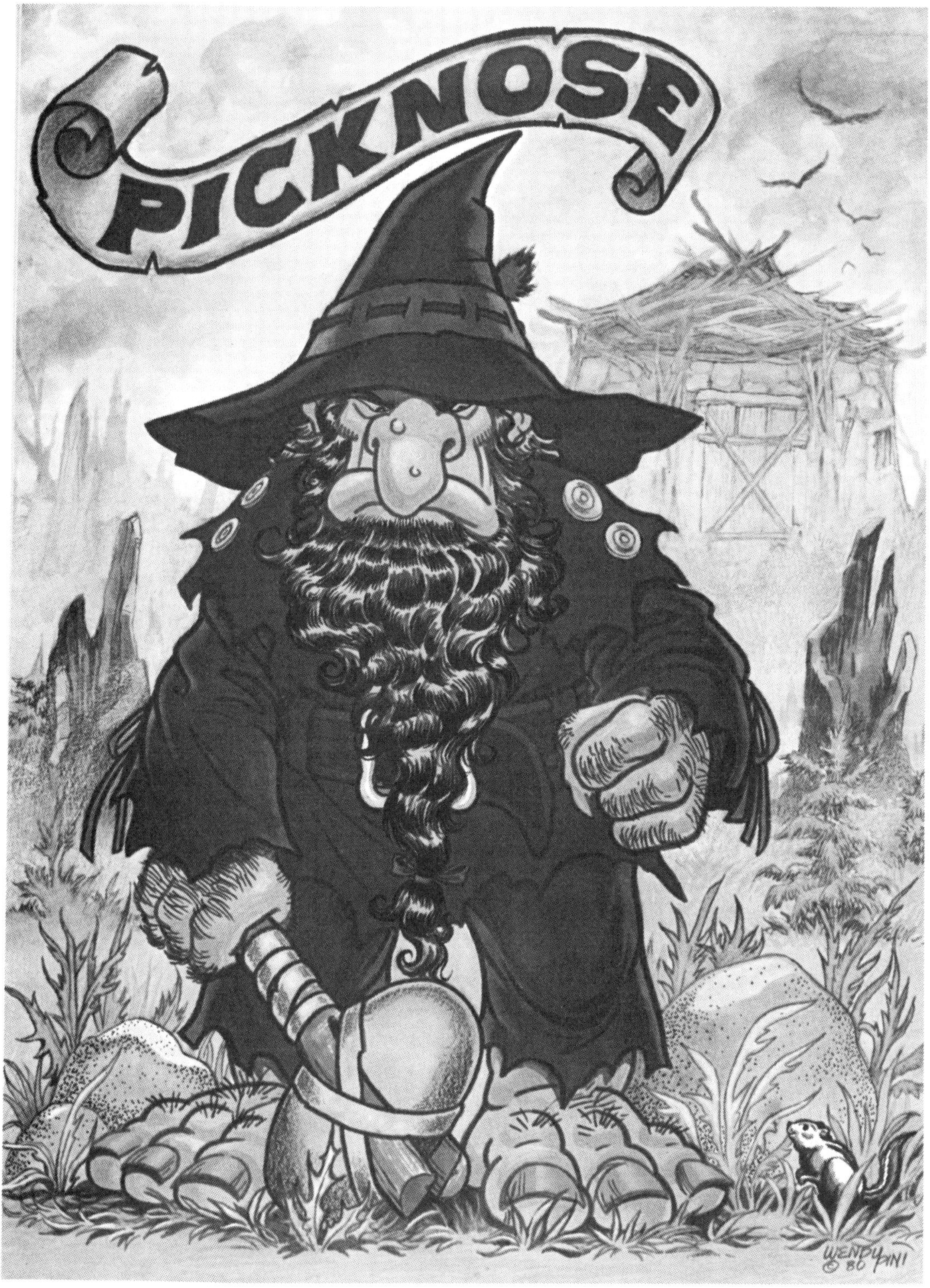
PICKNOSE
WENDY PINI
© 80

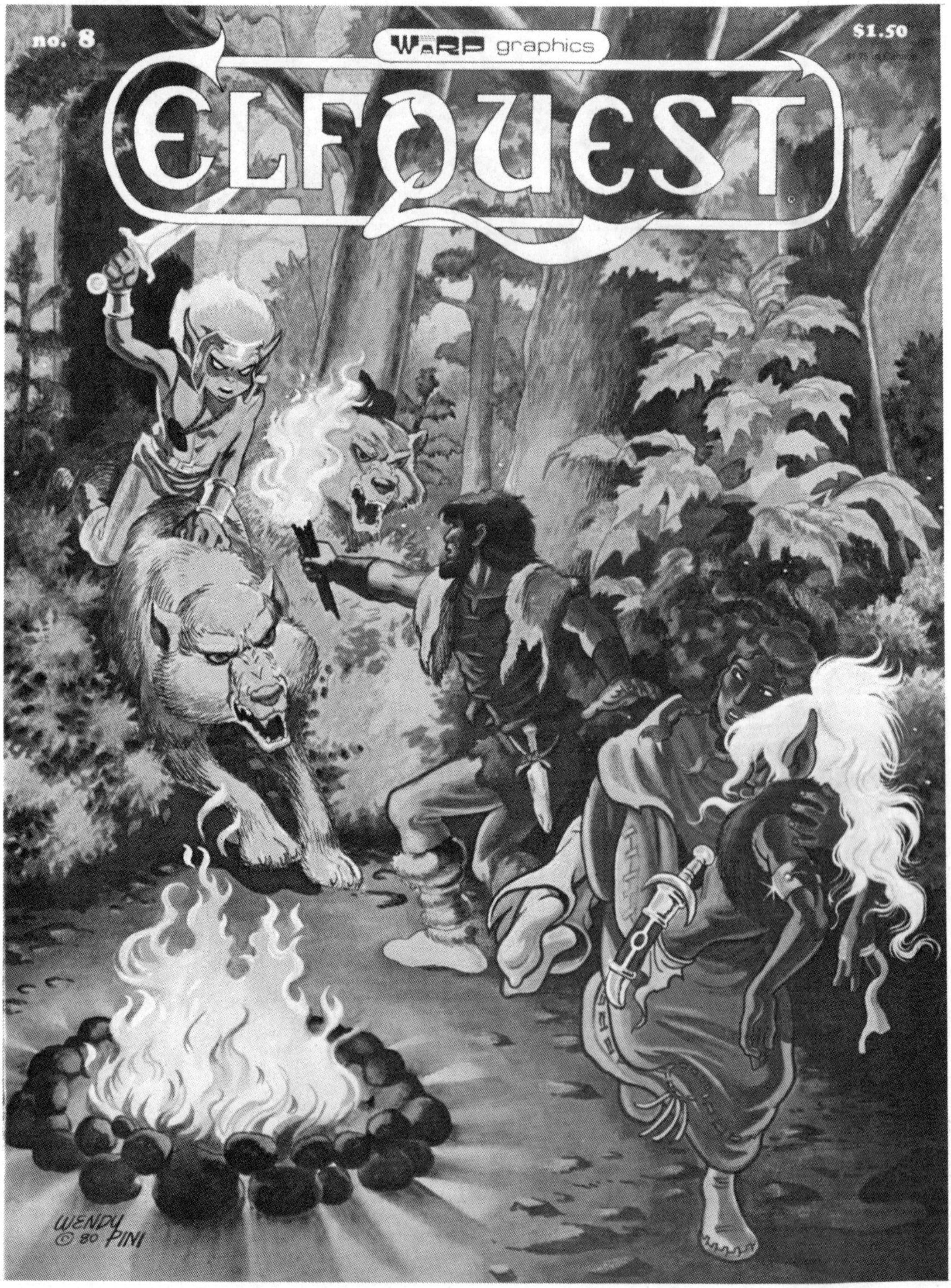
no. 8
WaRP graphics
$1.50
ELFQUEST
WENDY © 80 PINI

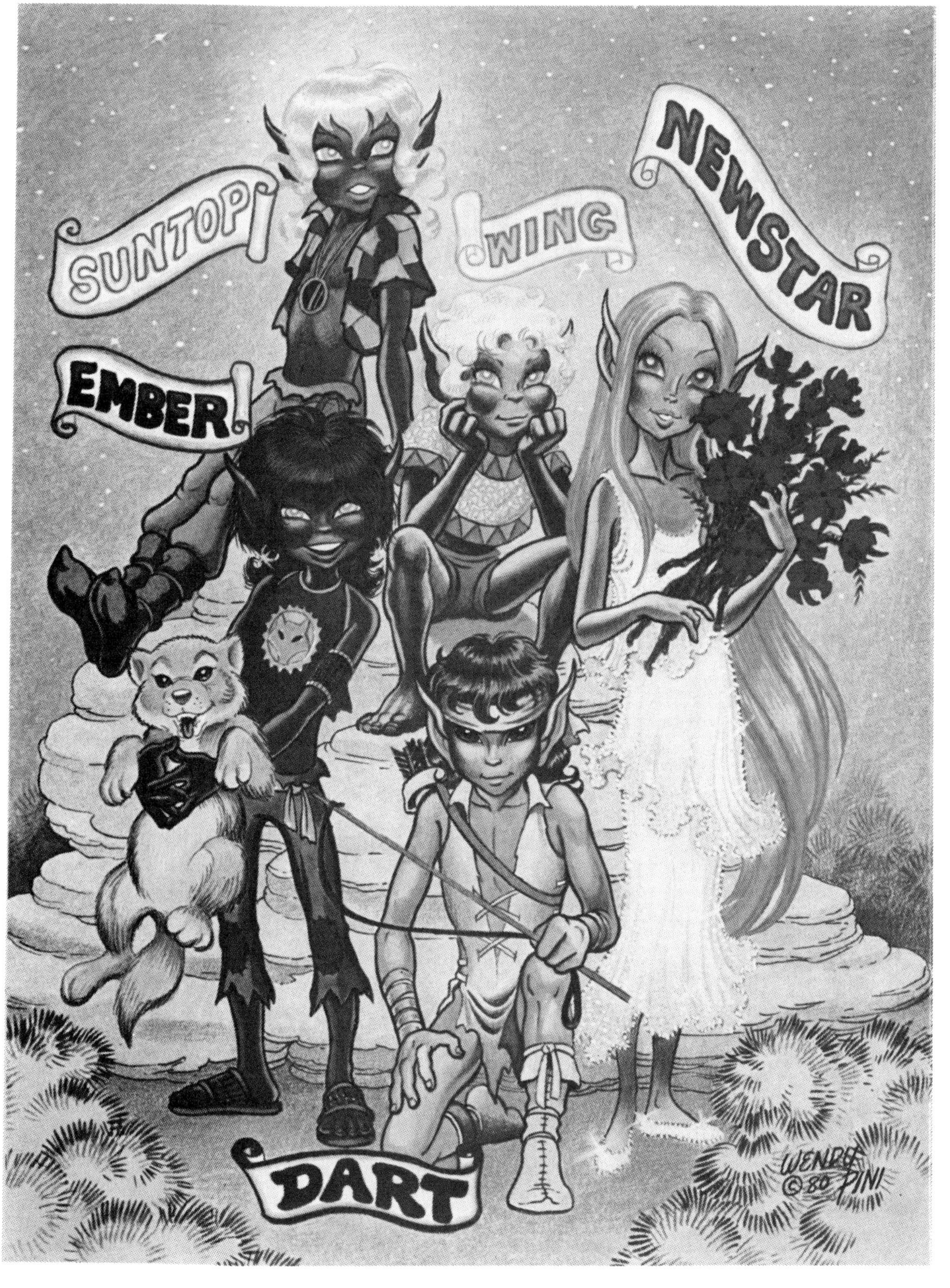
SUNTOP
WING
NEWSTAR
EMBER
DART
WENDY PINI
© 80

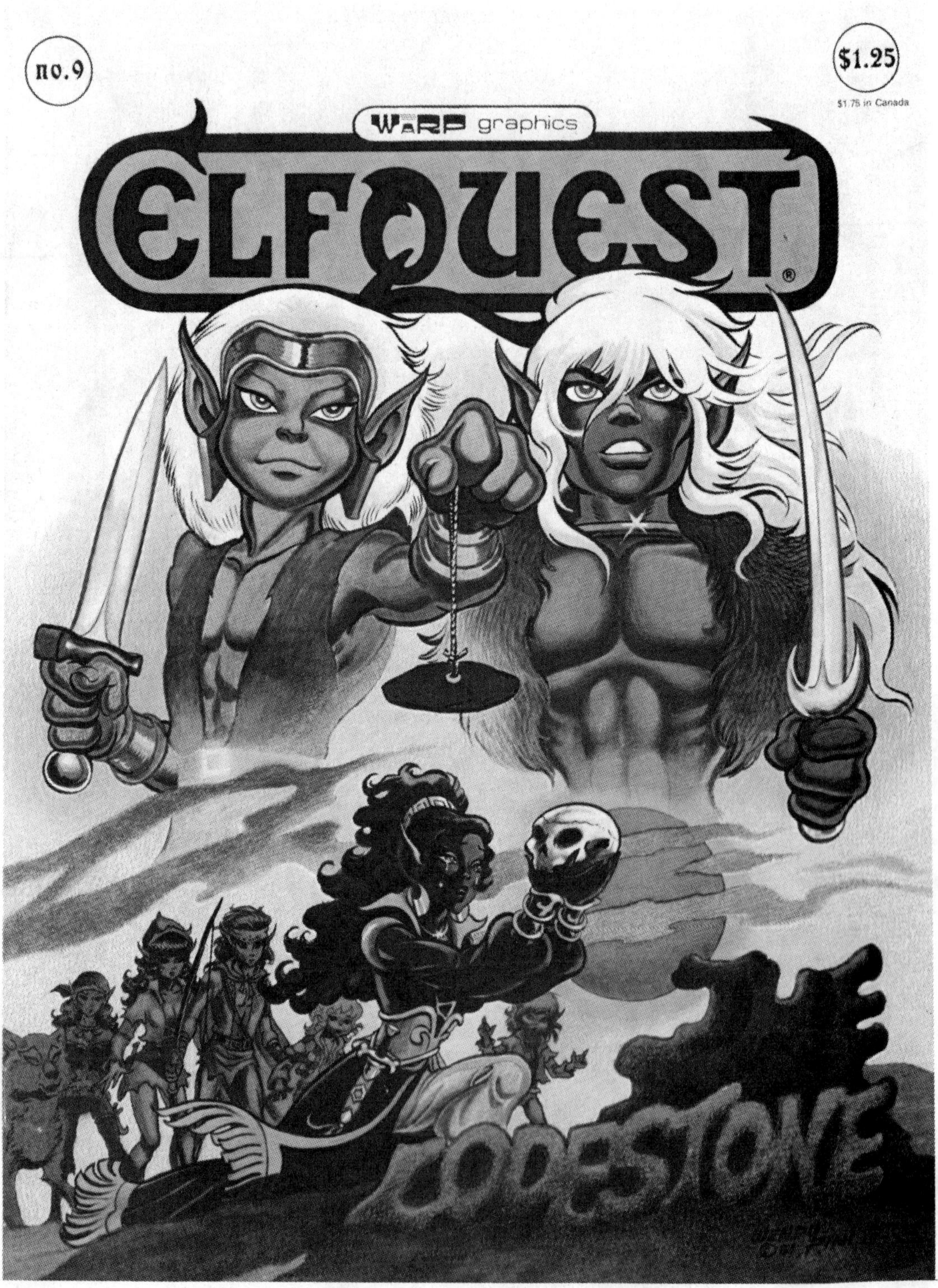
no.9
$1.25
$1.75 in Canada
WaRP graphics
ELFQUEST
LODESTONE

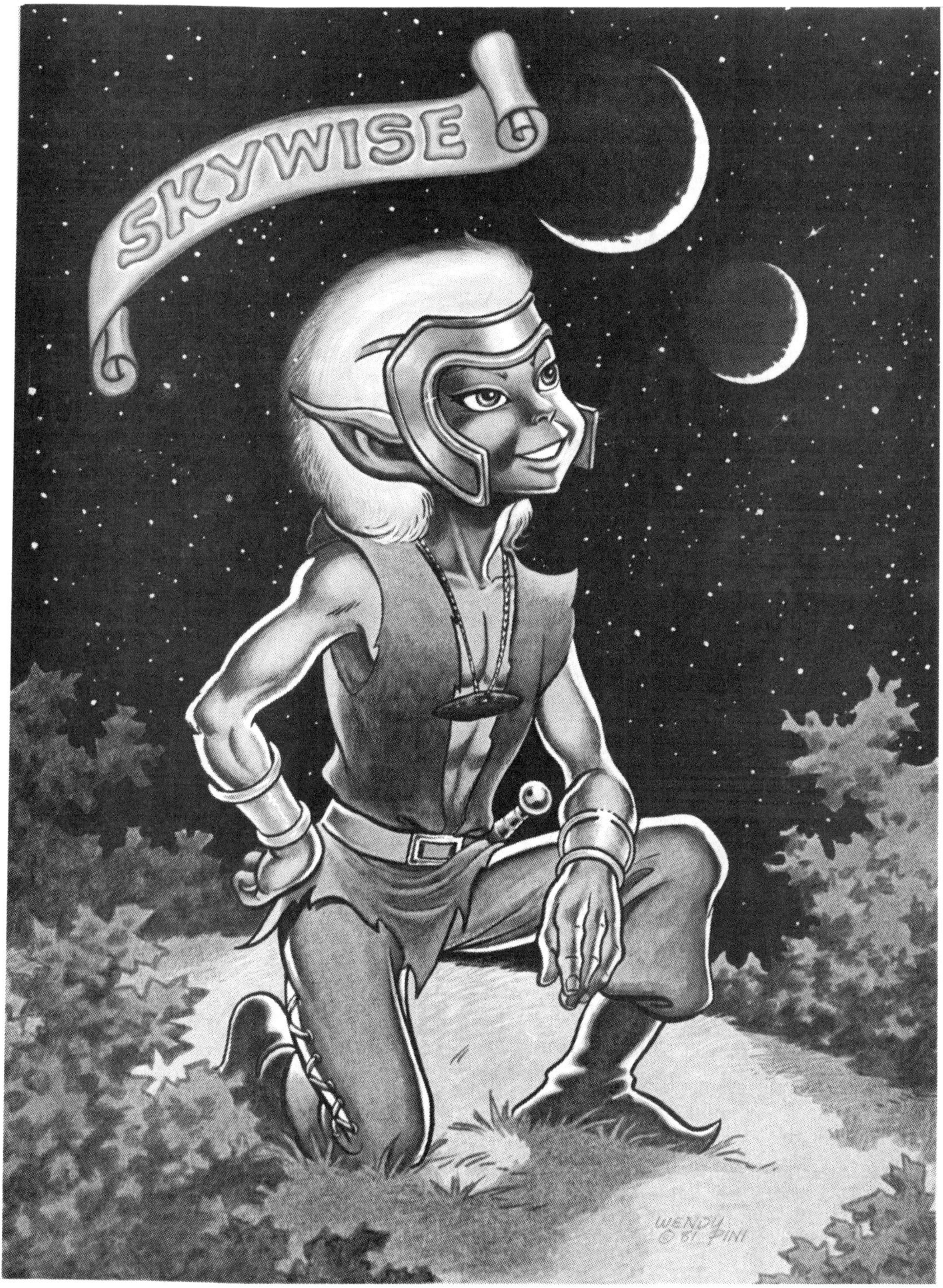
SKYWISE
WENDY
© 81 PINI

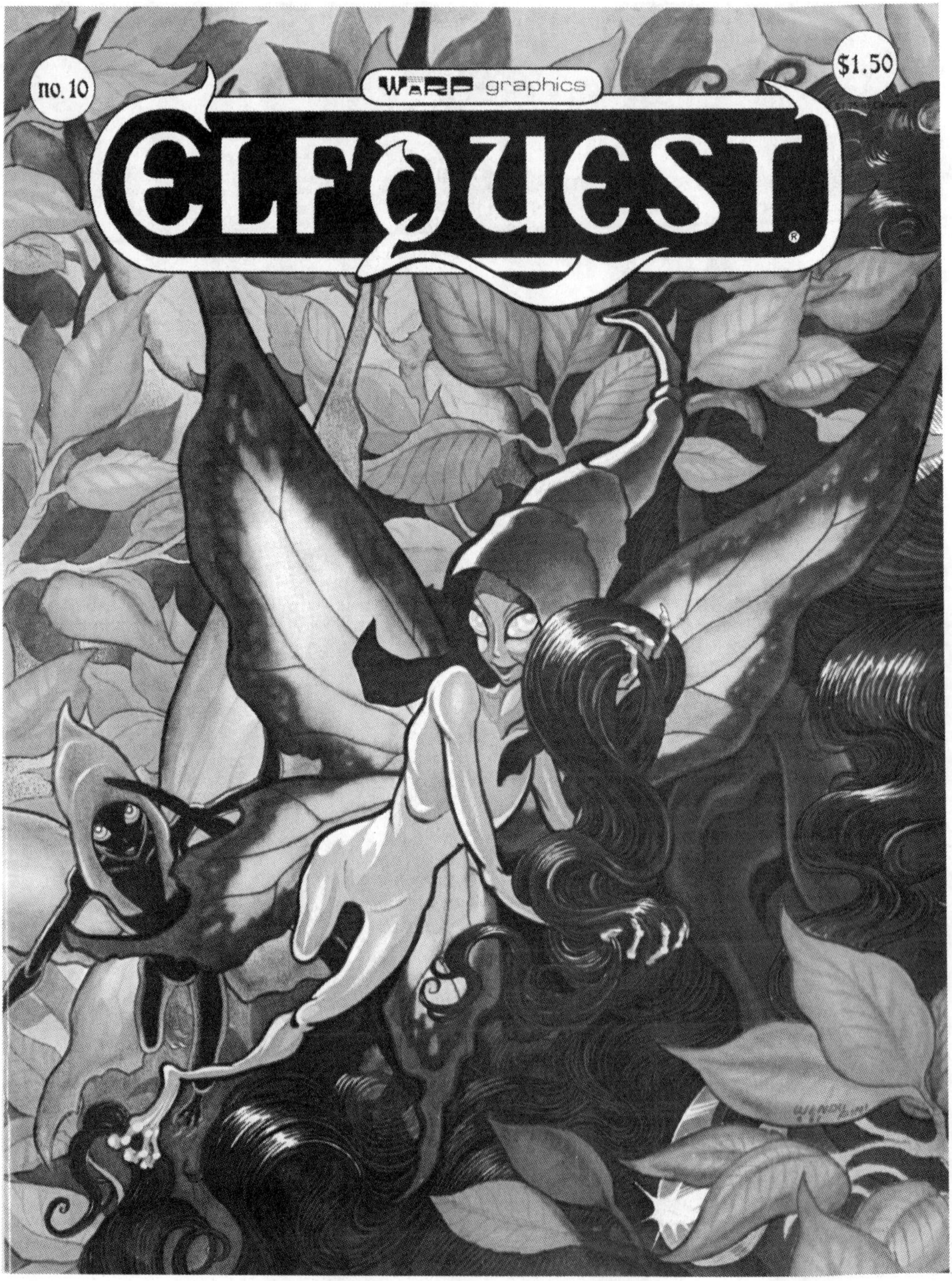
no. 10
WaRP graphics
ELFQUEST
$1.50

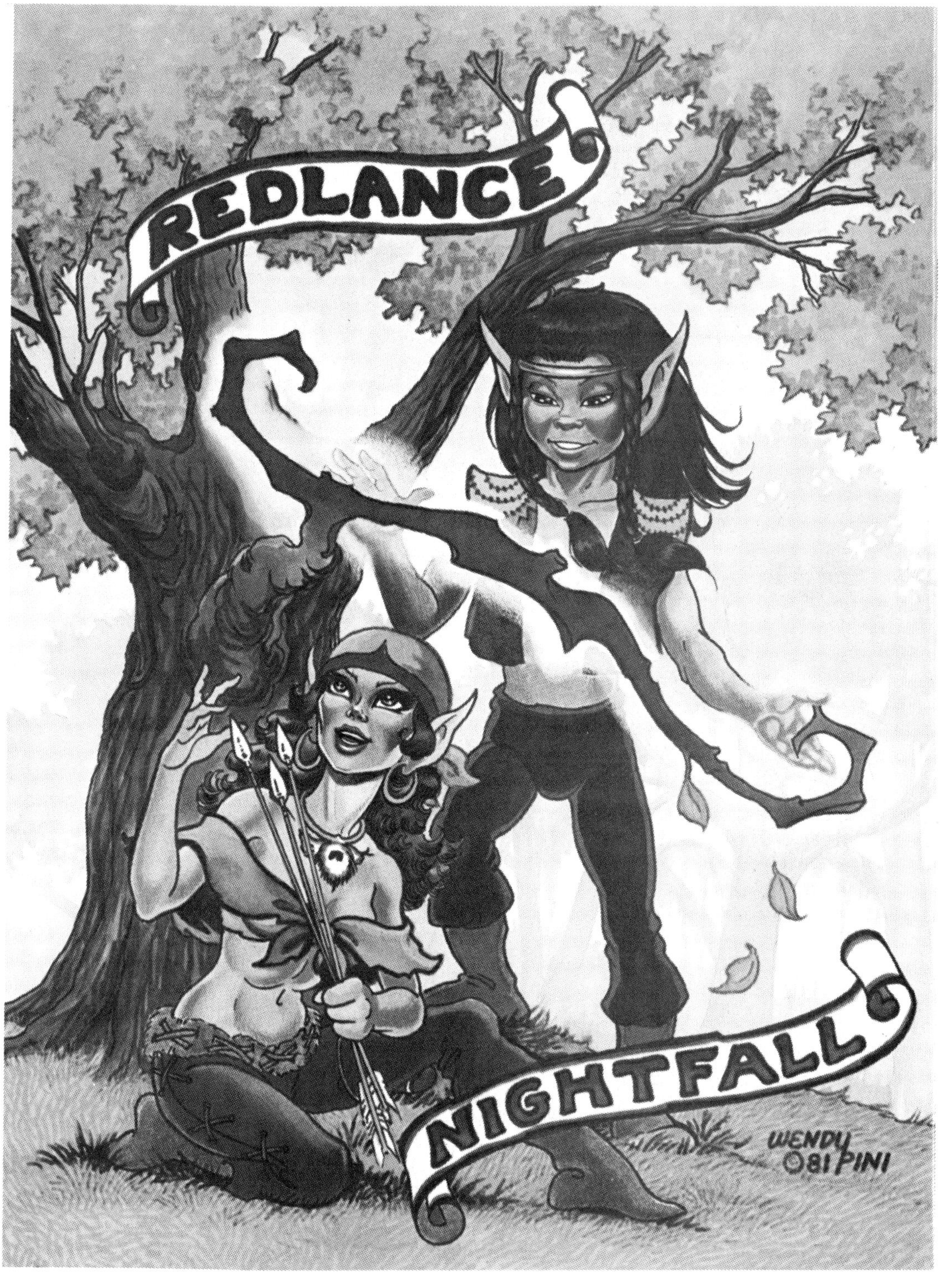
REDLANCE
NIGHTFALL
WENDY
©81 PINI